G000242915

# Fighting the US Youth Sex Trade

Campaigns against the prostitution of young people in the United States have surged and ebbed multiple times over the last fifty years. *Fighting the US Youth Sex Trade: Gender, Race, and Politics* examines how politically and ideologically diverse activists joined together to change perceptions and public policies on youth involvement in the sex trade over time, reframing "juvenile prostitution" of the 1970s as "commercial sexual exploitation of children" in the 1990s, and then as "domestic minor sex trafficking" in the 2000s. Based on organizational archives and interviews with activists, Baker shows that these campaigns were fundamentally shaped by the politics of gender, race, and class, and by global anti-trafficking campaigns. The author argues that the very frames that have made these movements so successful in achieving new laws and programs for youth have limited their ability to achieve systematic reforms that could decrease youth vulnerability to involvement in the sex trade.

Carrie N. Baker, J.D., Ph.D., is a professor and director of the Program for the Study of Women and Gender at Smith College. Baker's primary areas of research are women's legal history, gender and public policy, and women's social movements. Her first book, *The Women's Movement against Sexual Harassment* (Cambridge, 2007), won the National Women's Studies Association Sara A. Whaley book prize in 2008. Baker has published in many leading journals, including *Violence Against Women, Journal of Women, Politics & Policy*, and *The Journal of Women's History*. Baker also writes for *Ms.* magazine and is co-chair of the *Ms.* Committee of Scholars.

# Fighting the US Youth Sex Trade

*Gender, Race, and Politics*

**CARRIE N. BAKER**
*Smith College, Massachusetts*

CAMBRIDGE
UNIVERSITY PRESS

# CAMBRIDGE
## UNIVERSITY PRESS

University Printing House, Cambridge CB2 8BS, United Kingdom

One Liberty Plaza, 20th Floor, New York, NY 10006, USA

477 Williamstown Road, Port Melbourne, VIC 3207, Australia

314–321, 3rd Floor, Plot 3, Splendor Forum, Jasola District Centre,
New Delhi – 110025, India

79 Anson Road, #06–04/06, Singapore 079906

Cambridge University Press is part of the University of Cambridge.

It furthers the University's mission by disseminating knowledge in the pursuit of
education, learning, and research at the highest international levels of excellence.

www.cambridge.org
Information on this title: www.cambridge.org/9781316510223
DOI: 10.1017/9781108225045

First published 2018

Printed in the United States of America by Sheridan Books, Inc.

*A catalogue record for this publication is available from the British Library.*

*Library of Congress Cataloging-in-Publication Data*
NAMES: Baker, Carrie N., author.
TITLE: Fighting the U.S. youth sex trade : gender, activism, and politics / Carrie N. Baker.
DESCRIPTION: New York : Cambridge University Press, 2018.
IDENTIFIERS: LCCN 2018012048 | ISBN 9781316510223 (hardback)
SUBJECTS: LCSH: Child prostitution – United States – History. | Child trafficking – United
States – History. | Child prostitution – United States – Prevention.
CLASSIFICATION: LCC HQ144 .B3295 2018 | DDC 306.74/5–dc23
LC record available at https://lccn.loc.gov/2018012048

ISBN 978-1-316-51022-3 Hardback
ISBN 978-1-316-64961-9 Paperback

# Contents

*List of Figures*                                                    *page* vi
*Acknowledgments*                                                         vii
*List of Abbreviations*                                                    ix

Introduction                                                               1

1   "My God! If Only I Could Get Out of Here": Roots
    of Contemporary Activism Against the US Youth Sex Trade              14

2   "Teeny Hookers" and the "Chicken Hawk Trade":
    Organizing against Juvenile Prostitution in the 1970s                38

3   Survivor Activism and Global Connections: The US Campaign
    against Commercial Sexual Exploitation of Children in the 1990s      63

4   "Our Daughters" in Danger: Leveraging the Anti-Trafficking
    Framework in the Early 2000s                                        92

5   To Rescue or Empower: Building a Collaborative Adversarial
    Movement                                                           120

6   "Locked in Like a Dog in a Kennel": Expanding Tactics,
    Challenging Systems                                                161

7   "Quick Fixes and Good Versus Evil Responses": Criticisms
    of the Movement                                                    200

Conclusion: Ending the US Youth Sex Trade?                             220

*Select Bibliography*                                                   240
*Index*                                                                248

# Figures

1.1 Ernest A. Bell, *Fighting the Traffic in Young Girls or War on the White Slave Trade*, 1910      *page* 21

2.1 Cover of Robin Lloyd's best-selling book *For Money or Love*, 1976      41

2.2 Cover of *The Minnesota Connection* by Al Palmquist with John Stone, 1978      51

4.1 FBI Innocence Lost National Initiative promotional image, www.fbi.gov      106

4.2 Mayor Shirley Franklin, Dear John ad campaign, Atlanta, Georgia, 2006      116

5.1 Image used to promote GEMS youth leadership program in 2012      125

5.2 Young Women's Empowerment Project, Street Youth Rise Up! campaign image. Artwork by Christy C. Road      127

5.3 Shared Hope International sponsored an "end demand" protest in Las Vegas in June 2009      132

5.4 Truckers Against Trafficking Everyday Hero poster      133

5.5a, b Promotional images for the films *Very Young Girls* (2007) and *Playground* (2009)      140

5.6 Arrests of juveniles for prostitution and commercialized vice, 1980–2014. ©Nest Foundation      142

5.7 Image of trafficker in *The Candy Shop* (2010)      147

6.1 Use of "Child Prostitution" and "Child Sex Trafficking" in US Newspapers, 2000–2016      171

# Acknowledgments

In the fall of 2005, I attended a Feminist Majority Foundation young feminist conference at Spelman College in Atlanta, Georgia. During a session on child prostitution, I met Stephanie Davis, who was working with a group of local women on the issue of girls in the sex trade in Atlanta. Inspired by what I learned, I later wrote an article on the burgeoning movement against the prostitution of girls for *Ms.* magazine. I interviewed activists around the country, including Rachel Lloyd at Girls Educational and Mentoring Services in New York City, Atlanta Mayor Shirley Franklin, who was at the time leading the charge against child prostitution in Atlanta, and Texas attorney Karen Harpold, who was working on appealing the prostitution conviction of a thirteen-year-old girl to the Texas Supreme Court. Published in the summer of 2010, the article, titled "Jailing Girls for Men's Crimes," was the first time that *Ms.* magazine had dedicated a feature piece to the issue of girls involved in prostitution. I received a tremendous response to the article. As activism against the involvement of youth in the sex trade increased in the following years, I became curious about the history of this issue and decided to write this book, which first germinated in classroom discussions with my wonderful students at Smith College.

I would like to thank many people who helped me throughout the process of researching and writing this book, starting with Michele Kort, Michel Cicero, and Katherine Spillar at *Ms.* magazine for their fire, insight, and wit. I thank the activists who agreed to be interviewed for that article, including Rachel Lloyd, Shirley Franklin, Stephanie Davis, Caffie McCullough, Karen Harpold, and Deborah Richardson, as well as those interviewed for this book, including Lois Lee, Trudee Able-Peterson, Carol Smolenski, Vednita Carter, Laura Barnitz, Sandy Skelaney, Sienna Baskin, Priscilla Alexander, Keeli Sorenson, Brittany Vanderhoof, and Sara Gould. Thanks also go to the many dedicated friends and colleagues who read drafts of all or part of the manuscript, including Susan Van Dyne, Nancy Whittier, Alice Hearst, Ambreen Hai, Beth Reingold, Mary Odem, Karen Worthington, Sienna Baskin, Amy Davidson, Andrea

Pincus, Harvey Hill, and the anonymous readers. I would especially like to thank my editor at Cambridge, Sara Doskow, who was encouraging from the start and so helpful along the way, and those who helped produce and promote the book, including Claire Sissen, Jayavel Radhakrishnan, Ursula Acton, and Jim Diggins. I'd like to thank Andrew Maurer in the Imaging Center at Smith and the librarians at Smith College who helped me, including Miriam Neptune, and staffs at the Sophia Smith Collection and the Schlesinger Library on the History of Women in America. Thanks also go to my student research assistants who helped me on this book, including Tegan Waring, Monica Reifenstein, Sarah Evans, Carrie Lee Lancaster, Emily Bellanca, and Leah Parker-Bernstein. Finally, I would like to thank my family, especially Harvey Hill, for all the support they have given me in numerous ways over the years for this project and many others.

I dedicate this book to my students, who give me hope for the future.

# Abbreviations

| | |
|---|---|
| CAPTA | Child Abuse Prevention and Treatment Act |
| CATW | Coalition Against Trafficking in Women |
| CSEC | Commercial Sexual Exploitation of Children |
| COYOTE | Call Off Your Old Tired Ethics |
| ECPAT | End Child Prostitution in Asian Tourism (1990–1997); then later, End Child Prostitution and Trafficking |
| GEMS | Girls Educational and Mentoring Services |
| HIPS | Helping Individual Prostitutes Survive |
| HRPG | Human Rights Project for Girls (Rights4Girls) |
| IJM | International Justice Mission |
| MLMC | My Life My Choice |
| MNWRC | Minnesota Native Women's Resource Center |
| NCMEC | National Center for Missing and Exploited Children |
| OJJDP | Office of Juvenile Justice and Delinquency Prevention |
| PRIDE | From Prostitution to Independence, Dignity and Equality |
| SAGE | Standing Against Global Exploitation |
| SHI | Shared Hope International |
| SOS | Sisters Offering Support |
| TVPA | Trafficking Victims Protection Act |
| WAVPM | Women Against Violence in Pornography and Media |
| WHISPER | Women Hurt in Systems of Prostitution Engaged in Revolt |
| WAP | Women Against Pornography |
| YAPI | Youth Advocates Program International |
| YWEP | Young Women's Empowerment Project |

# Introduction

After she waved over an unmarked car on a Texas roadside, thirteen-year-old B.W., as she was called in court records, offered an undercover police officer oral sex for twenty dollars. The officer arrested B.W. and charged her as an adult with the crime of prostitution. When a background check revealed she was only thirteen, police refiled the charges in family court—juvenile delinquency for the offense of prostitution. During an interview with a state psychologist, B.W. revealed a history of sexual and physical abuse, including several sexually transmitted diseases, two abortions, and untreated substance abuse. She had run away from foster care repeatedly and at the time of her arrest had been living with her thirty-two-year-old "boyfriend," as she described him, for a year and a half. Despite evidence that he had coerced her into prostitution, police did not investigate or attempt to apprehend this man, whom she identified by name. The trial court ruled that B.W. was delinquent and placed her on probation for eighteen months. Represented by Houston-based criminal defense attorney Michelle W. Bush with support from Karen Clark Harpold of the child advocacy organization Children at Risk, B.W. appealed her case.[1]

B.W.'s attorneys argued that prosecuting a thirteen-year-old girl for prostitution was inconsistent with the unrebuttable presumption in Texas's statutory rape law that minors under the age of fourteen cannot consent to sex with an adult as a matter of law. Therefore, Texas' prosecution of B.W. led to "the inherently inconsistent result that a child is at the same time both legally capable and legally incapable of consenting to sex."[2] Furthermore, they argued that Texas violated B.W.'s due process rights by refusing to investigate whether an adult encouraged or compelled her to engage in prostitution. They contended that the state had an affirmative obligation to investigate facts indicating child abuse. Attorneys for the State of Texas responded that B.W.'s position "could arguably encourage enterprising, but amoral, juveniles to engage in

---

[1] *In re B.W.*, 313 S.W.3d 818 (Tex. 2010).
[2] Petitioner's Brief on the Merits, *In the Matter of B.W.*, 7.

prostitution."[3] Lock-down custody was necessary for the protection of youth engaged in prostitution, they asserted, and police had no obligation to investigate the man involved.

On June 18, 2010, the Texas Supreme Court issued a groundbreaking decision that Texas law did not allow the State to prosecute a thirteen-year-old child for prostitution because she could not consent to sex as a matter of law. In a 6–3 opinion, the majority ruled that the Texas statutory rape law and the recently enacted state anti-trafficking law that defined sex trafficking to include any commercial sex act involving a minor indicated the legislature's belief in "the extreme importance of protecting children from sexual exploitation, and the awareness that children are more vulnerable to exploitation by others even in the absence of explicit threats or fraud."[4] The Court recognized the developmental differences between adolescents and adults, particularly with regard to their capacity to appreciate the significance and consequences of agreeing to participate in prostitution, and that these differences affected culpability. The Court reasoned:

It is difficult to reconcile the Legislature's recognition of the special vulnerability of children, and its passage of laws for their protection, with an intent to find that children under fourteen understand the nature and consequences of their conduct when they agree to commit a sex act for money, or to consider children quasi-criminal offenders guilty of an act that necessarily involves their own sexual exploitation.[5]

Sergeant Byron A. Fassett of the Dallas Police Department starkly described this paradox to a *New York Times* reporter: "If a 45-year-old man had sex with a 14-year-old girl and no money changed hands, she was likely to get counseling and he was likely to get jail time for statutory rape ... If the same man left $80 on the table after having sex with her, she would probably be locked up for prostitution and he would probably go home with a fine as a john."[6] The case of B.W. inspired a statewide campaign in Texas to cease criminal prosecution of all minors for prostitution and to provide services to youth instead.

The Texas campaign was one of many that arose across the United States in the 2000s inspiring a shift away from treating youth engaged in the sex trade as delinquents and toward regarding them as victims of sexual abuse. For the last fifty years, many youth involved in prostitution have been arrested and prosecuted for prostitution or other crimes. With the expansion of the prison industrial complex, especially in the 1990s, they were likely to spend time in prison. But by 2015, youth in the sex trade came to be considered by many as victims of "domestic minor sex trafficking." On February 12, 2015, the United States Senate passed a resolution stating that "there is no such thing as a 'child

---

[3] State's Response to Petitioner's Brief on the Merits, *In the Matter of B.W.*, Supreme Court of Texas, No. 08–1044 (September 9, 2009), 13.

[4] *In re B.W.*, 313 S.W.3d 818 (Tex. 2010), 821.     [5] Ibid. 820.

[6] Ian Urbina, "For Runaways, Sex Buys Survival," *New York Times* (October 27, 2009), A1.

prostitute.'" The resolution insisted that "children trafficked for sex in the United States should not be treated or regarded as child prostitutes" but rather as "victims or survivors of rape and sex trafficking." The resolution emphatically concluded, "children in the United States are not for sale."[7] This shift in understanding was accompanied by new public policies and increased services targeted to youth identified as at risk of or involved in the sex trade. As of fall 2015, thirty-four states had passed "safe harbor" laws intended to divert youth found engaging in prostitution into social services and away from delinquency proceedings.[8] By the end of 2015, there were at least seventy-four state and local task forces and working groups fighting against "domestic minor sex trafficking" around the country.[9]

In this book, I examine the social movement behind these shifts in perceptions and policy. Some of the questions explored are: When and why did activism against the involvement of youth in the sex trade emerge, and what were the roots of this activism? Who were the leaders of these campaigns, and what were their backgrounds? How did they frame the causes and solutions to the problem, and what strategies did they use to fight the youth sex trade? How did the movement leverage an anti-trafficking framework to advance their cause? What assumptions about childhood, especially girlhood, undergirded the legal treatment of minors, particularly those with experiences in the sex trade, and how did the movement against the youth sex trade challenge these assumptions, or not? How were gender, race and class mobilized implicitly or explicitly in the movement? How have public discourses and media portrayed youth in the sex trade over time? What have been the impacts of the movement and critiques of it?

Answers to these questions reveal how the movement against the youth sex trade in the 2000s convinced many lawmakers and members of the public that youth involved in the sex trade were worth helping rather than punishing. To achieve this change, there emerged an ideologically diverse social movement composed of survivors and social service providers, feminists and evangelical Christians, sex worker advocates and human rights activists, politicians, professionals, and celebrities. Building on the 1970s feminist anti-rape movement and the 1980s movements against child sexual abuse and pornography, activists challenged widespread attitudes and public policies that blamed youth for involvement in the sex trade, reframing them as victims rather than perpetrators of prostitution and portraying the issue as an urgent social problem warranting public attention and resources.

---

[7] Senate Resolution 81, Cong. Rec., Vol. 161, No. 24, S1009 (February 12, 2015).
[8] Polaris Project, *Human Trafficking Issue Brief: Safe Harbor* (Washington, DC: Polaris Project, 2015).
[9] FBI, Innocence Lost National Initiative, Statistics (September 30, 2016), at www.fbi.gov/investigate/violent-crime/cac.

The ideological diversity of this movement encompassed opposing understandings of the problem and the most effective solutions. Some feminists framed the issue as a form of violence against women and girls rooted in a sexual double standard, male sexual entitlement, and the devaluation of females. Conservatives condemned the violation of girls' innocence and the moral bankruptcy of a sexualized American culture. Some activists focused on the sexual victimization of marginalized girls, especially girls from low-income communities and girls of color, and argued that racism and classism contributed to both their involvement in prostitution and to the way police and courts treated them as delinquents rather than victims. Some focused attention on the involvement of boys and LGBT youth in the sex trade. With regard to solutions, some urged expanding criminal prosecution of adult facilitators and buyers, while others pushed for increased government support for youth services. Some advocated for reforming the criminal justice system's treatment of youth in the sex trade, while others pushed for improving the social conditions that made youth vulnerable to sexual exploitation in the first place, like poverty, sexism, and homophobia. Despite their differences, activists were unified in their opposition to the criminalization of youth involved in prostitution. Appealing to different constituencies, activists in the movement collaborated across their different identities, ideologies, and strategic orientations to pursue this shared goal. In this way, they were able to generate widespread support for changing laws and providing services to youth. However, some frames resonated more widely than others and were more likely to be promoted by the media, and lawmakers pursued some of the proposed solutions while ignoring others. The following pages delve into how and why the issue resonated and policy developed so rapidly in the way that it did in the 2000s.

Placing the contemporary movement against the US youth sex trade in a broader historical context helps to identify factors that likely contributed toward increased concern about this issue at particular historical moments. These factors include the sexual revolution, the expansion of the commercial sex industry, the development of technologies such as home video in the 1970s and the internet in the 1990s that facilitated the proliferation and increased visibility of pornography and prostitution, and the increasing media sexualization of women and, especially, girls. Furthermore, the vulnerability of youth to involvement in the sex trade increased with the rise of neoliberal economic policies that stressed families and communities by contributing to high child poverty rates, a shrinking welfare state, growing wealth inequality, and the explosion of mass incarceration. Politically, the challenges to white heterosexual male supremacy posed by the civil rights, women's rights, and gay liberation movements generated a backlash in the form of the growing political engagement of evangelical Christians who allied with the New Right beginning in the 1960s and who focused on social issues relating to sexuality, especially youth sexuality. Finally, shifting demographics, including immigration, racial integration, and rising rates of premarital sex and divorce, increased the likelihood of interracial and nonmarital sexual relations, which became an intense concern for "family values" conservatives. While all of these factors influenced the ebb and flow of activism related to youth involvement in the sex trade over the fifty-year period under study, I argue that societal changes related to sex, gender, sexuality, and race in particular fueled anxieties about this issue.

Capitalizing on these anxieties, many activists against the US youth sex trade as well as journalists covering the issue used gendered and racialized narratives about the commercial sexual exploitation of youth, which resonated with long-standing cultural narratives about race and sexual victimization. Despite dissenting voices and contradicting facts about how minors became involved in prostitution, these dominant discourses disproportionately shaped policy responses in the late twentieth century and the early twenty-first century. Across the decades, mainstream campaigns against youth involvement in the sex trade repeatedly framed the issue as an "urban" problem that was invading white middle-class communities – men of color luring young and naïve white girls from suburban and rural areas into the city and forcing them into prostitution. This framing echoed a deeply entrenched historical narrative of foreign and black men sexually exploiting and assaulting young white women – one that had fueled lynching in the nineteenth century and "white slavery" campaigns against prostitution in the early twentieth century. In both the 1970s and the 2000s, gendered and racialized rescue narratives shaped public discourse and policy regarding the US youth sex trade, which focused strongly on "protection and rescue" of girls and criminal prosecution of "pimps" and traffickers more than on addressing the social conditions that made youth vulnerable to entering the sex trade.

In the 2000s, criticism of campaigns against the US youth sex trade emerged from both inside and outside the movement. Critics argued that many activists and media portrayed the issue in simplistic, sensationalist, and inaccurate ways. They criticized the movement's focus on young cisgender girls and called attention to the many boys and transgender youth involved in the sex trade. They also challenged the assumption that youth in the sex trade were always controlled by third party facilitators, arguing instead that many were engaging in commercial sex independently to support themselves because of the failures of families, schools, and child welfare systems. Critics condemned the movement for being too focused on criminal justice solutions that ignored the deeper causes of youth involvement in the sex trade like poverty, racism, sexism, homophobia, and transphobia. Others argued that funding to address the problem disproportionately went to law enforcement and criminal prosecution, thereby feeding the bloated prison industrial complex, while social support services for youth remained woefully inadequate. Furthermore, critics argued that legal reforms often still allowed for the arrest and detention of youth, and that they ignored the real needs of youth, like affordable housing and fair wage jobs. Sex worker rights activists argued that law-and-order responses to the youth sex trade had negative impacts on adult women in the sex trade. Some even argued that youth have a right to engage in sex work in order to support themselves, especially in the absence of an adequate social safety net.

Based on this study of the history of activism against the US youth sex trade, I offer several arguments about the movement and its impact. Activism against the US youth sex trade has surged during times of social change related to gender, sexuality, race, economics, and immigration, which fueled adult concerns about the safety and sexuality of youth, especially girls. To generate interest and support for the issue, many movement advocates, journalists and policymakers exploited these concerns by using gendered and racialized narratives of victimization that have exaggerated and sensationalized the US youth sex trade, relied on and reinforced traditional gender, sexual, and racial ideologies, and obscured the heterogeneity of youth experiencing prostitution. Furthermore, the harsh effects of neoliberal economic policies in the United States, as well as the embedded racism and sexism of these policies, have increased the vulnerability of youth to involvement in the sex trade and exacerbated its harms to American youth. Nevertheless, rather than challenging these underlying economic and social conditions, many activists and policymakers have relied upon and reinforced neoliberal approaches to the problem by focusing on individual perpetrators and criminal justice solutions to the problem. These approaches have exacerbated the very conditions that create the problem by bolstering the racialized prison industrial complex that has harmed many communities and families rather than creating policies and programs that address the structural vulnerabilities of youth to involvement in the sex trade. While some activists against abuse of youth in the sex trade have challenged these systems, most have not, so overall the movement's impact has been limited.

## METHODOLOGICAL CONSIDERATIONS

Sources for this interdisciplinary study include state and federal laws, legislative hearings and reports, case law, administrative actions and policies, activist organizations' records, interviews with activists, and books, films, media coverage, and research on youth involved in the sex trade from 1970 to 2015. Black feminist theory, as well as social movement theory, inform the analysis. Black feminist theory's concept of intersectionality, coined by Kimberlé Crenshaw in 1989, examines how the intersections of gender, race, class, sexuality, nationality, and other aspects of identity shape not only individual experience, but also social institutions, including politics, law, public policy, and the media.[10] These aspects of identity are not

---

[10] Kimberlé Crenshaw, "Demarginalizing the Intersections of Race and Sex: A Black Feminist Critique of Antidiscrimination Doctrine, Feminist Theory, and Antiracist Politics," *University of Chicago Legal Forum* 1 (1989), 139–167; Kimberlé Crenshaw, "Mapping the Margins:

"unitary, mutually exclusive entities, but rather ... reciprocally constructing phenomena" that interact on multiple levels.[11] Oppressive systems like racism, sexism, and classism do not function independently, but are interconnected, creating systems of oppression. Because laws and policies usually address only one form of oppression at a time, the intersections of oppressions are obscured and denied. Similarly, social movements have historically focused on singular forms of oppression – racism in the civil rights movement or sexism in the women's movement – thereby ignoring intersecting oppressions experienced by women of color. Intersectionality is a dynamic analysis of structures, social processes, ideologies and representations used to understand the complex, multidimensional power hierarchies in society. These intersections have heavily influenced activism against the US youth sex trade as well as related political discourse and public policy since the 1970s.

In addition to Black feminist theory, I use social movement theory on how activists frame issues in order to gain support, how they leverage political and cultural opportunities, and how they mobilize resources to build a movement. Collective action frames are the "meaning work" of social movements, whereby activists develop and promulgate particular ways of understanding issues in order to gain support and mobilize constituents. "By simplifying and condensing aspects of the 'world out there,'" movements seek to build a shared understanding of a social problem that identifies who is to blame, articulates a solution to the problem, proposes strategies for change, and motivates people to act collectively.[12] Movements construct individual and collective identities for their participants in order to generate support and mobilize people to their cause. Political opportunity theory focuses on how changes in the political structure, like the election of a new president or the appointment of an ally to a key position in government, can advance a social movement. Social movements can also take advantage of cultural opportunities – the "extant stock of meanings, beliefs, ideologies, practices, values, myths, narratives, and the like ... which constitute the cultural resource base from which new cultural elements are fashioned."[13] Finally, resource mobilization theory focuses on how successful movements mobilize resources, including people, money, and legitimacy, to achieve their goals. This social movement theory illuminates how the movement against youth involvement in the sex trade succeeded in gaining public attention and changing laws and policies.

Intersectionality, Identity Politics, and Violence Against Women of Color," *Stanford Law Review*, 43.6 (July 1991), 1241–1299.
[11] Patricia Hill Collins, "Intersectionality's Definitional Dilemmas," *Annual Review of Sociology*, 41 (2015), 1–20.
[12] Robert D. Benford and David A. Snow, "Framing Processes and Social Movements: An Overview and Assessment," *Annual Review of Sociology* 26 (2000), 615, 622.
[13] Ibid. 628.

Finally, I use sociologist Nancy Whittier's concept of a "collaborative adversarial movement" to analyze this ideologically diverse movement. Collaborative adversarial movements consist of social movement organizations that have differing collective action frames and identities and do not coordinate strategically, but who share specific or even long-term goals. Activism against the sex trade has often manifested as a collaborative adversarial movement. In the 1970s and 1980s, some feminists worked alongside conservatives to pass laws restricting the pornography and prostitution, while other feminists strenuously opposed these policies on free speech or right to work grounds.[14] In what was called the feminist "sex wars," "sex-positive" feminists fought bitterly with anti-prostitution feminists about the meaning of sex work/prostitution. Again, in the 1990s, some feminists worked alongside conservatives to pass the Trafficking Victims Protection Act of 2000 and then expand restrictions on trafficking in the 2000s, while other feminists and leftists vigorously criticized the anti-trafficking movement for conflating sex trafficking with sex work and ignoring labor trafficking as well as promoting policies that harmed sex workers, bolstered the prison industrial complex, and violated free speech. Critics, both scholars and activists, characterized the anti-trafficking movement as a "moral crusade" or a "sex panic" through which the Right was advancing its anti-sex and pro-criminal justice agendas.

Similar conflicts have influenced debates and policymaking relating to youth involvement in the sex trade. Feminists seeking to abolish the sex trade have worked side by side with conservatives and evangelical Christians to fight the US youth sex trade, although they have very different motivations and rarely directly collaborate. Conservatives use the issue to push a law-and-order agenda, calling for building up of the criminal justice system, whereas evangelical Christians frame the issue in terms of the moral breakdown of American culture and society. Feminists who believe that women are victimized by prostitution and seek to abolish the sex trade are able to garner broader support among feminists and the general public by focusing on girls' involvement in prostitution rather than that of adult women. Others, including sex workers, who advocate for the decriminalization of the sex trade, have supported some of the campaigns of the movement like laws to decriminalize youth or expunge the criminal history of trafficked people, but have opposed other efforts, like end demand campaigns and attacks against online websites advertising sex for sale. Scholars and journalists researching and writing on sex trafficking and youth involvement in the sex trade also often have strong investments in one side or the other, sometimes searingly critical of the movement and other times generating studies and resources to support

---

[14] Nancy Whittier, "Rethinking Coalitions: Anti-Pornography Feminists, Conservatives, and Relationships between Collaborative Adversarial Movements," *Social Problems* 61.2 (2014), 1–19.

campaigns against the youth sex trade. In this book, I navigate this politically fraught terrain by attempting to fairly depict the movement against youth involvement in the sex trade and its critics, with attention to the historical, political, and economic context of this activism. As a scholar of feminist social movements and their impact on the law, I seek to understand the origins of this movement, what propelled it forward, its politics, and its effects on the lives of young people. I focus, in particular, on how the ideologies underlying these campaigns, the resulting laws and policies, and their implementation are shaped by the intersections of gender, race, and class. These are the questions at the heart of this study.

A final methodological consideration is language. Language related to the sex trade is highly politicized, carrying assumptions about the impact of commercial sex on participants, as well as about culpability for any harms that might result. "Prostitution" means engaging in a sex act with someone for payment. In 1978, women working in the sex trade coined the phrase "sex work" as an alternative to the stigmatizing term "prostitution" often used in criminal laws.[15] "Sex work," which emphasizes that working in the sex trade is a form of labor, is sometimes understood to include a wide range of commercial sexual acts, including erotic dancing, pornography, phone sex, webcam sex, and live sex shows. The "sex trade" refers to this broader range of conduct. Whereas sex worker rights activists usually seek to decriminalize the selling and buying of sexual services, "abolitionists" oppose decriminalization and seek to abolish the sex trade. They also often use the word "slavery" to refer to sex trafficking and prostitution. Others have objected to the use of "abolition" and "slavery" in the context of prostitution/sex work as an "appropriation of black suffering."[16] According to federal law, "sex trafficking" is defined as inducing a person to engage in a commercial sex act by force, fraud, or coercion, or when the person is under the age of eighteen.[17] Abolitionists equate prostitution and sex trafficking because they believe that all or most women involved in the sex trade are coerced and abused. They often use the passive voice – "prostituted women" – to highlight this abuse, or refer to people in the sex trade as "sex trafficking victims." Many activists define themselves as survivors of prostitution and trafficking. Feminist anti-rape activists developed the term "survivor" in order to avoid defining people by their victimization and to avoid the negative connotations of victims as passive, helpless, and weak. Survivor language emphasizes strength, agency, resistance, and hope. When

---

[15] The phrase "sex work" was coined by Carol Leigh. Carol Leigh, "Inventing Sex Work," in Jill Nagle (ed.), *Whores and Other Feminists* (New York, NY: Routledge, 1997), 225–231. Many people in the sex trade today describe themselves as "sex workers."

[16] Robyn Maynard, "#Blacksexworkerslivesmatter: White-Washed 'Anti-Slavery' and the Appropriation of Black Suffering," *The Feminist Wire* (September 9, 2015).

[17] 22 USC § 7102 (9)(A) (2015).

discussing particular organizations or people, I reflect the language that they use, but I also examine controversies around language throughout the book.

Youth involvement in the sex trade has been called child prostitution, teen prostitution, juvenile prostitution, commercial sexual exploitation of children (CSEC), domestic minor sex trafficking, and child sex work. This language has both an historical and political registrar. For example, "child prostitute," which was used commonly in the 1970s but is today relatively rare, describes an identity that defined the child as inherently at fault. "Commercial sexual exploitation of children," on the other hand, which came into widespread use in the 1990s after the First World Congress on the Commercial Sexual Exploitation of Children, frames youth involved in the sex trade as victims of exploitation.[18] "Domestic minor sex trafficking," coined by anti-trafficking advocates in 2009, leverages the language of federal anti-trafficking law to frame youth in the sex trade as victims rather than perpetrators of prostitution. Other advocates use the language "prostituted youth" to emphasize the purported coercion and lack of agency of young people involved in the sex trade. In contrast, some refer to youth in the sex trade as "child sex workers" to emphasize youth agency.[19] In this book, I reflect the language of the time period, organization, or advocate that I'm discussing. In the movement, the term "children" is often used to refer to anyone under the age of eighteen, although others reserve the term "children" for preadolescents and use "youth" for adolescents from puberty to legal adulthood or even up to age twenty-one or older. I use "youth" to refer to people under the age of legal majority (eighteen). Until recently, most advocates against the youth sex trade focused on cisgender girls and boys. I identify the youth targeted as cisgender for programs and policies that do not attend to the particular needs of transgender youth.

Language for buyers and facilitators of people in the sex trade is also varied and politicized. Buyers have been referred to as johns, tricks, clients, customers, consumers, or "the demand." When minors are involved, buyers have also been referred to as pedophiles, child abusers, child rapists, and sex traffickers. Many have criticized the term "john" for normalizing buying sex and obscuring the harm caused to women and particularly youth, while others have criticized this gendered term for erasing the existence of female buyers of sex. People who facilitate others' involvement in the sex trade have been called pimps, sex traffickers, and third-party facilitators. The term "pimp" often collapses a range of behavior from economic dependence on someone else's prostitution, to helping someone voluntarily engage in prostitution or

[18] Penelope Saunders, "How 'Child Prostitution' Became 'CSEC,'" in Elizabeth Bernstein and Laurie Schaffner (eds.), *Regulating Sex: The Politics of Intimacy and Identity* (London, England; Routledge, 2005), 167–188, at 183.
[19] See, for example, Noah Berlatsky, "Child Sex Workers' Biggest Threat: The Police," *The New Republic* (January 20, 2016).

providing support such as security or bookings, to managing someone in prostitution like an employer/employee relationship, to controlling, abusing, or exploiting someone engaged in prostitution. "Pimp" is the widely used slang term for people who manage sex workers, but is also a racialized term for making something look fashionable or impressive, as in the MTV series "Pimp My Ride." In this book, I trace the political contests and evolution of this language at different points in time. I use the language of particular eras, organizations, or individuals when they are discussed but otherwise will attempt to use neutral language such as "youth involved in the sex trade," "buyers," and "facilitators." Because of its racialized connotation, I avoid using the term "pimp" unless reflecting the language of advocacy organizations or activists.

My focus is youth involvement in the sex trade within the United States, not on international trafficking of youth. While these phenomena are related, they are often addressed differently in law and by activists. The federal anti-trafficking law passed in 2000 defined sex trafficking to include US youth involved in the sex trade, but offered remedies only for international trafficking survivors. Policymakers were concerned about youth involvement in prostitution abroad, but ignored the youth sex trade within US borders. They tended to see US youth as blameworthy, delinquent, or already adequately served. This book explores how the politics of gender, race, class, and nation shaped these attitudes and priorities, and how activists fought to change them.

## PLAN OF THE BOOK

The first three chapters provide the historical and political context for contemporary activism against the US youth sex trade. Chapter one explains late nineteenth and early twentieth century campaigns to protect and control young women's sexuality, as well as the mid-century social and political shifts that provided fertile ground for the rise of activism against the youth sex trade in the 1970s. Chapter two describes campaigns against juvenile prostitution that emerged in the late 1970s and stretched into the 1980s. Activists mobilized public concern by stoking adults' anxieties about youth sexuality during a time of seismic shifts in norms related to sex, gender, sexuality, and race, as well as increased immigration and the proliferation of neoliberal economic policies that intensified income inequality and insecurity in the United States. Taking advantage of these cultural and political opportunities, activists were able to inspire new state and federal laws against sexual exploitation of youth, and innovative services and programs specifically focused on juveniles involved in prostitution. Chapter three chronicles the 1990s emergence of survivor activists who connected with the growing global movement against the commercial sexual exploitation of children. Mobilizing their individual and collective identities as survivors, these activists worked with the growing US movement against international sex trafficking to pass the Trafficking Victims Protection Act (TVPA) of 2000.

The next three chapters explain how activists reframed youth involvement in the sex trade as domestic minor sex trafficking in the 2000s. Chapter four describes how activists leveraged the political opportunities created by the passage of the TVPA to push for new laws at the federal, state, and local levels to assist US youth involved in the sex trade. Chapter five documents the growing ideological diversification of the movement later in the decade, with expanded participation of evangelical Christians, survivor activists, sex worker advocates, and youth empowerment groups. This chapter argues that these activists formed a collaborative adversarial movement, working side-by-side, sometimes at arm's length, to achieve common goals such as the passage of safe harbor laws and laws to allow vacating records of prostitution convictions, while maintaining different frames and strategies. Chapter six explains how in the 2010s activists mobilized the increased resources available to the movement to call for reform of the criminal justice and child welfare systems, as well as to engage in campaigns to "end demand" and stop online advertising of sex for sale.

Chapter seven describes the critiques of activism against the youth sex trade both from inside the movement and from journalists, academics, and activists on the left. The book concludes with a reflection on the recurrent narratives about widespread commercial sexual exploitation of youth. Across the decades, the same claims about youth involvement in the sex trade have recurred – claims that hundreds of thousands of youth are involved and that they are entering prostitution at younger and younger ages – despite lack of evidence to support these claims. I argue that the ebb and flow of campaigns against the US youth sex trade over time is rooted in Americans fears about social change and the future. These campaigns gain steam when they can tap into adults' anxieties about youth sexuality resulting from changing social norms related to gender, race, and sexuality and during times of economic stress or perceived external threats. Narratives about the youth sex trade – what are presumed to be the causes, who are the victims, who are the perpetrators, what the youth sex trade means, and what are the solutions – have shifted in some respects over time, but in other ways have remained strikingly consistent. They have recycled some of the same tropes of lost innocence and called for the same solutions over and over, yet blaming young people for their involvement in the sex trade has persisted, with some exceptions when the issue is framed to resonate with dominant cultural narratives around gender, race, and sexuality. The nineteenth century white slavery campaigns are echoed in the dominant racialized narratives of youth involvement in the sex trade in the 1970s and 2000s. The issue is framed as naïve white girls victimized by men of color. Boys, on the other hand, have generally been invisible, except during the 1970s panic about boys being targeted by gay pedophiles. The emergence of survivor leadership, and especially youth survivor leadership from girls of color in the

2000s, has been innovative, resisting traditional victimization narratives that focus only on individual perpetrators, and calling for reform of social, legal, and economic systems that have made them vulnerable to sexual exploitation. But they are fighting upstream against deeply entrenched cultural narratives about guilt and innocence, blameworthiness and responsibility – narratives inflected by gender, race, class, and sexuality. To combat these narratives, activists have produced diametrically opposed narratives of victimization, but still leveraged traditional ideologies of gender, sexuality, and race. Some activists have attempted to navigate a middle path between blame and victimization, to recognize vulnerability and victimization of youth while also respecting youth agency and resilience. But these narratives have had less traction, less cultural resonance, and so have not won the political support necessary to gain policy solutions that address youth vulnerabilities, especially at the systemic level. Instead, policymakers have relied heavily on a criminal justice response to the youth sex trade without adequately addressing the economic and social problems that make youth vulnerable to entering the sex trade. Until activists and policymakers engage with the complexity of the issue and address the root causes, they are not likely to achieve their goal of ending the youth sex trade.

I

# "My God! If Only I Could Get Out of Here": Roots of Contemporary Activism Against the US Youth Sex Trade

A girl named McConnell, only sixteen years old, and a girl named Shubert, three years older, were taken by two Jews, Brodsky and Jacobson, to a resort kept by one Weinstein in South Chicago. The girls were lured from an amusement park in the suburb of Forest Park, where they were unattended by parents or friends – fair game for the white slaver.

Ernest Bell, Illinois Vigilance Association

*Fighting the Traffic in Young Girls.* 1910[1]

Moral reformers in the United States have waged multiple campaigns across the centuries to fight the sexual abuse of young people, particularly girls. In nineteenth-century social purity campaigns, Christian reformers sought to "revise the law in order to protect, manage, and/or control the sexuality of young women."[2] Evolving ideas about childhood paired with societal changes related to gender, sexuality, class, race, and nation inflamed anxieties about youth sexuality. Whereas colonial America viewed children as inherently sinful and sexual, mid-nineteenth-century middle-class white parents developed sentimentalized notions of children as innocent, naïve and in need of protection from corruption. As the country industrialized and birthrates fell, middle-class parents "regarded their children not as sources of labor but as 'social capital' requiring substantial investments of time and resources."[3] The value of children in American society shifted from economic to sentimental, first in the urban middle-class, and later in the working class.[4]

---

[1] Ernest A. Bell, *Fighting the Traffic in Young Girls or War on the White Slave Trade* (Chicago, IL: L.H. Walker, 1910), 247.

[2] J. Shoshanna Ehrlich, *Regulating Desire: From the Virtuous Maiden to the Purity Princess* (Albany, NY: SUNY Press, 2014), 3.

[3] Steven Mintz, *Huck's Raft: A History of American Childhood* (Cambridge, MA: Belknap Press of Harvard University, 2004), 77.

[4] Viviana A. Zelizer, *Pricing the Priceless Child: The Changing Social Value of Children* (Princeton, NJ: Princeton University Press, 1985), 5–6; Mintz, *Huck's Raft*, 75–93.

In the late nineteenth and early twentieth centuries, laws instituting compulsory education and prohibiting child labor extended children's period of dependency on adults. This "sacralization of child life," argues sociologist Viviana Zelizer, supported a "normative ideal of the child as an exclusively emotional and affective asset," who "belonged in a domesticated, nonproductive world of lessons, games and token money."[5]

Views of children as innocent, vulnerable, and dependent, however, were shaped by gender, race, class, and nation. For moral reformers of all races, efforts to protect children often focused on girls and the preservation of female chastity. But dominant ideas of childhood innocence were racialized through a "cultural system linking innocence to whiteness through the body of the child."[6] Many moral reform campaigns arose in response to economic change and increased immigration that threatened the dominance of native-born middle-class white people. Concern about the moral corruption of children grew from white middle-class parents' anxieties that their children would "fail to replicate or exceed their parents' social position ... It tapped into the fear that their own children could fall prey to vice and ultimately live in disgrace."[7] Responding to white people's fears about increasing immigration, many moral reformers employed a nationalist discourse that "capitalized on racialized and sexualized fears of national decline and asserted a causal relationship between sexual immorality, Anglo-Saxon decline, and national decay."[8] As a result of these intersecting concerns, late nineteenth-century social purity campaigns against sexual abuse and prostitution often focused on white, middle-class girls and young women and bolstered white supremacy. African American moral reformers, on the other hand, rejected racist discourses of childhood innocence, focusing their energy on resisting white male sexual privilege and abuse of African American girls and women.[9]

Occurring during times of social, economic, and political change, social purity campaigns in the late nineteenth and early twentieth centuries both challenged *and* reinforced a racialized sexual double standard embedded in laws and society. This double standard accepted white boys' sexuality and encouraged their active exploration of sex, which was considered a mark of manhood and a sign of masculinity. On the other hand, dominant ideologies held that white women and girls were naturally asexual, unmarried women

---

[5] Zelizer, *Pricing the Priceless Child*, 11.

[6] Robin Bernstein, *Racial Innocence: Performing American Childhood from Slavery to Civil Rights* (New York, NY: New York University Press, 2011), 6, 29.

[7] Nicola Beisel, *Imperiled Innocents: Anthony Comstock and Family Reproduction in Victorian America* (Princeton, NJ: Princeton University Press, 1998), quote from https://press.princeton .edu/titles/5899.html.

[8] Sara Moslener, *Virgin Nation: Sexuality Purity and American Adolescence* (New York, NY: Oxford University Press, 2015), 8.

[9] Estelle E. Freedman, *Redefining Rape: Sexual Violence in the Era of Suffrage and Segregation* (Cambridge, MA: Harvard University Press, 2013), 73–124.

were expected to be virgins, and women had a social and moral responsibility to restrain men's sexual behavior. Sexually active women were regarded negatively. This sexual double standard underlay the longstanding police practice of more frequently arresting women selling sex than men buying sex. At common law, a woman's credibility hinged on her chastity, which made rape prosecutions hard to win. In calling for protection of female virginity from male sexual aggression, social purity reformers reinforced the importance of female chastity. These ideas about sexuality, however, were racialized.[10] In 1875, Congress passed the Page Act excluding Asian women on the grounds that they were prostitutes.[11] Similarly, white Americans stereotyped African American women as sexually promiscuous "jezebels." On the other hand, rape prosecution against white men for assaulting black women were rare while whites used the specter of African American men raping white women to justify brutal lynching.[12] As a result, African American reformers, led by Ida B. Wells, organized anti-lynching campaigns that challenged racialized notions of sexual purity and perpetration.[13]

Weaving narratives of sexual danger and female victimization, white social purity reformers sought to harness the state to intervene on behalf of young white women to protect them from male sexual aggression by challenging the sexual double standard in law and society that left women alone responsible for the consequences of sexual behavior. In the mid-nineteenth to early twentieth centuries, growing urban centers were attracting increasing numbers of working-class women and girls for employment and leisure activities. As part of a larger moral reform crusade to "cleanse the nation of sin," reformers had a "multipronged strategy for rewriting the sexual script in order to save young women from ruin."[14] Challenging the idea that young women were equally or more so responsible for men's sexual behavior and that their immorality made them unworthy of compassion, female reformers told a new story of male sexual predation and victimization of vulnerable girls, who deserved protection and rescue rather than condemnation and abandonment. Through criminal liability, reformers hoped to reshape male behavior by holding them responsible for the consequences of their behavior.

The first organized campaign to protect young women's sexuality in America was launched by the American Female Moral Reform Society in 1838. Fueled by evangelical Christian ideas of moral sin and anxieties generated from the

---

[10] Mary E. Odem, *Delinquent Daughters: Protecting and Policing Adolescent Female Sexuality in the United States, 1885–1920* (Chapel Hill, NC: University of North Carolina Press, 1994), 27.

[11] Eithne Luibheid, *Entry Denied: Controlling Sexuality at the Border* (University of Minnesota Press, 2002), 45.

[12] Patricia Hill Collins, *Black Feminist Thought: Knowledge, Consciousness, and the Politics of Empowerment* (New York, NY: Routledge, 2000), 69–96.

[13] Paula Giddings, *Ida: A Sword Among Lions: Ida B. Wells and the Campaign Against Lynching* (New York, NY: Amistad Publishing, 2009).

[14] Ehrlich, *Regulating Desire*, 8.

dislocations of urbanization and industrialization, as well as the increasing visibility of prostitution in cities, reformers concerned with protecting young women from sexual coercion and preserving their virginity pushed for laws to criminalize seduction – defined as when a man promised marriage to persuade a chaste young woman to have sex but then abandoned her. Female moral reform periodicals were "filled with seduction narratives in which a sexually aggressive male destroyed the life of an innocent and trusting young woman."[15] Relying on tragic tales of "unsuspecting young women from the countryside who had been drawn to the cities in pursuit of work or possibly by their glamorous allure"[16] and were then deceived and defiled by devious men, reformers reinforced a belief in the importance of female virginity, while also challenging male sexual privilege and irresponsibility. In addition to legislative campaigns for criminal seduction laws and civil litigation for damages, moral reformers called on mothers to "develop appropriate standards of behavior in their children," and they exposed and shunned the men who exploited young women.[17] In 1848, reformers convinced the New York legislature to pass a law to make it a crime for any person, "under promise of marriage" to seduce and have sexual intercourse with a female of "previous chaste character."[18] By the turn of the century, many other states had passed anti-seduction laws.[19] These campaigns helped establish a "new gender ideology which located sexual aggressiveness in men and victimhood in women."[20]

In contrast to white moral reformers, African American female moral reformers shied away from campaigns to create new criminal laws that might target African American men, focusing instead on challenging the racialized sexual double standard in law and society. Black women and girls experienced rampant sexual exploitation and assault during and after slavery, particularly from white men, who justified their behavior using stereotypes of African American female promiscuity. Black women had limited recourse to the legal system for relief, but they resisted individually and collectively.[21] Led by Ida B. Wells beginning in the 1870s, African American women organized against the terrorization of African American men and women through anti-lynching campaigns. These campaigns challenged white supremacist stereotypes about the innate promiscuity of African American women and the racial stereotype of African American men as rapists. Black reformers participated in the social purity movement through Women's Christian Temperance Union (WCTU), although they often formed separate chapters from white women, organizing educational

---

[15] Ibid. 17.　　[16] Ibid. 12.　　[17] Ibid. 19, 21.　　[18] Laws of New York, Chapter 111 (1848).
[19] Ehrlich, *Regulating Desire*, 29.　　[20] Ibid. 30.
[21] See, e.g., Rebecca Hall and Angela Harris, "Hidden Histories, Racialized Gender, and the Legacy of Reconstruction: The Untold Story of *United States v. Cruikshank*," in Elizabeth Schneider and Stephanie Wildman (eds.), *Women and Law Stories* (New York: Foundation Press, 2011), 21–55.

programs for African American youth to teach moral behavior and creating travelers' aid societies for working girls.[22]

In the late nineteenth century, white social purity reformers led by the WCTU launched a campaign to raise the age of consent for sex, which at the time was ten in most states – inherited from English common law. These campaigns included feminists and suffragists, religious leaders, and white working women.[23] Using narratives of sexual danger to female virtue, these reformers circulated petitions, which they presented to legislators, pressing them to raise the age of consent to eighteen or even twenty-one.[24] They argued that the state had a duty to protect young and innocent girls from predatory men who sought to take advantage of them because the loss of virginity outside of marriage was considered ruinous for young women. Reformers noted the irony that the law fixed the age of majority significantly higher than the age of consent, so that young women could consent "to their own ruin" at a much younger age than they could control property or sign a contract. They argued that "the age of legal protection for the person be made at least equal to that of property." They also "sought to enshrine the existing middle-class version of respectable sexuality into law"[25] by codifying the legal impossibility of young women consenting to sexual relations, a notion which some young women resisted. These campaigns were largely successful, resulting in what are now called statutory rape laws across the nation. African American women reformers, however, did not join age of consent campaigns because they feared that these laws would target African American men and would not prevent white men from sexually exploiting black girls in the south.[26] In fact, race did influence the enforcement of these laws: prosecutors were much more likely to bring statutory rape cases against African American men.[27]

Young white women were also the subject of "white slavery" campaigns in early twentieth-century America. Concern about "white slave trade" first emerged in England in the mid-nineteenth century. Moral reformers crafted a narrative of "fresh-faced young women snatched from their innocence and femininity to feed the cruel sexuality of powerful and unfeeling men," who were cast as "foreign, frequently Jewish, sometimes French, but seldom English."[28]

[22] Freedman, *Redefining Rape*, 73–124; Giddings, *Ida*; Paula Giddings, *When and Where I Enter: The Impact of Black Women on Race and Sex in America* (New York, NY: Amistad Publishing, 1984), 85–94; Odem, *Delinquent Daughters*, 27.

[23] Carolyn E. Cocca, *Jailbait: The Politics of Statutory Rape Laws in the United States* (Albany, NY: State University of New York, 2004), 14; Freedman, *Redefining Rape*, 125–146.

[24] Odem, *Delinquent Daughters*, 27; Cocca, *Jailbait*, 11; Ehrlich, *Regulating Desire*, 46.

[25] Ehrlich, *Regulating Desire*, 52, 55.    [26] Freedman, *Redefining Rape*, 143.

[27] Odem, *Delinquent Daughters*, 26–30; Freedman, *Redefining Rape*, 151–157; Cocca, *Jailbait*, 13; Michele Goodwin, "Law's Limits: Regulating Statutory Rape Law," *Wisconsin Law Review* (2013), 481–530, at 492–499.

[28] Philippa Levine, *Prostitution, Race, and Politics: Policing Venereal Disease in the British Empire* (New York, NY: Routledge, 2003), 245–246.

Characterizing child prostitution as a form of "white slavery," social reformers Josephine Butler, Catherine Booth, and William Stead successfully campaigned to raise the age of consent in England from twelve to thirteen in 1875. Later, Stead and Bramwell Booth of the Salvation Army joined forces to expose the growth in child prostitution. In 1895, Stead published "Maiden Tribute of Modern Babylon" in the newspaper he edited, *The Pall Mall Gazette*, recounting how he purchased a thirteen-year-old daughter of a chimney-sweep for five pounds to show how easy it was to procure young girls for prostitution. He was later criminally prosecuted for this act and spent three months in jail, but the publicity from his case led to the passage of the Criminal Law Campaign Act that raised the age of consent from thirteen to sixteen.[29]

In late nineteenth- and early twentieth-century America, the increasing visibility of red light districts led to the rise of a US movement against "white slavery," which argued that foreign men seduced, coerced, lured, tricked, or forced girls and young women into brothels far from their homes.[30] In 1909, muckraker George Kibbe Turner from Chicago published an article in *McLure's Magazine* on how Eastern European immigrants, particularly Jewish men, had lured "poorly paid young mill girls" from the industrial towns of New England and Pennsylvania and, later, girls from the tenement districts of the East Side into the "white slave trade."[31] White reformers claimed that thousands of girls were involved and that they were irreversibly harmed by their involvement in the sex trade. In response, Congress passed the White Slave Traffic Act in 1910, popularly known as the Mann Act after its main Congressional proponent Representative James Mann. The Act prohibited the interstate transportation of any woman or girl for "prostitution or debauchery, or for any other immoral purpose."[32]

These campaigns occurred at a time of increasing industrialization, urbanization, and immigration, as well as increasing female participation in the labor force, which generated anxieties about shifting gender and race relations.[33] In the nineteenth century, according to historian Nicola Beidel, "the anti-vice movement succeeded when its leaders connected concerns about the moral corruption of children, occasioned by changes in gender roles

[29] Stephanie A. Limoncelli, *The Politics of Trafficking: The First International Movement to Combat the Sexual Exploitation of Women* (San Francisco, CA: Stanford University Press, 2010), 44–46.

[30] Jessica R. Pliley, *Policing Sexuality: The Mann Act and the Making of the FBI* (Cambridge, MA: Harvard University Press, 2014).

[31] George Kibbe Turner, "The Daughters of the Poor: A Plain Story of the Development of New York City as a Leading Centre of the White Slave Trade of the World, under Tammany Hall," *McClure's Magazine* 34 (November 1909), 45–61; see also George Kibbe Turner, "The City of Chicago: A Study of the Great Immoralities," *McClure's Magazine* 28 (April 1907), 575–592.

[32] Ch. 395, 36 Stat. 825 (1910) (codified as amended at 18 U.S.C. §§ 2421–2424 (2006)).

[33] Ruth Rosen, *The Lost Sisterhood: Prostitution in America, 1900–1918* (Baltimore, MD: John Hopkins University Press, 1982), 15; Pliley, *Policing Sexuality*.

and the social meaning of sexuality, to threats to the social position of upper and middle classes. The latter concern resulted from the growing numbers, social presence, and political power of immigrants."[34] The white slave trade narrative portrayed young white women held against their will by foreign men, particularly Jews and men from southern Europe, who were not considered white at the time, and men from Asia.[35] The cover art of the 1911 book, *Fighting the Traffic in Young Girls* by Ernest A. Bell, for example, portrays a glowing white girl behind bars with her hands prayerfully folded in front of her looking imploringly skyward with the caption, "My God! If Only I Could Get Out of Here," while a shady figure of a man lurks in the background, rubbing his hands together in a gesture of avarice, or perhaps lust (see Figure 1.1). This image is surprisingly similar to images used in contemporary anti-trafficking campaigns.[36]

Despite widespread concern about the "white slave trade" in the United States and abroad, there has been little documented evidence that very many females were coerced into the sex trade at the time.[37] Most scholars agree that the involvement of girls and young women in prostitution was overstated and that these campaigns were moral panics based in anxieties about social changes like immigration, urbanization, and shifting gender roles.[38] Sociologist Brian Donovan argues that white slavery narratives "performed the ideological work necessary for gender and racial formation ... they clarified the boundaries of racial categories and allowed native-born whites to speak of a collective 'us' as opposed to a 'them.'"[39] White people then used these racial fabrications to claim moral superiority and to justify segregation and economic exploitation of African Americans and immigrants. Some claim that current campaigns against sex trafficking are similarly exaggerated and used to justify the expansion of law enforcement and the prison industrial complex in the United States.[40]

Criminal seduction, age of consent, and white slavery campaigns assumed that young white women were the passive victims of sexually aggressive and lustful men whom the state should restrain, but by the early twentieth century

---

[34] Beisel, *Imperiled Innocents*, 4.

[35] Karen Brodkin, *How Jews Became White Folks and What that Says about Race in America* (New Brunswick, NJ: Rutgers University Press, 1998).

[36] See, e.g., www.pinterest.com/mcc005/human-trafficking/?lp=true.

[37] Levine, *Prostitution, Race and Politics*, 249.

[38] See, for example, Christopher Diffee, "Sex and the City: The White Slavery Scare and Social Governance in the Progressive Era," *American Quarterly* 57.2 (June 2005), 411–437; Jo Doezema, "Loose Women or Lost Women? The Re-Emergence of the Myth of White Slavery in Contemporary Discourses of Trafficking in Women," *Gender Issues* 18.1 (Winter 2000), 23–50.

[39] Brian Donovan, *White Slave Crusades: Race, Gender, and Anti-Vice Activism, 1887–1917* (Chicago, IL: University of Illinois Press, 2006), 129.

[40] Jo Doezema, *Sex Slaves and Discourse Masters: The Construction of Trafficking* (London: Zed Books, 2010).

FIGURE 1.1 Ernest A. Bell, *Fighting the Traffic in Young Girls or War on the White Slave Trade*, 1910.

the narrative of sexual danger shifted.[41] White reformers in moral protection campaigns began pushing for laws to protect girls from themselves by supporting the passage of "incorrigible girl" statutes that authorized the detention of girls "in danger of becoming morally depraved." The goal of these laws was to "redirect the illicit impulses of the sexually nonconforming female delinquent into more normative channels."[42] These laws were targeted in particular at immigrant and working class adolescent girls living in tenement districts, and were a form of addressing the potential "moral degradation" of overcrowded and impoverished homes, morally suspect employment environments, and the "alluring world of commercial amusements."[43] Sometimes, however, working-class and immigrant parents themselves would turn to courts to control rebellious daughters. Girls engaged in sexual improprieties were charged for "being incorrigible or disorderly," allowing the state to regulate girls' sexual conduct by placing them in juvenile reformatories where they could be trained to become good wives and mothers. The number of reformatories for delinquent girls and young women expanded in the early twentieth century, rising to fifty-seven across the country by 1924.[44] According to historian Mary Odem, "the extensive system of courts, special police, detention centers, and reformatories established by purity reformers continued to monitor and regulate the sexuality of young women and girls throughout most of the twentieth century."[45] At the time, courts exhibited an "intense preoccupation with girls' sexuality and their obedience to parental authority."[46] Girls appearing before family courts in the early twentieth century were almost always charged with "immorality or waywardness," frequently related to sexual behavior, for which they experienced severe sanctions. For offenses like running away from home or truancy, over which courts had wide discretion in imposing sanctions, girls were much more likely than boys to be detained, and for much longer periods of time. This sexual double standard reflected a gender bias in the juvenile justice system that continued throughout the twentieth century. According to MacDonald and Chesney-Lind, courts have had "particular difficulty with persistent female defiance."[47]

The campaigns during this early period are remarkably similar to the campaigns that emerged in the late twentieth century. Spurred by some of the

---

[41] Freedman, *Redefining Rape*, 147–167.
[42] Ehrlich, *Regulating Desire*, 62; Odem, *Delinquent Daughters*, 95–127; see also John C. Spurlock, *Youth and Sexuality in the Twentieth-Century United States* (New York, NY: Routledge, 2016), 22.
[43] Ehrlich, *Regulating Desire*, 71.
[44] Odem, *Delinquent Daughters*, 113–121; Spurlock, *Youth and Sexuality*, 21.
[45] Odem, *Delinquent Daughters*, 189.
[46] John M. MacDonald and Meda Chesney-Lind, "Gender Bias and Juvenile Justice Revisited: A Multiyear Analysis," *Crime & Delinquency* 47.2 (April 2001), 173; see also Odem, *Delinquent Daughters*, 1–7.
[47] MacDonald and Chesney-Lind, "Gender Bias and Juvenile Justice Revisited," 189.

same types of social changes and dislocations that had inspired the earlier campaigns, late twentieth-century reformers told a racialized tale of female victimization and need for protection. Nineteenth and early twentieth century campaigns called for people across ideological and political belief to unify against the "Apollyon of evil" that was the commercial sexual exploitation of young girls.[48] They made parallels between the "white slave trade" and African slavery; they bemoaned that "our girls" were being lured from the countryside and debauched; and they objected to the focus on immigrant girls to the neglect of "American-born girls," imploring their audiences to realize that the "white slave trade" was not just a problem in other countries, but was right here in American cities.[49] These arguments were repeated in surprisingly similar ways in the late twentieth and early twenty-first century campaigns against the US youth sex trade.

## SEXUAL LIBERATION AND YOUTH ENDANGERMENT

A range of social, legal, and cultural changes across the century spurred 1970s activism against the US youth sex trade. By the 1960s sexual revolution, youth had liberalized attitudes toward premarital sex and displayed a greater willingness to openly discuss sex. In 1900, only about six percent of US women who were nineteen years old had engaged in premarital sex but by 1976 that rate had climbed to 55.2 percent. These rates increased especially fast in the 1970s. Rates of premarital sexual activity of girls aged fifteen to nineteen increased from 26.8 percent in 1971 to 34.9 percent in 1976.[50] National surveys of youth showed that the majority of teenage girls believed that sex before marriage was a legitimate choice. Commentators at the time concluded that the norm of premarital chastity was "effectively defunct."[51] These changes in behavior created great anxiety among parents and policymakers. Alarmed headlines announced increasing rates of premarital sex and pregnancy.[52]

---

[48] Bell, *Fighting the Traffic in Young Girls*, 29–30 (from quotation of anti-trafficking activist William Alexander Coote).

[49] Ibid. 47, 68–70, 105–106, 134, 181–182, 186–187, 261.

[50] Jeremy Greenwood, Jesús Fernández-Villaverde, and Nezih Guner, "From Shame to Game in One Hundred Years: An Economic Model of the Rise in Premarital Sex and its De-Stigmatization," *Vox* (February 20, 2010); Melvin Zelnik and John F. Kantner, "First Pregnancies to Women Aged 15–19: 1976 and 1971," *Family Planning Perspectives* 10.1 (January/February 1978), 12; Melvin Zelnik and John F. Kantner, "Sexual and Contraceptive Experience of Young Unmarried Women in the United States, 1976 and 1971," *Family Planning Perspectives* 9.2 (March–April 1977), 55–71.

[51] Melvin Zelnik, John F. Kantner, and Kathleen Ford, *Sex and Pregnancy in Adolescence* (Beverly Hills, CA: Sage, 1981), 47, 65. See also, Carolyn Bronstein, *Battling Pornography: The American Feminist Anti-Pornography Movement, 1976–1986* (New York, NY: Cambridge University Press, 2011), 1–24.

[52] See, for example, "Premarital Sex, Pregnancy Jumps 33%," *Daytona Beach Morning Journal* (January 31, 1978).

According to Carolyn Bronstein, "parents worried that a generation of fifteen- and sixteen-year-olds girls had become sexual prey for eighteen- and nineteen-year-old men."[53] More generally, the 1960s and 1970s were a time when youth intensely questioned adult authority through student movements and protests of the Vietnam War. Runaway youth and youth homelessness skyrocketed.[54] Young people were integrally involved in the broiling social movements of the day – the civil rights movement, the women's movement, and the gay liberation movement – which challenged traditional beliefs and public policies affecting the most intimate parts of American lives, including marriage, reproduction, and sexuality.

Legal norms relating to sexuality were also shifting, increasing youth control over their reproductive lives. In 1965, the Supreme Court ruled that married couples had a constitutional right to use contraception, which they later expanded to single people. Two years later, Congress passed Title X of the Public Health Services Act establishing a comprehensive federal family planning program.[55] In 1973, the Supreme Court ruled that women had a constitutional right to access abortion. Three years later, the Court struck down a Missouri statute that required girls to obtain parental consent for an abortion (although three years after that the Court would allow states to require parental consent as long as they provided a judicial bypass procedure).[56] In 1977, the Supreme Court invalidated a New York law that banned the distribution of nonprescription contraceptives to youth under the age of sixteen,[57] and a year later Congress required federal family planning clinics to offer free services to teenagers without parental notification.[58] These surprising developments were fueled by perceptions of a teen pregnancy "epidemic" although, in fact, teen pregnancy rates were at an all-time low. Historian Shoshanna Ehrlich attributes adults' spike in concern about teen pregnancy to the increasing visibility of pregnancy among middle-class white girls, who were more likely to refuse to give up their babies than previously. As legislators recognized teen pregnancy as a problem affecting the "girl next door," and not just the racialized other, they responded by passing laws to support pregnant and parenting teens as well as to provide confidential family planning services.[59]

Other societal changes in medicine, law and culture challenged traditional gender, racial, and sexual hierarchies as well. In 1960, the FDA approved the contraceptive pill, which became widely available by the late 1960s. For the first time, women had a highly reliable method of avoiding pregnancy that they

---

[53] Bronstein, *Battling Pornography*, 32.

[54] Karen Staller, *Runaways: How the Sixties Counterculture Shaped Today's Policies and Practices* (New York, NY: Columbia University Press, 2006).

[55] *Connecticut v. Griswold*, 381 U.S. 479 (1965); *Eisenstadt v. Baird*, 405 U.S. 438 (1972); 42 U. S.C. § 300(a), Hist. & Stat. Note 1978.

[56] *Roe v. Wade*, 410 U.S. 113 (1973); *Planned Parenthood of Central Missouri v. Danforth*, 428 U.S. 52 (1976); *Bellotti v. Baird*, 443 U.S. 662 (1979).

[57] *Carey v. Population Services*, 431 U.S. 678 (1977).

[58] 124 Congressional Record H37, 044 (1978).    [59] Ehrlich, *Regulating Desire*, 87–110.

controlled, separating heterosexual intimacy from procreation. Procreation and childrearing was increasingly separated from marriage as out-of-wedlock birth rates rose and marital dissolution became more common as a result of the legalization of no-fault divorce. This reshaped expectations about marriage by undermining the traditional economic bargain between a male breadwinner and female homemaker. After Congress approved the Twenty-Sixth Amendment in 1971 lowering the voting age to 18, states began to lower the age of majority to 18.[60] This combined with a rising average age of first marriage meant that young people had more independence earlier, and parents had less control over them. Furthermore, women's labor force participation rate soared in the 1970s, spurred by a changing economy with an expanding service sector and new job opportunities for women resulting from anti-discrimination laws. The Civil Rights Act of 1964 prohibited race and sex discrimination in the workplace, Title IX of the Educational Amendments of 1972 prohibited sex discrimination in federally funded educational institutions, and affirmative action programs opened doors to nontraditional occupations for women of color, white women, and men of color.[61] In addition to laws against race discrimination, the 1965 Immigration and Nationality Act greatly increased the number of immigrants, particularly from Latin America and Asia, which likely increased anxieties about racial integration.[62] In 1967, the Supreme Court ruled in *Loving v. Virginia* that the state's ban on interracial marriage was unconstitutional.[63] On issues of sexuality, the Supreme Court significantly narrowed the ability of states to restrict pornography under the first amendment in 1973 and not until 1982 did the Court rule that states could restrict child pornography.[64] The commercial sex industry grew significantly in the 1970s and became more visible. The hardcore feature film *Deep Throat*, released in 1972, spent ninety-six weeks on *Variety's* list of the top-grossing films and earned more than $100 million worldwide. Mainstream popular culture experienced an "explosion of sexuality and sexual content," from the *Love Boat*, to *Charlie's Angels*, to *Three's Company*.[65] Finally, in 1979, the American Psychological Association declassified homosexuality as a mental disorder in the *Diagnostic and Statistical Manual*.

In response to these changing sexual norms, as well as attitudes and behaviors of youth, parents expressed concern about losing control over their

---

[60] Staller, *Runaways*, 20.
[61] Civil Rights Act of 1964, Pub. L. 88–352, 78 Stat. 241, enacted July 2, 1964; Education Amendments of 1972, Public Law No. 92-318, 86 Stat. 235 (June 23, 1972); U.S Executive Order 11246 (1965); U.S. Executive Order 11375 (1967).
[62] Pub. L. 89–236, 79 Stat. 911, enacted June 30, 1968; Michael Lind, *The Next American Nation: The New Nationalism and the Fourth American Revolution* (New York, NY: The Free Press, 1995), 133.
[63] *Loving v. Virginia*, 388 U.S. 1 (1967).
[64] *Miller v. California*, 413 U.S. 15 (1973); *New York v. Ferber*, 458 U.S. 747 (1982).
[65] Bronstein, *Battling Pornography*, 65.

teenage daughters, who were becoming what historian Rickie Solinger has described as "threatening emblems of sexual and reproductive insubordination."[66] Public concern about sexually transmitted diseases among youth, particularly venereal disease, added fuel to the fire. In 1978, a letter writer to the *Chicago Tribune* bemoaned the "problem of sexual freedom among teenagers" and suggested "putting both the guilty boy and girl into an institution where they are not allowed freedom to come and go, combined with compulsory work and study programs."[67] The New Right mobilized these anxieties to recruit evangelical Christians into political campaigns to reestablish morality and "family values." They objected to government interference in the family and argued that parents should be able to impart moral values to children, particularly with regard to sexuality. The first target of this campaign was public school sex education and government-funded family planning for teens in the 1970s. But this later expanded to restricting abortion, attacking pornography and the sex industry, and opposing gay rights. Concern about boys in the sex trade bolstered homophobia through actions like Anita Bryant's "Save Our Children" crusade, which "warned that young boys were being recruited into homosexual rings to serve adult men."[68] Evangelicals tied fear of sexual immorality with "national security and impending apocalypse," thereby positioning themselves as the saviors of civilization.[69] Campaigns against juvenile prostitution in the late 1970s became a way that evangelical Christians, seeking to stem the "tide of social and moral decay brought on by the liberation movements of the previous decade," organized against changing sexual mores.[70]

## THE RUNAWAY YOUTH PROBLEM, SHIFTING PUBLIC POLICY, AND UNINTENDED CONSEQUENCES

In addition to changing social conditions, the rise in activism against juvenile prostitution was fueled by public concern about increasing youth homelessness in the 1960s and 1970s. At first this concern focused on the predominantly middle-class, white, hippie "flower children" (who were mostly in their late teens and early 20s) who fled to the Haight-Ashbury district of San Francisco during the 1967 "summer of love" to smoke marijuana and protest the Vietnam War. The next year, hippies gathered in Boston and, in 1970, they congregated in Boulder. Newspapers and magazines ran many stories about teenagers

---

[66] Rickie Solinger, *Pregnancy and Power: A Short History of Reproductive Politics in America* (New York, NY: New York University Press, 2005), 239.

[67] William A. Nott, "Morality, Contraception, and Teen Sex," *Chicago Tribune* (December 22, 1979), W10.

[68] Bronstein, *Battling Pornography*, 241.     [69] Moslener, *Virgin Nation*, 5.

[70] Bronstein, *Battling Pornography*, 241.

running away to join the hippie movement, and cities reported high numbers of homeless youth and missing children.[71]

If media presented youth on the streets as alienated children of the middle class, scholarly studies documented the more frequent reality of working-class youth fleeing familial abuse and poverty. The oil crisis, the economic recession that started in 1973, and growing unemployment exacerbated youth homelessness. A 1975 study prepared for the Department of Health, Education and Welfare reported that there had been a marked increase in the number of runaway youth between 1968 and 1972. Concern about the runaway youth problem spiked in 1973 in Houston when a serial murderer targeting homeless youth killed twenty-three young boys.[72] By focusing on white, middle-class runaways and shocking stories of abuse, the media mobilized public concern about youth homelessness, leading to increased social services and government responses.[73]

Social service agencies scrambled to provide help to homeless youth. Runaway centers like Huckleberry House in San Francisco and Runaway House in Washington, DC, formed to provide temporary shelter and services to youth and help youth reconnect with their parents. A network of "grassroots 'alternative' agencies" sprung up across the country, including hotlines and crisis intervention centers, organized by religious organizations and citizen groups. These centers were separate from law enforcement and the juvenile justice system because many believed that runaways should not be handled by the police or courts; it was deemed a "family problem" that should be solved by the family with the help of social service agencies. However, social services were often inadequate and many families were ill-equipped to deal with troubled youth.[74] There were also organizations formed within the LGBT community to

[71] Deborah Klein Walker, *Runaway Youth: An Annotated Bibliography and Literature Overview* (Washington, DC: Department of Health, Education and Welfare, May 1975); David Crystal and Irwin H. Gold, "A Social Work Mission to Hippieland," *Children*, 16.1 (1969), 28–32; David E. Suddick, "Runaways: A Review of the Literature," *Juvenile Justice* 24 (August 1974), 47–54; D. Kelly Weisberg, *Children of the Night: A Study of Adolescent Prostitution* (Lexington, MA: Lexington Books, 1985), 3–4.

[72] Richard Bock and Abigail English, *Got Me on The Run* (Boston, MA: Beacon, 1973) (documenting the lives of working-class runaway youth); Clifford J. English, *On the Streets: A Participant Observational Study of an Adolescent Subculture* (Doctoral Dissertation, University of Michigan, 1972); Bibi Wein, *The Runaway Generation* (New York, NY: McKay, 1970); Mary Reinholz, "The Throwaway Children," *Youth Reporter* (December 1973), 7; Walker, *Runaway Youth*; Weisberg, *Children of the Night*, 2–5.

[73] Kerwin Kaye, "Male Prostitution in the Twentieth Century: Pseudohomosexuals, Hoodlum Homosexuals, and Exploited Teens," *Journal of Homosexuality* 46.1/2 (2003), 39; see also, Staller, *Runaways*, 49–50 (arguing that public discourses about runaways evolved over time from harmless in the early 1960 to unsafe in the mid-to-late 1960s to a public problem in the late 1970s).

[74] Walker, *Runaway Youth*, 31; Dodie Butler, Joe Riener, and Bill Treanor, *Runaway House: A Youth-Run Service Project* (Washington, DC: National Institute of Mental Health, 1974); Celeste MacLeod, "Street People: The New Migrants," *The Nation* (October 22, 1973), 395;

support homeless LGBT youth engaged in the street economy. For example, under the auspices of Glide Memorial Church, gay male and transgender female youth formed a group called Vanguard in San Francisco's Tenderloin district in the late 1960s to support each other and engage in political actions.[75] In the early 1970s, STAR (Street Transvestite Action Revolutionaries), founded by Sylvia Rivera, supported transgender youth in New York City.[76]

Concern about runaways and youth homelessness inspired public policy shifts at the federal and state levels that changed the relations of the state to youth. At the time, most states had runaway laws that forbade youth from leaving home without parental consent. These laws usually applied to youth under twenty-one, although some states had gendered statutes declaring different ages of majority for boys and for girls, which were declared unconstitutional in 1975. These laws often provided for police intervention to retrieve youth. Legal doctrines of "in loco parentis" gave schools authority over children and "parents patriae" exempted juvenile courts from the normal procedural protections that adults enjoyed. Traditionally, the law allowed police to detain youth for status offenses, like running away from home, "ungovernability," "incorrigibility," being a truant, being in danger of becoming "morally depraved," or being a "person in need of supervision" – acts that if committed by an adult would not be a crime. In the 1970s, many American youth were in juvenile detention facilities across the country, but a significant portion of these incarcerated youth were held for status offenses.[77]

Girls were much more likely to be detained for status offenses than boys because of the belief that girls needed to be protected from the danger of leading "an idle, dissolute, lewd, or immoral life," which was considered ruinous to girls but not to boys.[78] Girls could end up confined to state facilities for years, until they turned eighteen or in some cases twenty-one. For example, in 1966, a Connecticut court sentenced a seventeen-year-old girl to four years at the Connecticut State Farm for Women under a Connecticut law that allowed

---

Lillian Ambrosino, *Runaways* (Boston, MA: Beacon, 1971); Larry Beggs, *Huckleberry's for Runaways* (New York, NY: Ballantine, 1969); Jeffrey D. Blum and Judith E. Smith, *Nothing Left to Lose* (Boston, MA: Beacon, 1972), 44.

[75] Jennifer Worley, "'Street Power' and the Claiming of Public Space: San Francisco's 'Vanguard' and Pre-Stonewall Queer Radicalism," *Captive Genders: Trans Embodiment and the Prison Industrial Complex*, ed. by Eric A. Stanley and Nat Smith (Oakland, CA: AK Press, 2011), 41–56.

[76] *Street Transvestite Action Revolutionaries: Survival, Revolt, and Queer Antagonist Struggle* (Untorelli Press, 2011); Leslie Feinberg, "Street Transvestite Action Revolutionaries," *Lavender & Red*, Part 73 (Workers World, September 24, 2006).

[77] Mark J. Green, "Runaways on the Legal Leash," *Trial* 7.5 (1971), 28–29; *Stanton v. Stanton*, 421 U.S. 7 (1975); Gorden A. Raley, "The JJDP Act: A Second Look," *Juvenile Justice* 2:2 (Fall/Winter 1995), 11–18; Staller, *Runaways*.

[78] MacLeod, "Street Girls of the '70s," 486; Barry C. Feld, "Violent Girls or Relabeled Status Offenders? An Alternative Interpretation of the Data," *Crime & Delinquency* 55.2 (April 2009), 241–265 at 244, 257.

detention if a young woman was in "manifest danger of falling into habits of vice." On appeal, the circuit court upheld the sentence, reasoning that due process was inapplicable because the proceedings were civil in nature and the purpose of the statute was protective rather than punitive.[79] LGBT youth were also more likely to end up incarcerated for gender non-conforming and non-normative sexual behaviors.[80] In 1967 the Presidential Task Force Commission on Law Enforcement and the Administration of Justice issued a report recommending major reforms of the juvenile court systems, including eliminating noncriminal conduct from juvenile courts' jurisdiction and establishing community-based youth service bureaus to provide services and counseling to troubled youth.[81]

At the same time, advocates for children's rights pushed for expanding the rights of juvenile offenders.[82] A series of Supreme Court cases established due process rights for youth in juvenile courts, including the right to notice of charges, the right to counsel, and a "beyond a reasonable doubt" standard of proof.[83] At the state level, several high court decisions also established due process rights for children.[84] Other cases successfully challenged laws that allowed the jailing of juveniles purportedly for their protection. For example, the 1971 California case, *Gonzales v. Mailliard*, held that a statute allowing the detention of a juvenile deemed "in danger of leading an immoral life" was unconstitutionally vague.[85] These rights-based reforms, however, existed in tension with the philosophical underpinnings of care in juvenile court proceedings and with other trends in the 1970s, like an emphasis on protecting communities, retribution and individual responsibility, as well as the influence of developmental psychology and the notion of adolescents' diminished culpability.[86]

The trend toward deinstitutionalization and enhanced due process rights for juveniles led some states to close juvenile detention centers. By 1972,

---

[79] *Mattiello v. Connecticut*, 4 Conn. Cir. 55 (App. Div. 1966), *cert. denied*, 154 Conn. 737 (1966).

[80] Wesley Ware, "'Rounding up the Homosexuals': The Impact of Juvenile Court on Queer and Trans/Gender Non-Conforming Youth," in *Captive Genders: Trans Embodiment and the Prison Industrial Complex*, ed. by Eric A. Stanley and Nat Smith (Oakland, CA: AK Press, 2011), 77–84.

[81] President's Commission on Law Enforcement and Administration of Justice, *The Challenge of Crime in a Free Society* (1967), 83–84.

[82] Patrick T. Murphy, *Our Kindly Parent – the State: The Juvenile Justice System and How It Works* (New York, NY: Viking, 1974), 9; Green, "Runaways on a Legal Leash," 28–29.

[83] *Kent v. United States*, 383 U.S. 541 (1966); *In re Gault*, 387 U.S. 1 (1967); *In Re Winship*, 397 U.S. 358 (1970).

[84] See, for example, *Harris v. Caledine*, 160 W. Va. 172 (1977); *Doe v. Norris*, 751 S.W.2d 834 (Tenn. 1988).

[85] No. 50424 (N.D. Cal. Feb. 9, 1971).

[86] Shelby Schwartz, "Harboring Concerns: The Problematic Conceptual Reorientation of Juvenile Prostitution Adjudication in New York," *Columbia Journal of Gender and the Law* 18.1 (2009), 235–280.

Massachusetts had closed all of its juvenile institutions and New York City closed three of its four secure juvenile facilities, placing juveniles into foster or group homes instead. Advocates working with runaway youth argued against large juvenile institutions that maintained an authoritarian atmosphere and did not provide individualized care and attention. Policymakers feared that youth exposed to the juvenile court system were more likely to return.[87] In a 1972 book, *Nothing Left to Lose*, about the runaway youth problem, youth advocates Jeffrey Blum and Judith Smith argued that youth "do not come out unscathed [from state corrective institutions]. They adapt to survive: they become cynical, manipulative, amoral."[88] Even judges and police in the early 1970s spoke out against addressing the runaway problem through law enforcement and the juvenile justice system. The National Association of Sheriffs condemned the practice of jailing runaways and Philadelphia's Judge Lisa Aversa Richette published a book, *The Throwaway Children*, calling for the deinstitutionalization of runaway youth and the creation of community-based programs that would provide individualized care and services to youth, including housing, education, and employment.[89] There was a push for more independence for young people that the system had failed. In the early 1970s, for example, Connecticut created an independent living program where the state would pay for a room in a motel for minors for whom other alternatives had not worked.[90] This proliferation of community-based organizations addressing the needs of runaway and homeless youth joined together in 1974 to form the National Network of Runaway and Youth Services (later the National Network for Youth) in Washington, DC, to lobby for federal policy on youth homelessness.[91]

In response to this lobbying and the clear need for juvenile justice reform, Senator Birch Bayh drafted the Runaway Youth Act, first introduced in 1971 and passed in 1974 as Title III of the Juvenile Justice and Delinquency Prevention Act.[92] This law focused on prevention of delinquency and rehabilitation of youth, rather than punishment, by requiring states to remove all status offenders from juvenile detention and correctional facilities and place them into community-based group homes and nonresidential treatment

---

[87] Holden and Kapler, "Deinstitutionalizing Status Offenders," 3; *Juvenile Delinquency Act, Hearings Before the General Subcommittee on Education of the House Committee on Education and Labor*, 90th Cong., 1st Session (1967), 16 (testimony of HEW Secretary John Gardner).

[88] Blum and Smith, *Nothing Left to Lose*, 80.

[89] MacLeod, "Street Girls of the '70s," 488; Lisa Aversa Richette, *The Throwaway Children* (New York, NY: Dell Publishing, 1969), 317–327.

[90] William Cockerham, "Kate is Veteran Prostitute at 17," *The Hartford Courant* (July 16, 1978).

[91] National Network for Youth, About, at www.nn4youth.org/about/.

[92] Juvenile Justice and Delinquency Prevention Act of 1974, Pub. L. No. 93–415; see Gwen A. Holden and Robert A. Kapler "Deinstitutionalizing Status Offenders: A Record of Progress," *Juvenile Justice*, 2:2 (Fall/Winter 1995), 3–10.

programs. The Act also created financial incentives for states to work on prevention of juvenile delinquency and to divert youth away from the juvenile justice system and into community-based treatment programs. Congress authorized the Department of Health, Education and Welfare to spend ten million dollars each year for three years for the creation of shelters and counseling programs for homeless youth.[93] Furthermore, the Act created the Office of Juvenile Justice and Delinquency Prevention, which supported the diversion of status offenders from the juvenile justice system and provided resources for states to accomplish this.[94] Finally, the Act enhanced due process rights of juvenile defendants and provided for more effective sealing of juvenile records.

In the years following the passage of Runaway Youth Act, some states adopted legislation requiring the deinstitutionalization of status offenders and, in 1977, Congress increased funding for delinquency prevention and amended the Act to remove the requirement that deinstitutionalized youth be placed in shelter facilities. By 1978, the Office of Juvenile Justice and Delinquency Prevention's budget topped $100 million a year. The Act contributed to the closure of many juvenile jails, detention centers, and correctional institutions. By the 1980s, the number of status offenders detained in juvenile detention facilities across the country had decreased by fifty percent and the Act was funding 169 runaway and homeless youth programs in all fifty states and the District of Columbia.[95] The number of status offenders held in secure facilities declined by 95% between 1974 and 1988.[96]

In response to the high numbers of runaway and homeless youth in the late 1960s and early 1970s, and the deinstitutionalization of status offenders as a result of state and local policy shifts, the need for youth services increased dramatically. By 1970, most cities had hotlines and free clinics for runaway youth, but only five cities had halfway houses to shelter youth.[97] With funds

---

[93] United States Senate, United States Congress, *The Runaway Youth Act Report (Accompanies S. 645) Together with Additional Views*. Report # 93–191 (Calendar No. 181), 93rd Congress, 1st Session, June 4, 1974.

[94] Karlyn Carroll and Keith Boggs, *Diversion of Youth From The Juvenile Justice System: Project Orientation Resource Handbook* (Washington, DC: US Dept. of Justice, Law Enforcement Assistance Administration, Office of Juvenile Justice and Delinquency Prevention, 1980); Alicia Rooney Yowell, *Deinstitutionalization Of Status Offenders: A Program Planning Guide* (Washington, DC: US Dept. of Justice, Law Enforcement Assistance Administration, Office of Juvenile Justice and Delinquency Prevention, 1980).

[95] *Juvenile Justice Amendments of 1980, Hearings Before the Subcommittee on Human Resources of the House Committee on Education and Labor*, 96th Cong., Second Sess. (1980), 43 (testimony of Ira M. Schwartz, Office of Juvenile Justice and Delinquency Prevention); *Problems of Runaway Youth, Hearings Before the Subcommittee on Juvenile Justice of the Senate Committee on the Judiciary*, 97th Cong., 2d Sess. (1982) [hereinafter *Problems of Runaway Youth Hearings, 1982*], 50–51 (testimony of Professor D. Kelly Weisberg).

[96] Feld, "Violent Girls or Relabeled Status Offenders?" 245.

[97] Lillian Ambrosino, "Runaways," *Today's Education* 60 (1971), 26–28.

from the 1974 Runaway Youth Act as well as state and private support, social service organizations working with homeless youth proliferated, providing street outreach and shelter to youth. Many of them created special programs for youth involved in prostitution. One of the earliest providers offering specific services to youth in prostitution was Bridge Over Troubled Waters, founded in 1970 in Boston to serve runaway youth and which established a dedicated staff position to reach the city's gay youth involved in prostitution.[98] Covenant House, founded in New York City by Reverend Bruce Ritter in 1972, was a charity providing services to homeless youth. In 1977, Ritter began to focus on prostitution and pornography, and opened a large shelter for homeless youth by Port Authority Bus Terminal. Ritter conducted street outreach, aggressively confronted "pimps and pornographers" in Times Square, and solicited funds with dramatic stories of sexual exploitation of youth. According to historian Peter Wosh, extensive media coverage of Ritter's advocacy "contributed to the social redefinition of youth homelessness in the popular consciousness, tying it inextricably to prostitution and pornography."[99] These programs provided important services to youth but, as the director of Bridge Over Troubled Waters later testified before Congress, the funding was sorely inadequate for the number of youth served.[100]

By the late 1970s, several programs emerged that focused exclusively on youth in the sex trade. Two such programs, whose founders later became national leaders in the movement against youth prostitution, were Children of the Night in Los Angeles and the Paul and Lisa Program in Connecticut. Children of the Night in was founded by Lois Lee in 1979 after, as a young Ph.D. student conducting research into the police treatment of prostitutes beginning in 1976, she encountered police refusal to come to the aid of a seventeen-year-old girl, who was later murdered by the Hillside Strangler. Lee initially housed young women seeking shelter in her two-bedroom apartment and in the homes of volunteers. She later set up a drop-in center and eventually a shelter and recovery center.[101] Lee received funding from the Irvine Foundation and the Giles W. and Elise G. Mead Foundation, as well as significant support and publicity from Hugh Hefner and the

---

[98] Bruce Fisher, Ernest Fazio, D. Kelly Weisberg, Edwin Johnson, Toby Marotta, and Sally Jones, *Juvenile Prostitution: A Resource Manual* (San Francisco, CA: Urban and Rural Systems Associates, July 1982), 86.

[99] Ibid. 86, 103–104; Wosh, *Covenant House*, 104. In 1990, Ritter was forced to resign because of reports that he had engaged in sex with youth under his care and because of financial improprieties.

[100] *Problems of Runaway Youth Hearings, 1982*, 77 (prepared statement of Sister Barbara Whelan, Director, Bridge Over Troubled Waters).

[101] Children of the Night, Who We Are, at www.childrenofthenight.org/who-we-are/; Gregory Ahart, *Sexual Exploitation of Children—A Problem of Unknown Magnitude. Report to the Chairman, Subcommittee on Select Education, House Committee on Education and Labor* (Washington, DC: General Accounting Office, 1982), 38.

Playboy Foundation.[102] The Paul and Lisa Program formed in 1980 in Westbrook, Connecticut, by businessman Frank Barnaba. Barnaba, a sales executive with a water-treatment company, met a young woman named Lisa when they were stranded in a snowstorm at an all-night restaurant in Connecticut. According to Barnaba, she "opened up like a ton of bricks" about her life as a prostitute. Barnaba and his wife helped Lisa get into therapy, out of prostitution and off drugs, but she was later found dead. Barnaba decided to create an organization to help young women like Lisa. He obtained start-up funds from St. Paul's Church in Westbrook, and named the organization the Paul and Lisa Program after the church and the young woman he had been unable to save.[103] The Program offered services, shelter, and educational programs to youth. These two programs served thousands of youth over the following decades, and were models for new programs that developed as federal and state funds became available for this work.

## THE POLITICAL ROOTS OF ACTIVISM AGAINST JUVENILE PROSTITUTION

The growing women's movement contributed toward creating conditions ripe for activism against juvenile prostitution. Several campaigns within the women's movement set the stage for the emergence of concern about juvenile prostitution, including the anti-rape movement, the child sexual abuse movement, the sex workers' rights movement, and feminist opposition to pornography and prostitution. The feminist anti-rape movement grew out of radical feminist consciousness-raising groups in the early 1970s. A 1971 speak-out on rape and an anti-rape conference in New York City, as well as the formation of rape counseling collectives and hotlines in the early 1970s, politicized rape by reframing sexual assault as a "political problem that functions to keep women subordinate to men" rather than a "personal problem for which women should feel shame or guilt."[104] To address the problem, feminists sought to reform rape law by broadening the definition of rape, dividing it into a series of graded offenses with varying degrees of severity based on circumstances such as the amount of force, the seriousness of the act (penetration versus touching), the extent of injury inflicted on the victim, the age of the victim, and the incapacity of the victim. Feminists supported the elimination of the marital rape exemption, corroboration

[102] Interview with Lois Lee, September 7, 2016 (on file with author); Children of the Night, 2010 Founder's Hero of the Heart Award, at www.childrenofthenight.org/pdf/Hugh_Hefner_Founders_Hero_of_the_Heart_Award.pdf.

[103] Paul and Lisa Program, About Us, at www.paulandlisa.org/aboutus.html#; Elizabeth Greene, "A Businessman's Charity Uses Education and Dedication to Aid Teenagers," *Chronicle of Philanthropy* 14.2 (November 1, 2001), 12; Mark Stuart Gill, "Night Stalker: Hitting the Streets in the Name of Corporate Philanthropy," *Business Month* 135:6 (June 1990), 42.

[104] Maria Bevacqua, *Rape on the Public Agenda: Feminism and the Politics of Sexual Assault* (Boston, MA: Northeastern University Press, 2000), 31.

requirements, and prompt reporting requirements, and they advocated for the enactment of rape shield laws, which restricted the admissibility of evidence regarding the victim's sexual history to prove consent or undermine a victim's credibility. Feminists challenged the idea that "real rape" was stranger rape involving extreme violence, naming and bringing attention to "acquaintance rape" and "date rape."[105] Feminists engaged in public education campaigns to challenge societal attitudes that blamed victims for sexual assault. These changes in rape law and the growing public awareness of sexual assault contributed to a shift toward the acknowledgement of the widespread existence and severe impact of sexual assault, and to the idea that a person's appearance, dress or social status should be irrelevant to the determination of whether that person was a victim of sexual assault. These developments provided a basis upon which advocates against the commercial sexual exploitation of youth could build.

Another important influence on these activists was the 1970s movement against child sexual abuse. This movement of child sexual abuse survivors, feminists, professionals and other advocates spurred a revolution in attitudes and policies toward child sexual abuse. Awareness of the issue of child sexual abuse grew out of the anti-rape movement of the early 1970s, first developing in consciousness raising groups of the women's liberation movements. Feminists analyzed child sexual abuse as a "social and political problem rather than an individual pathology," linking it to patriarchy and male power, particularly the "cultural legitimation of fathers' sexual access to their daughters."[106] At the time, child sexual abuse was considered a rare occurrence, but feminist activists argued that it was widespread, and backed up this claim with grassroots and experiential research. Florence Rush, a psychiatric social worker who participated in a consciousness-raising group in early 1971, developed the first extensive feminist analysis of incest, which she presented at a 1971 conference on rape sponsored by the New York Radical Feminists, and later published as an article in the 1974 book *Rape: A Sourcebook for Women* and expanded into the 1980 book *The Best Kept Secret: Sexual Abuse of Children*.[107] Feminists developed self-help techniques, challenging and eventually transforming professional therapeutic treatment of child sexual abuse survivors. Over time, the movement expanded to include politicians from across the political spectrum, physicians and mental health practitioners, and a diverse range of survivors. As non-feminists joined the movement, there was a shift away from a political analysis toward viewing the issue as a medical and criminal problem. Activists used the discourse of trauma and recovery, as opposed to empowerment, and offenders were portrayed as unredeemable and

[105] Susan Estrich, *Real Rape* (Boston, MA: Harvard University Press, 1987).     [106] Ibid. 23.
[107] Ibid.; Lynn Sacco, *Unspeakable: Father-Daughter Incest in American History* (Baltimore, MD: The Johns Hopkins University Press, 2009); Florence Rush, *The Best Kept Secret: Sexual Abuse of Children* (New York, NY: McGraw-Hill Book Company, 1981).

untreatable. Activists pushed for harsher laws for child sexual abuse, including sex offender registries and community notification. Whereas feminists focused on how child sex abuse derived from and reinforced patriarchal systems of male power, non-feminist reformers depoliticized the issue by focusing on individual victims and perpetrators. These activists leveraged ideas about childhood innocence that had deep roots in American culture. Over time this movement had a significant influence on mainstream culture and institutions, as well as the political and cultural landscape.[108] While focused primarily on noncommercial sexual behavior, this movement was an important foundation for campaigns against the US youth sex trade in the late twentieth and early twenty-first centuries because it raised awareness about the extent and harm of child sex abuse.

A third important locus of activism out of which grew concern about juvenile prostitution in the 1970s was women's movement organizing for and against the sex trade. Many feminists in the women's liberation movement, including leaders like Kate Millett and Susan Brownmiller, supported the decriminalization of women in prostitution, but considered prostitution to be exploitation and a form of male violence against women, so their long-term goal was the elimination of prostitution. Some women in the sex trade, on the other hand, argued for full decriminalization in the name of sexual freedom and women's right to control their bodies. Tensions exploded between these two groups in December 1971 at a conference on prostitution at Chelsea High School in New York City organized by women's movement leader Kate Millet. The conference culminated with a panel titled "The Elimination of Prostitution." Feminist prostitutes' rights activists angrily interrupted the panel, protesting against the elimination of their livelihoods and limiting their sexual freedom.[109] The same year on the West Coast, Margo St. James formed Whores, Housewives and Others (WHO) in San Francisco, seeking to bring women together to engage in consciousness raising about laws restricting sexual freedom, including prostitution laws. Two years later, St. James formed the first prostitutes' rights group COYOTE (Call Off Your Old Tired Ethics) in San Francisco, along with Priscilla Alexander, with the goal of decriminalizing sex work and combatting stigma against prostitutes.[110] Later in the 1970s, feminists on both sides of the issue were some of the first to address the issue

---

[108] Nancy Whittier, *The Politics of Child Sexual Abuse: Emotion, Social Movements and the State* (New York, NY: Oxford University Press, 2009), 4.

[109] Melinda Chateauvert, *Sex Workers Unite: A History of the Movement from Stonewall to SlutWalk* (Boston, MA: Beacon Press, 2013), 33–41; Ruth Rosen, *The World Split Open: How the Modern Women's Movement Changed America* (New York, NY: Penguin Books, 2000), 188–191.

[110] COYOTE won an initial grant from the Point Foundation of Glide Memorial Church, which also supported a group called Vanguard for gay and transgender female youth engaged in the sex trade. Valerie Jenness, "Sex as Sin to Sex as Work: COYOTE and the Reorganization of Prostitution as a Social Problem," *Social Problems*, 37.3 (1990), 406–407.

of youth involvement in the sex trade. COYOTE member Jennifer James, for example, conducted research into why youth people entered prostitution in 1976 and COYOTE founder Margo St. James raised the issue of girls in prostitution at the first International Tribunal on Crimes Against Women in Brussels in 1976.[111] The New York-based feminist anti-pornography group Women Against Pornography (WAP) protested the sexualization of girls in the media, including the popular 1978 film *Pretty Baby*, featuring 12-year-old Brooke Shields portraying a teenage prostitute, and the Broadway production of Vladimir Nabokov's 1958 novel, *Lolita*, which portrayed a sexual relationship between a middle-aged man and his twelve-year-old stepdaughter.[112] While feminists did not lead the campaigns against juvenile prostitution that emerged in the late 1970s, the impact of their work on rape, incest, prostitution, and the sexualization of girls contributed to public concern and understandings about sexual abuse of women and children.

CONCLUSION

In the late 1960s and early 1970s, influenced by the freedom movements of the era as well as an economic recession, young people were more likely to run away from home, and youth homelessness spiked. Around the same time, historic shifts were occurring in the juvenile justice system, including a move to deinstitutionalize youth status offenders and place them in community-based group homes, and also the recognition of due process rights for youth. As a result, it became harder for states to detain youth, but communities often lacked social services to help runaway and homeless youth. These factors combined into a perfect storm: vulnerable youth with few opportunities or social supports on the streets supporting themselves, often by engaging in the street economy, including selling sex, or recruited by adults into prostitution or pornography. Meanwhile, a myriad of social movements were challenging gender and sexual norms as well as racial hierarchies in society. Changing gender roles, increasing racial integration, and the increased visibility of the commercial sex trade made adults anxious to protect youth from what they perceived as growing sexual threats. All of these changes made the 1970s ripe for the emergence of activism against juvenile prostitution.

The movement that emerged at the end of the 1970s built upon the legacies of the late nineteenth and early twentieth-century movements to protect young women, particularly age of consent laws and the Mann Act, as well as early 1970s feminist activism opposing male sexual violence against women and girls.

[111] Jennifer James, "Motivations for Entrance into Prostitution," in Laura Crites (ed.), *The Female Offender* (Lexington, MA: Lexington Books, 1976), 177–205; Diana E.H. Russell and Nichol Van de Ven, *The Proceedings of the International Tribunal on Crimes Against Women* (Millbrae, CA: LES FEMMES, 1976), xiii, 180, 219.
[112] Bronstein, *Battling Pornography*, 217, 265–266.

Adult anxieties about youth sexuality were stimulated by some of the same factors that had prevailed in earlier periods where girls' sexuality became a focus of reform efforts – economic turbulence, high immigration, changing norms regarding gender and sexuality, and challenges to white supremacy. Like in earlier times, activists in the 1970s drew upon cultural notions of childhood innocence and racialized sexual double standards, and they used rhetoric and stories surprisingly similar to nineteenth-century criminal seduction and white slave trade captivity narratives to motivate communities to organize and policymakers to act against youth involvement in the sex trade. This activism was distinct, however, in that it focused not only on girls but also on boys involved in prostitution and pornography.

# 2

# "Teeny Hookers" and the "Chicken Hawk Trade"

## Organizing against Juvenile Prostitution in the 1970s

"Veronica's Short, Sad Life – Prostitution at 11, Death at 12" rang the headline on the front page of the *New York Times* on October 3, 1977. The story reported that Veronica Brunson had died in a "mysterious plunge ... from the 10th floor of a shabby midtown hotel frequented by pimps."[1] According to the story, Brunson had lived in a "fatherless home" with her mother and three brothers, supported by a monthly welfare check of $318. The first time she was arrested for prostitution in the fall of 1976, she gave her real age and identity. Under a police policy of diversion to keep youth out of criminal courts, the arresting officer referred Brunson to counseling. But there was little follow-up. The next summer she was arrested for prostitution again, but this time did not give her real name and claimed to be eighteen. She pled guilty and was released after spending a night in jail. She was arrested for prostitution and pled guilty ten more times that summer. For two of the convictions she spent a total of twelve days in an adult prison. According to Officer Warren McGinniss of the Youth Aid Division, "Even a baby-faced obvious child who claims she is 18 can parade through the entire process – arrest, fingerprinting, arraignment – without anyone asking any questions." Reverend Bruce Ritter, the director of Covenant House, a youth runaway shelter, opined, "The juvenile-justice and child-welfare systems in the city are chaotic. Programs just don't exist and everyone knows it."[2]

The Veronica Brunson story was one of many stories that ran in newspapers and magazines across the country in the 1970s that fueled concern and a wave of activism against the youth sex trade. The story emphasized her family background, the failures of social services and the courts, and the dire consequences of these failures. News stories quoted activists warning about the proliferation of child prostitution, linking the phenomena explicitly or

---

[1] Selwyn Raab, "Veronica's Short Sad Life – Prostitution at 11, Death at 12," *New York Times* (October 3, 1977), 1.
[2] Ibid.

implicitly to social changes occurring in society like increasing single parenthood and "fatherlessness," the growing runaway and homeless youth problems, and the expanding commercial sex trade, including both pornography and prostitution. Activists took advantage of cultural opportunities – ideologies of childhood innocence, anxieties about changing gender and sexual norms, and racialized narratives of sexually endangered white girls during a time of changing race relations – to stoke moral outrage about youth involvement in the sex trade. This chapter will chronicle the 1970s wave of activism against juvenile prostitution, the policy and social service responses to the issue, and the government retrenchment in the 1980s as a result of the Reagan administration's budget cuts and "law and order" approach to social problems.

## PUBLIC DISCOURSE ON YOUTH PROSTITUTION IN THE 1970S

Similar to the "white slave trade" campaigns earlier in the century and to the later twenty-first-century campaigns against "domestic minor sex trafficking," media in the 1970s framed juvenile prostitution as a vast and deadly social problem linked to societal changes related to gender, sexuality, and race. Alarming stories about girls and boys as young as eleven or twelve on the streets selling sex appeared in newspapers and magazines across the country. Newspapers were peppered with shocking headlines: "Little Ladies of the Night" in the *New York Times*, "Youth for Sale on the Streets" in *Time* magazine, and "Child Sex" in the *Chicago Tribune*.[3] A 1972 *Time* magazine article reported on "teeny hookers" in Manhattan's East Village.[4] In 1974, *The Nation* published an article, "Street Girls of the '70s," about runaway and homeless girls who survived on the street by exchanging sex for food and shelter.[5] A 1975 *New York Times* article described the transformation of youth runaways: "Today's runaway is no Norman Rockwell tyke. Instead, she may well be ... a 14-year-old girl in platform shoes and hot pants on a street corner on Eighth Avenue, asking passers-by whether they want a good time."[6] Several news stories told stories of the murder of young girls like the cases of Veronica Brunson and fifteen-year-old Karen Baxter.[7] The issue even reached television. In March of 1977, the drama *Police Story* ran an episode on

[3] Ted Morgan, "Little Ladies of the Night," *New York Times* (November 16, 1975), 34; "Youth for Sale on the Streets," *Time* 100.22, (November 28, 1977), 27; George Bliss and Michael Sneed, "Child Sex: Square Block in New Town Tells It All," *Chicago Tribune* (May 16, 1977).

[4] "White Slavery, 1972," *Time* 99.23 (June 5, 1972), 26.

[5] Celeste MacLeod, "Street Girls of the '70s," *The Nation* (April 20, 1974), 486; see also Michael Baizerman, Jacquelyn Thompson, and Kinaka Stafford-White, "Adolescent Prostitution," *Children Today* (September/October 1979), 20–24.

[6] Morgan, "Little Ladies of the Night," 34.

[7] Ibid. (Baxter was killed by a man buying sex from her).

teenage prostitution and *60 Minutes* aired a special report in 1979 on juvenile prostitution titled "Runaways, Throwaways."[8]

Media in the 1970s focused on girls, but gave significant attention to the prostitution of boys as well, likely responding to homophobia resulting from an increasingly visible gay rights movement at the time.[9] In 1977, for example, *The New York Times* published an article on the "chicken hawk trade" in the pinball arcades of Forty-Second Street.[10] George Bliss and Michael Sneed of the *Chicago Tribune* published a series of articles on boys in pornography and prostitution in Chicago and throughout the United States after investigating the issue for three months.[11] These articles were carried in more than 200 newspapers across the United States.[12] The series portrayed child pornography as a way that thousands of juveniles were being drawn into prostitution. In 1976, journalist Robin Lloyd published *For Money or Love* about prostitution of boys in the United States, and the book became a best seller that was republished in paperback as a Book-of-the-Month Club alternative selection.[13] Senator Birch Bayh, chair of the Senate Subcommittee to Investigate Juvenile Delinquency and sponsor of The Runaway Youth Act, wrote an introduction to the book. This book, adorned with a drawing of an innocent-looking, pre-adolescent white boy on the cover of the first edition, estimated that there were 300,000 boys engaged in prostitution in the United States (see Figure 2.1).

News stories reported huge numbers of sexually exploited youth based on Lloyd's estimate, which some questioned as speculative and unfounded. This number was referenced repeatedly in governmental hearings and media reports on juvenile prostitution, and then doubled or sometimes tripled to include girls. When investigators from the Illinois Legislative Investigating Commission later questioned Lloyd about how he arrived at this figure, Lloyd admitted that it was just a "gut hunch." The Illinois Commission concluded, "too much information

---

[8] "Ice Time," *Police Story* (dir. Robert Scheerer), aired March 8, 1977; Peter J. Wosh, *Covenant House: Journey of a Faith-Based Charity* (Philadelphia, PA: University of Pennsylvania Press, 2005), 105.

[9] Kerwin Kaye, "Male Prostitution in the Twentieth Century: Pseudohomosexuals, Hoodlum Homosexuals, and Exploited Teens," *Journal of Homosexuality* 46.1/2 (2003), 1–77, at 42–46.

[10] "'Chicken-Hawk' Trade Found Attracting More Young Boys to Times Square," *New York Times* (February 14, 1977), 24.

[11] See, for example, George Bliss and Michael Sneed, "U.S., Illinois Lawmakers Tackle Child Pornography," *Chicago Tribune* (June 10, 1977), 1, 18; George Bliss and Michael Sneed, "Dentist Seized in Child Sex Filming; Carey Sets Probe," *Chicago Tribune* (May 17, 1977), 1, 8; Bliss and Sneed, "Child Sex," 18.

[12] *Protection of Children Against Sexual Exploitation Hearings on S. 1585, on S. 1585 before the Subcommittee on Juvenile Delinquency of the Senate Committee on the Judiciary*, 95th Cong., 1st Sess. (May 27, 1977), 56 (hereinafter *Protection of Children Against Sexual Exploitation Hearings, 1977*).

[13] Robin Lloyd, *For Money or Love* (New York, NY: Vanguard Press, 1976); republished as a mass-market paperback by Ballantine Books in 1977.

FIGURE 2.1  Cover of Robin Lloyd's best-selling book *For Money or Love*, 1976.

contained in this unsupported document [Lloyd's book] made its way to the media without interference, creating the probable illusion of young boys prostituting themselves on every street corner of the country."[14] New stories and activists also repeatedly stated that the problem was increasing. Estimates that huge numbers of youth experienced prostitution suggested a vast substratum of youth potentially at risk. Repeated in the media and at legislative hearings both in the 1970s and in the later resurgence of widespread activism against the US youth sex trade in the 2000s, these estimates served activists' desire to garner public attention and spark moral outrage, yet they were also used by critics to undermine the credibility of advocates against youth involvement in the sex trade.

In addition to using unsubstantiated claims about the scope of youth involvement in the sex trade, advocates and the media often promoted a racialized narrative of predatory African American men cajoling and coercing white girls into prostitution, claims that echoed the earlier "white slavery" campaigns. By the 1970s, the civil rights movement had achieved stunning successes in the United States against Jim Crow segregation and opened up new educational and employment opportunities for African Americans. Nevertheless, many news articles about juvenile prostitution warned about the dangers of racial tolerance and integration. A common theme in these articles was that many of the youth involved in prostitution were lured from rural and suburban areas to big cities. The racialized subtext was that urban African American men were luring white suburban and rural girls to the cities. Numerous *New York Times* articles reported on girls being transported from the Midwest to New York City for prostitution.[15] But the media also warned of prostitution spreading from the cities into small towns across America. A 1977 *Time* magazine article warned that "a new and alarming wave of prostitution by teenagers and young children has struck the US, not only in the big cities but also in the small towns of the Dakotas, the Minnesota iron range, Kentucky, New England and elsewhere."[16] These news stories reported that youth were being moved from city to city across the country, suggesting the involvement of organized crime. Some news stories presented an explicitly racialized narrative of exploitation. For example, a 1972 front-page *Minneapolis Tribune* article quoted a local police officer commenting on shifts in the composition of prostitutes in Minneapolis over time:

In 1967, a negligible percentage of those arrested for prostitution were minors. So far this year more than 25 percent of the prostitutes arrested have been juveniles ... Young,

---

[14] Illinois Legislative Investigating Commission, *Sexual Exploitation of Children: A Report to the Illinois General Assembly* (Chicago, IL: State of Illinois, August 1980), 8–9.

[15] See, for example, Selwyn Raab, "Pimps Establish Recruiting Link to the Midwest," *New York Times* (October 30, 1977), 1, 6; Nathaniel Sheppard, "Money, Not New York, Lures Minnesota Prostitutes," *New York Times* (November 25, 1977), A18.

[16] "Youth for Sale on the Streets," *Time*, 27.

white runaways may have become a bigger target for pimps, most of whom are black, because fewer black women are going into prostitution ... the racial composition of prostitutes in Minneapolis has gone from being 60 to 70 percent black to being 80 percent white.[17]

A 1975 *New York Times* article reported that "nearly all the pimps are black; nearly all the out-of-town [girls] are white."[18] The article then quoted police officer Warren McGinniss saying, "The kid has been brought up not to have any racial bias and she's bending over backward to show she's not prejudiced when she's accosted by this nicely dressed, sweet-talking, perfumed Black man; she's so conscious that she shouldn't put him down that she forgets she's being picked up by a street hustler."[19] The article suggested that anti-racist attitudes were contributing to juvenile prostitution.

Activists, policymakers, and the media in the 1970s sometimes used the explicitly racialized language of "white slavery" from the early twentieth century. For example, a 1972 *Time* magazine article was titled "White Slavery, 1972."[20] The 1978 book, *The Minnesota Connection*, claimed to tell the story of the "white slave trade between the midwestern cities and New York" and how one preacher/cop was "winning the fight against teenage white slavery."[21] In a 1979 press release announcing the creation of a shelter for prostituted youth, the New York City-based Odyssey Institute quoted its founder Judianne Densen-Gerber describing the men who exploit children in prostitution as "true white slavers."[22] A 1980 report by the Illinois Legislative Investigating Commission also used the phrase "white slavery activist" in referencing people fighting juvenile prostitution.[23] These framings reveal how racial anxieties may have fueled concern about juvenile prostitution in the 1970s.

In addition to racialized framings of the issue, some media stories suggested gender-based social changes occurring in society at the time contributed to youth involvement in the sex trade because of a lack of discipline and structure in the family, related particularly to the absence of fathers in the home. A 1976 WNBC news documentary, *Requiem for Tina Sanchez*, recounted the true story of a young girl who ran away from her family at

---

[17] Greg Schmidt, "Runaways Lured into Prostitution in City 'Work' the Streets of N.Y.," *Minneapolis Tribune* (November 19, 1972), 1.

[18] Morgan, "Little Ladies of the Night," 34. *Little Ladies of the Night*, a made-for-TV movie based on Morgan's article, aired in January of 1977. *Little Ladies of the Night*, dir. Marvin J. Chomsky, Spelling Goldberg Productions, 1977, at www.imdb.com/title/tt0076318/.

[19] Morgan, "Little Ladies of the Night."

[20] "White Slavery, 1972," *Time* 99.23 (June 5, 1972), 26.

[21] Al Palmquist with John Stone, *The Minnesota Connection* (New York, NY: Warner Books, 1978), back cover.

[22] COYOTE Records, 1962–1989; Odyssey Institute, Press Release: Dr. Judianne Densen-Gerber Calls for Legislative Hearing on Child Prostitution in New York State, January 10, 1979; 81-M32 – 90-M1. Schlesinger Library, Radcliffe Institute, Harvard University, Cambridge, MA.

[23] Illinois Legislative Investigating Commission, *Sexual Exploitation of Children*, 1989, 5.

eleven, entered prostitution at thirteen, and died at fifteen.[24] The documentary focused on the "Minnesota strip," a section of Eighth Avenue between Fortieth and Fiftieth Streets described as a "tawdry section of New York City where pimps make money exploiting the bodies of the young ... hundreds of midwestern middle-class girls, mostly white, many under 16, runaways," which the narrator described as "a new breed of prostitutes."[25] Despite describing the girls as middle class, the film focuses on the stories of two girls from poor single-mother families. The program featured two white police officers, including Warren McGinniss, who explained,

today children are running from a situation ... [in which] we don't have much structure in the home ... We're a materialist and very permissive society and many youngsters can't deal with that because they are after all youngsters and they are looking for guidelines and they are looking for discipline. They are expecting some structure in their homes and their lives.[26]

McGinniss suggests that the absence of a father results in lack of structure in the family, which makes girls vulnerable to prostitution. After McGinniss detained a girl suspected of prostitution, a woman interviewing the girl asked her, "Do you blame your mother for what happened?" to which the girl replied affirmatively, saying her mother never loved her. Later in the documentary, a friend of Tina Sanchez was shown saying that the girl's mother prostituted her and didn't love her. The program's narrative of fatherless white girls saved by middle-aged white men from African American "pimps" and neglectful mothers suggested white male supremacy as the solution to juvenile prostitution, a theme used repeatedly in public discourses in late 1970s.

Finally, homophobia infused public discourses relating to the prostitution of boys. Media coverage and political discussions of child pornography involving boys in the late 1970s often linked "homosexuality" with child sexual abuse and targeted the gay community more generally. William Kelly of the Illinois Gay Rights Task Force in written testimony submitted to Congress in 1977 objected to the "repeated insinuations and sometimes overt allegations by some of the news media and some State and local officials that gayness is in any way synonymous with any form of child abuse."[27] In the early 1970s, the gay liberation movement was gaining steam, having recently convinced the American Psychological Association to remove "homosexuality" from the Diagnostic and Statistical Manual of Mental Disorders. The conflation of homosexuality and pedophilia was a way that conservatives resisted the legitimization of gay identity in the 1970s.

Resonating with deep-seated anxieties about societal changes relating to race, gender and sexuality, media coverage of youth involvement in the sex trade generated public attention to the issue, mobilizing both feminists concerned

---

[24] *Requiem for Tina Sanchez*, dir. Patricia K. Lynch, WNBC-TV, 1976.    [25] Ibid., 1:40.
[26] Ibid., 5:10.    [27] *Protection of Children Against Sexual Exploitation Hearings, 1977*, 68.

about male violence against women and girls, as well as conservatives worried about moral decline in society.[28] By linking the issue to changes in the family, racial integration, and gay liberation, media representations tapped into ideological and political debates about hot-button issues of the day.[29] This broad appeal quickly moved the issue to the top of the legislative agenda.

## FROM SHIRLEY TEMPLE TO JODIE FOSTER: GOVERNMENT RESPONSES TO THE YOUTH SEX TRADE

In early 1977, two media-savvy activists – a New York heiress and a midwestern academic – captured the attention of the public and lawmakers with shocking images and dire predictions. They were Dr. Judianne Densen-Gerber, a psychiatrist, lawyer, and founder of the Odyssey House drug treatment centers in New York City, and Frank Osanka, a sociology professor at Lewis University in Illinois where he taught a class on child abuse. Several Supreme Court rulings in the late 1960s and early 1970s had expanded First Amendment protection for pornography, which led to the proliferation in the mid-1970s of adult bookstores, many selling child pornography.[30] Osanka became aware of child pornography from his students who worked in law enforcement.[31] Meanwhile, Densen-Gerber's New York office at Odyssey received an anonymously mailed copy of the child pornography magazine *Moppets* with a note asking, "Are you aware of this?" Odyssey staff investigated adult bookstores and found an abundant supply of magazines and movies featuring children, girls and boys, engaged in sexual acts with each other and with adults.[32]

---

[28] See Jenny Kitzinger, *Framing Abuse: Media Influence and Public Understanding of Sexual Violence Against Children* (London, England: Pluto Press, 2004), 6; Kathleen M. Blee and Kimberly A. Creasap, "Conservative and Right-Wing Movements," *Annual Review of Sociology* 36 (2010), 273–276 (discussing factors motivating conservative political engagement, including economic competition, changing racial composition of a population, and evolving gender roles and sexual norms); Emma Renold and Jessica Ringrose, "Feminisms Re-Figuring 'Sexualisation,' Sexuality and the 'The Girl,'" *Feminist Theory* 14.3 (2013), 248 (discussing how "public and private anxieties over the eroticized child have long circulated throughout history," especially during times of "big societal and cultural change, such as seismically shifting sexual and gender relations").

[29] Tanya Horeck, *Public Rape: Representing Violation in Fiction and Film* (New York, NY: Routledge, 2004), 7; see also Sujata Moorti, *Color of Rape: Gender and Race in Television's Public Spheres* (Albany, NY: State University of New York Press, 2002); Sarah Projansky, *Watching Rape: Film and Television in Postfeminist Culture* (New York, NY: New York University Press, 2001).

[30] *Stanley v. Georgia*, 294 U.S. 557 (1969); *Miller v. California*, 413 U.S. 15 (1973). The Court later approved restrictions on child pornography in *New York v. Ferber*, 458 U.S. 747 (1982) and *Osborne v. Ohio*, 495 U.S. 103 (1990).

[31] *Protection of Children Against Sexual Exploitation Hearings, 1977*, 26 (written testimony of Frank Osanka).

[32] Helen Dudar, "America Discovers Child Pornography," *Ms.* (August 1977), 43–47, 80.

With these shocking images in hand, Densen-Gerber and Osanka initiated a national campaign for legal reform, staging press conferences and public demonstrations. On February 4, 1977, they held a closed press conference in Chicago, where they shared examples of the child pornography that they had collected. This inspired journalists for the *Chicago Sun-Times* and the *Chicago Tribune* to investigate the issue and publish a slew of articles on child pornography and prostitution, particularly involving boys. One of these articles quoted Densen-Gerber dramatically describing the impact of child pornography and prostitution on children: "They are destroyed by these experiences. They are emotionally and spiritually murdered."[33] Frank Osanka led a campaign against child pornography in Illinois, speaking before the Illinois legislature and the Chicago City Council, organizing protest pickets outside Chicago adult bookstores that sold child pornography, and speaking repeatedly to the press. Protests were held outside adult bookstores in other cities across the country, including New York City, Portsmouth, New Hampshire, Shreveport, Louisiana, Highland Park, Michigan, and Salt Lake City, Utah.[34]

On February 14, Densen-Gerber held a press conference in Washington, DC, calling for Congress to act. Within a few weeks, more than one hundred cosponsors introduced two bills, drafted with the help of Odyssey lawyers, proposing twenty-year sentences for traffickers in child pornography. Densen-Gerber consulted with lawmakers around the country and, by the end of the summer, similar legislation had been introduced in more than twenty states. In Congress, committees in the House and the Senate held hearings on child pornography and prostitution. On May 27, 1977, the Senate Judiciary Subcommittee to Investigate Juvenile Delinquency held hearings in Chicago, at which Chicago's mayor, a police officer, a state attorney, *Chicago Tribune* journalists Bliss and Sneed, two former pornographic filmmakers, and a seventeen-year-old boy who had experience in prostitution and pornography testified. The boy reported that he knew more than fifty other boys between the age of twelve and seventeen in the Chicago area who engaged in prostitution and pornography. Expressing disapproval of "widespread increase in teenage sexual promiscuity," Senator John Conyers (D-MI) stated that "the Shirley Temple of yesterday has become the Jodie Foster of today," referring to the popular 1976 movie *Taxi Driver* in which Jodie Foster played a teenage prostitute.[35] The Subcommittee followed up with a hearing in Washington, DC, on June 16,

---

[33] Ray Moseley, "Child Pornography: Sickness for Sale," *Chicago Tribune* (May 15, 1977), 1.

[34] Judianne Densen-Gerber, "What Pornographers Are Doing to Children: A Shocking Report," *Redbook* 149 (August 1977), 86; Clifford L. Linedecker, *Children in Chains* (New York, NY: Everest House Publishers, 1981), 34; *Protection of Children Against Sexual Exploitation Hearings*, 1977, 26, 66, 130–158.

[35] *Sexual Exploitation of Children: Hearing on H.A 8059 before the Subcommittee on Crime of the House Committee on the Judiciary*, 95th Cong., 1st Sess. (May 23, 25, June 10 and September 20, 1977), 9 (hereinafter *Sexual Exploitation of Children Hearing*, 1977).

1977, which included the testimony of a law professor, attorneys from the Department of Justice and the American Civil Liberties Union (ACLU), and several senators.[36]

The House also held multiple hearings from May to September of 1977 where witnesses testified that there existed a vast industry of child sexual exploitation in the United States. The House Judiciary Subcommittees on Crime and Select Education traveled to Chicago, Los Angeles, and New York City to hear testimony about the problem, and held hearings in Washington, DC, as well. A broad range of people testified – social service providers, psychologists, law enforcement officers, a postal inspector, a customs official, politicians, law professors, journalists, and activists, including Densen-Gerber, Osanka, and Reverend Bruce Ritter, as well as representatives from the ACLU and the National Organization for Women.[37] They testified that child pornography was a multimillion-dollar industry controlled by organized crime, that "pimps" were recruiting young girls for prostitution, and that large numbers of youth runaways were engaging in prostitution to support themselves. Densen-Gerber testified that there were more than 1 million commercially sexually exploited youth in the United States and that 264 monthly child pornography publications were available in the United States, a figure that government investigations later showed to be exaggerated "by several orders of magnitude."[38] Opposition to regulation came from *Hustler* magazine publisher Larry Flynt and an attorney for the ACLU, who testified that restricting child pornography infringed on the First Amendment right to free speech. These hearings led lawmakers to conclude that children were being harmed in prostitution and pornography and that existing federal laws did not do enough to protect children from these activities.

---

[36] "Around the Nation: Group Protests Child Use in Pornographic Material," *New York Times* (February 15, 1977), 12; Judianne Densen-Gerber, "Child Prostitution and Child Pornography: Medical, Legal, and Societal Aspects of the Commercial Sexual Exploitation of Children," in Barbara McComb Jones, Linda L. Jenstrom, and Kee McFarlane (eds.), *Sexual Abuse of Children: Selected Readings* (Washington, DC: US Department of Health and Human Services, 1980), 77–81; *Protection of Children Against Sexual Exploitation Hearings, 1977,* 1–158.

[37] Feminists did not prioritize the issue of child pornography at the time, but in August of 1977, *Ms.* magazine published a cover story on the issue written by Gloria Steinem with a companion article by Helen Dudar, which explicitly linked child pornography and juvenile prostitution. Gloria Steinem, "Is Child Pornography ... About Sex?" *Ms.* (August 1977), 43–44; Dudar, "America Discovers Child Pornography," 45–47, 80. Two years later, *Ms.* published an article on sexual slavery that mentioned child prostitution in the United States. Kathleen Barry, "Terror and Coercion: The Female Sexual Slave Trade," *Ms.* (November 1979), 62.

[38] Illinois Legislative Investigating Committee, Sexual Exploitation of Children, 4; *Sexual Exploitation of Children Hearing, 1977,* 45; Douglas Martin, "Dr. Judianne Densen-Gerber Is Dead at 68; Founded Odyssey House Group Drug Program," *New York Times* (May 14, 2003). In 1983, Densen-Gerber was accused of financial irregularities in her management of Odyssey House and stepped down as director.

In response, Congress unanimously passed the Protection of Children Against Sexual Exploitation Act of 1977,[39] which established federal criminal penalties specifically targeting the commercial production and dissemination of obscene visual or print depictions of minors under sixteen engaged in sexually explicit conduct. The Act also outlawed the interstate transport of minors for prostitution, which had previously been illegal for females in some circumstances under the Mann Act but not for males, and funded research into the commercial sexual exploitation of youth.[40] This Act inspired states to pass similar laws prohibiting the sale of child pornography. In the early 1980s, police and postal inspectors across the country reported a drastic decrease in commercial child pornography, which they attributed to stronger laws and tougher enforcement of obscenity laws. These laws led many adult bookstores and publishers that had dealt in child pornography as a sideline to their principal business of adult pornography to end this practice as too risky.[41] In addition to the 1977 Act, Congress passed the Child Abuse Prevention and Treatment and Adoption Reform Act the same year, which expanded the federal definition of child abuse in the Child Abuse Prevention and Treatment Act (CAPTA) to include sexual abuse and prostitution and authorized special state grants related to sexual abuse.[42] A year later, Congress amended CAPTA again to require reporting of juvenile prostitution as child abuse.[43] At the state and local levels, lawmakers turned to the issue as well. Many states, including New York, Minnesota, and California, passed laws against inducing minors to become prostitutes and deriving support from child prostitution, with harsher penalties for people exploiting younger victims. Some states increased penalties if adults used force, threat, or intimidation to coerce a juvenile into prostitution. States also reformed civil child abuse statutes to increase the identification of juveniles engaged in prostitution in order to facilitate prevention and treatment.[44]

---

[39] Pub. L. No. 95–225, 92 Stat. 7 (codified as amended at 18 U.S.C. §§ 2251–2252, 2256, 2423 [2006]).

[40] See D. Kelly Weisberg, *Children of the Night: A Study of Adolescent Prostitution* (Lexington, MA: Lexington Books, 1985), 85–151, for a review of this early research, much of which was federally funded. See, for example, Arthur Young and Company, *Juvenile Prostitution: A Federal Strategy for Combatting Its Causes and Consequences, Report Submitted to the Youth Development Bureau, Office of Human Development Services, Department of Health, Education and Welfare* (June 1978).

[41] Gregory Ahart, *Sexual Exploitation of Children – A Problem of Unknown Magnitude. Report to the Chairman, Subcommittee on Select Education, House Committee on Education and Labor* (Washington, DC: General Accounting Office, 1982), 28–31, 40; Dudar, "America Discovers Child Pornography," 46.

[42] 42 U.S.C. §§ 5102, 5104(b)(3)(A) (1977).

[43] Child Abuse Prevention and Treatment and Adoption Reform Act of 1978, Public Law 95–266, April 24, 1978, 42 U.S.C. § 5102 (1978); Weisberg, *Children of the Night*, 208–209.

[44] D. Kelly Weisberg, "Children of the Night: The Adequacy of Statutory Treatment of Juvenile Prostitution," *American Journal of Criminal Law* 12.1 (1984), 39–45; Karen Staller, *Runaways:*

One of the most active states was Minnesota, but a close look at what happened there reveals that attention to youth prostitution was fueled, at least in part, by myths and misinformation about the issue. In December of 1977, police raided a Minneapolis photography studio that was a front for the largest call-girl service in the city after the parents of a fourteen-year-old runaway who allegedly worked there complained to police. Police at the time estimated that about 25 percent of the 1,500 prostitutes in Minneapolis-St. Paul area were aged 17 and younger.[45] They expressed concern that runaway youth from small Minnesota towns were recruited into prostitution in Minneapolis and then sent to cities across the country, including New York City, New Orleans, and Denver, which police called "the Minnesota pipeline." In Manhattan, pimps allegedly brought girls from Minneapolis to the "Minnesota Strip" because there was a demand for "young 'Nordic' type prostitutes," according to the *New York Times*.[46] In the fall of 1977, three teenaged girls from Minnesota testified before the New York legislature's Select Committee on Crime about their experiences of having been lured to New York City for prostitution by promises of "romance and money."[47] Press accounts attributed this phenomenon to more lenient laws against prostitution in New York City than Minnesota. In the early 1970s, the Minnesota legislature made a second prostitution offense punishable by a mandatory ninety-day sentence, whereas New York merely imposed a fine. The committee also heard testimony about Mafia involvement in prostitution and about a nationwide circuit of facilitators who transported youth from city to city.[48]

These alarming stories were amplified by a Minnesota police officer and preacher named Al Palmquist, who became a media celebrity on the issue of juvenile prostitution in the late 1970s. Inspired to work on juvenile prostitution when he saw the *Police Story* episode about the issue, Palmquist opened a safe house in Minneapolis for teenagers exiting prostitution and declared his mission to "search and expose, rescue and restore."[49] It was Palmquist who organized the young women's testimony at the 1977 New York hearing, and he himself testified that up to 400 juveniles a year were transported from Minneapolis to

*How the Sixties Counterculture Shaped Today's Policies and Practices* (New York, NY: Columbia University Press, 2006), 143–149 (New York passed the Runaway and Homeless Youth Act of 1978 appropriating funds for private organizations to provide crisis shelter and services).

45 Nathaniel Sheppard, Jr., "Minneapolis Steps Up Fight on Prostitution," *New York Times* (February 7, 1978), 6.

46 "Midwest Teen-Agers Tell of Forced Vice," *New York Times* (November 15, 1977), 29; "Youth for Sale on the Streets," *Time*, 27.

47 Ibid.; Nathaniel Sheppard, Jr., "Teen-Age Runaways Turn to Prostitution as Rebellion," *New York Times* (November 14, 1977), 20.

48 Morgan, "Little Ladies of the Night," 273.

49 Rosemary Rawson, "The 'Minnesota Pipeline' Sends Teenage Hookers to New York, and Al Palmquist Wants to Plug It," *People Magazine* 8.25 (December 19, 1977); Tom Davies, "Study Disputes Ideas about Teenage Prostitution," *Minneapolis Tribune* (August 18, 1978), 49.

New York for prostitution, which he dubbed "the Minnesota Connection."[50] A year later, he published a book of the same name, a first-person account of his campaign to stop the transportation of teenage girls from Minnesota to New York's commercial sex trade.[51]

In the book, Palmquist portrayed the issue in starkly racialized and gendered terms, similar to some of the media portrayals of the day. He focused on young white girls, as young as fourteen, exploited by African American men. The cover drawing as well as photographs within the book made these racial dynamics clear (see Figure 2.2). Palmquist repeatedly described the girls as blonde or Scandinavian and churchgoing before their fall into prostitution. According to Palmquist, the "average prostitute" was an unwilling participant: "Trapped, forced and threatened with torture or death, she has little chance to escape."[52] He described the African American men's exploitation of white girls as "slavery" or "bondage," and included several scenes of graphic sexualized violence and torture in the book and two photographs of murdered girls.[53]

In addition to clear racial dynamics, gender played an important role in his portrayal of the issue. Palmquist characterized the girls as coming from "fatherless" homes or having weak or inattentive fathers. The girls, he argued, were in need of "discipline" and responsible male control over their lives. He repeatedly made specific reference to Christianity and the power of religion to save young girls. Palmquist portrayed himself as hypermacho, "strapping on a gun," driving a "fast sports car," and crashing in the door of a "pimp." He described traveling to New York twice to find girls on the "Minnesota strip" to return home, but when he found few girls and none willing to go with him, he blamed police corruption, media publicity, and discomfort with his religious message. Palmquist's campaign against juvenile prostitution garnered national media coverage. He and two young survivors went on a speaking tour in the Midwest and appeared on the *Phil Donahue Show* and on the Christian evangelical program *The P.T.L. Club*. In 1978, there was a Broadway musical – *Runaways* – about juvenile prostitution, with a song titled "The Minnesota Strip: Song of a Child Prostitute."[54] On May 2, 1980, ABC aired a television movie, *Off the Minnesota Strip*, about a mid-Western teenage runaway's struggles to readjust to home and family life after living as a prostitute in New York City.[55]

Despite Palmquist's claims, research conducted on juvenile prostitution in Minnesota at the time did not find that many girls traveled out of the state for prostitution. The Minnesota Governor's Crime Commission created a Task

---

[50] "Youth for Sale on the Streets," *Time*, 27.    [51] Palmquist, *Minnesota Connection*.
[52] Ibid., 50.    [53] Ibid., 11, 50, 52, 57, 92.
[54] Elizabeth Swados, *Runaways* (New York, NY: Samuel French, Inc.: 1978).
[55] *Off the Minnesota Strip* (ABC Monday Night Movie), dir. Lamont Johnson, aired May 2, 1980 (the writer, David Chase, won an Emmy in 1980 for Outstanding Writing in a Limited Series or Special).

FIGURE 2.2 Cover of *The Minnesota Connection* by Al Palmquist with John Stone, 1978.

Force on Juvenile Prostitution that commissioned a study in 1976 that was published in 1978. Based on interviews with eighty Twin Cities women who experienced prostitution as teenagers, the study gave a conservative estimate of between 150 and 250 juveniles working as prostitutes in the Twin Cities area at any given time. Of those surveyed, about half had worked for third parties and half had experienced violence by the third parties or customers. The study, however, did not support the existence of a Minnesota to New York "pipeline," although ten of the minors had traveled to New York City. The study reported that most youth felt like they were not forced into prostitution by third parties but had voluntarily entered prostitution, and a third reported they had been attracted to prostitution because of "the glamour and excitement."[56] About a third felt trapped in prostitution but the remaining two-thirds did not. Many of the women reported experiencing sexual abuse within their families before becoming involved in prostitution. Respondents reported their first sexual experience at around twelve years old, and more than two-thirds had been raped. According to the study, many young people had been arrested for prostitution or loitering, sometimes multiple times. Palmquist's characterization of youth prostitution clearly did not conform to the reports of youth in the Task Force study.

Based on this research the Task Force recommended that courts refrain from criminally charging juveniles involved in prostitution or labeling them as delinquent, but instead direct them to child protection services through a dependency petition. However, the report explicitly opposed abolishing status offenses because then "the state, police and courts would have little ability to offer protection for these minors,"[57] meaning that they could not hold them against their will purportedly for their own safety. The report recommended that the state train youth service workers to deal openly with the sexual experiences of young women, create a pilot residential program for girls involved in prostitution, and fund a public information campaign to educate young people "to identify the discrepancies between the glamour image portrayed about the life and the reality" as well as to understand physical and sexual abuse and available resources.[58]

In response to the Task Force recommendations and the work of a large coalition of youth social service workers, the Minnesota legislature passed a law in 1978 that defined juveniles experiencing prostitution as victims rather than delinquents, a groundbreaking approach that would years later be adopted in many other states.[59] This shift in perception of minors encouraged the development of services geared toward youth in prostitution. One such program was sponsored by The Bridge for Runaway Youth in Minneapolis,

---

[56] Enablers, *Juvenile Prostitution in Minneapolis: The Report of a Research Project* (St. Paul, MN: The Enablers, 1978), 56.
[57] Ibid., 130.    [58] Ibid., 128–129.    [59] Minn. Stat. Ann. § 626.556 (1978).

which created a residential program specifically for adolescent females in the sex trade in 1978, funded in part as a demonstration project by the Youth Development Bureau of the Department of Health and Human Services and in part by private corporations. This public–private approach to services for youth leaving the sex trade would become widespread in the 2000s. The next year, the Minneapolis Youth Diversion Program created a residential treatment program for juvenile females in prostitution called North Star, which provided a nonresidential outreach program as well.[60] At the same time PRIDE (From Prostitution to Independence, Dignity and Equality), a nongovernmental organization, was founded in the Twin Cities in 1978 to assist survivors of prostitution.[61]

In addition to the Task Force study, other research at the time disproved alarmist claims appearing in the media and on the floor of legislative chambers about the extent and character of juvenile involvement in prostitution. In a 1977 resolution authorizing a study of juvenile prostitution, the Illinois House of Representatives stated that 300,000 children were engaged in pornography and prostitution nationwide, that some parents offered their children to film producers to make child pornography, that Chicago was a transfer point for the movement of children for pornography and prostitution, and that organized crime was involved.[62] After a three-year investigation, the Illinois Legislative Investigating Commission issued a report to the Illinois General Assembly in August of 1980 concluding that there was no evidence to substantiate most of these claims and that "most children involved in prostitution had chosen to do so on their own,"[63] a position that challenged the claim of people like Al Palmquist that youth were always coerced into prostitution. A 1982 Government Accountability Office study found the estimates given by police and social service workers about the extent of juvenile prostitution in New York City were not supported by the existing documentation and suggested that a smaller number of children were involved in prostitution.[64] The research in both cases, however, revealed that youth were engaged in prostitution, and the Illinois study concluded that police had not developed an aggressive approach for dealing with sex crimes against children. Based on its study, the Illinois Legislative Investigating Commission made a wide range of suggestions for how to minimize the prostitution of youth directed at parents, schools, communities, the news media, legislators, and law enforcement officials. These recommendations included progressive structural reforms like ending sex discrimination, enhancing sex education in schools, and providing job skills and employment opportunities for girls, as well as more traditional and

---

[60] Weisberg, *Children of the Night*, 254–255.
[61] The Advocates for Human Rights, *Sex Trafficking Needs Assessment for the State of Minnesota* (Minneapolis, MN: The Advocates for Human Rights, 2008), 6 n. 29.
[62] House Resolution 41, Illinois House of Representatives, March 23, 1977.
[63] Illinois Legislative Investigating Commission, *Sexual Exploitation of Children* (1980).
[64] Ahart, *Sexual Exploitation of Children*, 40.

individualistic recommendations, like teaching values and ethics of sexual behavior and increasing prosecution of adults involved in the prostitution of youth.

Despite these attempts to help youth involved in the sex trade, police in many states were not sympathetic to them. Research on police treatment of juvenile prostitution in the 1970s revealed that while police were generally compassionate toward victims of child abuse and neglect, juvenile prostitution was usually handled by vice divisions that had a punitive approach, treating youth as offenders rather than victims because of their involvement in the street economy and their streetwise behaviors. Police rarely referred youth involved in prostitution to services, if available, and if police were aware of them. Youth would often claim they were of age, and if they did admit they were minors, transferring them to juvenile court involved significant paperwork for police officers. Building cases against adult facilitators was difficult because youth often were not willing to testify against them and buyers were rarely arrested. Police were found to be pessimistic about the usefulness of rehabilitation and were frustrated with the deinstitutionalization of status offenders, which meant that runaways could return immediately to the streets.[65]

A 1982 Government Accountability Office investigative report that focused on prostitution and child pornography in California and Illinois found that police did not focus much effort on child prostitution in the late 1970s and early 1980s. In California, juveniles arrested for prostitution were often released to an adult with their case referred to the probation department, which usually closed the case, or police transferred the case to another department like child welfare, which would find a suitable placement for the child if necessary.[66] In New York, the Public Morals Division of the New York Police Department enforced prostitution laws. The Manhattan South precinct, which included Times Square, established a "Pimp Squad" in 1976 to help people get out of prostitution. The squad considered identification of child prostitutes incidental to their mission and they reported that less than two percent of their prostitution arrests involved juveniles. They arrested approximately twenty to thirty youth under sixteen years old each year for the misdemeanor of prostitution, and they referred the cases to the Manhattan Family Court.[67] However, a much higher number of youth were issued summonses for "loitering for prostitution." Police estimated that they issued up to ten thousand such violations each year, but they rarely referred these youth to social services.[68] A 1979 study by Dorothy Heid Bracey based on in-depth interviews with 120 teenage girls in custody and on the streets in New York City concluded that "the juvenile justice system tends to regard a young prostitute as the perpetrator of a crime. However, everything we have learned about the lives of these girls leads us to think of them as victims. Until they are perceived as

---

[65] Weisberg, *Children of the Night*, 229–233.   [66] Ibid. 36–37.
[67] Ahart, *Sexual Exploitation of Children*, 43.   [68] Ibid. 41.

victims, efforts to help them will meet with little success." She argued that these beliefs were based on the idea that a "'good' female adolescent is not sexual" and therefore youth involved in prostitution were blamed for their situations.[69] Bracey's argument would later become a core contention of the movement against the US youth sex trade.

Some police departments, however, developed specialized units to deal with sexual exploitation of youth, including prostitution. Police departments in Indianapolis, Los Angeles, Seattle, and Washington D.C. were some of the first to develop child sexual exploitation units. The Los Angeles Police Department created a task force on sexual exploitation of children in 1976, which conducted an eight-month investigation into child pornography and prostitution. This led to the creation of the Sexually Exploited Child Unit in 1977 to investigate commercial exploitation of children under the age of sixteen.[70] The Washington D.C. Metropolitan Police Juvenile Prostitution Unit, created in 1976, had two officers searching for youth on the 14th Street "prostitution strip," three blocks from the White House. A reduction in force closed the unit in 1981, but attempts were later made to reopen it.[71] In another program, the Exploited and Missing Child Unit in Louisville, Kentucky, police and social workers collaborated to provide support services to victims and develop investigations of perpetrators. The program did not use the terms "runaway" or "juvenile prostitute," but used "exploited child" or "missing child" to reduce the stigma for youth. The program had success in prosecuting facilitators and even buyers. The director of this program, John Rabun, went on to become the Deputy Director of the National Center for Missing and Exploited Children in Washington D.C.[72] The Louisville program resulted from the recommendation of a local interagency, intergovernmental task force on child prostitution and pornography initiated by Jefferson County Judge Mitchell McConnell. The task force established a 24-hour hotline for reports of child prostitution and pornography. A statewide task force in Kentucky was also formed, which held public hearings throughout the state and made recommendations.[73]

## RETRENCHMENT BUT ONGOING CONCERN ABOUT JUVENILE PROSTITUTION IN THE 1980S

Media coverage of juvenile prostitution peaked in the late 1970s and by the early 1980s had decreased significantly as priorities shifted with the advent of the Reagan era.[74] A significant political backlash to progressive social changes

---

[69] Dorothy Heid Bracey, *"Baby-Pros": Preliminary Profiles of Juvenile Prostitutes* (New York, NY: John Jay Press, 1979), 60.
[70] Illinois Legislative Investigating Commission, *Sexual Exploitation of Children*, 7–8.
[71] Weisberg, *Children of the Night*, 233.    [72] Ibid. 234.    [73] Ibid. 256–257.
[74] See, e.g. Cheryl McCall, "Streets of the Lost: Runaway Kids Eke Out a Mean Life in Seattle," *Life Magazine* (July 1983), 36–42; *Streetwise*, dir. Martin Bell, Angelika Films, 1983.

in the 1960s and 1970s swept Ronald Reagan into the White House in 1980. Once in office, the Reagan administration advanced neoliberal social and economic policies, including cutting taxes, decreasing social welfare spending, deregulating business, and expanding the criminal justice system. Motivated by African American uprisings after the assassination of Martin Luther King, Jr., and increased violent crime in the 1960s and 1970s, "law and order" conservatives supported a stricter criminal justice system, including longer terms of imprisonment and "three-strikes" laws that imposed life sentences after three felony convictions.[75] With Reagan's support, Congress passed the Sentencing Reform Act that led to mandatory federal sentencing guidelines, removing federal judges' discretion in sentencing criminal defendants, and abolishing parole for federal prisoners. Conservatives policymakers in the states likewise passed "tough on crime" policies that supported "proactive policing, and aggressively addressing minor disorder and law violations."[76] As a result, the number of people incarcerated in the United States tripled from 500,000 in 1980 to 1.5 million in 1994, with more than five million under criminal justice supervision.[77]

For young people, these policies shifted the pendulum back toward blaming youth for their involvement in prostitution rather than addressing the social factors making youth vulnerable to the sex trade, like the lack of social services for homeless youth. Reagan reframed issues like poverty, drug addiction, and juvenile delinquency as individual misbehavior or irresponsibility rather than social problems to be addressed through government programs. In this "get tough on crime" political climate, conservatives portrayed troubled youth as "dangerous, violent offenders from whom the community needs protection."[78] As a result, state and federal governments enacted more punitive policies toward youth.[79] For example, in response to the deinstitutionalization mandates of the Juvenile Justice and Delinquency Prevention Act of 1974, the juvenile justice system began to relabel female status offenders as delinquents in order to detain them "by lowering the threshold of what behavior constitutes an assault, especially in the context

---

[75] "Law and order" conservativism emerged in the 1960s in response to African American uprisings after the assassination of Martin Luther King and to an increase in violent crime in the 1960s and 1970s. Michael W. Flamm, *Law and Order: Street Crime, Civil Unrest, and the Crisis of Liberalism in the 1960s* (2005).

[76] Barry C. Feld, "Violent Girls or Relabeled Status Offenders? An Alternative Interpretation of the Data," *Crime & Delinquency* 55.2 (April 2009), 260.

[77] Jodi M. Brown, Darrell K. Gilliard, Tracy L. Snell, James J. Stephan, and Doris James Wilson, *Correctional Populations in the United States, 1994* (Washington, DC: US Department of Justice, June 1996).

[78] Gordon A. Raley, "The JJDP Act: A Second Look," *Juvenile Justice* 2.2 (Fall/Winter 1995), 17–18; Feld, "Violent Girls or Relabeled Status Offenders?" 245.

[79] Katherine Beckett and Theodore Sasson, "The Origins of the Current Conservative Discourse on Law and Order," in Palak Shah (ed.), *Defending Justice* (Somerville, MA: Political Research Associates, 2005), 43–68.

of domestic conflict."[80] Furthermore, states began to prosecute juveniles as adults in criminal courts. In 1980, Congress backtracked on the deinstitutionalization mandate of the 1974 Act under pressure from the National Council of Family and Juvenile Court Judges. Congress amended the JJDP Act by creating a loophole to the prohibition of incarceration of youth for status offenses, the Valid Court Order (VCO) exception, which allowed youth to be detained if they violated a court order prohibiting them from committing enumerated status offenses.[81] Several states chose not to do this, but most states did. Amendments to the JJDP Act in 1984 shifted the focus from delinquency prevention to criminal law enforcement by encouraging the prosecution of juvenile offenders and creating mandatory and tougher sentencing for juveniles.[82] In addition to harsher criminal justice responses to juvenile delinquency, social services for at-risk youth dwindled. In the 1980s, the Reagan administration decreased funding for homeless youth programs.[83] The budget of the OJJDP was reduced between 1981 and 1989 by a third of the 1978 high to $66 million. As a result of these shifts, many social service agencies helping youth in the sex trade lost funding and folded in the 1980s.[84]

In this new political context, Congress continued to investigate child prostitution and pornography and pass new laws in the 1980s, albeit with a focus on expanding criminal justice responses rather than funding social service programs. These initiatives were supported by a New Right grassroots campaign against pornography, which was framed as indecent and harmful to the traditional family. In 1981, the Senate Judiciary Committee's Juvenile Justice Subcommittee held more hearings on the prostitution of boys, including the testimony of a survivor and Reverend Bruce Ritter of Covenant House.[85] In 1983, the House Judiciary Committee's Crime Subcommittee held a hearing on child pornography.[86] The next year, Congress passed the Child Protection Act,[87] which expanded the federal prohibition on child pornography to cover to noncommercial pornography, eliminated the need for the material to

---

[80] Feld, "Violent Girls or Relabeled Status Offenders?" 242.

[81] Pub. L. 96–509, codified as amended at 46 U.S.C. §5603(16).

[82] Raley, "The JJDP Act," 14–15.   [83] Ibid. 29.

[84] Although overall funding for child abuse services decreased, a greater percentage of remaining child abuse funds were directed toward child sexual abuse programs. Nancy Whittier, *The Politics of Child Sexual Abuse: Emotions, Social Movements and the State* (New York, NY: Oxford University Press, 2011), 80–85.

[85] *Sexual Exploitation of Children, Hearing Before the Subcommittee on Juvenile Justice of the Committee of the Judiciary, United States Senate*, 97th Cong., 1st Sess., November 5, 1981, Serial No. J-97-78.

[86] *Protection of Children Against Sexual Exploitation Hearing Before the Subcommittee on Crime of the Committee of the Judiciary, House of Representatives*, 98th Cong., 1st Sess., June 16, 1983, Serial No. 138.

[87] Pub. L. No. 98–292, 98 Stat. 204, May 21, 1984 (codified as amended at 18 U.S.C. §§ 2251–2252).

be obscene, raised the age of protection to include all youth under eighteen, and established the National Center for Missing and Exploited Children to help find missing children and prevent child victimization.[88] In 1985, Reagan appointed Attorney General Edwin Meese to chair a commission to study pornography, which issued a report in 1986 concluding that pornography was harmful, particularly to children.[89] At the time, some anti-pornography feminists who opposed violence against women in pornography worked alongside New Right conservatives with moral opposition to pornography in a collaborative adversarial movement that was a precursor to coalitions against sex trafficking in the 1990s and 2000s.[90]

Despite decreasing federal funds for youth homelessness in the 1980s and the resulting shuttering of many programs, some programs serving youth involved in prostitution continued.[91] The Paul and Lisa Program, for example, thrived with support from foundations, corporations, and individuals, as well as some government support. They provided assistance to youth in the sex trade, conducted educational programs in high schools, universities, detention centers, and on the streets, supported an alternative sentencing program for people arrested for prostitution, and offered shelter. Their educational programs focused on preventing recruitment into the sex industry, discouraging young people from becoming customers of the sex industry and challenging the glamorous portrayal of prostitution in popular culture.[92]

New programs formed as well. In 1984, Trudee Able-Peterson created Streetwork Project at the Victim Services Agency in New York City to serve homeless youth in Times Square, many of whom were involved in the sex trade.[93] Able-Peterson, who was a survivor of prostitution herself, started working on the issue of youth involved in the sex trade in 1976 in Minneapolis, then became the first female supervisor at Covenant House in New York City in 1977. In 1981, she published a book, *Children of the Evening*, about her own experiences in prostitution and her work with youth

---

[88] 28 U.S.C. § 534 (1982); Senate Report No. 583, 97th Congress, 2nd Session 3 (1982).

[89] Attorney General's Commission on Pornography, *Final Report* (Washington DC: U.S. Department of Justice, July 1986) (Bruce Ritter sat on the Commission).

[90] Bornstein, *Battling Pornography*; Nancy Whittier, "Rethinking Coalitions: Anti-Pornography Feminists, Conservatives, and Relationships between Collaborative Adversarial Movements," *Social Problems* 61.2 (2014), 1.

[91] Trudee Able-Peterson and June Bucy, *The Streetwork Outreach Training Manual* (Washington, DC: US Department of Health and Human Services, 1993), 147–148; Sheila Pires and Judith Tolmach-Silber, *On Their Own: Runaway and Homeless Youth and Programs that Serve Them* (Washington, DC: CASSP TA Center, 1991).

[92] The founder of the Paul and Lisa Program, Frank Barnaba, later founded the Barnaba Institute to carry on this work.

[93] Able-Peterson and Bucy, *The Streetwork Outreach Training Manual*, 22; Safe Horizon, Streetwork Project: Helping Homeless Youth, at www.safehorizon.org/page/streetwork-project-helping-homeless-youth-68.html. Streetwork Project later become a part of Safe Horizon.

involved in the sex trade, including the story of a young girl she was working with who had been murdered.[94] According to Able-Peterson, she wanted to tell her story because she was hoping "that it would help people to understand that prostitution was a crime against women and that it was a horrible life."[95] Able-Peterson became a public speaker, presenting at public and parochial schools about the sexual abuse of youth. When counseling youth with histories of sexual abuse or involvement in the sex trade, Able-Peterson pioneered a method of "nonjudgmental engagement," which was a precursor to harm reduction methods. In addition to counseling youth, she trained staff from the Paul and Lisa Program and also testified for the Minneapolis anti-pornography ordinance proposed by Catherine MacKinnon and Andrea Dworkin in 1983.

Several other organizations that worked with youth in the sex trade were founded around this time. Evelina Giobbe, also known as Sarah Wynter, founded WHISPER (Women Hurt in Systems of Prostitution Engaged in Revolt) in 1985 in New York City, later moving the organization to Minnesota.[96] Led by survivors of prostitution, WHISPER developed a Juvenile Prostitution Prevention Program with volunteer speakers that conducted presentations for teens on prostitution and pornography.[97] In Detroit, Alternatives for Girls opened in 1985 as a volunteer-run shelter in a neighborhood church for youth involved in prostitution.[98] In Charleston, West Virginia, community-members concerned about juvenile prostitution formed New Connections in 1983 to provide direct services to commercially sexually exploited youth.[99] Some new programs developed as a result of funding that became available for HIV/AIDS prevention work in the 1980s. In 1988, Planned Parenthood founded Project Street Beat to serve youth in the South Bronx, later expanding to Brooklyn in 1990.[100] Outreach teams operated two minivans and a thirty-one-foot mobile medical van at night in areas where

---

[94] Trudee Able-Peterson, *Children of the Evening* (New York NY: G.P. Putnam's Sons, 1981).

[95] Interview with Trudee Able-Peterson, October 30, 2016 (on file with author).

[96] The Advocates for Human Rights, *Sex Trafficking Needs Assessment for the State of Minnesota*, 6 n. 29.

[97] Kathleen Barry, *The Prostitution of Sexuality* (New York, NY: New York University Press, 1995), 4; National Center for Missing and Exploited Children, *Female Juvenile Prostitution: Problem and Response* (Washington, DC: National Center for Missing and Exploited Children, December 1992), 60; Sarah Wynter, "WHISPER: Women Hurt in Systems of Prostitution Engaged in Revolt," in Frédérique Delacoste and Priscilla Alexander (eds.), *Sex Work: Writings by Women in the Sex Industry* (San Francisco, CA: Cleis Press, 1987), 266–270, at 268.

[98] By 2002, the program was a multiservice agency with over fifty employees. Alternatives for Girls, History, at https://alternativesforgirls.org/history/.

[99] Daniel S. Campagna and Donald L. Poffenberger, *The Sexual Trafficking in Children: An Investigation of the Child Sex Trade* (Dover, MA: Auburn House Publishing Co., 1988), 196–199.

[100] Able-Peterson and Bucy, *The Streetwork Outreach Training Manual*, 119–120; Planned Parenthood of New York City, Our History, at www.plannedparenthood.org/planned-parenthood-new-york-city/who-we-are/our-history.

youth congregated in order to provide for basic survival needs, medical testing, and counseling.[101]

In addition to these efforts, some states initiated campaigns against the prostitution of youth in the 1980s. In 1987, the California Office of Criminal Justice Planning (OCJP) created a Child Sexual Exploitation Intervention Program, which funded three comprehensive projects – The Storefront run by San Diego Youth and Community Service, Project Turnaround run by Central City Hospitality House in San Francisco, and Project PACE (People Against Child Exploitation) run by the Division of Adolescent Medicine of the Los Angeles Children's Hospital. These projects provided comprehensive services, including counseling, temporary safe shelters, outreach services, and training in independent living and survival skills. In the first three years, the projects served five thousand youth. The Program added a fourth project in 1990 – the Bill Wilson Center in Santa Clara. The OCJP conducted a rigorous evaluation of these projects in 1991 to serve as a step-by-step guide for how to plan and implement a successful project to address juvenile prostitution. The detailed guide emphasized the importance of involving a wide cross-section of the community, including youth engaged in prostitution, at every step. The guide explained how to determine if juvenile prostitution existed in a community, how to assess the needs of a community, how to organize a community task force, and how to develop and implement a program. Finally, the guide addressed resource development, relationships with law enforcement, and use of volunteers, and included an ethnographic study of twenty sexually exploited youth in San Francisco.[102]

In addition to these state campaigns, researchers continued to study youth homelessness and juvenile prostitution. In 1985, sociologist D. Kelly Weisberg published a study on adolescent prostitution based on ethnographic research in six cities.[103] The same year, Gitta Sereny published a book comparing prostitution in three countries – United States, West Germany, and Great Britain – with the goal of understanding these "invisible children" and the societies that neglect them.[104] Sereny conducted in-depth interviews with sixty-one youth, twelve of whom she profiled in her book, and attempted to understand what she described as the widespread and growing problem of

---

[101] Nadine Brozan, "Van is Hope for Bronx 'Throwaways,'" *New York Times* (October 6, 1989), B3.

[102] California Office of Criminal Justice Planning, *Confronting Sexual Exploitation of Homeless Youth: California's Juvenile Prostitution Intervention Projects* (Sacramento, CA: California Office of Criminal Justice Planning, 1991), 13–16, 67–98; Able-Peterson and Bucy, *The Streetwork Outreach Training Manual*, 81–82.

[103] Weisberg, *Children of the Night*; see also Donald Allen, "Young Male Prostitutes: A Psychosocial Study," *Archives of Sexual Behavior*, 9.5 (1980), 399–426.

[104] Gitta Sereny, *The Invisible Children: Child Prostitution in America, West Germany and Great Britain* (New York, NY: Knopf, 1985).

child prostitution. In 1988, scholars Daniel Campagna and Donald Poffenberger published a book on the child sex trade based on five-years of field research including interviews, field observations, and case studies.[105] In 1989, the Council on Scientific Affairs of the *Journal of the American Medical Association* published a study identifying widespread prostitution among homeless youth.[106] These academic studies portrayed youth involved in the sex trade more sympathetically than previous eras.[107]

## CONCLUSION

In the 1970s, activism against youth involvement in the sex trade generated media coverage of the issue, which fueled widespread public concern and led to federal and state action to address the issue. Activists took advantage of cultural opportunities to draw attention to the youth sex trade – deeply ingrained notions of childhood innocence and anxieties generated by social changes occurring in society. Activists and the media linked an alleged rise in juvenile prostitution to shifting family forms, including increased divorce and single parenthood; the sexualization and sexual independence of young women; the increasing size and visibility of the commercial sex market; the rise of the gay rights movement; and changing race relations as a result of the civil rights movement, much of which challenged white male heterosexual dominance and control in the family and in society. Some men involved in fighting the US youth sex trade, like Warren McGinniss and Al Palmquist, expressly linked juvenile prostitution to the waning centrality of fathers in families, which supposedly led to a lack of "structure," discipline, and protection of children. Reviving long-standing gendered and racialized narratives of sexual danger and a newer narrative of adult male predation of boys, journalists and activists told stories of African American men exploiting naïve white girls and gay men targeting young boys, which effectively mobilized public concern about juvenile prostitution. In this sense, the movement exploited the growing political backlash against progressive social change, in particular the growing economic and sexual independence of women and girls, to generate attention, concern, and action against the US youth sex trade.

Despite these racialized and gendered constructions of the problem of juvenile prostitution, most studies done at the time concluded that the problem existed but was overstated, and many teens were not coerced or controlled by third parties but were fleeing sexual abuse, homophobia, or poverty at home. Many, like Veronica Brunson, were vulnerable to

---

[105] Campagna and Poffenberger, *The Sexual Trafficking in Children.*
[106] Council on Scientific Affairs, "Healthcare Needs of Homeless and Runaway Youth," *Journal of the American Medical Association*, 262.10 (1989), 1358–1361.
[107] Kaye, "Male Prostitution in the Twentieth Century," 46–47.

prostitution because of failing social systems – her school, the criminal justice system that arrested her, and the child welfare system that did not follow up with her. Nevertheless, these powerful narratives activated lawmakers, who addressed some of these problems but left others – like homophobia and poverty – unaddressed. Congress and state legislatures prohibited child pornography, passed increased penalties for facilitation of youth involvement in the sex trade, and funded some social services to help youth. The 1970s saw the development of programs across the country to assist youth in prostitution, but very little structural change to address youth vulnerabilities to the sex trade. With budget cuts and a growing "law and order" approach to youth ushered in by the Reagan administration in the 1980s, juvenile prostitution dropped off the public agenda, although community based work on the issue continued. The issue, however, was raised in a global context in the 1990s, and US survivor-activists concerned about the commercial sexual exploitation of youth connected with these international conversations, bringing back to the United States new strategies and ideas to combat the problem.

# 3

# Survivor Activism and Global Connections: The US Campaign against Commercial Sexual Exploitation of Children in the 1990s

"My story began in New York when I was just five years old. Older men in the neighborhood park would give me money to view pornography and do to them what was shown in the pornography."[1] So began the story of Norma Hotaling, which she shared at a conference on "Sex for Sale" at Yale Law School in 2006. Hotaling, founder of the San Francisco-based service provider Standing Against Global Exploitation (SAGE), described how she was sexually abused by older boys and became addicted to heroin as a teenager. From the age of twelve, described Hotaling, she was "in and out of jails, mental health hospitals, emergency rooms, and drug treatment programs," yet, "[n]o one ever asked me about my life, about prostitution, about being raped, or about being kidnapped. No one asked me about the metal plate and the screws in my head from the beatings, about my suicide attempts, or about my desperation. No one asked me if I hurt, or why I hurt. No one ever treated me like a person. I was just a whore, a drug addict, and a criminal."[2] After a twenty-five-year heroin addiction, Hotaling went cold turkey while in jail, where she met an outreach worker who was also a survivor of prostitution and who suggested that she try street outreach work. After her release, Hotaling became an HIV outreach and education worker in a program funded by the Centers for Disease Control. She graduated from San Francisco State University with a degree in Health Education in 1992 and became coordinator for the San Francisco Department of Public Health's HIV testing program for women in prostitution. In 1995, Hotaling founded SAGE because, as she said, "there were no services at the time to help women and girls like me get off the streets."[3]

Norma Hotaling was one of several survivor activists who emerged as leaders in the movement against the commercial sexual exploitation of youth in the United States in the 1990s. These activists constructed individual and collective

---

[1] Norma Hotaling, "Sex for Sale: The Commercial Sexual Exploitation of Women and Girls: A Service Provider's Perspective," *Yale Journal of Law and Feminism* 18 (2006), 182.
[2] Ibid. 181–182.  [3] Ibid. 183.

identities as survivors, which gave them credibility and authority on the issue of juvenile prostitution. Through sharing their own excruciating stories of exploitation and escape from prostitution, survivor activists were able to generate support and to mobilize people to their cause. These activists deployed techniques developed in the 1970s women's movement – speaking out about sexual abuse, connecting with other women who had similar experiences, and then organizing to challenge male abuse. Increasing concern about HIV/AIDS bolstered their campaigns, and federal funds made available to address the disease through the CDC, especially those targeted toward sex workers, provided resources for people and organizations working against the US youth sex trade. These activists also took advantage of the political opportunities offered by emerging international movements against commercial sexual exploitation of children and sex trafficking to reframe US youth involvement in the sex trade as a form of child sexual abuse.

## COMING OUT, SPEAKING UP: THE US SURVIVOR MOVEMENT AGAINST COMMERCIAL SEXUAL EXPLOITATION OF YOUTH

In the 1990s, welfare reform eviscerated the social safety net and forced single mothers into long hours of low-paid employment without adequate childcare.[4] The 1990s also saw a steep increase in the number of Americans incarcerated in prisons, which removed parents and caregivers from communities and swelled the number of children in foster care.[5] These changing conditions contributed to increasing vulnerability of youth to commercial sexual exploitation. In response, several new organizations dedicated to helping youth involved in the sex trade were formed, many by survivor-activists, joining older organization like Lois Lee's Children of the Night in Los Angeles and Frank Barnaba's Paul and Lisa Program in Connecticut, which both continued to thrive in this period. With the continued support of Hugh Hefner and the Playboy Foundation, as well as support from corporations and Johnny Carson, Lois Lee opened a $2-million home for prostituted youth in the San Fernando Valley of California in 1992.[6] The home, which housed up to twenty-four residents at a time, received youth from all over the United States and offered case management, an on-site school, and recreational outings.[7] By 1992, the Paul and Lisa Program had four full-time and eight part-time staff members and twenty volunteers. They offered over one hundred prevention education

---

[4] Jane L. Collins and Victoria Mayer, *Both Hands Tied: Welfare Reform and the Race to the Bottom of the Low-Wage Labor Market* (Chicago, IL: University of Chicago, 2010), 2–3.

[5] Elizabeth Hinton, *From the War on Poverty to the War on Crime: The Making of Mass Incarceration in America* (Cambridge, MA: Harvard University Press, 2016).

[6] John Johnson, "Group That Shelters Teen-Age Prostitutes Expands into Suburbs," *Los Angeles Times* (June 14, 1992), VBC20; Children of the Night, 2010 Founder's Hero of the Heart Award, at www.childrenofthenight.org/pdf/Hugh_Hefner_Founders_Hero_of_the_Heart_Award.pdf.

[7] Children of the Night, Who We Are, at www.childrenofthenight.org/who-we-are/.

programs to over 6,000 people a year and their street work outreach program
made over two hundred contacts a year with youth involved in prostitution on
the streets of New York City.[8] In the mid-1990s, the Paul and Lisa Program
worked with the Midtown Community Court in Manhattan to launch an
alternate sentencing program.

Between 1995 and 1998, survivors like Hotaling founded four new service
organizations that worked with youth involved in prostitution – Breaking Free
in Minneapolis, Sisters Offering Support (SOS) in Honolulu, and Girls
Educational and Mentoring Services (GEMS) in New York City, in addition
to SAGE. The founders of these organizations became leaders in the movement
against commercial sexual exploitation of youth in the United States, each
bringing their own approach to the problem. Norma Hotaling of SAGE
advocated for peer counseling and pioneered "john schools" to discourage
men from buying sex. SAGE provided outreach and services to women and
girls, as well as advocacy and public awareness programs.[9] Rather than relying
on professional counselors, SAGE developed a Peer Educator Training
Program, which taught survivors to counsel clients desiring to leave the sex
trade. By 2001, fifteen of its eighteen employees were survivors.[10] SAGE also
pioneered the country's first "john school," which allowed first offenders
charged with soliciting prostitution to have their charges dropped if they paid
a fine and participated in a six-hour course designed to discourage future
solicitation.[11]

Vednita Carter, who had worked for WHISPER and founded the
Minneapolis-based Breaking Free in 1996, focused on the role that race
played in prostitution. Breaking Free offered transitional housing and life
skills training to women leaving the sex trade, with a special youth program
for girls aged 14 to 18. Breaking Free offered a twelve-week intensive
educational program, called "Save Our Sisters" or SOS, which examined the

---

[8] National Center for Missing and Exploited Children, *Female Juvenile Prostitution: Problem and Response* (Washington, DC: National Center for Missing and Exploited Children, December 1992), 37; Richard Weizel, "Friends Guide Prostitutes Off the Streets," *New York Times* (January 26, 1992), CN1; Mark Stuart Gill, "Savior on the Streets," *Reader's Digest* 139 (July, 1991), 111–115; Mark S. Gill, "Night Stalker: Hitting the Streets in the Name of Corporate Philanthropy," *Business Month* 135 (June 1990), 42–46.

[9] Marcia I. Cohen, Mark C. Edberg, and Stephen V. Gies, *Final Report on the Evaluation of the SAGE Project's LIFESKILLS and GRACE Programs* (May 2011), 1–2.

[10] Norma Hotaling, Autumn Burris, B. Julie Johnson, Yoshi M. Bird, and Kirsten A. Melbye, "Been There Done That: SAGE, A Peer Leadership Model Among Prostitution Survivors," in Melissa Farley (ed.), *Prostitution, Trafficking, and Traumatic Stress* (Binghamton, NY: Hawthorne Press, 2003), 255–265.

[11] Michael Shively, Sarah Kuck Jalbert, Ryan Kling, William Rhodes, Peter Finn, Chris Flygare, Laura Tierney, Dana Hunt, David Squires, Christina Dyous, and Kristin Wheeler, *Final Report on the Evaluation of the First Offender Prostitution Program: Report Summary* (Cambridge, MA: Abt Associates, March 2008).

role that race played in prostitution.[12] Carter published several articles arguing that the intersection of racism, classism, and heterosexism made African American women particularly vulnerable to sexual exploitation by white men and called on African American women and men to "unlearn the lessons of slavery" and to "deprogram ourselves."[13] Under Carter's leadership, Breaking Free had a Christian orientation and worked closely with churches in Minneapolis.[14]

Kelly Hill, who founded Sisters Offering Support (SOS) in Honolulu in 1996, condemned the role that popular culture played in fostering prostitution. SOS offered a crisis hotline, peer counseling, and other services to help women and girls exit the sex trade.[15] In 1998, SOS developed the Prostitution Intervention Project (PIP), a peer-based alternative sentencing program for adult and juvenile prostitution offenders. Hill argued that popular culture was "one of the biggest challenges we face in helping these girls get out. Because a lot of the values that they are developing as teenagers are coming from the media."[16] She condemned the media for "glamorizing pimping" and prostitution, mentioning MTV and World Wrestling Federation in particular. She also supported raising Hawaii's age of consent, which was 14, which she said had an impact on girls being lured into the sex industry.[17]

Rachel Lloyd, who founded Girls Educational and Mentoring Services (GEMS) in New York City in 1998, developed an empowerment model that focused on youth survivor leadership and policy advocacy. Lloyd came to the United States in 1997 as a missionary to work with women exiting the sex trade.[18] In this work, she encountered many commercially sexually exploited girls for whom there were no appropriate social services, so she formed GEMS to provide services for these girls. GEMS began by offering transitional and crisis housing to young women exiting the sex trade, including counseling, job training, and access to health care. Lloyd and the youth at GEMS later became instrumental in policy developments at the state and federal level.

---

[12] Julian Sher, *Somebody's Daughter: The Hidden Story of America's Prostituted Children and the Battle to Save Them* (Chicago, IL: Chicago Review Press, 2011), 288.

[13] Vednita Carter and Evelina Giobbe, "Duet: Prostitution, Racism and Feminist Discourse," *Hastings Women's Law Journal* 10 (1999), 55; Vednita Carter, "Providing Services to African American Prostituted Women," *Journal of Trauma Practice* 2.3/4 (2003), 213–222; Vednita Carter, "Prostitution: Where Racism and Sexism Intersect," *Michigan Journal of Gender and Law* 1 (1993), 81–89.

[14] Interview with Vednita Carter, July 27, 2017 (on file with author).

[15] Elizabeth Greene, "Charity Run by Former Prostitutes Steers Girls Away from the Streets," *Chronicle of Philanthropy* 14:2 (November 1, 2001), 10. SOS operated until 2006. Mary Vorsino, "Sisters Offering Support Closing," *Honolulu Advertiser* (September 23, 2006).

[16] Christine Donnelly, "Under the Surface: It's Not All as Seen on TV," *Honolulu Star-Bulletin* (August 23, 2000).

[17] Christine Donnelly, "Hawaii's Age of Consent Is Too Low, Advocates Say," *Honolulu Star-Bulletin* (August 25, 2000).

[18] Rachel Lloyd, *Girls Like Us* (New York, NY: Harper Collins, 2011), 22.

In addition to these new organizations, survivor Trudee Able-Peterson continued to work with youth survivors through Streetwork Project, now affiliated with Safe Horizon, in New York City. Able-Peterson was a strong advocate of a "harm reduction" approach to assisting youth in the sex trade, which focused on reducing the negative effects of certain behaviors, like participation in the sex trade, but still allowing individuals to make their own decisions about whether to cease the behavior. Streetwork Project offered street-based outreach services to youth. Able-Peterson encouraged outreach workers to adopt a non-judgmental attitude toward youth by meeting their self-defined needs rather than by telling them what to do.[19] Between 1991 and 1994, Able-Peterson worked for the Empire State Coalition on a federally funded street outreach project for youth, some of whom were involved in the sex trade, in rural areas and small cities in New York.[20] In 1993, Able-Peterson and June Bucy of the National Network of Runaway and Youth Services published a streetwork outreach training manual promoting harm reduction approaches to youth in the sex trade. They encouraged streetworkers to "not think they can, or feel they have to, save young people ... streetworkers open the doors for the kids to save themselves." Able-Peterson and Bucy condemned predominant attitudes that youth are to blame for exploitation and rape because they had chosen to live on the streets. Able-Peterson and Bucy criticized people who "locate problems in the pathology of individuals" and fail to appreciate how economics and employment conditions prevented youth from supporting themselves without resort to the street economy.[21] They also addressed the impact of stratification according to class, race, nationality, and sexual orientation and advocated "cultural competence" for service providers.

Whereas many of the founders of the organizations serving youth in the 1970s, like Lois Lee and Frank Barnaba, were not survivors, by the 1990s survivors were founding many of the new organizations. These advocates used their identities as survivors to mobilize concern about the issue of youth in the sex trade. These survivor advocates emphasized a range of tactics to help girls, including peer counseling, youth empowerment, and harm reduction, and they offered varying analyses of the sex trade, including critiques of the role of racism and popular culture in fostering prostitution. However, they all strongly supported the central importance of survivors' voices in service provision and in the development of public policy. They were also all abolitionists: they sought to end the sex trade. They opposed the criminal prosecution of women and girls involved in prostitution but supported the criminal prosecution of men buying

---

[19] Trudee Able-Peterson and June Bucy, *The Streetwork Outreach Training Manual* (Washington, DC: US Department of Health and Human Services, 1993). Social worker Terrie William, founder of Washington, DC-based Helping Individual Prostitutes Survive (HIPS), also used a harm reduction approach. HIPS History at www.hips.org/history.html.

[20] Interview with Trudee Able-Peterson, October 30, 2017 (on file with author).

[21] Able-Peterson and Bucy, *The Streetwork Outreach Training Manual*, 85.

sex. In addition to speaking out about their own experiences, survivor activists connected with a growing global movement against the commercial sexual exploitation of children in the 1990s, bringing back to the United States theories and strategies to address the issue at home.

## FINDING ALLIES ABROAD: THE GLOBAL MOVEMENT AGAINST COMMERCIAL SEXUAL EXPLOITATION OF CHILDREN

"For the first time, the scope and horror of the buying, selling, trafficking, and exploitation of children was revealed to the world," reported Norma Hotaling after attending the First World Congress Against the Commercial Sexual Exploitation of Children in Stockholm, Sweden, in 1996. "Testimony after testimony described the stories of brutally stolen childhoods."[22] The five-day Congress, attended by 1,300 participants from 136 countries, was co-sponsored by End Child Prostitution in Asian Tourism (ECPAT) in partnership with UNICEF, Rights of the Child, and the government of Sweden.[23] ECPAT, based in Bangkok, Thailand, was formed in 1990 by activists from four Asian countries concerned about extensive prostitution of children in Thailand, which had become a hub of sex tourism in Southeast Asia after the US military's rest and recuperation program for soldiers during the Vietnam war.[24] The conference was part of a growing child rights movement, epitomized by the United Nations adoption in 1989 of the Convention on the Rights of the Child, which addressed child prostitution under article 34 calling on nations to "protect children from all forms of sexual exploitation, including prostitution and involvement in pornography."[25]

In 1990, the United Nations High Commission on Human Rights established the office of the UN Special Rapporteur on the Sale of Children, Child Prostitution and Child Pornography that, along with the UN Committee on the Rights of the Child, was tasked with identifying problems and monitoring progress regarding the rights of children in countries that had ratified the Convention on the Rights of the Child. After a two-year investigation, special rapporteur Vitit Muntarbhorn, a Thai law professor, issued a report in 1992

---

[22] Hotaling, "Sex for Sale," 181.

[23] ECPAT International, *Commercial Sexual Exploitation of Children: Report of the First Year Following the Congress Against the Commercial Sexual Exploitation of Children Held in Stockholm, Sweden, August 1996* (Bangkok, Thailand: ECPAT International, August 1997), 6, 27.

[24] ECPAT International, *ECPAT 25 Years: Rallying the World to End Childhood Sexual Exploitation* (Bangkok, Thailand: ECPAT International, May 2015), 8; see also Heather Montgomery, *Modern Babylon? Prostituting Children in Thailand* (New York, NY: Berghahn Books, 2001), 47–49.

[25] United Nations Treaty Collection, Status of Treaties, Convention on the Rights of the Child, at https://treaties.un.org/Pages/ViewDetails.aspx?src=TREATY&mtdsg_no=IV-11&chapter=4& lang=en.

concluding "the sale of children, child prostitution and child pornography are undoubtedly global in nature" and "are much more extensive than is apparent at first glance" because "it is often invisible or only marginally visible, shielded by the cloak of a pervasive underworld."[26] Child prostitution was also addressed at a 1993 UNESCO conference on prostitution and human rights in Brussels held by the Council of Europe and at the United Nations Fourth World Conference on Women in Beijing in September of 1995.[27]

Despite UN concern about trafficking, ECPAT leaders could not get the United Nations to hold a meeting on the issue of child prostitution, so they organized the First World Congress Against the Sexual Exploitation of Children, where participants met to share research and best practices and to develop a strategy to address the problem.[28] Delegates representing 122 governments (not including the United States) adopted a sweeping declaration that child prostitution was a widespread and growing problem and agreed to allocate more resources to counter child prostitution, expand international cooperation, and improve their laws. The resulting *Declaration and Agenda for Action* provided the first working definition of commercial sexual exploitation of children and youth: "sexual abuse by the adult and remuneration in cash or kind to the child or a third person or persons."[29] The Congress adopted a resolution urging all governments to develop a National Plan of Action to address commercial sexual exploitation of children in their home countries that would contain indicators of progress toward reducing the number of children vulnerable to commercial sexual exploitation, with set goals and time frames for implementation. In addition to Hotaling, US anti-pornography activist Laura Lederer attended the Congress and presented research she had conducted on laws relating to child prostitution and pornography around the world.[30] In 1997, ECPAT expanded its mission beyond Asia and adopted the name ECPAT-International, changing the meaning of their acronym to End Child Prostitution, Child Pornography and the Trafficking of Children for Sexual Purposes, and later to End Child Prostitution and Trafficking. ECPAT-International now serves as the hub of a global network of

---

[26] Vitit Muntarbhorn, *Rights of the Child: Sale of Children* (New York, NY: United Nations Economic and Social Council, 1992), 1.

[27] Marlise Simons, "The Sex Market: Scourge on the World's Children," *New York Times* (April 9, 1993), A3; Roger Matthews, *Prostitution, Politics and Policy* (New York, NY: Routledge-Cavendish, 2008), 16; United Nations Fourth World Conference on Women, Platform for Action, Beijing China, September 1995, Strategic Objective L.2. section 277 d.

[28] Ron O'Grady, *The Road to Rio* (Bangkok, Thailand: ECPAT, 2008); Cameron W. Barr, "World Congress Sets Goals to End Sexual Exploitation of Children," *Christian Science Monitor* (August 30, 1996), 1.

[29] *Declaration and Agenda for Action*, First World Congress Against the Commercial Sexual Exploitation of Children, Stockholm, Sweden, August 27–31, 1996; William Adams, Colleen Owens, and Kevonne Small, "Effects of Federal Legislation on the Commercial Sexual Exploitation of Youth," *OJJDP Juvenile Justice Bulletin* (July 2010), 1.

[30] Laura J. Lederer, "Poor Children Targets of Sex Exploitation," *National Catholic Reporter* (November 22, 1996).

over eighty organizations fighting commercial sexual exploitation of youth in more than seventy countries.[31]

The First World Congress was an important moment for young survivors in the movement to combat the commercial sexual exploitation of youth. Seventeen child and youth delegates from eight countries (not including the US) attended the Congress, but there was little time allocated for their voices. The youth participants held their own meeting at the Congress and developed *An Appeal of Children and Young People*, calling for a range of actions, including punishment of offenders rather than children and public education. They demanded full participation of young people themselves in conversations about commercial sexual exploitation of youth. The youth committed themselves to building a network of children and young people across the world and called for governments to create a CSEC Fund for Youth to support these efforts.[32] One of the invited delegates to the Congress was Cherry Kingsley, a young Shuswap indigenous woman and Canadian activist with experience in the sex trade.[33] Kingsley noticed a lack of youth participation at the Congress. So, she along with Canadian delegate Senator Landon Pearson, who shared her concern, organized the first international summit of sexually exploited youth in March of 1998 in Victoria, British Columbia.

The gathering, titled Out from the Shadows: International Summit of Sexually Exploited Youth, was cohosted by University of Victoria's Institute for Child Rights and Development, the Office of the Ombudsman for British Columbia, and non-governmental organization PEERS (Prostitutes' Empowerment Education and Resource Society).[34] Sponsors included UNICEF, ECPAT-International and the Canadian International Development Agency (CIDA). In preparation for the summit, consultations were held with young people who had direct experience in the sex trade in sixteen sites across the Americas and the Caribbean and two youth from each consultation were invited to attend the summit. During the summit, attended by fifty-five youth delegates, participants shared their stories through music, drama, art, and creative writing. According to Rachel Lloyd, who was a representative from the United States, the purpose of the summit was to "ensure that survivor voices

---

[31] ECPAT-International, Who We Are, at www.ecpat.org/where-we-work/.

[32] ECPAT International, *Report of the World Congress III Against Sexual Exploitation of Children and Adolescents* (Bangkok, Thailand: ECPAT International, September 2009), 11, 15. CSEC stands for commercial sexual exploitation of children.

[33] Laura A. Barnitz, *Commercial Sexual Exploitation of Children: Youth Involved in Prostitution, Pornography, and Sex Trafficking* (Washington, DC: Youth Advocate Program International, 1998), 29; James Brooke, "Sex Web Spun Worldwide Traps Children," *New York Times* (December 23, 2001), A12.

[34] Lisa E. Goulet, *Out From the Shadows: Good Practices In Working With Sexually Exploited Youth in the Americas* (Victoria, BC: University of Victoria, 2001), 15 (conference follow-up report describing best practices). See also, *Report on Out From the Shadows: International Summit of Sexually Exploited Youth* at http://o3559de.netsolhost.com/vicreport-e.htm.

are no longer silenced, and that our expertise on our own experiences is heard by policy makers and others in power."[35] Attendees, including Lloyd, drafted a *Declaration and Agenda for Action*. Lloyd and Kingsley presented the declaration at the United Nations, where it was later ratified by 130 countries due in large part to the activism of youth.[36]

The agenda they developed demonstrated a new narrative of youth involvement in the sex trade grounded in survivor activism and human rights. The *Agenda for Action* explicitly called for change in the legal treatment of commercially sexually exploited young people: "We believe that, as sexually exploited children and youth, our laws must protect us and no longer punish us as criminals." They declared that "the term child or youth prostitute can no longer be used" and called for "severe penalties" to be imposed on all those profiting from the sexual exploitation of children and youth. They stated that sexually exploited children and youth had a right to resources to meet their diverse needs, including safe and adequate housing and 24-hour help lines. Calling attention to the fact that girls were not the only victims of commercial sexual exploitation, they declared, "We believe that as children and youth, we are all vulnerable to sexual exploitation whether male, female or transgender." And they highlighted the importance of their participation in the development of solutions to commercial sexual exploitation of children and youth: "We believe that the voices and experience of sexually exploited youth must be heard and are central to the development and implementation of action. We must be empowered to help ourselves." The *Agenda* supported harm reduction and the elimination of societal stereotypes surrounding sexually exploited children and youth, declaring that the media "has a responsibility to educate the public" and calling for the development of forums where the voices of children could be heard.[37] This declaration and agenda became the blueprint for the movement against the commercial sexual exploitation of youth. Since the 1998 summit, participation of young people in policy development on the commercial sexual exploitation of youth has grown significantly.[38] Out of the 1996 First World Congress and the 1998 Out From the Shadows Summit emerged a global consensus against the commercial sexual exploitation of youth and a call for youth survivor leadership.

[35] Lloyd, *Girls Like Us*, 238; see also, Lynette Jackson, Out From the Shadows Youth Delegates, and Cherry Kingsley, *Moving Forward Together To Stop the Sexual Exploitation of Children and Youth, Educational Guide to Out From the Shadows: First International Summit of Sexually Exploited Youth* (Victoria, BC: Save the Children, 1998).

[36] Lloyd, *Girls Like Us*, 240.

[37] Youth Delegates of Out From the Shadows: International Summit of Sexually Exploited Youth, *Declaration and Agenda for Action of Sexually Exploited Children and Youth*, March 12, 1998, Victoria, B.C.; Goulet, *Out From the Shadows*, 31, 35, 44, 80.

[38] Claire Feinstein and Clare O'Kane, "Children's and Adolescents' Participation and Protection from Sexual Abuse and Exploitation," *Innocenti Working Paper 2009–10* (Florence, Italy: UNICEF Innocenti Research Centre, February 2009).

   This international organizing fueled the growing US movement against the youth sex trade by providing allies, strategies and analysis of the issue from around the world. Inspired by the formation of ECPAT in 1990, several Americans from faith-based communities, including Carol Smolenski of the Christian Children's Fund, formed ECPAT-USA in 1991.[39] The organization incorporated in 1994 and Smolenski became the Executive Director in 1996.[40] ECPAT-USA and Smolenski initially focused on "child sex tourism," as it was called at the time, but broadened their mission to the prostitution of American youth in the United States in the 2000s. According to Carol Smolenski, the international meetings and World Congresses were helpful because they gave activists new ideas and new connections, as well as an international consensus condemning the commercial sexual exploitation of children and a government commitment to work on the issue.[41] In addition to encouraging US campaigns, the global activism against child prostitution led to increased media coverage of the issue, which raised public awareness within the United States.

## LOOKING THE OTHER WAY: US MEDIA COVERAGE OF YOUTH INVOLVEMENT IN PROSTITUTION IN THE 1990S

In the 1990s, US media reported extensively on child prostitution around the world, especially in Southeast Asia and Eastern Europe, often attributing its occurrence to "third world backwardness" or flawed societies, all the while remaining silent about youth prostitution within the United States.[42] Newspapers and magazines reported dramatic stories about Cambodian parents selling their young daughters for cash to buy television sets or young boys servicing Western male tourists on Thai beaches. Child prostitution in Southeast Asia was linked to the end of the Vietnam war and the growth of sex tourism in the region, while the phenomenon in Eastern Europe was linked to economic dislocation resulting from the dissolution of the Soviet Union.[43] According to a 1994 *New York Times* magazine feature, "All over the world, the child sex trade is booming, thanks to mercenary parents, indifferent

---

[39] ECPAT International, *ECPAT 25 Years*, 25.

[40] ECPAT-USA, History of ECPAT-USA, at www.ecpatusa.org/history-alt/; Chris David, "Carol Smolenski/ECPAT-USA," *Means: The Art of Social Justice* (December 2, 2015).

[41] Interview with Carol Smolenski, July 21, 2017 (on file with author).

[42] Julietta Hua, *Trafficking Women's Human Rights* (Minneapolis, MN: University of Minnesota Press, 2011), 55.

[43] See, for example, William Branigin, "Children for Sale in Thailand: Poverty, Greed Force Girls Into Prostitution," *Washington Post* (December 28, 1993), A1; Marlise Simons, "East Europeans Duped into West's Sex Trade," *New York Times* (June 9, 1994), A1; Uli Schmetzer, "Philippine Town Haven for Touring Pedophiles," *Chicago Tribune* (April 9, 1992), N31; Joyce Liu, "Prostitution Snares Taiwan Children," *Los Angeles Times* (August 19, 1990), A11; Michael S. Serrill, "Prostitution: Defiling the Children," *Time Magazine* (June 21, 1993), 52–55; Marlise Simons, "The Sex Market: Scourge on the World's Children," *New York Times* (April 9, 1993), A3.

customers and government officials who look the other way."[44] According to author Marlise Simons, the girls came from villages in northern Thailand where old men had the "thin, spent demeanor of longtime opium smokers" and "everyone craves televisions and other consumer goods."[45] Few young girls remained in these villages, reported Simons, giving a detailed account of a father who sold his 13-year-old daughter for $320. "Agents pay an advance, perhaps the price of a TV set, to the parents of a child who is then left in virtual bondage."[46] In addition to blaming greedy and heartless parents, Simons attributed the problem to corrupt police officials and the "clients" who bought sex from children. Asian men, she reported, sought sex from young girls because they believed they were less likely to have AIDS or because they believed that sex with virgins would "rejuvenate" them. Accompanied by a photograph of a young Thai boy massaging the leg of an older white man on a beach, the story reported that "gay and pedophile guidebooks and newsletters" direct Western men to Sri Lanka and Thailand for "very young boys on the cheap."[47] Other photographs portrayed girls despondent or cowering in brothels and shelters, or boys being chased or arrested by the police. Attributing child prostitution in Southeast Asia to callous and greedy parents, corrupt police, ignorant Asian men, and gay westerners, Simons portrayed the issue as the moral failure of individuals, rarely mentioning the broader political and economic factors contributing to the problem, such as ethnic conflict and displacement, poverty, and development policies that encouraged tourism, including sex tourism.[48] Meanwhile, prostitution of youth in the United States was rarely mentioned.

Sometimes the media was called out for its myopia. On August 25, 1996, the eve of the First World Congress on Commercial Sexual Exploitation of Children, the *New York Times* published an editorial condemning child prostitution in Southeast Asia.[49] A few days later, a letter to the editor appeared written by Richard Haymes of New York City's Community Health Project in which he suggested that the editorial board "venture over to 10th Avenue to witness the tragedy of child prostitution first hand."[50] He challenged the "stereotypical image of young girls running away from home only to be pounced upon by a pimp," arguing instead that most street youth forced to engage in sex to survive were youth of color from the five boroughs or

---

[44] Marlise Simons, "The Littlest Prostitutes," *New York Times* (January 16, 1994), SM30–35.

[45] Ibid. SM34.

[46] Ibid. SM35; see also, Nicholas Kristof, "Asian Childhoods Sacrificed to Prosperity's Lust," *New York Times* (April 14, 1996), 1.

[47] Simons, "The Littlest Prostitutes," 33.

[48] For an excellent analysis of some of the structural causes of child prostitution, see Julia O'Connell Davidson, *Children in the Global Sex Trade* (Malden, MA: Polity Press, 2005).

[49] "Prostituted Children," *New York Times* (August 26, 1996), A14.

[50] Richard Haymes, "Under Streetlights, the Vulnerable Huddle," *New York Times* (September 1, 1996), E8.

neighboring areas and that they were overwhelmingly lesbian, gay, and bisexual. He noted that funding for community-based organizations to help young people was being slashed by city and state agencies. He praised the *Times* for its concern about prostituted youth abroad, but suggested that they pay attention to the same activities occurring *within* the United States.

An exception to media's tendency to focus on child prostitution in other countries while ignoring the same problem in the United States were several articles included in a series of over thirty articles that ran in the *Christian Science Monitor* from August through October of 1996, titled "The Child Sex Trade: Battling a Scourge," which was part of a larger series entitled "Safeguarding Our Children." The child sex trade series of articles was inspired by the First World Congress on the Commercial Sexual Exploitation of Children in 1996. While most of the articles in the *Christian Science Monitor* series focused abroad, the series also covered "child prostitution" into and within the US, challenging the common perception that youth involvement in prostitution was only a foreign problem. One article quoted the president of the Palo Alto-based Global Fund for Women, Kavita Ramdas, saying, "it is as much an issue for us here in the United States as it is in my home country [India], as it is in Nepal and China and the Philippines."[51] Another article quoted the head of Vancouver's Downtown Eastside Youth Activities Society Josh Turvey saying, "Canadians and Americans should quit wagging fingers at Asia and instead take a hard look at the fast-growing business of renting children for sex in their own North American backyard."[52] Lois Lee was quoted in one article stating, "We have a lot of it [child prostitution] in this country, and a lot of powerful, wealthy people are involved in it. You've got teen prostitutes working three blocks from the White House. We're not any better than any other country – and we don't handle it any better. We've got to wake up to the problem before we can solve it."[53] The articles on juvenile prostitution within the United States reported on Minneapolis, the west coast "Pacific circuit" from Vancouver to Los Angeles, and New York City. The articles repeatedly quoted US activist/experts, including Lee, Barnaba, and Hotaling, as well as youth survivors.[54]

When covering child prostitution in the United States, the *Christian Science Monitor* series echoed the common refrain from the 1970s that the phenomena was spreading from big cities to suburbs and small towns. For example, an October 23, 1996, article quoted Lois Lee of Children of the Night in Los Angeles saying, "The circuit used to be the big cities ... Now the circuit has

---

[51] Brad Knickerbocker, "Prostitution's Pernicious Reach Grows in the U.S.," *Christian Science Monitor* (October 23, 1996), 1.

[52] Mark Clayton, "Sex Trade Lures Kids From Burbs," *Christian Science Monitor* (August 30, 1996), 9.

[53] Mark Clayton, "In United States, Canada, New Laws Fail to Curb Demand for Child Sex," *Christian Science Monitor* (September 5, 1996), 10.

[54] Cameron W. Barr, "Getting Adults to Think in New Ways," *Christian Science Monitor* (September 16, 1996), 9.

switched to the suburbs. The prostitution subculture has become very, very mobile."[55] In an August 30 article titled "Sex Trade Lures Kids from Burbs," Frank Barnaba was quoted saying, "pimps used to recruit in the city. But they discovered it's much easier to work the burbs. The kids are naïve, materialistic, and vulnerable to the pimp's message."[56] Barnaba described working with youth recruited from "the shopping malls and fast-food restaurants of the Midwest – heartland places like San Antonio, Cleveland, or Wichita, Kansas,"[57] and one article quoted him saying that girls came to New York from Connecticut, Florida, Massachusetts, Texas, Oklahoma, California, Cleveland, Minneapolis, Poughkeepsie, and Westchester County, Long Island. Ericka Moses of Minneapolis-based PRIDE was quoted saying, "A lot of the time naïve suburban girls come to the city to hang out and have fun, and within six months they're on the streets prostituting."[58] The series repeatedly characterized the problem as not only in the cities, but also in "America's heartland."[59] These characterizations of the issue were strikingly similar to the media's portrayal of the issue in the 1970s.

Also similar to the 1970s, the *Christian Science Monitor* series described "child prostitution" as increasingly common and as "one of the great hidden scourges of human society."[60] The articles cited some of the same speculative statistics from the 1970s, such as the claim that 100,000 to 300,000 children were involved in prostitution in North America. The articles claimed that the average age of entry into prostitution was getting younger and that homeless youth were often approached by "pimps" within forty-eight hours of being on the street, a claim that would reappear repeatedly in coverage of the issue in the 2000s, despite the lack of reliable studies to support this claim.[61] Unlike the 1970s, the series overwhelmingly focused on girls, although boys were sometimes mentioned. One article told the story of Kenny, who "cross-dressed as a young girl" in Minneapolis, although she may have been a transgender girl.[62] The series paid particular attention to the vulnerability of youth to HIV/AIDS.

Reminiscent of feminist arguments in the 1970s, the series portrayed popular culture as contributing to the problem of youth prostitution by sexually

[55] Knickerbocker, "Prostitution's Pernicious Reach Grows in the U.S.," 1.
[56] Clayton, "Sex Trade Lures Kids from Burbs," 9.
[57] Mark Clayton, "Prostitution 'Circuit' Takes Girls Across North America," *Christian Science Monitor* (August 23, 1996), 10.
[58] Ibid.
[59] See, for example, Mark Clayton, "Minneapolis 'Shouldn't Have to Sell Its Daughters,'" *Christian Science Monitor* (August 30, 1996), 11.
[60] Cameron W. Barr, "Sexually Exploited Youths Draws World's Vigilance," *Christian Science Monitor* (August 22, 1996), 10.
[61] Clayton, "Sex Trade Lures Kids from Burbs," 9; see also *Hofstede Committee Report, Juvenile Prostitution in Minnesota* (St. Paul: Minnesota Attorney General's Office, November 1999), 6.
[62] Clayton, "Minneapolis 'Shouldn't Have to Sell Its Daughters,'" 11.

objectifying women and girls, glamorizing the sex trade, and instilling materialistic values into children. In a September 13, 1996, article titled "Popular Culture Paves the Way," journalist Mark Clayton describes the increasing sexual objectification of young girls in advertising, movies, and television programs, giving as an example 15-year-old Brooke Shields' Calvin Klein advertisement ("nothing comes between me and my Calvins") as well as popular films *Pretty Woman* and *Milk Money*, described as portraying prostitution in "glamorous terms" and generating a "'Pretty Woman' syndrome" by "making it socially acceptable."[63] The series also criticized the sexual attitudes of men for contributing to increased youth prostitution and reported on activists' attempts to shift perceptions of youth in the sex trade from seeing them as promiscuous to seeing them as vulnerable and naïve, not as perpetrators but as victims.[64]

In contrast to the *Christian Science Monitor* coverage, mainstream newspapers coverage of the issue of juvenile prostitution in the United States was limited, mostly covering particular cases. For example, in 1997, the *New York Times* published a story about four young girls in Brooklyn who were allegedly forced into prostitution and required to earn $1000 a night.[65] In 1999, the *Minneapolis Star Tribune* published a series of articles about the federal prosecution of the Twin Cities-based Evans family for running a child prostitution ring and another Minneapolis case involving a King Mafia Crip gang member.[66] These stories sometimes followed the racialized tropes that appeared in mainstream coverage of the issue in the 1970s. Several stories focused on blonde, Midwestern girls. For example, a 1992 *New York Times* story about the Paul and Lisa Program began with a story of a "blonde Midwesterner" whom the program had successfully transformed from a girl dressed in a "miniskirt, fishnet stockings and six-inch heels" into a girl described as having a "shy polite manner" and who "could have easily passed for a cheerleader."[67] An August 19, 1999, *Star Tribune* article on the Evans prosecution reported that the Midwest was a "major recruiting center" because "blue-eyed, blonde girls are considered valuable," according to one police sergeant, and Midwest girls "have a higher degree of vulnerability" and

---

[63] Mark Clayton, "Pop Culture Paves the Way," *Christian Science Monitor* (September 13, 1996), 10.

[64] See, for example, Barr, "Getting Adults to Think in New Ways," 9; Mark Clayton, "Girls Entering the Sex Trade May Say It's a 'Choice' ... But Experts See Them as Victims of Master Manipulators," *Christian Science Monitor* (September 13, 1996), 10.

[65] Kit R. Roane, "Man Accused of Forcing Four Girls to be Prostitutes: The Youngest Victim is 11 Years Old," *New York Times* (August 13, 1997), B3.

[66] Paul Gustafson, "Guilty Plea in Gang Prostitution Case," *Minneapolis Star Tribune* (August 6, 1999), B3; Rosalind Bentley and Richard Meryhew, "Turning Girls into Prostitutes is an Easy Task, Experts Say," *Minneapolis Star Tribune* (August 19, 1999), B1.

[67] Richard Weizel, "Friends Guide Prostitutes Off the Street," *New York Times* (January 26, 1992), CN1.

were "a little more naïve" than girls elsewhere, according to a social worker.[68] This article repeated the stereotypical portrayal of vulnerability and abuse: "recruitment involved a predictable interplay of a young girl's vulnerability, a pimp's smooth talking and then, physical and emotional abuse."[69] The recurrent framing of the problem as affecting middle-class white girls from suburban areas targeted by African American men was effective in mobilizing concern from mainstream white readers and generating sympathy for some youth involved in the sex trade.

## A POLITICAL OPPORTUNITY: THE US MOVEMENT AGAINST INTERNATIONAL SEX TRAFFICKING

Despite the media's downplaying of youth prostitution in the US, increased media coverage of international sex trafficking and a growing US movement against international trafficking provided a political opportunity for activists concerned about commercial sexual exploitation of youth in the United States, who attempted to leverage concern about international trafficking to raise the issue of the involvement of US youth in the sex trade. The US-based movement against international trafficking was initiated by feminist activists Kathleen Barry, Laura Lederer, Dorchen Leidholdt, and Norma Ramos, all of whom were leaders in the feminist anti-pornography movement in the 1970s and 1980s.[70] In 1988, members of Women Against Pornography and the Minneapolis-based anti-prostitution organization WHISPER organized the Global Conference Against Trafficking in Women, which was held in New York City at Martin Luther King High School in October and attended by over five hundred women from around the world. Lederer, who was a program officer at the Scaggs Foundation at the time, provided the seed money for the conference.[71] The Coalition Against Trafficking in Women (CATW) was founded at this conference by Barry, Leidholdt, and Ramos.[72] CATW sought to increase awareness of international sex trafficking and to push for legal reforms. In 1989, CATW was granted Category II Consultative Status

---

[68] Bentley and Meryhew, "Turning Girls into Prostitutes is an Easy Task, Experts Say," B1.

[69] Ibid.

[70] Jennifer Suchland, *Economies of Violence: Transnational Feminism, Postsocialism, and the Politics of Sex Trafficking* (Durham, NC: Duke University Press, 2015), 33; Carolyn Bronstein, *Battling Pornography* (New York, NY: Cambridge University Press, 2011), 248. See also Kathleen Barry, Charlotte Bunch, and Shirley Castley, *International Feminism: Networking Against Female Sexual Slavery* (New York, NY: International Women's Tribune Centre, Inc., 1984).

[71] Dorchen Leidholdt, "Keynote Address: Demand and the Debate," in Morrison Torrey (ed.), *Demand Dynamics: The Forces of Demand in Global Sex Trafficking* (Chicago, IL: DePaul University College of Law, 2004), 5.

[72] Coalition Against Trafficking in Women, Asia Pacific, Herstory, at www.catw-ap.org.ph/herstory.html; Kathleen Barry, *The Prostitution of Sexuality* (New York, NY: New York University Press, 1995), 5.

with the United Nations Economic and Social Council, the highest status granted by the United Nations to non-governmental organizations, thereby allowing them to participate in the work of the United Nations. In 1991, CATW collaborated with UNESCO in a meeting at Penn State on the development of a new international human rights treaty against sex trafficking.[73] In the following years, CATW held conferences and regional meetings around the world, including in the Philippines and Bangladesh, and eventually formed national coalitions in over fifteen countries.[74] CATW organized the International Human Rights Network (IHRN), a coalition of more than 140 nongovernmental organizations, to advocate for a broad definition of sex trafficking that included not just victims forced to participate in prostitution, but all women and children involved in prostitution. IHRN was an abolitionist organization that equated all prostitution with sex trafficking, as opposed to the International Human Rights Law Group, which distinguished between prostitution and sex trafficking.[75]

Another organization that was central to the US movement against international sex trafficking was The Protection Project, founded in 1997 by Laura Lederer. In 1976, Lederer co-founded the San Francisco-based Women Against Violence in Pornography and Media (WAVPM) along with Kathleen Barry and Diana Russell, among others. Lederer served as national coordinator of WAVPM from 1976 to 1980 and edited *Take Back the Night: Women on Pornography*,[76] a widely read and influential collection of feminist anti-pornography essays.[77] The Protection Project, which was originally based at Harvard University's Kennedy School of Government and later at Johns Hopkins University School of Advanced International Studies, was a leading legal research institute for the study of human trafficking. The Project led a coalition of organizations that played an important role in the passage of the Trafficking Victims Protection Act of 2000. As head of the Protection Project, Lederer researched laws on sex trafficking in over two hundred countries, documented trafficking routes, and collected the stories of trafficking survivors, which she published in a 2001 report.[78] Lederer's focus,

---

[73] Barry, *The Prostitution of Sexuality*, 5.

[74] Coalition Against Trafficking in Women, History, at www.catwinternational.org/WhoWeAre/History.

[75] Kamala Kempadoo, Jyoti Sanghera, and Bandana Pattanaik, *Trafficking and Prostitution Reconsidered: New Perspectives on Migration, Sex Work and Human Rights* (New York, NY: Routledge, 2011).

[76] Laura Lederer, *Take Back the Night: Women on Pornography* (New York, NY: Harper Perennial, 1980).

[77] Bronstein, *Battling Pornography*, 247.

[78] Laura Lederer, *Human Rights Report on Trafficking of Women and Children: A Country-by-Country Report on a Contemporary Form of Slavery* (Washington, DC: Paul H. Nitze School of Advanced International Studies, Johns Hopkins University, 2001). See also, Allen D. Hertzke, *Freeing God's Children: The Unlikely Alliance for Global Human Rights* (New York, NY: Rowman & Littlefield Publishers, 2004), 319.

however, was international sex trafficking; her report only briefly mentioned prostitution of American youth within the United States.

A third feminist organization that played an important role in the US movement against international sex trafficking was Equality Now, an international women's rights organization founded in 1992 by Jessica Neuwirth in New York City. Neuwirth, who had worked for Amnesty International in the early 1990s, became disillusioned with human rights groups because they avoided "cultural or 'commercial' abuses" such as "female genital mutilation" and sex trafficking. She disagreed with feminists who advocated for the legalization of prostitution, which she believed would just contribute to more sex trafficking. She founded Equality Now to address these types of issues that received short shrift from human rights groups. Equality Now initiated a campaign against sex tourism in 1996 and became an important player in the anti-trafficking movement.[79] But feminists weren't the only ones concerned about international sex trafficking.

As in the late nineteenth and early twentieth centuries, religious groups worked on the issue as well. Evangelical Christian Gary Haugen founded The International Justice Mission (IJM) in 1997 in Washington, DC. A former Justice Department lawyer who had directed the UN genocide investigation in Rwanda, Haugen founded IJM to help victims of violence and forced labor around the world by pressuring local police and courts to enforce existing laws. Sex trafficking was the major focus of the organization in the late 1990s and early 2000s and Haugen used undercover investigations to expose child prostitution throughout Asia.[80] He later became a leader in the campaign to pass the Trafficking Victims Protection Act (TVPA) in the United States.[81] Haugen was part of a broader move by evangelical Christians into international human rights work.

In the mid-1990s, some evangelicals made a strategic decision to turn their attention away from divisive domestic issues on which they had not made significant headway, like abortion, school prayer, and pornography. According to Reverend Richard Cizik, the vice president for governmental affairs of the National Association of Evangelicals, "We made a lot of statements in the 1980s and got zip."[82] Therefore, they looked instead to the international arena: the persecution of Christians abroad. In the 1990s, led by Michael Horowitz who was at the time a fellow at the Hudson Institute, evangelical groups worked with human rights organizations and Jewish groups to pass the International Religious Freedom Act of 1998 and to pressure the US government to work toward ending the war in Sudan. Then

---

[79] Equality Now, Campaigns, at www.equalitynow.org/campaigns/ending-sex-tourism; Hertzke, *Freeing God's Children*, 320–321.

[80] See, for example, *Children for Sale*, NBC Dateline, 2005.

[81] Hertzke, *Freeing God's Children*, 319–320.

[82] Elisabeth Bumiller, "Evangelicals Sway White House on Human Rights Issues Abroad: Liberal Join Effort on AIDS and Sex Trafficking," *New York Times* (October 26, 2003), N1.

they turned to sex trafficking in 1998, again led by Horowitz, who brought in a wide range of religious groups to fight for the TVPA.[83]

The activists concerned about international sex trafficking had very different political orientations, but they worked together collaboratively to pass the TVPA. The movement included religious conservatives, anti-prostitution feminists, and human rights advocates.[84] On the right, Michael Horowitz of the Hudson Institute brought in religious activists like Miriam Bell of Prison Fellowship, Richard Cizik of the National Association of Evangelicals, John Busby of the Salvation Army, and William Bennett and Richard Land of the Southern Baptist Convention. On the left, Laura Lederer and Jessica Neuwirth brought in mainstream feminists like Patricia Ireland of the National Organization for Women, Gloria Feldt of Planned Parenthood, Eleanor Smeal of the Feminist Majority Foundation, and Gloria Steinem of *Ms.* magazine.[85] Anti-prostitution feminists agreed with religious conservatives that sex trafficking should be defined to include "the transport of human beings for the purpose of sexual exploitation . . . regardless of whether or not such persons have 'consented' to their exploitation."[86] Human rights groups, such as Amnesty International and Human Rights Watch, joined the coalition but pressed for the inclusion of labor trafficking in the TVPA.[87] Lederer and Haugen worked together, testifying multiple times at Congressional hearings on the anti-trafficking legislation, and they brought in women who had survived sex trafficking to tell their stories to legislators.[88] Legislators supporting the bill were ideologically diverse, including Representatives Chris Smith (R-NJ) and Sam Brownback (R-KS), and Senators Paul Wellstone (D-MN) and Barbara

---

[83] Hertzke, *Freeing God's Children*; Margaret McDonnell, *Case Study of the Campaign to End "Modern-Day Slavery"* (US Coalition for Child Survival, March 2007), 2; Tony Carnes, "'Odd Couple' Politics: Evangelicals, Feminists Make Common Cause Against Sex Trafficking," *Christianity Today* (March 6, 2000), 24; Nicole Footen Bromfield, *The Hijacking of Human Trafficking Legislation During Its Creation* (Saarbrücken, Germany: VDM Verlag Dr. Müller, 2010), 114–116; Bumiller, "Evangelicals Sway White House on Human Rights Issues Abroad," N1.

[84] Alicia W. Peters, *Responding to Human Trafficking: Sex, Gender, and Culture in the Law* (Philadelphia, PA: University of Pennsylvania Press, 2015), 50; Bromfield, *The Hijacking of Human Trafficking Legislation During Its Creation*, 114–116.

[85] Hertzke, *Freeing God's Children*, 321–322, 324, 328, 330.

[86] Letter to Senator Paul Wellstone from Jessica Neuworth et al., International Trafficking of Women and Children Victim Protection Act of 1999 (S.600, Analysis of Protection Act by Dorchen Leidholdt, April 14, 1999, at www.bayswan.org/traffick/antiwellstone.html). Peters, *Responding to Human Trafficking*, 53.

[87] Bromfield, *The Hijacking of Human Trafficking Legislation During Its Creation*, 89, 126–128.

[88] *Trafficking of Women and Children in the International Sex Trade, Hearing Before the Subcommittee on International Operations and Human Rights of the Committee on International Relations of the House of Representatives*, 106th Congress, 1st Session, September 14, 1999; *The Sex Trade: Trafficking of Women and Children in Europe and the United States, Hearing Before the Commission on Security and Cooperation in Europe*, 106th Congress, 1st Session, June 28, 1999.

Mikulski (D-MD). The coalition also had the support of First Lady Hillary Clinton, who had first raised the issue of trafficking at the 1995 UN Conference on Women in Beijing. The Clintons' support was a significant factor in moving the issue forward within the United States.[89] The media regularly commented on the "odd couple" politics of feminists and evangelicals working together against sex trafficking.[90] Activists drew attention to their unlikely alliance to gain media attention. Michael Horowitz of the Hudson Institute was quoted in *Christianity Today*, saying "This is an amazing, somewhat vulnerable, but remarkably cohesive coalition of feminists and church groups."[91] This diverse movement consciously adopted strategies and tactics to accommodate and leverage their differences. The campaign focused narrowly on the single goal of passing the TVPA and they communicated separately to their diverse constituencies to raise awareness and press Congress to act.[92] They also recruited celebrities like Bono, Sigourney Weaver, and Angelina Jolie and humanitarians like Elie Wiesel and Muhummad Yunus to be spokespersons for the campaign, further raising the profile of the issue. Finally, they had the support of President Bill Clinton.

This coalition, however, focused on international sex trafficking, including international child sex trafficking, and labor trafficking, but not US youth involved in the sex trade.[93] Nevertheless, advocates for commercial sexually exploited youth in the United States saw a political opportunity to raise the issue of juvenile prostitution within the United States. Legislators and public policy advocates were condemning the sexual exploitation of children in countries around the world, and even condemning sex trafficking of children brought *into* the United States, but they were ignoring the commercial sexual exploitation of US youth. Advocates for youth in the US sex trade highlighted this contradiction to put their issue on the public agenda.

## THE US CAMPAIGN AGAINST COMMERCIAL SEXUAL EXPLOITATION OF CHILDREN

As organizations focused on international trafficking began to lobby Congress for a federal anti-trafficking law in the 1990s, activists against the US youth sex trade organized to support the effort with the hope that their cause would benefit from federal anti-trafficking legislation. Survivor-founded service providers came together to form the US Campaign Against Commercial

---

[89] Bromfield, *The Hijacking of Human Trafficking Legislation During Its Creation*, 100, 108.

[90] See, for example, Shenon Philip, "Feminist Coalition Protests U.S. Stance on Sex Trafficking Treaty," *New York Times* (January 13, 2000), A5.

[91] Carnes, "'Odd Couple' Politics," 24.

[92] McDonnell, *Case Study of the Campaign to End "Modern-Day Slavery,"* 4–5.

[93] Bromfield, *The Hijacking of Human Trafficking Legislation During Its Creation*, 151 (people testifying for the legislation at Congressional hearings gave significant attention to the exploitation of children).

Sexual Exploitation of Children, coordinated by Laura Barnitz of Youth Advocate Program International, Inc. (YAPI). YAPI, founded in 1994 in Washington, DC, with several state affiliate programs, were advocates of children's rights and strong supporters of the UN Convention on the Rights of the Child. In 1998, Laura Barnitz, initially under contract and later hired at YAPI, published a booklet compiling research on commercial sexual exploitation of children across the globe and reporting on the First World Congress Against the Commercial Sexual Exploitation of Children. In researching this issue, Barnitz interviewed staff at youth service provider organizations like Children of the Night, ECPAT, Breaking Free, GEMS, and Washington, DC-based HIPS (Helping Individual Prostitutes Survive, a sex worker rights organization founded with AIDS prevention funds from the CDC in the early 1990s), as well as law enforcement in New York, Los Angeles, and Texas. In the introduction, YAPI Director Nancy Nye noted that sexually abused children were often seen as victims, unless they were abused in the commercial sex business, in which case they were seen as perpetrators of criminal acts. But, she argued, "YAPI takes the position that all children who are sexually exploited, whether in homes and schools or in hotels and brothels, are victims."[94] The pamphlet discussed the experiences of youth in the commercial sex trade in countries across the globe *and* within the United States. In her analysis, Barnitz adopted the First World Congress' child rights perspective on the issue of commercial sexual exploitation of children, condemning the criminalization of exploited youth and calling for services for youth rather than incarceration. YAPI then attempted to realize this perspective in US public policy by creating a coalition of advocates against commercial sexual exploitation of youth to lobby Congress on the issue.

In the late 1990s, on behalf of YAPI, Laura Barnitz invited advocates working with commercially sexually exploited youth to form the US Campaign Against the Commercial Sexual Exploitation of Children. The purpose of the Campaign was to lobby Congress to pass the TVPA with the hope of generating resources to support services for US youth in the sex trade. The Campaign's steering committee included Norma Hotaling of SAGE, Carol Smolenski of ECPAT-USA, Vednita Carter of Breaking Free, Rachel Lloyd of GEMS, and Kelly Hill of Sisters Offering Support.[95] There were over twenty-five organizations in the Campaign, including service providers, foundations, faith-based groups, and international organizations. Members included CATW, Children of the Night, the Paul and Lisa Program, and HIPS. The Campaign worked closely with Ernie Allen of the National Center for Missing and Exploited Children, and maintained a website that served as an

---

[94] Barnitz, *Commercial Sexual Exploitation of Children*, v. The pamphlet was part of a series also covering child soldiers and child labor.

[95] Interview with Laura Barnitz, April 3, 2016, at 47:45 (on file with author); Interview with Vednita Carter, July 27, 2017.

information and resource clearinghouse for advocates and law enforcement working on commercial sexual exploitation of US youth.[96]

Campaign representatives lobbied Congress to pass the Trafficking Victims Protection Act by organizing meetings on Capitol Hill with lawmakers from both political parties and other governmental officials to raise awareness about the commercial sexual exploitation of youth in the United States. According to Barnitz, one of the most effective techniques for getting governmental officials to take this issue seriously was to bring youth survivors to speak with legislators about their experiences on the streets. Kelly Hill of SOS, Rachel Lloyd of GEMS, and Norma Hotaling of SAGE brought survivors from their organizations – mostly girls, although there was one boy – to Washington, DC, to tell their stories to legislators and law enforcement personnel. According to Barnitz, this personal testimony played an important role in convincing governmental officials to act on the issue. Advocacy groups in Washington and New York organized police ride-alongs for politicians to show them youth on the streets so that they could better understand what was going on. Advocates for sexually exploited youth in the US sometimes had difficulties convincing legislators that commercially sexually exploited youth in the United States were victims. According to Barnitz, people would often dismiss commercially sexually exploited youth as drug addicts, and she believed that race was at least part of the reason. Barnitz said that when attempting to convince conservative members of Congress of the importance of this issue, activists selected victims strategically to tell their stories of exploitation. When approaching conservative North Carolina Senator Jesse Helms, for example, she said that they knew they needed "to have a young white woman to speak about her experiences for him to get on board or it's not going to happen."[97] This strategy likely reinforced the racialized narrative that came to dominate discussions of minors involved in the sex trade.

The US Campaign members worked effectively together, but sometimes there were tensions among their members. Some did not like the Campaign's approach of separating out youth, but instead wanted to focus on sexually exploited adults as well. But, according to Barnitz, "we came to a conclusion as a group that we could make huge strides forward if we kept the focus on youth at this point and in time that would actually benefit everyone eventually. It was an incremental approach, but that is what we could move people on."[98] There was also a division between those organizations that had a law-and-order approach, calling for criminal prosecution of facilitators and buyers, and those that had more of a social service approach and supported harm reduction strategies. HIPS pushed for the Campaign to explicitly address the needs of LGBT youth, but the Campaign did not do this because of concerns that it would not have been politically viable.

According to Barnitz, advocates in the campaign were very aware of the systemic issues that needed to be addressed in order to deal with the commercial

---

[96] Interview with Laura Barnitz, April 3, 2016, at 47:45.     [97] Ibid. at 27:45.
[98] Ibid. at 16:01.

sexual exploitation of youth, like the inadequate child welfare systems and child poverty, but they knew that these issues were much harder to address. Because the issue of commercial sexual exploitation of American youth was not on anyone's radar screen at the time, they made a strategic decision to define the issue in a way that made the problem clear and the solution achievable in order to succeed in changing attitudes about the problem. According to Barnitz, "we knew the issue was much more complicated and there were huge systemic issues that we had to deal with, but if we were to take advantage of this sudden interest in trafficking, we had to be crystal clear about what we were asking people to do."[99] They defined the problem as the exploitation and abuse of young people who could not protect themselves, which then led to more problems in their lives. Barnitz acknowledged that this "completely oversimplified the picture" but contended that this was "necessary in order to get people behind it."[100] Their goal was to pass the bill and get more resources for youth. They understood the complexity of the problem, but believed that they first had to get people to see youth in the sex trade as victims rather than delinquents, so they simplified their message and rhetoric. Advocates for US youth lobbied side by side with organizations that focused on international trafficking, like CATW, Protection Project, and IJM.

Systemic change was particularly unlikely because President Bill Clinton had continued the expansion of neoliberal policies of the Reagan and Bush eras. While in office, President Clinton signed the 1994 Violent Crime Control and Law Enforcement Act, significantly expanding the criminal justice system and prison industrial complex; the 1996 Personal Responsibility Act – welfare reform – which eviscerated the social safety net for impoverished families in the United States; and the North America Free Trade Agreement, which dismantled barriers to capital flow across borders while maintaining barriers to the mobility of labor. The anti-trafficking law fit well within Clinton's agenda of expanding the criminal justice system, especially in light of the fact that it contained only modest spending for victim services.

The mainstream women's movement, which throughout the 1990s focused on violence against women, also supported the anti-trafficking law. Earlier in the decade, the movement had achieved a long-term goal with passage of the Violence Against Women Act (VAWA) of 1994. Several high-profile incidents propelled the 1994 law to passage, including Anita Hill's 1991 sexual harassment allegations against Supreme Court nominee Clarence Thomas; the 1992 Tailhook scandal where eighty-three women and seven men alleged that

---

[99] Ibid. at 1:19:10. See Davis S. Meyer and Suzanne Staggenborg, "Thinking About Strategy," in Gregory M. Maney (ed.), *Social Movements, Protest, and Contentions: Strategies for Social Change* (Minneapolis, MN: University of Minnesota Press, 2012), 3–22, for a discussion of how activists experience "constraints on strategic choices." In other words, activists are limited by what choices are actually possible in a particular political context and time.

[100] Interview with Laura Barnitz, April 3, 2016, at 1:19:44.

more than one hundred male US Navy and United States Marine Corps aviation officers sexually assaulted them at a naval aviators' convention in Las Vegas; and the 1994 trial of OJ Simpson for allegedly murdering his wife Nicole Brown Simpson and her friend Ron Goldman. VAWA created new federal crimes related to violence against women, authorized funding for police investigation and prosecution of crimes against women, funded victim services, and created a federal civil rights remedy for gender-based violence against women (later ruled unconstitutional by the Supreme Court). While some feminists, particularly women of color, critiqued the growing alliance between the women's movement and the criminal justice system because of the longstanding and deep racism of law enforcement and the devastating impact of the expanding prison industrial complex on communities of color, others welcomed the new source of funding for domestic violence services and for increased police training on violence against women. In 2000, when Congress was considering the anti-trafficking bill, anti-violence advocates were also seeking reauthorization of the Violence Against Women Act.

It was in this context that the anti-trafficking movement succeeded in convincing Congress to pass the Trafficking Victims Protection Act (TVPA) of 2000, which passed along with a reauthorization of the Violence Against Women Act in the same bill.[101] The TVPA, which created federal criminal penalties for sex and labor trafficking, defined sex trafficking to be "the recruitment, harboring, transportation, provision, or obtaining of a person for the purpose of a commercial sex act," although the operative provisions of the Act applied only to "severe forms of trafficking in persons," which is defined as inducing a person to engage in a commercial sex act by "force, fraud or coercion" or if they are under the age of eighteen. The Act did not require the transportation across international borders, or even state borders. Therefore, the Act defined inducing a minor into the sex trade as a severe form of human trafficking. This was a major victory for advocates of US youth involved in prostitution, but one that would not manifest in any concrete change for many years.[102]

Despite this broad definition, Congress directed the remedies under the act exclusively to international victims of trafficking. The Act provided visas and

---

[101] Trafficking Victims Protection Act of 2000, Pub. L. No. 106–386, § 101, 22 U.S.C. § 7102 et seq. For an analysis of the diverse coalitions involved in the passage of the TVPA, see, Bromfield, *The Hijacking of Human Trafficking Legislation During Its Creation*, 109–116.

[102] During the same year that the TVPA was passed, the United Nations adopted the Protocol to Prevent, Suppress and Punish Trafficking in Persons, especially Women and Children, otherwise known as the "Palermo Protocol." Protocol to Prevent, Suppress and Punish Trafficking in Persons, Especially Women and Children, Supplementing the United Nations Convention Against Transnational Organized Crime, Nov. 15, 2000, 2237 U.N.T.S. 343. As a result of the TVPA and the Palermo Protocol, countries around the world began to pass anti-trafficking laws. In 2000, the UN also passed an Optional Protocol to the Convention on the Rights of the Child on the sale of children, child prostitution and child pornography, which the US signed in 2000 and ratified in 2002.

access to services for international human trafficking survivors, as well as grant money for NGOs working abroad, but provided nothing for US citizen survivors in the United States or organizations working with them. Advocates had failed to convince members of Congress that the issue of US youth in the sex trade was a significant problem or that there was a need for resources to address this issue. The TVPA focused on international human trafficking, framing the problem as a crime control issue that demanded criminal justice solutions. The Act pressured nations to prohibit and prosecute trafficking offenses by requiring the Secretary of State to issue an annual Trafficking in Persons Report ("TIP Report"), which rated any country deemed to be a country of origin, destination, or transit of victims of severe forms of trafficking on whether that country was making appropriate efforts to combat the trafficking and imposing sanctions if they failed to do so. Beginning in 2001, the Secretary of State issued a TIP report every year, evaluating countries across the globe but, interestingly, not evaluating efforts to combat trafficking within the United States itself. Only in the 2010 TIP report, after pressure from several NGOs and under the leadership of Secretary of State Hillary Rodham Clinton, did the State Department assess United States' efforts to comply with the Act.

This focus on international victims of sex trafficking meant that advocates for US youth initially received no concrete benefits from the Act, despite their hard work to get it passed. Funds went to groups working internationally, like Shared Hope International, founded in 1998 by Representative Linda Smith (R-WA), to provide shelter and services to victims of sex trafficking in India. According to Barnitz, members of the US Campaign Against the Commercial Sexual Exploitation of Children resented the fact that groups working with US youth did not receive funds. She said legislators believed that the social safety net available to US youth adequately met their needs – a claim she contested. Nevertheless, Barnitz worked through the Campaign's organizational affiliates to inform state and local law enforcement about the new trafficking bill, how it would affect them, and what resources or organizations could help youth found in the sex trade. YAPI also continued to serve as a clearinghouse for information on the new trafficking law. The goals of the Campaign included raising public awareness about the commercial sexual exploitation of children; developing educational programs for youth as well as law enforcement, social workers, and other professionals; expanding services for survivors; and finding ways to prevent men from buying sex from youth. The Campaign members also continued to meet with legislators. For example, Barnitz and Laura Lederer of the Protection Project met with Senator Sam Brownback in 2001 to encourage him to push for funding for US youth involved in the sex trade.[103] In 2001, Laura Lederer became Deputy Senior Advisor to the

---

[103] Greene, "Charity Run by Former Prostitutes Steers Girls Away from the Streets"; Interview with Laura Barnitz, April 3, 2016.

Secretary of State and helped set up the Office to Monitor and Combat Trafficking in Persons at the US Department of State. Then from 2002 to 2007, she served as Senior Advisor on Trafficking in Persons to Under Secretary of State for Democracy and Global Affairs, which provided a beneficial political opportunity to anti-trafficking advocates in the 2000s. And in fact, some of the money Congress allocated under the TVPA did end up funding research into domestic sex trafficking, including the sexual exploitation of youth, which helped build the movement against the US youth sex trade.[104]

## FEDERAL AND STATE ACTION ON JUVENILE PROSTITUTION IN THE 1990S

Despite the failure of the TVPA to provide funding to help American youth in the sex trade, there were several federal initiatives in the 1990s that addressed the issue. The Violence Against Women Act of 1994 established the Education and Prevention Services to Reduce Sexual Abuse of Runaway, Homeless, and Street Youth Program, a program that created a funding stream for the prevention of sexual abuse of runaway and homeless youth, including a Street Outreach Program. While not specifically mentioning abuse in prostitution, this provision benefitted US youth involved in the sex trade. The Act also required that people convicted of soliciting minors to enter prostitution must register as sex offenders.[105] In September of 1995, the United States Department of Labor sponsored a symposium on child prostitution in Washington, DC. The symposium focused on child prostitution globally, but gave some attention to child prostitution in the United States.[106] Robert Flores of US Department of Justice's Child Exploitation and Obscenity Section gave a presentation on how the United States had "a huge problem on both coasts with thousands of runaway children and throwaway children engaging in prostitution." He challenged the stereotype of child prostitution as involving a young child violently kidnapped and forced to work the streets, arguing that in reality it involved older teens, "who do not have families to go home to, have long arrest records, have a history of drug abuse of one form or another, and have very few social skills that would allow them to function in the world of most Americans."[107] Flores argued against incarceration of these teens, instead advocating for "multidisciplinary teams made up of professionals who are experts in the areas of social work, medicine, psychiatric health, and law

---

[104] See, e.g., Janice G. Raymond and Donna M. Hughes, *Sex Trafficking of Women in the United States: International and Domestic Trends* (New York, NY: Coalition Against Trafficking in Women, 2001).

[105] *Violent Crime Control and Law Enforcement Act of 1994*, Public Law 103–322, September 13, 1994, 42 U.S. 5712d, sec. 6702 and 42 U.S. 14071, sec. 170101.

[106] US Department of Labor, *Forced Labor: The Prostitution of Children* (Washington, DC: US Department of Labor, 1996).

[107] Ibid. 41.

enforcement,"[108] and he supported increased prosecution of facilitators. Flores' view of youth involvement in the sex trade was more consistent with the research available at the time than the sensationalized media portrayals of white middle-class suburban girls lured from malls.[109]

The federal government also put in place several initiatives against child pornography. Congress attempted to limit minors' access to pornography through the Communications Decency Act of 1996 and the Child Online Protection Act of 1998, both of which were struck down by courts for violating the First Amendment free speech guarantee.[110] In the meantime, the Office of Juvenile Justice and Delinquency Prevention funded forty regional task forces to combat child pornography and, in 1998, sponsored a CyberTipline, run by the National Center for Missing and Exploited Children (NCMEC), to whom internet service providers were required to report child pornography on their systems. The FBI's Innocent Images National Initiative targeted crimes conducted via the internet and a US Postal Service program focused on child obscenity sent through the mail.[111]

At the state level, Minnesota again distinguished itself by proactively addressing the issue as it had in the 1970s. In 1998, the Minnesota legislature directed the Attorney General's Office to investigate juvenile prostitution.[112] The Alliance for Speaking Truths on Prostitution (A-STOP) of the Minnesota Attorney General's Office formed a committee chaired by Former Minneapolis Mayor Albert Hofstede with members from PRIDE, Breaking Free (including Vednita Carter), Catholic Charities, and Project Offstreets to investigate juvenile prostitution in Minnesota and make recommendations for how the government should address the issue. The Hofstede Committee Report, published in November of 1999, described the existing research on the nature and extent of commercial sexual exploitation of youth and recommended more severe penalties against facilitators and people who purchased sex from youth, increased prosecutorial authority and resources for police investigation, increased civil enforcement of nuisance laws to shut down businesses facilitating juvenile prostitution, and increased emergency and transitional housing and services for homeless youth at risk of experiencing prostitution.[113] The Report explained that efforts to address juvenile

[108] Ibid. 44.
[109] See studies cited in chapter 2 and Enablers, *Juvenile Prostitution in Minneapolis: The Report of a Research Project* (St. Paul, MN: The Enablers, 1978), and D. Kelly Weisberg, *Children of the Night: A Study of Adolescent Prostitution* (Lexington, MA: Lexington Books, 1985).
[110] *Reno v. ACLU*, 521 U.S. 844 (1997); *ACLU v. Makasey*, 534 F.3d 181 (3d Cir. 2008), *cert. denied*, 555 U.S. 1137 (2009).
[111] Michael B. Mukasey, Cybele K. Daley, and David G. Hagy, *Commercial Sexual Exploitation of Children: What Do We Know and What Do We Do about It?* (Washington, DC: US Department of Justice, Office of Justice Programs, 2007), ii.
[112] S.F. 3345, 80th Leg. Sess., Reg. Sess. (Minn. 1998).
[113] *Hofstede Committee Report, Juvenile Prostitution in Minnesota*, 17–19.

prostitution in the 1970s and 1980s had been successful, but that in the 1990s police efforts were diverted away from juvenile prostitution to other crimes, like drugs, and that as a result juvenile prostitution had increased again. The Report characterized juvenile prostitution as "an underground, highly mobile, and complex network of organized crime," facilitated by the internet and targeting "virtually anyone's child."[114] The Report warned about a "growing number of suburban teen-aged girls involved in prostitution," recruited from places like the Mall of America and the Minneapolis City Center. The report also addressed the prevalence of GLBT youth in prostitution, citing a 1999 study by the Partnership for GLBT Youth. In the late 1990s, Minnesota formed a statewide Pimp/Juvenile Prostitution Task Force to develop collaboration and communication among police, state and federal prosecutors, and community organizations. In the summer of 1999, the FBI and Minneapolis police arrested fifteen members of the Evans family for running a multi-million-dollar juvenile prostitution ring in Minneapolis, recruiting girls as young as fourteen and forcing them into prostitution.

Two Minnesota organizations that advocated for survivors of prostitution – PRIDE and WHISPER – worked to raise awareness about juvenile prostitution. They were quoted repeatedly in the series of articles in the *Christian Science Monitor* in the fall of 1996. WHISPER produced a video in 1995 called "Where the Lies Take You," containing the stories of youth with experience in the sex trade, and narrated by actresses. The video was targeted at youth with the goal of shocking them and scaring them away from the sex trade. One of WHISPER's best-known campaigns was a sarcastic help-wanted ad for prostitution, highlighting how poor women, single mothers, and women of color were targeted, and the severe dangers of the job.[115]

In other states, police departments set up special units to address child prostitution, including in Las Vegas, Dallas, and Lexington, Kentucky. In 1994, Las Vegas Metropolitan Police Department set up Operation STOP – Stop Turning Out Child Prostitutes – to address the increasing prevalence of minors in prostitution in Las Vegas. It started with four officers, expanded to eight by 2003, and later had the largest city police team in the country devoted exclusively to prostituted youth. Sergeant Bryon Fassett, head of the Child Exploitation Unit in Dallas, Texas, noticed in the mid-1990s that the number of prostituted children in the Dallas area was growing. He approached a prosecutor in the district attorney's office, Tim Gallagher, and they worked together to prosecute adults who facilitated youth involvement in the youth sex trade by devoting police department and prosecutor office resources to the issue.[116] But the

---

[114] Ibid. 2.
[115] Sher, *Somebody's Daughter*; Melissa Farley, "Prostitution, Trafficking, and Cultural Amnesia: What We Must Not Know in Order to Keep the Business of Sexual Exploitation Running Smoothly," *Yale Journal of Law and Feminism* 18.1 (2006), 111 n. 11.
[116] Sher, *Somebody's Daughter*, 43–47.

majority of states continued to address the issue as they always had – by ignoring it or by arresting and prosecuting youth for the crime of prostitution.

CONCLUSION

In the 1970s, most of the prominent activists working against commercial sexual exploitation of youth were motivated by having known someone who was exploited. By contrast, many of the leading advocates in the 1990s, like Norma Hotaling whose story began this chapter, were themselves survivors of commercial sexual exploitation and they articulated their belief in the important role to be played by survivors both in providing services to commercially sexually exploited youth, but also in developing public policies on the issue. Activists constructed individual and collective identities as survivors to generate support and mobilize people to their cause. Survivor-activists formed organizations that provided outreach and shelter to youth involved in prostitution and staffed these organizations with survivors themselves. In lobbying for a federal anti-trafficking law, they brought youth survivors to Washington, DC, to testify about their experiences. The central role of survivors in the 1990s movement began a trend that developed significantly in the years that followed and became a defining characteristic of the movement in the 2000s.

Survivor activists took advantage of political opportunities that were available in the 1990s with the expanding international women's movement, the emergence of a global movement against the commercial sexual exploitation of children, and a US-based movement against international sex trafficking. US activists participated in the First World Congress and the first International Summit for Sexually Exploited Youth. These and other international meetings, 'as well as the formation of a US branch of the international organization ECPAT, enabled US activists to find allies across the world and to develop support networks to address the commercial sexual exploitation of youth in the United States. Inspired by the 1996 Congress, activists formed the US Campaign Against the Commercial Sexual Exploitation of Children as a national clearinghouse for information on the issue and to lobby for the TVPA, which they hoped would benefit youth in the United States. Their central message was that youth involved in prostitution were victims, not delinquents, and that society had a responsibility to provide youth with support and services, rather than blaming and incarcerating them. Activists further argued that the adults involved in the exploitation of youth – both buyers and facilitators – should be held responsible for sexual abuse of minors.

Despite the efforts of advocates for US youth involved in prostitution, the media and policymakers in the 1990s focused mostly on international sex trafficking, especially in Southeast Asia and Eastern Europe. The exception was the *Christian Science Monitor* series on child prostitution, which covered the issue in the United States as well abroad, interviewing US activists and providing them a forum to share their analysis of the issue. The series challenged the idea that commercial sexual exploitation of children was only a problem in other countries, and described it as a widespread growing problem in the United States that involved younger and younger children. Similar to the 1970s, this series emphasized that the issue impacted white, middle-class girls from the suburbs. Activists, police, policymakers, and journalists decried a "new trend" – "the movement of organized prostitution into smaller cities and suburbs" and into "America's heartland" – in ways very similar to how the issue was portrayed in the 1970s. Concern about the "*Lolita* syndrome" of the 1970s evolved into the 1990s concern about the "*Pretty Woman* syndrome" – young girls lured by glamorized images of prostitution in the media.[117] Similar to the 1970s concern about girls being trafficked along the "Minnesota pipeline" from Minneapolis to New York City, concern in the 1990s centered on girls being trafficked along the "Pacific circuit" from Vancouver to Los Angeles. Some activists and media echoed the racialized and gendered narratives of sexual danger from earlier periods of activism against the US youth sex trade, but others made new arguments. Some critiqued prostitution as a racialized system of exploitation rooted in slavery and the history of race discrimination in the United States. Others analyzed prostitution as a system of male domination. These critiques were significantly expanded upon as the movement matured in the 2000s.

The Trafficking Victims Protection Act passed in 2000 but despite their best efforts activists working with US youth involved in prostitution did not immediately benefit from the Act. Reflecting the Congressional focus on international victims, the funds allocated by the Act went to organizations working on international sex trafficking. Policymakers were not concerned about the US youth sex trade, believing that this phenomenon was not common or that young Americans already had access to the resources they needed. Nevertheless, the Act defined sex trafficking broadly to include US youth involved in the sex trade, setting the stage for activists' reframing of this phenomena as "domestic minor sex trafficking" in a campaign to win resources and policy changes for these youth in the 2000s.

---

[117] Members of the feminist group Women Against Pornograhy (WAP) dubbed the "eroti-cized images of little girls which now flourish in every form of the media" as the "*Lolita* syndrome." Women Against Pornography Records, 1979–1989; Press Release, "The *Lolita* Syndrome," n.d., 90-M153-2003-M133, folder 114, box 8. Schlesinger Library, Radcliffe Institute, Harvard University, Cambridge, Mass.

# 4

## "Our Daughters" in Danger: Leveraging the Anti-Trafficking Framework in the early 2000s

In the afternoon of June 7, 2005, in Washington, DC, a young white woman, Leisa B., appeared before the US Commission on Cooperation and Security in Europe at the invitation of Co-Chair Representative Chris Smith (R-NJ).[1] Leisa, described by Smith as a "survivor of domestic trafficking for sexual exploitation," told how at the age of 17, while she was living with her parents in a "well-off, upper middle-class neighborhood" in Atlanta, she met a man on a local phone chat line who, as she testified, "sold me dreams of fancy cars, expensive clothes, lavish homes, and the freedom of running around in an adult's world."[2] She ran away to Washington, DC, with the man, who became her "pimp," as she described him. A month later, she was arrested for prostitution and placed in a juvenile detention center for a month, but returned to the streets when she was released, where she met another pimp who took her to Florida to work. She was arrested once again, this time spending a week in jail. Sick of "rapes and beatings," she returned to Washington, DC, where she met a third pimp. He was, she testified, "worse than the others," so she contacted her first pimp, who by that time was living in Brooklyn with four girls, and he came down to DC to get her. She described how he would "hire drug dealers to drive four of us in a van, while he followed behind with another girl in a van. He used to say it would look hot if there was [sic] five white girls and a black man driving a truck."[3] For another month she worked in New York, taking trips to Atlantic City to work "during the big fighting

---

[1] The Commission on Cooperation and Security in Europe is a US government agency consisting of representatives from the executive and legislative branches of government with the mission of promoting "human rights, military security, and economic cooperation in 57 countries in Europe, Eurasia, and North America." Commission on Cooperation and Security in Europe, Mission, at www.csce.gov/.

[2] *Exploiting Americans on American Soil: Domestic Trafficking Exposed, Hearing on H.R. 972 before the Commission on Security & Cooperation in Europe*, 109th Cong., 1st Sess. (June 7, 2005) [hereinafter *Exploiting Americans on American Soil Hearing, 2005*], 21–22.

[3] Ibid. 23.

events." Eventually, she called her parents, who arranged for a bus ticket for her return to Atlanta. The Paul and Lisa Program helped Leisa leave "the life."

Leisa's testimony before the Commission illustrates a shift that occurred in public discourses about sex trafficking by the mid-2000s. Whereas the focus in the 1990s had been almost exclusively on international sex trafficking, the 2000s saw the advent of increased concern about "domestic trafficking" of American girls. After the disappointment of being excluded from receiving support under the TVPA, activists fighting the US youth sex trade continued to push for recognition of the problem within the United States, gaining momentum over the decade. Existing organizations thrived and continued to connect globally, but new ones formed and US youth survivors emerged as important participants in the movement. These organizations formed in response to the continued vulnerability of youth to involvement in the sex trade and to law enforcement's harsh treatment of these youth, embedded within the continuing expansion of the prison industrial complex under the presidency of George W. Bush. By 2005, there were over 2.2 million people incarcerated in the United States, with over seven million people under state and federal supervision.[4] A recession in the early 2000s and welfare reform's evisceration of the social safety net left many young people more vulnerable than ever.

The political context both exacerbated the problem of youth involved in the sex trade but also highlighted the hypocrisy of the increasingly strident US global campaign against human trafficking, including child sex trafficking. With the tools created by the TVPA and with the support of George W. Bush, the United States Secretary of State began issuing an annual Trafficking in Persons Report, which evaluated countries around the world on whether they were adequately addressing human trafficking within their borders. After September 11, 2001, the "war on terror" and the US invasion of Afghanistan and later Iraq politicized the issue of human trafficking, which Bush embraced as a way to promote the United States as a human rights leader despite the fact that the US military was torturing suspected terrorists in violation of the Geneva convention. Bush also embraced the issue of human trafficking because it was important to his evangelical Christian base and he used it to funnel money to evangelical organizations.[5] Activists against the US youth sex trade, however, used this heightened awareness about international human trafficking to draw attention to "domestic trafficking" of American youth. The movement also built upon increasing awareness of child sex abuse in American society

---

[4] Danielle Kaeble, Lauren Glaze, Anastasios Tsoutis, and Todd Minton, *Correctional Populations in the United States, 2014* (Washington, DC: US Department of Justice, revised January 21, 2016).

[5] Nicole Footen Bromfield, *The Hijacking of Human Trafficking Legislation During Its Creation: A U.S. Public Policy Study* (Saarbrücken, Germany: VDM Verlag Dr. Müller, 2010), 175–177.

triggered by a 2002 Pulitzer Prize-winning *Boston Globe* series on the Catholic Church coverup of extensive priest abuse of children over decades.[6]

As in previous decades, many activists mobilized concern by focusing on narratives of innocent and naïve white, middle-class girls tricked and violently abused by African American men. Challenging the dominant belief that child sex trafficking happened primarily abroad or to non-US citizens, activists raised the alarm about "our daughters" and "our girls." This framing functioned to obscure the involvement of boys, girls from low-income families, and girls of color in the sex trade. It also inspired calls for criminal justice responses to child sex trafficking rather than solutions that addressed structural inequalities that made many young people vulnerable to involvement in the sex trade.

However, while much of the national-level attention to the issue focused on middle-class white girls, some local activists worked to help the girls more often involved in the sex trade – poor girls and girls of color. A groundbreaking campaign in Atlanta, Georgia, for example, brought widespread attention to youth involvement in the sex trade, with a particular focus on African American girls. This grassroots campaign led to legislative reform as well as increased public awareness and services for youth. In Chicago, youth in the sex trade organized Young Women's Empowerment Project (YWEP) to support each other and organize against discrimination and abuse by police and social service providers. In contrast to dominant discourses, YWEP focused on youth of color and empowerment rather than victimization and rescue. At the local and national levels, activism led to increased attention to and resources for youth involved in the sex trade in the early 2000s.

## GROWING AND CONNECTING, NATIONALLY AND GLOBALLY

Youth service organizations that formed in the 1990s thrived in the 2000s, as they amplified their message and attracted increasing resources. By 2001, SAGE had an annual operating budget of over $1 million and served over 300 women and girls a week.[7] In April of the same year, Oprah Winfrey honored Norma Hotaling with the "Use Your Life Award," which came with $100,000 in prize money. In 2004, Hotaling successfully lobbied the California legislature to pass a law that allowed prosecutors to charge facilitators and johns with child abuse if they prostituted a minor.[8] Sisters Offering Support in Honolulu also continued to grow. Founder and director Kelly Hill won an award – "America's Best Young Community Leader" – that came with $100,000 for

[6] Michael DiAntonio, *Mortal Sins: Sex, Crime, and the Era of Catholic Scandal* (New York, NY: Thomas Dunne Books, 2013).

[7] Elizabeth Greene, "Charity Run by Former Prostitutes Steer Girls Away from Streets," *Chronicle of Philanthropy* 14: 2 (November 1, 2001), 10.

[8] Norma Hotaling, "Sex for Sale: The Commercial Sexual Exploitation of Women and Girls: A Service Provider's Perspective," *Yale Journal of Law and Feminism* 18 (2006), 187; Meredith May, "Norma Hotaling Dies – Fought Prostitution," *San Francisco Gate* (December 20, 2008).

SOS.[9] In addition to helping four to five hundred individual clients a year, SOS conducted educational programs in Hawaii public schools and engaged in public policy reform.[10] In 2002, nineteen community organizations in Hawaii formed a coalition called Protect Our Children from Sexual Exploitation, which worked on educating the community about the sexual exploitation of children. In 2002, Hill spoke at a three-day conference on human trafficking, out of which emerged the Hawaii Task Force Against Human Trafficking.[11]

ECPAT-USA turned more attention to commercial sexual exploitation of youth in the United States in the early 2000s. In 2001, they produced a study on "prostituted youth" in New York City based on interviews with service providers and police. At the time, ECPAT was not yet referring to US youth in the sex trade as trafficked: the report used the term "trafficked" to refer to non-US citizen victims only, a usage that would soon broaden to include US victims. The report claimed an extraordinary number of victims, quoting the director of the Paul and Lisa Program estimating that up to 5,000 youth were involved in prostitution in New York City alone. The report speculated that there were as many as 400,000 prostituted children in the US.[12] Challenging the prevailing belief that youth involved in prostitution were "bad kids," that they "ask for it," or that "they like sex," the report noted that most had been sexually abused as children and argued that youth were forced or had few alternatives. ECPAT-USA's Executive Director Carol Smolenski spoke to many community groups in the early 2000s in order to raise awareness about the issue.[13]

In addition to this study, ECPAT partnered with the International Organization for Adolescents and GEMS to found the New York City Task Force on the Sexual Exploitation of Young People. The Task Force, which included service providers, elected officials, counselors, researchers, and others, sought to "raise the political profile of the problem of prostituted young people in New York City" through research, education, and public policy reform.[14] The Task Force explicitly sought to increase youth participation in policy and program development. In December of 2002, the New York City Council Women's Issues and Public Safety Committees held a hearing on teenage prostitution, where over a dozen witnesses appeared,

---

[9] Christine Donnelly, "Support Agency's Leader Wins $100,000," *Honolulu Star-Bulletin* (November 22, 2000).

[10] Mary Vorsino, "Sisters Offering Support Closing," *Honolulu Advertiser* (September 23, 2006).

[11] Diana Leone, "The Task Force to Fight Human Trafficking," *Honolulu Star-Bulletin* (November 15, 2002).

[12] Mia Spangenberg, *Prostituted Youth in New York City: An Overview* (ECPAT-USA, 2001), 1. ECPAT acknowledged in a 2005 report that they lacked "formal data" to support this claim. Sara Ann Friedman, *Who Is There to Help Us? How the System Fails Sexually Exploited Girls in the United States: Examples from Four American Cities* (New York, NY: ECPAT-USA, Inc., 2005), 2–3.

[13] Interview with Carol Smolenski, July 21, 2017 (on file with author).

[14] Spangenberg, *Prostituted Youth in New York City*, 2.

including the chief of the sex crimes bureau at the Brooklyn District Attorney's Office and a survivor escorted by Rachel Lloyd of GEMS.[15]

A few years later, ECPAT published another report, this time on the disparity of services available to foreign and US victims of trafficking and commercial sexual exploitation based on qualitative research in New York City, Atlanta, Minneapolis and San Francisco.[16] The report argued that the TVPA defined trafficking to include inducing a person under the age of eighteen to engage in commercial sex, without regard to consent, yet the Act's implementation in terms of prosecution and services had focused on foreign victims and ignored trafficked American girls. The original version of the report had a cartoon of several girls entering a door marked "foreign girls" next to a Caucasian girl walking away from a door marked "American girls" with a "closed" sign on it. After criticism that the cartoon was anti-immigrant and racist, a revised version of the report deleted the depiction of foreign girls, and just showed the American girls being turned away.[17] The report called for an "amber alert for 'our girls,'" explaining that the majority of prostituted girls do not see themselves as victims, but that they end up in prostitution out of "desperation or manipulation by adults." Referring to factors like childhood sexual abuse and abandonment, the report described the girls as "easy prey" and "unaware of the danger they face." The girls, according to the report, "often cling to the false belief that they are doing what they want." The report described "pimps," on the other hand, as "a kind of emotional executioner." In this report, ECPAT set up a dichotomy between "choice or coercion" and "victim or willing participant," coming down firmly on the side of youth as coerced victims. Explicitly disregarding the perspectives of youth themselves, and rejecting the possibility that youth might be both victims *and* willing participants, or something in between, ECPAT argued vigorously that the criminal justice system must treat prostituted girls as victims, not offenders.[18]

The US Campaign Against the Commercial Sexual Exploitation of Children, including Hotaling, Hill, Lloyd, and Smolenski, continued to connect activists working against the youth sex trade in the United States in the early 2000s. In preparation for the Second World Congress Against the Commercial Sexual Exploitation of Children in Yokohama, Japan, planned for December of 2001, the Campaign organized a meeting of the nongovernmental organization delegation in San Francisco in March of 2001. The meeting was cosponsored by YAPI; Sisters Offering Support; and the Fund for Nonviolence, a Santa Cruz, California, grant maker.[19] In early December, the United States, Canada, and

---

[15] Diane Cardwell, "Officials Say Sex Trade Lures Younger Girls," *New York Times* (December 7, 2002), B1.

[16] Friedman, *Who Is There to Help Us?*

[17] Alicia Peters, *Responding to Human Trafficking: Sex, Gender, and Culture in the Law* (Philadelphia, PA: University of Pennsylvania Press, 2015), 196.

[18] Friedman, *Who Is There to Help Us?* 1, 4–5, 7.

[19] Greene, "Charity Run by Former Prostitutes Steers Girls Away from the Streets"; interview with Laura Barnitz, April 3, 2016 (on file with author).

Mexico held a regional consultation on commercial sexual exploitation of children at the University of Pennsylvania School of Social Work.[20] Norma Hotaling was the convener for the US national delegation. Laura Barnitz of YAPI represented the US Campaign Against the Commercial Sexual Exploitation of Children. Attendees included Rachel Lloyd of GEMS, Cherry Kingsley of Save the Children Canada, and Susan Breault of the Paul and Lisa Program, as well as representatives from Equality Now and Safe Horizon. Research presented at this event included a study by Richard Estes and Neil Alan Weiner of University of Pennsylvania on the commercial sexual exploitation of children in the United States, Mexico, and Canada. The study was funded by the Department of Justice, as well as by the Fund for Nonviolence, the William T. Grant Foundation, and the University of Pennsylvania. Based on studies of data from the 1990s, Estes and Weiner estimated that between 244,000 and 325,000 youth were at risk of entering the commercial sex trade in the United States.[21] This study was cited widely in the press and in legislative hearings, and was extremely influential in generating concern about the commercial sexual exploitation of youth in the United States. However, the study was criticized for being mostly "educated guesses or extrapolations based on questionable assumptions."[22] Furthermore, the Estes and Weiner estimate was regularly miscited as an estimate of the number of juveniles involved in prostitution when in fact it was an estimate of the number of youth *at risk* of becoming involved in prostitution. Like in the 1970s, activists and the media repeated speculative numbers with little factual basis to generate public concern about youth involvement in the sex trade. Another important federally funded study, written by Janice Raymond and Donna Hughes of the Coalition Against Trafficking in Women, gave significant attention to sex trafficking of teenage girls in the United States.[23]

The 2001 Second World Congress in Japan was attended by 3,050 participants, with official delegations from 136 governments and representatives from 283 NGOs. At the time, over one hundred countries had developed national plans of action, which were presented at the Second World Congress, but the United States had not yet developed a plan. US NGO participants at the Congress included Laura Barnitz, Norma Hotaling, Rachel

---

[20] Nicole Ives, *Background Paper for the North American Regional Consultation on the Commercial Sexual Exploitation of Children* (Philadelphia, PA: University of Pennsylvania School of Social Work, December 2–3, 2001).

[21] Richard J. Estes and Neil Alan Weiner, *Commercial Sexual Exploitation of Children in the United States, Canada and Mexico, Full Report* (Philadelphia, PA: University of Pennsylvania, 2002), 144.

[22] Michelle Stransky and David Finkelhor, *How Many Juveniles Are Involved in Prostitution in the U.S.?* (Durham, NH: Crimes Against Children Research Center, 2008), 2.

[23] Janice G. Raymond and Donna M. Hughes, *Sex Trafficking of Women in the United States: International and Domestic Trends* (New York, NY: Coalition Against Trafficking in Women, 2001).

Lloyd, and Clare Nolan of CATW.[24] Youth participation expanded significantly over the First World Congress, with ninety-five children representing thirty-five countries attending the Second World Congress. Regions also made efforts to increase youth participation, by including holding pre-Congress regional forums for youth. On site right before the Congress started, youth attended a three-day preparation program. At the Congress, youth fully participated, offering a keynote, presenting a panel on "The Children and Young People's Voice on Moving Forward," managing several roundtable discussions and serving as workshop presenters and facilitators. The Congress had over 107 workshops covering a wide range of topics, including the role of the internet in facilitating commercial sexual exploitation of youth and the impact of AIDS on youth involved in prostitution.[25] The Congress worked on inter-governmental cooperation, but was not able to put in place mechanisms for monitoring progress on these issues or to provide resources to realize their proposals.[26] Participating nations adopted the *Yokohama Global Commitment 2001*, which was largely a restatement of the 1996 Stockholm goals.[27]

Within the United States, the most important new development was the increasing participation of youth in campaigns against the US youth trade, including in policy debates, as spokespersons in the movement, and as service providers. In 2003, GEMS and the US Campaign Against the Commercial Exploitation of Children organized the first national youth summit on the commercial sexual exploitation of children, Breaking the Silence, in Washington, DC, which was funded by the US Department of Justice Office of Juvenile Justice and Delinquency Prevention. About thirty youth survivors from around the country attended the summit along with twelve representatives from their sponsoring organizations, like Breaking Free, SAGE, the Paul and Lisa Program, and several others.[28] The youth participated in workshops, including a documentary film-making workshop, a creative-writing workshop with survivor David Henry Sterry, a visual art class with survivor Christine Stark, an advocacy class with Laura Barnitz, and a media workshop run by the anti-trafficking organization Polaris Project. The youth presented their creative projects to the entire group at the end of the summit. The youth also produced

---

[24] Coalition Against Trafficking in Women, *Coalition Report* (New York, NY: Coalition Against Trafficking in Women, 2001).

[25] Vitit Muntarbhorn, *Report of the Second World Congress Against Commercial Sexual Exploitation of Children* (Yokohama, Japan, December 2001), 4; see also, James Brooke, "Sex Web Spun Worldwide Traps Children," *New York Times*, (December 23, 2001), A12.

[26] Ron O'Grady, *The Road to Rio* (Bangkok, Thailand: ECPAT International, 2008).

[27] *Yokohama Global Commitment 2001*, Second World Congress Against the Commercial Sexual Exploitation of Children, Yokohama, Japan, December 17–20, 2001; ECPAT International, *ECPAT 25 Years: Rallying the World to End Child Sexual Exploitation* (Bangkok, Thailand: ECPAT International, May 2015), 78.

[28] Interview with Sandy Skelaney, May 27, 2016, at 7:00 (on file with author).

an agenda for action, which they presented to the Congressional Caucus on Missing and Exploited Children. They toured Capitol Hill, meeting with their Congressional representatives to educate them about CSEC and discuss solutions, and they held a huge press conference and a candlelight vigil at Dupont Circle.[29] In early 2004, five of the youth returned to Washington DC, for a Congressional briefing where they testified about their experiences of commercial sexual exploitation. According to organizer Sandy Skelaney, the summit played an important role in getting the issue of commercial sexual exploitation on the public agenda.[30]

In addition to meeting with lawmakers, survivors shared their voices in other contexts as well. Deborah Lake Fortson produced a documentary play, *Body and Sold*, based on interviews with youth survivors in Boston, Hartford, and Minneapolis. The play opened in Boston in 2005 and then was produced around the country as part of a national campaign to raise awareness about sex trafficking of American children and teens.[31] Forton originally wrote a play about child trafficking in India, but then learned that it happened to youth in the United States so instead focused on US youth. The play narrated the stories of six girls and two boys who "left home and were seduced, lured, kidnapped into a life of prostitution, "telling". About the trouble in their families which forced them from home, how they became prostituted, the daily violence in 'the life,' how they escaped, their struggle to survive."[32] The play was supported by Boston Women's Fund, The Department of Social Services in Boston, and the Haymarket Peoples' Fund. Survivor stories were a powerful tool to generate concern and sympathy for youth involved in the sex trade.

## NEW AND DIVERSIFIED SERVICE PROVIDERS

New service providers with new approaches to the issue entered the scene in the early 2000s, like Young Women's Empowerment Project (YWEP) in Chicago, My Life My Choice in Boston, and Sex Workers Project in New York City. Formed in 2001, YWEP was a survivor-led, youth-led membership organization of girls, including trans girls, aged twelve to twenty-three who had direct experience in the sex trade or street economy (including work, whether legal or illegal, where youth do not have to show identification and do not pay taxes).[33] They had "adult allies," but youth staffed the organization.

---

[29] Ibid. at 12:20; Shared Hope International, EPCAT-USA, & The Protection Project of John Hopkins University School of Advanced International Studies, *Report from the U.S. Mid-Term Review on the Commercial Sexual Exploitation of Children in America* (May 2006), 2–3.

[30] Interview with Sandy Skelaney, May 27, 2016, at 15:10.

[31] Deborah Lake Fortson, *Body and Sold* (Boston, MA: Tempest Productions, 2005).

[32] Bodyandsold.org, Motivation, at www.bodyandsold.org/motivation.htm.

[33] YWEP, *Girls Do What They Have to Do to Survive: Illuminating Methods Used by Girls in the Sex Trade and Street Economy to Fight Back and Heal* (Chicago, IL: Young Women's Empowerment Project, 2009), 7–8.

The first director was Claudine O'Leary. Their mission was to offer "respectful, free-of-judgment spaces for girls impacted by the sex trade and street economy to recognize their hopes, dreams, and desires."[34] Unlike most organizations working with youth in the sex trade, YWEP did not pressure youth to leave the sex trade, but sought to help them to stay safe no matter what they did to survive.[35] The Project provided peer-based services, including weekly meetings for youth in the sex trade, a clothing exchange, free condoms and safe sex supplies, and a youth-run syringe program. Their core values and strategies included empowerment, harm reduction, self-care, social justice, and popular education.

YWEP's "empowerment model" focused on youth leadership based on the idea that "girls are the experts in their own lives," not doctors, social workers, or judges. They believed that "young people in the sex trade deserve a spot at the table where decisions are made about our lives."[36] To teach empowerment, YWEP made decisions through a weekly group called Girls in Charge; members wrote zines and position papers about drugs, the sex trade, violence against girls, and social justice for distribution to the general public; they led workshops and presentations for other girls and service providers; and they hired girls as staff members. The Project provided a fifty-six-hour training course to build girls' knowledge on issues like sexual and reproductive health, street law, and positive options for health and safety for girls using drugs or active in the sex trade. Girls who graduated from the training would then be eligible to provide outreach support to other girls.

Harm reduction was YWEP's core belief. They did not try to pressure girls to exit the sex trade, but worked without judgment to help them find ways to stay safer when engaging in risky behavior. According to their value statement, "we believe that girls do what they have to do to survive and we don't question why a girl is involved in the sex trade or street economy, instead we ask them what they think they need to stay safe, feel supported and take care of themselves."[37] They did not think that telling girls to stop selling sex was effective: "we'd rather work with girls to realize their dreams than argue with them about what they are doing."[38] They emphasized that exit from the sex trade was a process that entailed addressing emotional as well as economic issues and so might take a long time. They respected the choices girls made, sought to help them to figure out what was best for them, and then supported them in achieving their goals. The Project embraced a philosophy of self-care that encouraged girls to take

---

[34] YWEP Website, About, at https://ywepchicago.wordpress.com/about/.

[35] Kari Lydersen, "Youth Sex Workers Organize for Their Rights," *Working in These Times* (June 19, 2012).

[36] YWEP, Letter to the Community, dated June 18, 2013, at https://ywepchicago.wordpress.com/.

[37] YWPE, Our Values, at https://ywepchicago.wordpress.com/our-values/.

[38] YWEP, Frequently Asked Questions, at https://ywepchicago.files.wordpress.com/2011/06/frequently-asked-questions.pdf.

care of their bodies, minds, and spirits and to regularly check in with themselves to see how they were doing.

YWEP also taught and advocated for social justice. Girls learned about how social systems like the criminal justice, health care, and foster care systems oppressed youth involved in the sex trade, and how racism, classism, sexism, and homophobia in society influenced these systems and impacted the lives of girls. They worked to improve systems, but also pursued transformative justice strategies – working outside these systems to find community-based solutions to problems. Finally, they engaged in popular education, encouraging girls to think critically about their lives and communities so they could act together to address inequalities and injustices. They produced zines and other creative projects, went to high schools to talk to girls, and conducted participatory action research, which trained girls to conduct research to improve their lives, their communities, and the institutions intended to serve them.

Another organization that used the language of empowerment but was quite distinct from YWEP is My Life My Choice (MLMC), founded by Lisa Goldblatt Grace in 2002 in Boston, Massachusetts, after the murder of a seventeen-year-old girl involved in the sex trade who had been living in a Child Protective Services-funded group home.[39] Since its founding, MLMC has followed what it calls an empowerment model by providing survivor-led services to commercially sexually exploited youth with the goal of educating youth "to find their voice and create a positive life path." According to their mission statement, "We believe that children have a fundamental human right to live their lives free from exploitation – without fear that adults will prey on their vulnerabilities. We empower youth to be agents of change in their own lives and in the movement to end the commercial sexual exploitation of children."[40] In addition to survivor services and mentorship, MLMC offered prevention education, provider training, and advocacy and leadership training, including the participation of youth in public policy debates.[41] MLMC originally only served girls aged twelve to seventeen, but eventually expanded services to include boys and transgender youth. Despite both using the language of empowerment, MLMC and YWEP developed distinct visions of empowerment: YWEP was youth-led and focused on harm reduction, whereas MLMC was run by adults and sought to end the involvement of youth in the sex trade.

Sex Workers Project (SWP) of the Urban Justice Center in New York City, founded in December of 2001, also worked with youth in the sex trade. SWP was formed to work with both sex workers and sex trafficking survivors by providing

---

[39] MLMC is part of the Justice Resource Institute, which was formed in 1973 to address issues arising from the deinstitutionalization of youth. Justice Resource Institute, Our Story, at https://jri.org/about/story.

[40] The Giving Common, My Life My Choice, Mission Statement, at https://www.givingcommon.org/profile/1127292/my-life-my-choice–a-division-of-justice-resource-institute/.

[41] My Life My Choice, History, at http://www.fightingexploitation.org.

legal and social services. Taking a harm reduction and human rights approach, SWP engaged in policy and media advocacy, community education, and human rights documentation.[42] While mostly focused on adults, they have worked with youth experiencing commercial sex.[43] In 2003, SWP published a research report on street prostitution in New York City based on interviews with thirty adult sex workers, eight of whom had entered the sex trade as minors.[44]

These new organizations diversified the movement. Most of the older service providers like SAGE, Breaking Free, and the Paul and Lisa Program were explicitly abolitionist: they believed that prostitution was always coercive and abusive, and their long-term goal was the abolition of the sex trade. Several of these new organizations, however, were explicitly not abolitionist. YWEP and SWP, in particular, added a new type of organization to the mix of service providers working with youth involved in prostitution – groups that not only had a harm reduction approach but also supported decriminalization of the sex trade. Similar to GEMS, YWEP focused on youth empowerment, but YWEP was also youth-led, whereas GEMS was adult-led like most other organizations working with youth involved in prostitution. Furthermore, GEMS worked with the courts and law enforcement, whereas YWEP was highly critical of the police, whom they saw as part of the problem, not part of the solution to the abuse of youth involved in sex work and the street economy. Despite these differences, some of these organizations sometimes worked together to achieve common goals, like when GEMS and SWP both supported safe harbor legislation in New York later in the decade. The movement would continue to diversify as the decade progressed.

## MEDIA COVERAGE OF TRAFFICKING IN THE EARLY 2000S

Despite ongoing activism against abuse of US youth in the sex trade in the early 2000s, public awareness and discussion still focused mostly on sex trafficking outside the United States.[45] For example, in 2005, Nicholas Kristof of the *New York Times* wrote a series of stories about girls in the brothels of Cambodia.[46] However, the same month, *New York Times* journalist Peter

---

[42] Sex Workers Project, Mission, at https://swp.urbanjustice.org/swp-mission.

[43] Interview with Sienna Baskin, April 22, 2016 (on file with author).

[44] Juhu Thukral and Melissa Ditmore, *Revolving Door: An Analysis of Street-Based Prostitution in New York City* (New York, NY: Urban Justice Center, 2003), 54.

[45] Editorial, "Putting the Sex Trade on Notice," *New York Times* (January 9, 2004), A18; David Binder, "In Europe, Sex Slavery is Thriving Despite Raids," *New York Times* (October 20, 2002), 8; Ronald Smothers, "6 Are Accused of Forcing Girls From Mexico Into Prostitution," *New York Times* (March 26, 2002), B5; Carlotta Gall, "Macedonia Village is Center of Europe Web in Sex Trade," *New York Times* (July 28, 2001), A1; Joel Brinkley, "U.S. Criticizes Major Allies in for Inaction in Slave Trade," *New York Times* (July 13, 2001), A8.

[46] Nicholas Kristof, "Sex Slaves? Lock Up the Pimps," *New York Times* (January 29, 2005), A19; Nicholas Kristof, "Stopping the Traffickers," *New York Times* (January 31, 2004), A17; Nicholas Kristof, "Loss of Innocence," *New York Times* (January 28, 2004), A25;

Landesman published an article, "The Girls Next Door," recounting the trafficking of under-aged girls from Mexico to a suburban New Jersey neighborhood, where adult men patronized their services at all times of the day.[47] This article cited an estimate that at least 10,000 sex trafficking victims entered the US each year, drawing disbelief and challenges.[48] This article, along with the Hollywood movie *Trade* based on the article, contributed to an increased awareness that trafficking was a problem not only in foreign countries, but in the United States as well.[49]

Some articles, however, addressed US-citizen youth involved in the sex trade. A *New York Times* article that ran in December of 2002 described the problem as growing and as affecting younger and younger girls. The article emphasized that youth involved in prostitution were often victims of sexual abuse at an early age, or had come from extremely troubled homes.[50] Another article asked whether incarcerating "child prostitutes" protected them, or whether it was counterproductive and needlessly punitive.[51] Often articles framed the issue in racialized ways, reminiscent of the 1970s. For example, in 2003, *Newsweek* ran a story titled, "This Could Be Your Kid," by Suzanne Smalley about suburban "teen prostitutes" who sold sex for designer clothes. The story featured a "cute, blond and chatty" teenage girl named Stacey from Minnesota, who was lured from the Mall of America where she liked to hang out after school. Stacey, described as living with her parents in an "upscale neighborhood" with "good grades in high school and plans to try out for the tennis team," was typical of a growing number of "teen prostitutes," warned Smalley.[52] The article characterized the problem as mainly involving girls, who were getting younger, were increasingly likely to come from middle-class homes, and were subjected to increasing violence from "pimps." The story quoted a Minneapolis detective, saying "Everyone thinks they are runaways with drug problems from the inner city. It's not true. This could be your kid." Smalley quoted a counselor from the Paul and Lisa Program, who said, "People say, 'We're not from the ghetto.' The shame the parents feel is incredible." The story used the racially-coded language of "inner city" and "ghetto" are racially coded terms.[53] By targeting white middle-class readers and emphasizing the disjunction

Nicholas Kristof, "Bargaining for Freedom," *New York Times* (January 21, 2004), A21; Nicholas Kristof, "Girls for Sale," *New York Times* (January 17, 2004), A15.

[47] Peter Landesman, "The Girls Next Door," *New York Times* (January 25, 2004), 30–39, 66–67, 72, 75.

[48] Jack Shafer, "The Sex Slavery Epidemic That Wasn't," *Slate* (September 27, 2007).

[49] *Trade*, dir. Marco Kreuzpaintner, Lionsgate, 2007.

[50] Cardwell, "Officials Say Sex Trade Lures Younger Girls," B1.

[51] Leslie Kaufman, "Determining the Future of a Girl with a Past," *New York Times* (September 15, 2004), B1.

[52] Suzanne Smalley, "This Could Be Your Kid," *Newsweek* 142.7 (August 18, 2003), 44–47.

[53] Ian Haney López, *Dog Whistle Politics: How Coded Racial Appeals Have Reinvented Racism and Wrecked the Middle Class* (New York, NY: Oxford University Press, 2014), ix.

between expectations about teen prostitutes – that they were "from the ghetto" – and the middle-class, white youth featured in the article, the article's underlying message was that readers should care about the issue because it was affecting people like them. The article characterized the Mall of America as a "huge recruiting center," and blamed "a culture that glorifies pimping," quoting the lyrics of the popular song "P.I.M.P." by rapper 50 Cent featured on MTV Music Video Awards in 2003. A writer for *Slate* magazine criticized the *Newsweek* article as "bogus trendspotting," questioning its claims that teen prostitution was increasing and that teens involved in prostitution were getting younger.[54] Police and mall owners disputed that the Mall of America was a center of teen recruitment into prostitution.[55]

Newspapers ran similar articles. One article warned parents about "the new middle-class teen sex industry," described by the FBI as an "epidemic that was attracting younger and younger kids. While traditionally "teen prostitution" was "mostly limited to runaways, abused children and children from poor inner-city areas who lacked parental supervision and often had drug addictions, emotional problems and learning disabilities," said the article, now they come from "stable, two-parent families who live in middle-class suburbs with no history of abuse or neglect. They are, it seems, doing it for kicks." According to Bob Flores, director of the Office of Juvenile Justice and Delinquency Prevention, "we've got kids in every major city and in suburbia all over the place being prostituted."[56] This framing echoed characterizations of the issue from previous decades – the 1990s, the 1970s, and even the 1910s. As the media increasingly focused on the US youth sex trade, so did public policymakers.

## FEDERAL INITIATIVES ON JUVENILE PROSTITUTION IN THE UNITED STATES

In the early 2000s, the primary focus of the federal government was still international sex trafficking, but there was growing attention to youth involvement in the sex trade in the United States. In response to pressure from advocates, including Lois Lee, the federal government began to prosecute adults who trafficked children.[57] In 2003, the Innocence Lost National Initiative was created by the Federal Bureau of Investigation (FBI) Violent Crimes and Major Offenders Section and the Department of Justice (DOJ) Child Exploitation and

---

[54] Jack Shafer, "Newsweek's Bogus Trendspotting," *Slate* (August 12, 2003).

[55] "Megamall, Officials Criticize Article About Pimps Recruiting Girls at Mall," *Minneapolis Star Tribune* (August 13, 2003).

[56] Marion McKeone, "US Rights Blames MTV for Teen Mall Sex Craze," *Sunday Tribune* (August 24, 2003), 24. See also Cynthia Fagan, "Oldest Profession Gets Younger," *The New York Post* (August 11, 2003), 17.

[57] Interview with Lois Lee, September 7, 2017 (on file with author).

Obscenity Section, in partnership with the National Center for Missing and Exploited Children.[58] The FBI identified fourteen cities thought to have the highest incidence of children in prostitution, including Chicago, New York, and San Francisco. They then notified the FBI field offices in these cities that prostitution against children was a high priority and directed them to determine whether these cities had a significant problem. The National Center for Missing and Exploited Children developed week-long trainings with an intensive curriculum entitled "Protecting Victims of Child Prostitution" for state and federal law enforcement agencies, prosecutors, and social service providers. By June of 2005, they had trained 263 individuals.[59] The Initiative also developed task forces specific to child trafficking and prostitution issues in these fourteen cities, later expanding to over thirty cities.[60] A fact sheet on the commercial sexual exploitation of children produced by the Initiative explained that a major obstacle to addressing juvenile prostitution was the attitudes many held about the girls involved: many did not see juvenile prostitution as a crime, but instead saw the girls involved as delinquents.[61] The Initiative treated facilitators like organized crime bosses and went after them with racketeering laws. By 2005, the FBI was clear that prostitution involving children was always exploitative. The FBI's Assistant Director of the Criminal Investigative Division Chris Swecker testified before Congress that "children can never consent to prostitution. It is always exploitation."[62] Furthermore, federal law enforcement recognized that criminally prosecuting youth was an ineffective way to obtain their cooperation in criminal prosecutions. Despite the fact that many of the youth they removed from prostitution were older teens, the FBI's Innocence Lost National Initiative logo used a silhouette of a young girl with pigtails, with the tagline, "America's Children Are Not for Sale" (see Figure 4.1).[63] This image leveraged ideologies of childhood innocence to mobilize concern and support about youth involved in the sex trade.

In addition to this FBI initiative, the Commission on Security and Cooperation in Europe chaired by Sam Brownback (R-KS) and Christopher Smith (R-NJ) held a hearing titled "Exploiting Americans on American Soil: Domestic Trafficking Exposed" on June 7, 2005. The hearing included testimony from representatives

[58] National Center for Missing and Exploited Children was established in 1984 as a private non-profit organization to serve as a national clearinghouse for missing and sexually exploited children. NCMEC has been authorized by Congress to run two programs that assist law enforcement, professionals and families in the recovery of missing children. National Center for Missing and Exploited Children, Programs and Services, at www.missingkids.org/Programs.

[59] *Exploiting Americans on American Soil Hearing*, 2005, 7.

[60] Julian Sher, *Somebody's Daughter: The Hidden Story of America's Prostituted Children and the Battle to Save Them* (Chicago, IL: Chicago Review Press, 2011), 51.

[61] Innocence Lost Working Group, *Commercial Sexual Exploitation of Children: A Fact Sheet* (March 2010) (citing research by feminist abolitionists Melissa Farley and Donna Hughes).

[62] *Exploiting Americans on American Soil Hearing*, 2005, 6.

[63] Federal Bureau of Investigation, Innocence Lost National Initiative Banner," at www.fbi.gov/investigate/violent-crime/cac.

FIGURE 4.1   FBI Innocence Lost National Initiative promotional image.

of the FBI and the Department of Health and Human Services; a young survivor of
domestic trafficking, Leisa B., whose story began this chapter; Norma Hotaling of
SAGE; Frank Barnaba of the Paul and Lisa Program; and Ernie Allen of the
National Center for Missing and Exploited Children. Hotaling recounted her
own story of surviving a life of abuse and prostitution and called for including
survivors in all aspects of policy and service development and implementation.
At the time, Congress was considering two pieces of proposed legislation – the
reauthorization of the TVPA and the End Demand for Sex Trafficking Act of
2005, which proposed treating buyers of sex as sex traffickers.[64]

Whereas previous trafficking hearings had only addressed non-US citizens,
this hearing was groundbreaking in that it focused on American youth within
the United States. Representative Smith cited the 2001 Estes and Weiner study
as an inspiration for the hearing. The central question of the hearing, as stated
by Representative Smith at the start, was whether the TVPA required US citizen
youth involved in prostitution to be treated as victims of trafficking under the
Act. While the language of the law clearly applied to US citizen youth involved
in the sex trade, states in fact often treated these youth as delinquents, not
victims, which clearly ran counter to the requirements of the Act. Because the
focus of the 2000 Act was international trafficking, and the resources the law
provided were directed entirely to non-US citizen victims, the applicability of
the Act to US citizen youth was unclear. Smith noted that he and Representative
Benjamin Cardin (D-Maryland) had introduced a bill to reauthorize the TVPA
that would explicitly define commercial sexual exploitation of American
citizens and nationals within the United States as domestic trafficking and
would authorize new funds to the FBI and to State and local law enforcement

[64] H.R. 2012, 109th Congress, 2005.

for investigations and prosecutions, as well as authorize grants for victim service providers to pilot residential rehabilitation facilities for domestic trafficking victims. The bill also authorized a study of best practices and a pilot program to reduce demand. The goal of the bill, according to Smith, was to "begin to shift the paradigm so that our own citizens who are exploited are seen and treated as victims of crime."[65] Nevertheless, Smith wavered in his call to decriminalize youth when he expressed concern about youth returning to abusive situations if they were not detained. He asked the witnesses about whether "some kind of benign lockup could be put into place for their own sake while they're getting over this sense that they want to get right back out on the street, back to, you know, the cycle of abuse, which hasn't been broken yet, in their own minds?"[66] One witness testified about a "more therapeutic" option, like mental health treatment facilities and social service facilities with locked doors.[67]

A major theme of the hearing was the spread of the commercial sexual exploitation of youth from poor kids in the city to wealthy, white children in the suburbs and rural areas. Class was addressed more explicitly than race, but both were driving themes of the hearing. The survivor chosen to testify, Leisa B., was a white woman who described herself as coming from an upper-middle-class family in Atlanta. Chris Smith noted that children from poor families were at higher risk of commercial sexual exploitation, but emphasized that "most of the street children encountered in the [Estes and Weiner] study [which in part inspired the hearing] were Caucasian youths who had run away from middle-class families."[68] Frank Barnaba most explicitly emphasized how the problem was spreading from the city into the wealthy suburbs. He testified, "Traffickers are no longer demons of the big city. They are infiltrating the small towns of America," then explained that seventy-five percent of youth served by his program were from "upper middle-class families living in rural areas," whom he described as "more vulnerable to exploitation and less streetwise than their city peers." He told the story of working with a "valedictorian from a very, very prominent Connecticut town" and warned that "pimps [were] coming right into their homes." Several of the speakers, including Chris Smith and Norma Hotaling, emphasized that it was "our citizens" and "our girls" who were being exploited. Hotaling described how "pimps" lured girls, emphasizing that "it's any girl, it's our girls."[69] References to class were explicit, but references to race were usually coded, except for once. The survivor who testified, Leisa B. referenced her pimp hiring a drug dealer to drive her and four other girls around because "it would look hot if there was five white girls and a black man driving a nice truck."[70] Several speakers acknowledged that girls from all racial and ethnic backgrounds were targeted for prostitution, yet the hearings focused on white, upper-middle-class girls.

---

[65] *Exploiting Americans on American Soil Hearing*, 2005, 2.    [66] Ibid. 16.    [67] Ibid. 17.
[68] Ibid. 3.    [69] Ibid. 32–34.    [70] Ibid. 23.

Much of the testimony in the 2005 hearing framed the issue as a criminal justice problem and the solution as more funding for investigation and prosecution of facilitators as well as training for federal, state, and local law enforcement. Chris Smith questioned the FBI representative as to whether he had enough resources to combat domestic trafficking. Ernie Allen testified that he would like to see the FBI receive significantly more resources to expand the Innocence Lost National Initiative and Barnaba agreed. Hotaling emphasized that criminal justice efforts should "go after the demand and go after them hard."[71] She supported the End Demand Against Sex Trafficking Act, which targeted buyers of sex. She argued that men who buy sex from under-aged girls should be charged with sexual abuse and statutory rape and should be required to register as sex offenders. She also argued that mandated reporters should be required to report child prostitution as abuse of children. She criticized the double standard whereby "We encourage the perpetrators by focusing on the behavior – supposed wrongs – of the children, and ignore the perpetrators."[72] Raising the issue of increased demand at sporting events and conventions, Chris Smith asked witnesses about whether there were any efforts to "sensitize and also scare" men about under-aged girls in prostitution, including threatening the men with jail time.[73] Both Hotaling and Barnaba encouraged public education campaigns. Hotaling suggested "little rings of educational material that goes around urinals that says, 'Buy a kid, go to jail.'"[74] Hotaling stated her support for "john schools" to educate men arrested for buying sex of the harm and danger of their behavior.

Most of the witnesses had a law-and-order approach to the commercial sexual exploitation of youth, but some also emphasized cultural change. Both Hotaling and Barnaba critiqued sexually explicit popular culture. Hotaling addressed the "myths and misunderstandings about prostitution," how it's "glamorized and romanticized" and how women and girls in prostitution are viewed as "criminal sexual deviants, socially inept and mentally deficient." She criticized the "loosened social norms concerning the sex industry" and its "huge marketing campaign" encouraging men to purchase sex.[75] In her written testimony, Hotaling placed the issue in historical context. She noted how societal beliefs about child sexual abuse and sexual assault of adult women were shifting, except within the context of prostitution. Throughout history, argued Hotaling, society denied the existence of sexual assault or blamed the victim, noting a case where a judge called a five-year-old rape victim "provocative" and "promiscuous." But now, she argued, sex without consent and adults having sex with children were crimes and society was more likely to acknowledge these crimes and be less likely to blame the victims of these crimes because of their appearance, dress, social status, or "the idea that some people are 'deserving' victims." But when it came to prostitution, Hotaling argued, "it's as if no changes have occurred. As long as someone is labeled as

[71] Ibid. 40.    [72] Ibid. 29.    [73] Ibid. 40.    [74] Ibid. 46.    [75] Ibid. 26, 28.

a prostitute – whether child or adult – we still say that it is OK to dehumanize, to mistreat, and to endanger that person." Hotaling argued, "we can end child prostitution by renaming and redefining it as child abuse and statutory rape."[76] She called for "dramatic legislative reform" to decriminalize children and increase prosecution of "pimps" and customers.

Hotaling also raised the underlying structural issues that trapped women and girls in prostitution, like the lack of affordable housing, treatment for drug and alcohol addiction, and access to education and vocational training. In her prepared statement, she expanded on the "social causes of prostitution," including extremes of poverty, gender inequality, racial stratification, and "gaping problems in our social response to child abuse within families and communities."[77] Hotaling's more complex analysis of child prostitution was not unique at the time, but was often overshadowed by criminal justice approaches to the problem that centered on punishing facilitators and buyers rather than decreasing the vulnerabilities of youth. These two approaches would become more deeply articulated and starkly contrasted by both activists and lawmakers in subsequent years.

In 2005, Congress passed the Trafficking Victims Protection Reauthorization Act.[78] In the Act, Congress acknowledged that United States' efforts to combat trafficking had focused primarily on international trafficking of persons, including the trafficking of foreign citizens into the United States, but not on the trafficking of US citizens.[79] In its findings, the Act stated that people were trafficked within United States borders and that many minors were vulnerable to commercial sexual exploitation.[80] The Act strengthened state programs to prosecute adults involved in prostituting youth by funding law enforcement and prosecution and as well as public education. The Act also provided modest funds for new programs to serve United States citizen victims of domestic trafficking, including a pilot program for sheltering minors.[81] Some of the first organizations to receive this money included SAGE in San Francisco ($121,979), Breaking Free in St. Paul, Minnesota ($110,000), GEMS in New York City ($109,473), Coalition to Abolish Slavery and Trafficking in Los Angeles ($75,000), and Alternatives for Girls in Michigan ($25,000). Federal funds helped grow these organizations so that they could offer more services to more youth, but it also enabled them to increase public advocacy on the issue.

---

[76] Ibid. 72–73.    [77] Ibid. 75.

[78] Trafficking Victims Protection Reauthorization Act of 2005, Pub. L. No. 109–164, § 2(3)-(5), 119 Stat. 3558, 3558–59 (2006) (codified as amended at 22 U.S.C. § 7101 (2006)).

[79] Trafficking Victims Protection Reauthorization Act of 2005, H.R. 972, Sec. 2(3) (passed December 14, 2005); see also Trafficking Victims Protection Reauthorization Act of 2005, Committee on the Judiciary Report, H.R. Rep. No. 109–317, pt. 2 (submitted by Rep. Sensenbrenner, Member, House Comm. on the Judiciary).

[80] H.R. 972, Sec. 2(4)-(6).    [81] H.R. 972, Sec. 203.

## GEORGIA CAMPAIGN AGAINST COMMERCIAL SEXUAL EXPLOITATION OF GIRLS

In addition to federal-level action against the youth sex trade, activists were working at the state and local levels. Whereas federal discussions on juvenile prostitution focused on middle-class, white girls, a particularly successful and well-organized state-level campaign in Georgia focused on African American girls. Concern about the commercial sexual exploitation of youth in Atlanta arose in the late-1990s when two Fulton County Juvenile Court Judges – Glenda Hatchett and Nina Hickson, both African American – noticed an increasing number of cases in the juvenile courts involving girls allegedly engaged in prostitution. The judges collected five years of data on cases involving child prostitution and noticed a marked increase in the number of cases in the previous eighteen months. They also noticed that the girls appearing before courts were becoming younger.[82] Hickson reported that she was adjudicating approximately thirty such cases each month, some involving kidnapping, assault, and torture of young girls.[83] Hickson was moved to action when she was faced with the cases of a ten-year-old girl and her eleven-year-old sister, both allegedly involved in prostitution.[84]

At the time, there was little public interest in spending scarce resources on girls assumed to be complicit in prostitution and therefore considered to be perpetrators of crimes, but Hatchett and Hickson were undaunted. Judge Hatchett took a delegation of concerned women to District Attorney Paul Howard's office to request increased legal scrutiny of adults involving youth in the sex trade.[85] As a result, Howard put together a task force to address child prostitution in Fulton County. Judge Hickson, along with the Director of Programs for the Juvenile Court Deborah Richardson, met with Fulton County Commissioner Nancy Boxill to discuss the problem. Judge Hickson expressed her frustration at the limited options she had to help these girls – sentencing them to detention, placing them under court supervision, or freeing them to return to the streets. There were no treatment programs for commercially sexually exploited girls in Atlanta at the time, and the only law to punish adults who prostituted youth was the misdemeanor offense of pandering, punishable by a fifty-dollar fine.

Convinced of the seriousness of the problem, Boxill called together a small group of diverse female leaders in July of 2000, including Hickson, Richardson,

---

[82] Nancy A. Boxill and Deborah J. Richardson, "Ending Sex Trafficking in Atlanta," *Affilia: Journal of Women and Social Work* 22. 2 (Summer 2007), 138–149, at 143.

[83] Nancy A. Boxill and Deborah J. Richardson, "A Community's Response to the Sex Trafficking of Children," *The Link* 3.4 (2005), 1, 3–4, 9, at 4.

[84] Boxill and Richardson, "Ending Sex Trafficking in Atlanta," 143.

[85] Child Interfaith Movement, *Child Sexual Exploitation and Trafficking in Georgia: A 10-Year Review of the Issue of Child Prostitution in Georgia with Special Emphasis on Child Prostitution in Atlanta* (Atlanta, GA: Child Interfaith Movement, August 2009).

Stephanie Davis – the founder and executive director of the Atlanta Women's Foundation – and community advocate Susan May. The group developed several goals: to raise awareness about the problem of child prostitution in Atlanta, to enhance penalties for prostituting a minor, and to raise public and private money to create a treatment facility and services for girls exiting prostitution.[86] They then held a meeting and invited women from a wide range of organizations across Atlanta, including "bridge clubs, garden clubs, professional and religious organizations, social clubs, sororities, and recreational clubs."[87] They mailed three hundred letters of invitation.

On a cold morning in November of 2000, more than eighty women showed up. The meeting began with a short video about the commercial sexual exploitation of girls in Atlanta, produced by a local network television station, and then the women gathered heard from a mother whose daughter had been kidnapped and prostituted. Afterwards, the group split into three working groups – the Public Awareness Group, the Legislative Group, and the Fundraising Group – to address the three goals the organizers had set out. The Public Awareness Group decided to recruit a reporter from the *Atlanta Journal-Constitution* to write a series of articles on the prostitution of children in Atlanta. They also decided to convene a series of town-hall meeting about the issue. The Legislative Group planned to identify a female attorney to draft legislation to make prostituting a child a felony, find legislators to introduce the bill, and organize lobbying days and a public relations campaign to support the bill. Finally, the Fundraising Committee strategized about how to raise money for a treatment facility for girls exiting prostitution. A federal prosecutor who attended the meeting reported that his office was investigating adults who prostituted minors in the Atlanta area, so the women's group formed an alliance with him.[88] This diverse coalition of women across race and class had remarkable success in achieving their goals.

Even before the November meeting, the effort to raise public awareness had begun. In June of 2000, Judge Hickson published an editorial in the *Atlanta Journal-Constitution*, where she called child prostitution in Atlanta "an epidemic of tragic proportions."[89] The following January, in 2001, as a result of the Public Awareness Group lobbying for coverage, the *Atlanta Journal-Constitution* published a five-part series of articles titled, "Selling Atlanta's Children," written by Jane Hansen and appearing on the front pages of the newspaper.[90] The series subtitle was, "Runaway girls lured into the sex trade are being jailed for crimes while their adult pimps go free." In her research for the articles, Hansen could not get reliable numbers on how many youth were

---

[86] Boxill and Richardson, "Ending Sex Trafficking in Atlanta," 146.    [87] Ibid. 147.
[88] Ibid. 147.
[89] Nina Hickson, "An Epidemic of Tragic Proportions," *Atlanta Journal-Constitution* (June 11, 2000), C7.
[90] Jane Hansen, "Selling Atlanta's Children," *Atlanta Journal-Constitution* (January 7–9, 2001).

involved in prostitution, but she discovered that between 1972 and 1999, 401 adults had been incarcerated for prostitution, almost all females, but not one person had gone to prison for the crime of pimping.[91] To find out more about the scope of the problem, Hansen convinced the *Atlanta Journal-Constitution* to commission a national survey of juvenile court judges, who reported that the problem of juvenile prostitution was growing, that the youth were getting younger, and that the adults involved were often not charged, prosecuted, or sentenced very severely.[92]

The *Atlanta Journal-Constitution* series raised many of the same issues that the earlier 1996 *Christian Science Monitor* series had raised: that sex trafficking was a not just a problem abroad but was a "home-grown American phenomena," that there existed a double standard where youth were arrested but the adults who prostituted them were not, that there were not enough services for youth exiting the sex trade, and that youth were victims of child prostitution, not perpetrators. The series alternated between the stories of individual girls and stories about the scope of the problem – how girls end up in prostitution and what was being done to address it, quoting judges, police, and social workers. The first article in the series began with a description of a ten-year-old runaway and alleged prostitute, in jailhouse garb and metal shackles around her ankles, appearing before an Atlanta Juvenile Court Judge.[93] Hansen later said she intentionally sought out a young victim in order to make "the exploitative nature of this problem ... more real to our readers," who saw these youth as "consenting participants."[94] The series quoted Judges Hatchett and Hickson, as well as activists, including Alesia Adams of Victims of Prostitution. The articles included a range of views about what to do about prostituted children, including send them to boot camp as a form of "tough love," shut down strip clubs, and crack down on hotels where adult men take children.[95] The series also reported on the need for specialized services for youth. Reflecting back on that time, Hansen later noted, "There were plenty of beds for bad children needing punishment, but practically none for young exploited victims needing help."[96] A recurrent theme in the series was the need for a change in attitudes toward prostituted youth away from seeing them as perpetrators and toward seeing them as victims. The series also had an article about how internet chat rooms were being used to lure youth

---

[91] Jane Hansen, "Selling Atlanta's Children: What Has and Hasn't Changed," *CNN Freedom Project* (July 18, 2015).

[92] Jane Hansen, "Prostitutes Getting Younger as Sex Trade Grows," *Atlanta Journal-Constitution* (January 8, 2001), A1.

[93] Jane Hansen, "Runaway Girls Lured into the Sex Trade Are Being Jailed for Crimes while Their Adult Pimps Go Free," *Atlanta Journal-Constitution* (January 7, 2001), A1.

[94] Hansen, "Selling Atlanta's Children: What Has and Hasn't Changed."

[95] Jane Hansen, "Feds, Police Elsewhere Finding Solutions," *Atlanta Journal-Constitution* (January 8, 2001), A8.

[96] Hansen, "Selling Atlanta's Children: What Has and Hasn't Changed."

into the sex trade.[97] The series encouraged readers to volunteer through a group called Victims of Prostitution, to contribute to a shelter program through the Atlanta Women's Foundation, and to lobby in support of a proposed law to make prostituting minors a felony.

In addition to the *Atlanta Journal-Constitution* series, local television stations covered the issue and several coalition members appeared on radio talk shows. Op-eds on child prostitution appeared several more times in the Sunday edition of the *Atlanta Journal-Constitution*. Members of the coalition met with the editorial board of the *Atlanta Journal-Constitution* and convinced them to take a strong editorial stance in support of legislative change and funding support.[98] The increased media coverage led to increased concern about the issue in the community. In April of 2001, more than three hundred people gathered for an "Emergency Citywide Summit on Child Prostitution" at Atlanta Metropolitan College, where youth survivors and their mothers spoke about their experiences of commercial sexual exploitation.[99] This activism quickly led to legislative action.

The coalition worked with an attorney to draft legislation, which was circulated among the Fulton County legislators in November of 2000. Female legislators introduced the Child Sexual Commerce Prevention Act in January of 2001. The coalition held a lobby day at the State Capitol on January 25 and a "Show Up and Be Counted" rally on January 31. The bill passed and was signed into law on March 27, 2001. The law made prostituting any child under age eighteen a felony, punishable by a prison term of five to twenty years and a fine of $2,500 to $10,000. The legislature passed another new law giving law enforcement the power to seize any property used to further a child prostitution business, including cars and homes.[100] The legislative group continued to pressure lawmakers to improve laws relating to child prostitution. The following year, the coalition held a candlelight vigil with students from seven area colleges and a second lobby day. Church groups also held rallies at the capital to support legislative reform.[101]

In addition to legislative change, government officials at all levels began to take action. On Tuesday, January 23, the US Attorney's Office, the FBI, and the Atlanta Police conducted a sweep targeting child prostitution in Atlanta, resulting in a federal grand jury indictment of fourteen people for luring

[97] Jane Hansen, "When Danger is as Close as a Phone Line," *Atlanta Journal-Constitution* (January 9, 2001), A1.

[98] Boxill and Richardson, "Ending Sex Trafficking in Atlanta," 148.

[99] Jane Hansen, "Police Plan Child Prostitution Unit," *Atlanta Journal-Constitution* (April 28, 2001), A1.

[100] Paul Menair. "Crimes and Offenses: Prostitution: Increase Penalties for Offenses of Pimping and Pandering Of A Minor," *Georgia State University Law Review* 18 (2001): 32.

[101] Alan Judd, "Capital Rally Targets Teen Prostitution," *Atlanta Journal Constitution* (August 12, 2001), 2E.

minors into prostitution, including some as young as ten years old.[102] They were charged and successfully prosecuted by attorney Janis Gordon for violations of the Racketeer Influenced and Corrupt Organizations Act of 1970 (RICO), the first time anyone had been convicted for prostituting minors under RICO in Georgia. At the local level, city officials were also acting to combat child prostitution. In April of 2001, Mayor Bill Campbell directed Atlanta Sheriff Beverly Harvard to create a special unit to identify victims and build cases against the adults exploiting them.[103]

Courts also expanded support systems for youth appearing before them. In 1999, Alesia Adams of the Fulton County Court Appointed Special Advocates had noticed, like Judge Hickson, the increasing number of prostituted girls in the system. Adams established a volunteer-based Victims of Prostitution program with the goal of eliminating youth prostitution in Fulton County by creating treatment options for youth and encouraging prosecution of adult exploiters.[104] In 2001, Deborah Richardson moved to the Juvenile Justice Fund and created the Center to End Adolescent Sexual Exploitation (CEASE) Program to advocate before the Fulton County Juvenile Courts for girls who were involved or at risk of being involved in commercial sexual exploitation.[105]

The third goal of the coalition was to raise funds for a treatment facility for youth exiting prostitution. The coalition was able to obtain seed funding through the Georgia legislature, but most of the funds were raised through private fundraising. Atlanta businesswoman Kayrita Anderson donated significant funds after reading the *Atlanta Journal-Constitution* series on commercial sexual exploitation of youth. The coalition opened Angela's House in late 2001, sixteen months after the coalition's first meeting.[106] Angela's House provided gender-specific programming and attention in all aspects of its design, including goals, daily schedule, volunteer recruitment, and staff training.[107] Foundations and civic groups contributed funds for capital improvements and women's social and professional groups provided the furnishings. The state provided half the operating budget, with the rest provided by donations from individuals, foundations, and faith-based

---

[102] Associated Press, "14 Indicted in Connection with Child Sex Trade," *Athens Daily News* (January 21, 2001).

[103] Associated Press, "Atlanta Police to Form Special Unit to Combat Child Prostitution," *Athens Daily News* (April 29, 2001).

[104] Alexandra Priebe and Cristen Suhr, *Hidden in Plain View: The Commercial Sexual Exploitation of Girls in Atlanta* (Atlanta, GA: Atlanta Women's Agenda, September 2005), 13.

[105] Youth Spark, Our Programs, at www.youth-spark.org/learn/our-programs/legacy-programs /cease/; *Domestic Minor Sex Trafficking, A Hearing Before the United States House Judiciary Subcommittee on Crime, Terrorism and Homeland Security*, 111th Cong., 2nd Sess. (September 25, 2010), 126.

[106] Boxill and Richardson, "Ending Sex Trafficking in Atlanta," 148.

[107] Boxill and Richardson, "A Community's Response to Sex Trafficking of Children," 3.

organizations. Angela's House provided a ninety-day program for girls. In the first four years of the program, seventy girls lived at Angela's House. All but seven successfully completed the full program and were sent home to relatives and three-fourths had no further involvement with the juvenile justice system.[108]

In 2001, Shirley Franklin became mayor of Atlanta and made child prostitution a priority issue for her administration. One of her first initiatives was to research the problem of child prostitution in Atlanta. Franklin's Atlanta Women's Agenda office, led by Stephanie Davis, sponsored a groundbreaking study titled *Hidden in Plain View: The Commercial Sexual Exploitation of Girls in Atlanta*, conducted by two researchers affiliated with the Centers for Disease Control and published in 2005. The study mapped child prostitution in Atlanta, estimating that nearly three hundred girls were commercially sexually exploited each month within the thriving "adult entertainment" industry in Atlanta, supported by the convention and sports events in the city. The report, which expressed particular concern about the health consequences of involvement in the sex trade on girls, especially STDs and HIV/AIDS, recommended expansion of services to victims, the launch of a major public education campaign, increased prosecution of facilitators and buyers of sex from youth, and a victim-centered approach to exploited youth.[109] This study led to a multifaceted prevention campaign by the Mayor's office, which centered on raising public awareness about the commercial sexual exploitation of youth.

The next year, Mayor Franklin launched her nationally acclaimed "Dear John" media campaign focused on the demand side of commercial sexual exploitation of girls. The Mayor's office retained the international public relations firm Edelman to develop the campaign, which featured Mayor Franklin imploring men to stop buying Atlanta's children (see Figure 4.2).[110] The campaign included print advertisements and radio and television public service announcements.[111] At the press conference introducing the campaign, Mayor Franklin explained her commitment to the issue of sexual exploitation of girls by recounting how she had been sexually abused by a friend's father when she was nine years old.[112] The print ads ran pro bono in a number of publications, including the *Atlanta Business Chronicle*, and the campaign soon caught the attention of the national press, including *New York Times'* Nicholas Kristof who wrote a column "Girls on the Streets," quoting Mayor Franklin.[113] A private foundation then donated $100,000 to run the ads for two

---

[108] Ibid. 9.  [109] Priebe and Suhr, *Hidden in Plain View*, 36–37.

[110] Shirley Franklin, "Human Trafficking," at shirley-franklin.com/?page_id=732.

[111] Soloflight Design, Case Studies, at www.soloflightdesign.com/casestudies/juvenile_justice_fund .html; Shirley Franklin, Dear John Campaign, April 5, 2009, at www.youtube.com/watch? v=fRsbo6g21hU.

[112] Rose Scott, "A Personal Mission Continues for Shirley Franklin in Combating Trafficking," *WABE* (radio interview) (November 9, 2012).

[113] Nicholas Kristof, "Girls on Our Streets," *New York Times* (May 7, 2009), 33.

FIGURE 4.2 Mayor Shirley Franklin, Dear John ad campaign, Atlanta, Georgia, 2006.[114]

[114] Soloflight Design, The Juvenile Justice Fund Asked for Help, at www.soloflightdesign.com /casestudies/juvenile_justice_fund.html.

years in the city's major publications.[115] The television PSAs, developed with the nonprofit Women in Film and Television Atlanta, won an Emmy award from the Southeast division of the National Academy of Television Arts and Sciences in 2007,[116] which then led the public service directors at three major networks in Atlanta to run the PSAs pro bono for several months.[117] In addition to this public awareness campaign, Franklin generated further media coverage with her effort to pressure Craigslist to remove the erotic services section of their website. Based on findings from the 2005 study that many trafficked girls were advertised on the internet, Franklin wrote a letter to Craigslist, requesting that they cease posting ads for under-aged girls. A front-page story in the *Atlanta Journal Constitution*, and subsequent *New York Times* coverage, propelled Franklin into the national spotlight.[118]

The campaign against the commercial sexual exploitation of youth in Georgia was a broad-based, innovative effort that included city officials, judges, activists, and community members working collaboratively to raise awareness about the issue and develop solutions. Aspects of this campaign, such as the Dear John ad campaign, were imitated in other states in subsequent years. Whereas the national discourse on youth involved in prostitution focused on white, middle-class girls, the campaign in Georgia centered on the lives of African American girls and girls from working-class and poor communities. In contrast to the national movement, led by white activists, the campaign in Atlanta was led by African American women, including Mayor Shirley Franklin and Judges Hickson and Hatchett. Despite these differences, both movements supported the decriminalization of girls involved in prostitution, the criminal prosecution of the adults involved in prostituting them, building public awareness about the issue, and raising funds to provide services to help youth involved in the sex trade.

## CONCLUSION

The early 2000s was marked by a growing number of activists working on the issue of youth involved in prostitution, and a growing diversity of approaches to the issue. While older groups like the Paul and Lisa Program and Children of the Night continued to thrive, newer organizations like SAGE and GEMS took center stage, and even newer organizations formed. Organizations that centered on youth empowerment like YWEP carved a new niche in the movement, and

---

[115] Stephanie Davis and Michael Shively, *An Overview of Anti-Demand Efforts in Atlanta: Summary Based Upon Research from the Study, "Developing a National Action Plan for Eliminating Sex Trafficking"* (August 16, 2010), 4.

[116] National Academy of Television Arts and Sciences, Southeast Chapter, Outstanding Achievement Television News Programming Excellence (2007), 14.

[117] Davis and Shively, *An Overview of Anti-Demand Efforts in Atlanta*, 4.

[118] Ibid. 2. Franklin continued to work on the issue of child sex trafficking after she left office in 2010. Scott, "A Personal Mission Continues for Shirley Franklin in Combating Trafficking."

the sex worker advocacy group, the Urban Justice Center's Sex Work Project, began helping youth in the sex trade. These latter groups brought a harm reduction approach to the problem. In addition to expanding activism, this period was also marked by the growing voices of youth survivor activists like Leisa B., who shared their stories with legislators and the public.

Some activists attempted to leverage the TVPA to argue for increased attention to domestic youth involved in the sex trade by framing this involvement as domestic sex trafficking. They argued that children were prostituted not only abroad, but in the United States as well, and they condemned the fact that youth were often criminalized while the adults who bought and sold them were not held accountable. Activists worked at the state and federal levels during these years in order to gain recognition for the problem of juveniles involved in prostitution and for more resources to address the needs of these youth.[119] Advocates argued that youth involved in prostitution were victims, not delinquents, and that the adults buying and selling children's bodies should be criminally prosecuted for sexual abuse. They succeeded in convincing Congress to include support for domestically trafficked youth in the 2005 reauthorization of the TVPA, which defined youth involved in prostitution as victims of domestic sex trafficking and allocated funds for pilot projects to provide services to youth. The organizations that had worked to pass the TVPA could finally directly benefit from it, helping them to grow their programs and provide services to more girls.

Common themes for the commercial sexual exploitation of youth in the early 2000s were framing the issue as a hidden problem that must be revealed and as an issue affecting "our children" – meaning white, American, middle-class suburban girls, not only youth in Southeast Asia, or poor girls of color in US cities. The issue was framed as a matter of "lost innocence" – young naïve girls, being taken advantage of by violent and manipulative men. Some, however, were critical of these framings. In 2005, Rachel Lloyd questioned why stories about "some poor little white girls from Kansas kidnapped by some older bad black pimp and taken to another big bad city like New York or Los Angeles are supposed to bring change ... as opposed to an African American girl who's grown up in her own neighborhood, whose aunt was probably a prostitute, whose father or cousin may be a pimp, and she's working four blocks down the street from where her mother lives."[120] Rachel Lloyd criticized the *Newsweek* article, "This Could Be Your Kid," because it "dismissed the real

---

[119] Some have criticized the anti-trafficking movement and law enforcement for focusing too much on sex trafficking to the neglect of labor trafficking. Peters, *Responding to Human Trafficking*, 90–126. Others have criticized the redirection of resources away from labor trafficking toward domestic minor sex trafficking. Denise Brennan, "Competing Claims of Victimhood? Foreign and Domestic Victims of Trafficking in the United States," *Sexuality Research & Social Policy: Journal of NSRC* 5.4 (December 2008), 52–53.

[120] Friedman, *Who Is There to Help Us?* 26.

issues of commercial sexual exploitation, such as race, poverty, homelessness, abuse, ineffective city systems, and a public policy that blames the victims."[121] In the years following, Lloyd would become a strong voice for these "less sympathetic" youth involved in the sex trade and a powerful critic of the social systems that allowed these youth to fall through the cracks.

[121] Lloyd, *Girls Like Us*, 44.

# 5

## To Rescue or Empower: Building a Collaborative Adversarial Movement

Testimony at two Congressional hearings on child prostitution and sex trafficking – one in February of 2010 before the House Subcommittee on Human Rights and the Law, and another in September of the same year before the Senate Subcommittee on Crime, Terrorism and Homeland Security – represented increasingly divergent framings of youth involvement in the sex trade within the movement. In February, a young African American survivor named Shaquana from New York City testified about how at age fourteen she met a man in her neighborhood who at first "seemed like a complete gentleman," but who later psychologically manipulated and physically abused her to sell her body. Shaquana described how she was arrested, sent to juvenile detention, and received no counseling. She was eventually mandated to GEMS when she got out of jail, but didn't manage to leave her abuser until two years later, when she was sixteen, after being beaten and nearly killed by a man who hired her for sex. Shaquana described how she went back to school, graduating valedictorian of her class at Brownsville Academy High School, went to college, and was working at GEMS as an educator and outreach worker. She concluded, the "commercially sexually exploited need support, not jail."[1]

At the hearing before the Senate subcommittee a few months later, Linda Smith of Shared Hope International testified about a girl she had "saved," whom she described as "a little Sunday school girl, hadn't even had a boyfriend," who was abducted on her thirteenth birthday and trafficked. Smith emphasized the girl's religion: "this little girl was – I call her a little church girl. Her whole week the week before she was abducted was going to church, going to Sunday school, going to youth group." The girl, whom she called Lacey, was coerced with threats of harm to her younger siblings. Smith

---

[1] *In Our Own Backyard: Child Prostitution and Sex Trafficking in the United States, A Hearing Before the United States Senate Judiciary Subcommittee on Human Rights and Law.* 111th Cong., 2nd Sess. (February 24, 2010) [hereinafter *In Our Own Backyard Hearing, 2010*], 19.

testified that Lacey was rescued when she was fifteen and was now "in protection."[2]

These two testimonies represent the disparate ways that the issue of youth involvement in the sex trade was framed by activists by 2010. The first was a story of victimization but also survival and empowerment – a woman telling her story of her long struggle to escape prostitution and rebuild her life. The second was a story of victimization and rescue – an adult telling a story of saving and protecting an innocent, vulnerable, and voiceless child. This chapter will describe how the movement against the US youth sex trade broadened and diversified between 2005 and 2010, embracing divergent stories about trafficking and acting as a collaborative adversarial movement that leveraged the international sex trafficking framework to place involvement of US youth in the sex trade on the public agenda.

This period was marked by the increasing presence of evangelical Christian activists and men within the movement against domestic sex trafficking. Under George W. Bush, the US government channeled significant federal funds toward faith-based anti-trafficking organizations, like Shared Hope International, which expanded their voice within the movement.[3] More generally in society, the politicization of white evangelical Christians expanded as the gay and lesbian rights movement began to win same-sex marriage rights in the United States and the American people elected the first African American president, Barack Obama, in 2008. In response, the Tea Party Movement emerged, energizing the right wing and accelerating conflict on a range of culture war issues like gay rights, abortion, social welfare programs, and race relations in the United States. Child prostitution was an issue like few others that could unite people across the political divide, although for varying reasons. Evangelical Christians organized around the issue as an example of the sexual revolution run amok whereas women's rights advocates framed the issue as a matter of male dominance, violence against women, and racism. Despite these differences, activists came together to support policy initiatives before Congress and in state legislatures.

## EXPANSION AND DIVERSIFICATION OF ACTIVISM AGAINST CHILD SEX TRAFFICKING

Contrasting frames for youth involvement in prostitution sprung from the increasingly ideologically diverse movement against the US youth sex trade as it expanded significantly between 2005 and 2010. More groups formed to

---

[2] *Domestic Minor Sex Trafficking, A Hearing Before the United States House Judiciary Subcommittee on Crime, Terrorism and Homeland Security*, 111th Cong., 2nd Sess. (September 25, 2010) [hereinafter *Domestic Minor Sex Trafficking Hearing, 2010*], 114.

[3] Nicole Footen Bromfield, *The Hijacking of Human Trafficking Legislation During Its Creation: A U.S. Public Policy Study* (Saarbrücken, Germany: VDM Verlag Dr. Müller, 2010), 175–177.

address the issue, and these groups had a wider array of perspectives and strategies. The movement encompassed liberal, moderate, and evangelical Christians, human rights and feminist groups, sex worker advocates, service providers, and youth empowerment groups. Some of these groups were abolitionist – they advocated for the abolition of the sex trade – while others supported the decriminalization of sex work for adults. Many had a law and order approach to the issue, calling for expanded arrest and prosecution of adults facilitating youth involvement in the sex trade. Some had a human rights approach to trafficking, analyzing the issue as part of a broader system of economic and social injustices. Some adopted a harm reduction approach to services, while others advocated a more protectionist approach. Some worked with law enforcement while others refused to.

With increasing support from federal, state, city, and private funders, organizations working with youth involved in prostitution were able to expand their services and increase their public education efforts. Children of the Night continued to run their shelter and on-site school in California, and the Paul and Lisa Program continued its street outreach, prevention education, and community-based court rehabilitation program. In 2006, Frank Barnaba created the Barnaba Institute to focus on public education, professional training seminars, and outreach to at-risk youth and young adults.[4] Barnaba was a leader in the campaign to pass a safe harbor law in Connecticut in 2010, working with ECPAT USA, Love146, and several Connecticut children's advocacy organizations. Both SAGE and Breaking Free created shelters for youth with specialized services in 2005 and 2006 respectively. In October of 2005, Hotaling helped to open SAGE House and Edgewood Academy, a six-room safe house in San Francisco for girls trying to leave prostitution.[5] SAGE worked with youth mandated to the program by the criminal justice and child welfare systems. SAGE provided a Life Skills Program for girls that met weekly. SAGE also provided outreach and training to law enforcement, service providers, and the community with funding from the federal government's Office for Victims of Crime. In 2006, Breaking Free opened a six-bedroom shelter in east St. Paul, called House of Hope. The same year, the mayor of St. Paul declared November 2 Breaking Free Day to honor the tenth anniversary of the organization.[6] Breaking Free also had a longer-term residence, a monthly john school to educate men arrested for solicitation, and a drop-in center on University Avenue in Minneapolis. Trudee Able-Peterson, now at Streetworks Outreach Collaborative for Homeless Youth in Minneapolis, continued her

[4] Barnaba Institute, About the Institute, at http://barnabainstitute.org/wordpress/?page_id=2.
[5] Norma Hotaling, "Sex for Sale: The Commercial Sexual Exploitation of Women and Girls: A Service Provider's Perspective," *Yale Journal of Law and Feminism* 18 (2006), 188. City funding cuts forced the house to close in 2007.
[6] Julian Sher, *Somebody's Daughter: The Hidden Story of America's Prostituted Children and the Battle to Save Them* (Chicago, IL: Chicago Review Press, 2011), 101.

harm reduction work with homeless youth and published a best practices manual in 2006.[7]

Hotaling and Carter, along with Kathleen Mitchell of the Catholic Charities' DIGNITY Program in Phoenix and Kristy Child of Veronica's Voice in Kansas City (both of whom served adult survivors of prostitution), founded the Survivor Services Education and Empowerment Network (SSEEN), a network of survivor-centered service providers.[8] The network was formed to "establish a strong foundation for a national movement of survivors who can combat commercial sexual exploitation by drawing on their own experiences to inform their work."[9] SSEEN opposed the distinction between prostitution and sex trafficking, arguing that all prostitution was coercive whether or not women appeared to be consenting, and supported prosecuting buyers as sex traffickers.[10]

In addition to her 2005 Congressional testimony, Hotaling published articles and spoke out in community and academic settings calling for systemic change to address the root causes of the commercial sexual exploitation of women and girls. At a 2006 symposium, "Sex for Sale," at Yale Law School, Hotaling argued, "we need to direct sustained attention to all the social causes of prostitution, including but not limited to: gaping problems in our social response to child abuse within families; extreme poverty; outdated legal doctrines and practices; gender inequality; racial stratification; and the horrifying societal tolerance for the notion that prostituted individuals are without value or legal and moral rights."[11] She argued for a redefinition of child prostitution as a matter of child safety and called for criminal prosecution of adults who sexually abuse children, including registration as sex offenders, as well as for resources for rehabilitation of children rather than criminal prosecution. She argued that services should not be contingent on victims testifying against their abusers. Finally, she called for "survivor-run programs that address the social, political, and economic contexts of clients' lives."[12]

---

[7] Trudee Able-Peterson and Richard A. Hooks Wayman, *Streetworks: Best Practices and Standards in Outreach Methodology to Homeless Youth* (Minneapolis, MN: StreetWorks Collaborative, 2006).

[8] Kristy Child founded Veronica's Voice in Kansas City in 2000 in honor of her friend Veronica Neverdusky, who had experienced commercial sexual exploitation and was murdered in 1993. Veronica's Voice, Our Story, at www.veronicasvoice.org/#!our-story/c1dcq. In the 1990s, survivor Kathleen Mitchell founded DIGNITY, with the support of Catholic Charities. Andrea Aker, "Prevailing Over Prostitution," *Kronkitezine* (Spring 2008).

[9] Hotaling, "Sex for Sale," 189.

[10] *Exploiting Americans on American Soil: Domestic Trafficking Exposed, Hearing on H.R. 972 before the Commission on Security & Cooperation in Europe*, 109th Cong., 1st Sess. (June 7, 2005) [hereinafter *Exploiting Americans on American Soil Hearing, 2005*], 30, 65 (testimony of Norma Hotaling).

[11] Hotaling, "Sex for Sale," 188.

[12] Ibid. 189; see also *Exploiting Americans on American Soil Hearing, 2005, 75*.

Norma Hotaling's analysis made an important intellectual and political contribution to the movement, but it was Rachel Lloyd's work at GEMS that would bring the issue to a wider, mainstream audience through film, music, and social media. In 2007, Lloyd produced a feature-length documentary titled *Very Young Girls* about the lives of the girls served by GEMS, most of whom were young African Americans.[13] The film received favorable reviews, including in the *New York Times,* and was widely distributed through Showtime and Netflix. In 2009, GEMS created a public awareness campaign called "Girls Are Not For Sale," that used the film as well as Facebook, Twitter, and YouTube to raise awareness about the commercial sexual exploitation of girls (see Figure 5.1). The campaign produced public service announcements, music videos, and other media.[14] In support of GEMS, Sinead O'Connor and Mary J. Blige recorded a song for GEMS, *This Is to Mother You,* which O'Connor performed on the David Letterman Show.[15] GEMS obtained support from celebrities, including from Demi Moore, Halle Berry, and Beyoncé Knowles, who became part of a network of supporters called the "Council of Daughters." In addition to public education, GEMS conducted training for law enforcement and service providers, and offered assistance to organizations around the country.

While SAGE, Breaking Free, and GEMS embraced an "abolitionist" politics – supporting the eradication of the sex trade altogether – and worked closely with law enforcement, YWEP developed their radical, transformative justice approach to youth in the sex trade during this period. YWEP continued their peer-based support services, drop-in center, and youth-run syringe exchange program, but they also initiated several participatory action research projects in order to understand how to help youth in the sex trade and street economy. Following a long tradition of social movements challenging expert knowledge, YWEP's research constructed new knowledge about youth in the sex trade based on the experiences and interpretation of the youth themselves.[16] YWEP then used their research to guide their social justice campaigns. Their first research project, which occurred in 2006 and was funded by the Cricket Island Foundation's Capacity Building Initiative, investigated the effectiveness of harm reduction on their outreach contacts, as well as who were girls' allies and how girls responded to other girls in leadership.[17] Their second project

[13] *Very Young Girls,* dir. David Schisgall and Nina Alvarez, Swinging T Productions, 2007.

[14] GEMS PSA, May 29, 2007, at www.youtube.com/watch?v=T7Z69YTPTHA; GEMS, Music and Video, at www.gems-girls.org/media-center/music.

[15] Sinéad O'Connor, "This Is to Mother You" (Live on Letterman), October 12, 2011, at www .youtube.com/watch?v=kPo-HWWmXBU.

[16] Nancy Whittier, *The Politics of Child Sexual Abuse: Emotion, Social Movements and the State* (New York, NY: Oxford University Press, 2009), 54.

[17] Young Women's Empowerment Project, *Girls Do What They Have To Do To Survive: Illuminating Methods Used by Girls in the Sex Trade and Street Economy to Fight Back and Heal* (Chicago, IL: Young Women's Empowerment Project, 2009), 16.

FIGURE 5.1 Image used to promote GEMS Youth Leadership Program in 2012.

researched what kind of institutional and individual violence girls in the sex trade experienced, how they resisted this violence, and how they could unite and fight back. They wanted to find out how girls took care of themselves without relying on systems that harm and oppress them, and how they rely on each other for support. Their data collection methods included ethnographic observations by their outreach workers, feedback from popular education workshops, and focus groups.

In their first research report, published in 2009, YWEP directly challenged expert authority, stating, "This research is a response to all of those researchers, doctors, government officials, social workers, therapists, journalists, foster care workers and every other adult who said we were too messed up or that we needed to be saved from ourselves." They emphasized that their research was "created by girls, collected by girls, and analyzed by girls" because "who knows us better than us?"[18] In their research, girls played an active role in developing both theory and practice about the causes and solutions for exploitation of youth in the sex trade. They criticized existing research for only viewing girls as powerless and as victims. Their research, by contrast, focused on girls' resilience and resistance to violence, how they fight back and recover from experiences of violence. They also criticized existing research for focusing on harm from individuals, especially facilitators and buyers, whereas they wanted to focus

[18] Ibid., 5.

on harm from institutions and social services, especially police, health care providers, and child protective services.

The main findings were that institutions often refused to help girls, making individual violence worse, but that healing through self-care and community building among girls enabled them to resist and fight back. As a result of this report, YWEP organized the "Street Youth Rise Up Campaign" – a youth-led campaign to "change the way Chicago sees and treats its homeless, home-free and street-based youth for doing what they have to do to survive" (see Figure 5.2).[19] Building on their 2009 participatory action research, the campaign had four components: The Bad Encounter Line, Chicago Street Youth in Motion, Healing in Action, and media projects. The Bad Encounter Line was a participatory action research project into the negative experiences youth have with institutions. They published their results in zines and in a research report in 2012, which was based on 146 reports collected between 2009 and 2012.[20] YWEP publicized the report through a street march in Chicago on September 30, 2011, with seventy-five youth and fifteen adult allies. After a two-mile march through the streets of Chicago, organizers held a speak out and announced the release of its Bad Encounter Line report. The march received coverage on Chicago Public Radio, which interviewed YWEP leader C. Angel Torre.[21] The Chicago Street Youth in Motion was a city-wide task force for street-based youth that developed a Street Youth Bill of Rights[22] outlining youth rights in four areas – health care, education, police, and social services. The campaign asked institutional representatives to sign on to the bill of rights and change their policies to be in compliance with it, which several organizations did.[23] Healing in Action taught youth how to take care of themselves outside institutional health care through workshops and a magazine.[24] YWEP taught girls to do their own self-exams, including how to use speculums, and to do breast, anal, and testicular checks. YWEP's self-care philosophy was based on their core principle that girls know what is best for themselves and their research finding that health care providers

[19] YWEP, "Our Campaign," at https://ywepchicago.wordpress.com/our-work/our-campaign/.

[20] YWEP, *Bad Encounter Line Zine #1 and #3*, at https://ywepchicago.files.wordpress.com/2011/07/bel-zine-13.pdf; YWEP, *Denied Help! How Youth in the Sex Trade & Street Economy Are Turned Away from Systems Meant to Help Us & What We Are Doing to Fight Back* (Chicago, IL: Young Women's Empowerment Project, 2012).

[21] Interview with C. Angel Torre, Vocalo, Chicago Public Radio, at https://ywepchicago.files.wordpress.com/2011/10/interview-with-c-angel.mp3.

[22] Chicago Street Youth in Motion Task Force, Street Youth Bill of Rights, at www.usprisonculture.com/blog/wp-content/uploads/2011/09/finalized-strret-youth-bill-of-rights.pdf.

[23] Kari Lydersen, "Youth Sex Workers Organize for Their Rights," *Working In These Times* (June 19, 2012).

[24] YWEP, *Universal Self-Exam*, at https://ywepchicago.files.wordpress.com/2011/07/universal-self-exam.pdf; YWEP, *Healing in Action Zine*, at https://ywepchicago.files.wordpress.com/2011/06/healing-in-action-zine.pdf.

FIGURE 5.2 Young Women's Empowerment Project, Street Youth Rise Up! campaign image (artwork by Cristy C. Road).

often interfered with girls' ability to heal. YWEP's media project publicized YWEP's research findings and campaign work.[25]

YWEP differed significantly from SAGE, Breaking Free, and GEMS in that they did not unilaterally condemn the sex trade, even for youth, but instead focused their critiques on the systems that abused youth and made them vulnerable to exploitation, and actively attempted to reform those institutions through research, accountability training, and direct pressure. Their empowerment approach differed from these other organizations by focusing on strategies like youth-led participatory action research, self-help strategies, and harm reduction approaches. Similar to the child sexual abuse survivors' movement, which "focused considerable attention on constructing new knowledge specifically aimed at challenging the expert knowledge that maintained the status quo,"[26] YWEP had an explicit strategy of creating new knowledge that challenged expert knowledge about youth involved in prostitution through their participatory action research. YWEP resisted the pathologization of youth involved in the sex trade, instead focusing on the

[25] Noy Thrupkaew, "A Misguided Moral Crusade," *New York Times* (September 22, 2012), SR 14.
[26] Whittier, *The Politics of Child Sexual Abuse*, 54.

ways that the systems that were supposed to help youth were in fact failing them. Other movement actors explained youth's inability to leave abusive relationships by making parallels to domestic violence[27] or by framing these relationships in terms of trauma bonding, involving "strong emotional ties that develop between two persons where one person intermittently harasses, beats, threatens, abuses, or intimidates the other."[28] By reframing participation in the sex trade as a survival strategy for youth, YWEP activists challenged common beliefs as well as professional knowledge that pathologized them.

SAGE, Breaking Free, GEMS, and YWEP grew significantly between 2005 and 2010, albeit in differing directions, and many new service providers joined them. In 2006, Nola Brantley, Adela Hernandez Rodarte, Sarai T. Smith-Mazariegos, and Emily Hamman founded MISSSEY (Motivating, Inspiring, Supporting & Serving Sexually Exploited Youth), a survivor-led, survivor-informed nonprofit organization serving mainly girls in Oakland, California.[29] Across the country, Sandy Skelaney founded Project GOLD at Kristi House Child Advocacy Center in Miami, Florida, in 2007[30] and survivor Tina Frundt founded Courtney's House in Washington, DC, in 2008.[31]

On the policy side, a major new player in the campaign against the US youth sex trade was Shared Hope International (SHI), an organization founded in 1998 in Vancouver, Washington, by Republican Representative Linda A. Smith to combat international sex trafficking. In 2005, Shared Hope began working on child sex trafficking within the United States.[32] Smith began her political career in 1983 in Washington State's House of Representatives, later serving in the Washington State Senate. She was well-known for her opposition to abortion and gay rights. She was elected to the US House of Representatives in 1995, serving there until 1999, when she ran unsuccessfully for a seat in the US Senate.[33] In 1998, after visiting the brothel district of Falkland Road in

[27] *In Our Own Backyard Hearing, 2010,* 15.

[28] Donald G. Dutton and Susan L. Painter, "Traumatic Bonding: The Development of Emotional Attachments in Battered Women and Other Relationships of Intermittent Abuse," *Victimology: An International Journal* 1:4 (1981), 139–155.

[29] MISSSEY, Mission/Beliefs/Demands, at http://misssey.org/about-us/mission-beliefs/.

[30] Kristi House, Chronology and Milestones, at www.kristihouse.org/kristi-house-chronology-and-milestones/. Skelaney had interned at ECPAT International while earning a Master's degree at Yale University in International Relations and later worked for GEMS in New York City, where she helped organize the first national summit for commercially sexually exploited youth, *Breaking the Silence,* in 2003. Interview with Sandy Skelaney, May 27, 2016 (on file with author).

[31] Courtney's House, Who We Are, at www.courtneyshouse.org/who-we-are.html.

[32] Another organization that started working on child sex trafficking in Southeast Asia but has expanded to include work in the United States is Love146, which does prevention education, professional training, research, advocacy, and survivor care programs in Connecticut and Houston. Love146, About US Survivor Care, at https://love146.org/programs/u-s-survivor-care/.

[33] "Linda Smith," *Biographical Directory of the United States Congress,* at http://bioguide.congress.gov/scripts/biodisplay.pl?index=S000587.

Mumbai, India, and encountering women and children in prostitution, Smith founded Shared Hope International with the goal of eradicating sex trafficking. SHI is a Christian organization with an explicit statement of faith that supports biblical infallibility, which has shaped the ideology and rhetoric of the organization.[34] SHI initially focused primarily on international sex trafficking. The organization supported shelter and services for survivors of international sex trafficking in the US and around the world, conducted research, training, and public education, and engaged in public policy advocacy. In 2001, Smith created the War Against Trafficking Alliance (WATA) to coordinate regional and international efforts to combat sex trafficking. In 2003, WATA and the US Department of State co-sponsored a World Summit on sex trafficking with one hundred and fourteen nations participating.

SHI turned to domestic sex trafficking in 2005 when the organization received funding from the US Department of State Office to Monitor and Combat Trafficking in Persons to conduct a study comparing sex trafficking and sex tourism markets in Japan, Jamaica, the Netherlands, and the United States.[35] In written testimony submitted at a 2010 Congressional hearing on child sex trafficking, Linda Smith testified that she was "stunned to discover much larger numbers of US citizen and lawful permanent resident minors being exploited through the commercial sex industry" than foreign national women trafficked into the United States.[36] She testified that this research, published in 2007, suggested a "national crisis," so Shared Hope International decided after years of working in other countries to "take action here in the United States."[37] Once SHI decided to focus on "domestic sex trafficking" of youth, the organization received substantial federal funds to conduct research and organize convenings on the issue, leap frogging over organizations and researchers with a much longer history of working on the US youth sex trade, a decision likely due to the appeal of SHI's evangelical orientation to the Bush administration.

With federal funding, SHI produced several influential reports on "domestic minor sex trafficking." In 2006, Shared Hope International teamed up with ECPAT-USA and The Protection Project of the John Hopkins University School of Advanced International Studies to publish a mid-term review of commercial sexual exploitation of children in the United States as a follow up to the Second World Congress Against the Commercial Sexual Exploitation of Children

---

[34] Shared Hope International, Statement of Faith, at https://sharedhope.org/about-us/our-mission-and-values/statement-of-faith/.

[35] Linda Smith was an evangelical Christian, which might explain why the Bush administration selected SHI to do this research, despite the fact that they were a relatively new organization and did not have any experience working on the domestic youth sex trade.

[36] *In Our Own Backyard Hearing*, 2010, 82.

[37] Shared Hope International, *Demand. A Comparative Examination of Sex Tourism and Trafficking in Jamaica, Japan, the Netherlands, and the United States* (Vancouver, WA: Shared Hope International, 2007); *In Our Own Backyard Hearing*, 2010, 83.

which occurred in 2001 in Yokohama, Japan.[38] As part of this mid-term review, these organizations sponsored a conference from April 3–4, 2006, in Washington, DC, bringing together over one hundred and twenty people, including government agency representatives, law enforcement officials, academics, private industry representatives, and non-governmental organization leaders. Organizations across the ideological spectrum participated, from YWEP to Focus on the Family. Many service providers like GEMS, SAGE, the Paul and Lisa Program, and Covenant House attended. Norma Hotaling spoke on a panel about supply and demand, and Rachel Lloyd participated on a panel about child trafficking. The meeting participants engaged in discussions on trafficking, prostitution, pornography, sex tourism, and supply and demand of children.

The conference resulted in a report with five recommendations: address demand through prevention and criminal prosecution; address the proliferation of child pornography, especially online; develop more effective and secure services for victims, especially shelter; increase cooperation between civil society and local and federal law enforcement; and further develop legislation, including decriminalizing exploited minors, reforming child protective services to address the needs of CSEC victims, raising the upper age for protection of child victims, and prosecuting all adult exploiters, including those who purchase sex from minors. The report distinguished child trafficking and child prostitution, the former involving international victims and the latter involving US citizens – a distinction that would later be abandoned in the movement. The report emphasized the importance of "educating public defenders and judges to view prostituted children as victims as opposed to criminals."[39]

In subsequent years, SHI became an aggressive campaigner for legal change relating to the commercial sexual exploitation of youth. In 2009, SHI published an influential report, *Domestic Minor Sex Trafficking: America's Prostituted Children*,[40] which assessed the incidence of commercial sexual exploitation of youth in ten cities across the United States and the community responses. Linda Smith introduced this report into the Congressional record when she testified before a Senate subcommittee in 2010. For a popular audience, Smith published in 2009 a book on child sex trafficking in the form of a novel, titled *Renting Lacey*, with explanatory commentary inserted throughout the text.[41] Beginning in 2010, SHI began the "Protected Innocence Challenge," a project that monitored each state's progress in passing anti-trafficking laws, issuing

---

[38] Shared Hope International, ECPAT-USA, and the Protection Project of the John Hopkins School of Advanced International Studies, *Report from the U.S. Mid-Term Review on the Commercial Sexual Exploitation of Children in America* (2006).

[39] Ibid. 15.

[40] Linda A. Smith, Samantha Healey Vardaman, and Melissa A. Snow, *Domestic Minor Sex Trafficking: America's Prostituted Children* (Vancouver, WA: Shared Hope International, 2009).

[41] Linda A. Smith with Cindy Coloma, *Renting Lacy: A Story of America's Prostituted Children* (Vancouver, WA: Shared Hope International, 2009).

"report cards" for each state similar to how the Department of State evaluated and ranked countries around the world in its annual Trafficking in Persons Report.[42] SHI evaluated whether states criminalized domestic minor sex trafficking, enhanced law enforcement and criminal justice tools to aid in investigations and prosecutions, and provided protection for child victims, including passing safe harbor laws.[43] From 2009 to 2011, SHI also conducted field assessments of service delivery to exploited youth in ten states and territories. Since these early reports, SHI has produced multiple reports each year monitoring legal developments, service provision to minors, and prosecution of people who buy sex from youth. In addition to research, SHI provided extensive training resources for law enforcement, social service workers, and the public, they developed a prevention program called "Chosen" to educate youth about sex trafficking, and they engaged in protests to "end demand" (see Figure 5.3).

SHI's work had a major impact on the growing movement to pass safe harbor laws, as well as the push for increasing punishment of facilitators and buyers. As opposed to the empowerment approach of groups like GEMS and YWEP, SHI used a rescue and protect approach. In their programs and rhetoric, they focused almost exclusively on cisgender girls, whom they framed as young, innocent, and vulnerable, as Linda Smith had in her Congressional testimony in 2010. They framed the issue in terms of protecting girls' innocence and saving them from exploitation. Much of the language they used and the way they framed the issue reflected Smith's religious orientation.

Another strand of activism that formed at this time was men organizing against sex trafficking. Shared Hope International created a program for men called The Defenders USA in June of 2006. Describing themselves as "the men of Shared Hope," The Defenders opposed all forms of commercialized sex. They asked men to pledge not engage in commercial sex, to promise to hold their friends "accountable for their actions toward women and children," and to "take immediate action to protect those I love from this destructive market."[44] Seeking to "reveal the link between pornography and demand" for commercial sexual services, The Defenders USA encouraged men to engage in "moral supervision" over other men by encouraging them to say no to commercial sex.[45]

---

[42] Shared Hope International, What We Do, at https://sharedhope.org/what-we-do/.
[43] Shared Hope International and American Center for Justice and Law, *Protected Innocence Legislative Framework: Methodology* (Vancouver, WA: Shared Hope International, 2010) and *Protected Innocence States Report Card* at https://sharedhope.org/what-we-do/bring-justice /reportcards/.
[44] The Defenders USA, Become a Defender, at http://sharedhope.org/join-the-cause/become-a-defender/.
[45] Shared Hope International et al., *Mid-Term Report*, 26; Shared Hope International, *Demand*, 105.

FIGURE 5.3 Shared Hope International sponsored an "end demand" protest in Las Vegas in June 2009

Another organization focused on men – Truckers Against Trafficking (TAT) – was founded in 2009 in Oklahoma, later moving to Colorado.[46]

---

[46] Truckers Against Trafficking, Who We Are, at www.truckersagainsttrafficking.org/who-we-are/.

FIGURE 5.4 Truckers Against Trafficking Everyday Hero poster.[47]

TAT was formed to educate truckers about sex trafficking and to teach them to recognize and report sex trafficking. TAT, which worked with law enforcement and trucking companies, produced brochures, posters, and decals that their

[47] MATTO, The Story, at http://mattoo.org/the-story-logo/.

members posted at truck stops and on trucks across the country. Another group, Men Against the Trafficking of Others (MATTO), was formed in 2010 in Minnesota to fight trafficking through public education, research, and public policy advocacy.[48] These organizations deployed traditional gendered images of heroic masculinity with men as defenders and saviors of women and girls (see Figure 5.4).[49] Gendered rescue narratives mobilized men to participate in the movement.

Activists from many of these organizations participated in the Third World Congress Against Sexual Exploitation of Children and Adolescents, which took place in Rio De Janeiro, Brazil, in November of 2008. Before the Congress, US and Canadian government officials and activists met from October 2–3, 2008, in Arlington, Virginia, for the Canada–United States Consultation in Preparation for World Congress III Against Sexual Exploitation of Children and Adolescents, hosted by Shared Hope International.[50] Government officials included members of the US Departments of State, Justice, Education, Health and Human Services, and Homeland Security. Activists attending included Carol Smolenski of ECPAT-USA, Shared Hope International's Linda Smith, who opened the meeting, Sandy Skelaney from Kristi House, Katherine Mullen of Legal Aid-New York City (who led New York's Safe Harbor Act campaign), Karen McLaughlin of the Boston Human Trafficking Task Force, Lina Nealon of Hunt Alternatives Fund, and representatives from the Protection Project, National Center on Missing and Exploited Children, Adults Saving Kids, Global Health Promise, Lutheran Immigration and Refugee Services, and The National Crime Prevention Council.

The Third World Congress, organized by ECPAT-International, UNICEF, and the NGO Group for the Convention on the Rights of the Child, was attended by one hundred and thirty eight governments, with over four thousand participants and nearly three hundred children and youth from ninety-four countries.[51] After four days of workshops, plenary sessions, speeches, panel discussions, and presentations, the Congress adopted the *Rio de Janeiro Pact to Prevent and Stop Sexual Exploitation of Children and Adolescents*, known as the Rio Pact, with a declaration and plan of action.[52]

---

[48] Carrie N. Baker, "Moving Beyond 'Slaves, Sinners, and Saviors': An Intersectional Feminist Analysis of U.S. Sex Trafficking Discourse, Law and Policy," *Journal of Feminist Scholarship* 4 (Spring 2013).

[49] Truckers Against Trafficking at www.truckersagainsttrafficking.org/get-our-materials/.

[50] Beyond Borders, ECPAT-USA, and Shared Hope International, *Report of the Canada–United States Consultation in Preparation for World Congress III Against Sexual Exploitation of Children and Adolescents*, October 2–3, 2008 (Arlington, VA: Beyond Borders, ECPAT-USA, and Shared Hope International, 2008), 16.

[51] ECPAT International, *ECPAT 25 Years*, 106.

[52] *The Rio de Janeiro Declaration and Call for Action to Prevent and Stop Sexual Exploitation of Children and Adolescents*, November 2008.

Youth delegates issued a separate statement, urging governments to take stronger action to prevent the sexual exploitation of youth.[53] This Congress once again provided an opportunity for US activists to connect with a global community working on commercial sexual exploitation of youth, to share experiences, and to bring back new ideas.

By 2010, many more organizations had become involved in the movement against youth sex trafficking in the United States, incorporating a more diverse array of ideologies and strategies. The movement included evangelical abolitionist public policy organizations like SHI, feminist abolitionist service providers like SAGE and Breaking Free, youth empowerment groups like GEMS, youth rights collectives like YWEP, and men's educational organizations like Truckers Against Trafficking. These groups had different constituencies, generating a broad base of support, and they used a wide range of strategies to advance their cause, including lobbying and litigation; public education through media, music and theater; training of professionals, including law enforcement, social workers, and health care workers; legal research and participatory action research; and services provision and leadership training.

This proliferation of diverse groups working on commercial sexual exploitation of youth created challenges but also opportunities for the movement. Despite these groups' different ideological and political positions, they still worked together in pursuit of shared goals. Social movement scholar Nancy Whittier has described "the relationships between collaborating, ideologically opposed movements" as *collaborative adversarial movements*.[54] Whereas coalitions rest on "compatible ideology or collective identity" as well as overlapping networks, coordinated actions, shared resources, and agreed-upon frames, collaborative adversarial movements consist of social movement organizations that do not have compatible ideologies, identities, frames, or strategies but may share common specific or even long-term goals for "different reasons and through different specific policies."[55] They are a "mixture of cooperation and conflict," says Whittier. Collaborative adversarial movements entail "reputational risks" to participants such as accusations of "sleeping with the enemy," which may motivate participants to engage in distancing strategies "such as keeping direct cooperation covert or advocating for their goal in different locations or through separate elite allies." These relationships also have the "potential to influence both sides' frames, strategies, or tactics."[56]

---

[53] Neha Bhandari, *Pulling a Face at Sexual Exploitation* (ECPAT, IIDAC, Plan International, Save the Children, UNICEF, Viração, World Vision, 2009), at www.unicef.org/brazil/pt/br_IIIWC_En.pdf.

[54] Nancy Whittier, "Rethinking Coalitions: Anti-Pornography Feminists, Conservatives, and Relationships between Collaborative Adversarial Movements," *Social Problems* 61.2 (2014), 1.

[55] Ibid. 4.  [56] Ibid.

As it grew and diversified, the movement against the US youth sex trade became an adversarial collaborative movement. While advocates often had opposing ideologies, they sometimes had similar goals and were able to work together on particular campaigns. For example, in New York, groups that supported the safe harbor law included abolitionist groups like Coalition Against Trafficking in Women, GEMS, and Polaris Project, but the Sex Workers Project (SWP) also supported the campaign. SWP worked with Polaris Project again a few years later on a bill to vacate prostitution convictions of survivors of trafficking into commercial sex, which was passed by the New York State Assembly in 2010.[57] SWP Executive Director at the time, Sienna Baskin, has noted that even though SWP and Polaris Project might not agree on all issues, she found it useful to work with them to achieve goals about which they did agree, noting that Polaris Project had tremendous clout.[58] Diverse activists later supported federal proposals to allow vacating convictions of trafficking victims.[59] On other issues, SWP differed from the anti-trafficking movement – like its focus on ending demand. In a 2007 position paper, SWP argued that focusing on the factors creating vulnerability to entering the sex trade, like poverty, unemployment, and gender inequality, was a much more effective way to protect the rights of sex workers and trafficked persons than attempting to curb demand.[60]

Another example of collaborative action by groups with adversarial ideological orientations was a 2010 campaign in support of federal legislation on domestic minor sex trafficking. A diverse coalition of organizations submitted a letter to Representatives John Conyers (D-MI) and Lamar Smith (R-TX), ranking members of the House Judiciary Committee, in support of the Domestic Minor Sex Trafficking Deterrence and Victims Support Act of 2010. The coalition included national and state organizations; religious, feminist, and service organizations; as well as several women's funds. For example, Feminist Majority Foundation (FMF) signed on alongside the evangelical Christian organization VineyardUSA and the National District Attorneys Association,

---

[57] Sex Workers Project, New York State Assembly Bill A7670/S4429 Summary, at http://sexworkersproject.org/campaigns/2009/new-york-vacating-convictions-bill/; Interview with Sienna Baskin, April 22, 2016 (on file with author).

[58] Interview with Sienna Baskin, April 22, 2016.

[59] See, for example, the Human Trafficking Survivors Relief and Empowerment Act of 2015, S. 642, 114th Congress (2014–2015) and the Trafficking Survivors Relief Act of 2016, Press Release: Senators Gillibrand, Portman and Blumenthal and US Representatives Wagner, Gabbard, and Jolly Announce Bipartisan Legislation to Clear Criminal Records of Human Trafficking Victims, September 28, 2016, at https://www.gillibrand.senate.gov/news/press/release/senators-gillibrand-portman-and-blumenthal-and-us-representatives-wagner-gabbard-and-jolly-announce-bipartisan-legislation-to-clear-criminal-records-of-human-trafficking-victims.

[60] Emilia Casella, Irene Martinetti, and Stephan Sastrawidjaja, *Critique of Focus on Demand in the Context of Trafficking in Persons: A Position Paper of the Sex Workers Project at the Urban Justice Center* (New York, NY: Urban Justice Center, 2007).

along with anti-trafficking organizations like ECPAT-USA, Polaris Project, and Shared Hope International.[61] On issues like abortion, FMF and SHI would be diametrically opposed, but they could both join together to support this anti-trafficking legislation.

Some scholars have criticized feminists within the anti-trafficking movement for working with conservatives[62] and movement feminists have sometimes explicitly tried to distance themselves from religious factions of the movement. For example, in a review of activism to end demand in Atlanta, feminist Stephanie Davis explained that organizers trying to shift media focus off victims and onto johns struggled with the question of how to "build a campaign that shifts a culture of tolerance [for prostitution] to one of intolerance that is more than a 'Bible-thumping, anti-sex crusade.'"[63] On the issue of pornography, Davis called for "a progressive analysis of pornography and free speech so as not to cross the line into censorship and anti-sex culture."[64] These comments show Davis trying to defend her reputation as a feminist by distinguishing herself from conservatives, while at the same time working alongside them and maintaining a strong critique of prostitution and pornography.

## EXPANDING MEDIA COVERAGE AND PUBLIC AWARENESS

The diversity of the movement, however, often did not appear in the significantly expanding newspaper, magazine, and television coverage of child sex trafficking between 2005 and 2010, which tended to frame the issue in simplistic ways that echoed the lost innocence and rescue narratives propagated by groups like SHI. The proliferation and increasing forms of media coverage raised awareness about the US youth sex trade, but this coverage usually focused on a subset of youth – those whom adults lured or forced into trading sex. This focus contributed to public policies, like the criminal prosecution of third-party facilitators, that addressed the situation of some youth, but ignored many others, like youth independently engaging in "survival sex" because families and social welfare systems had failed to support them.

Media coverage often related to legislative campaigns or criminal justice initiatives against child sex trafficking. The *New York Times* had many articles on child prostitution during this period, including coverage of the ongoing activism in Atlanta in a series of articles by Bob Herbert in 2006 and developments in the campaign for a safe harbor law in New York as well as

---

[61] Ibid. 281–283.
[62] Elizabeth Bernstein, "Militarized Humanitarianism Meets Carceral Feminism: The Politics of Sex, Rights, and Freedom in Contemporary Anti-Trafficking Campaigns," *Signs*, 36 (2010), 45–71.
[63] Stephanie Davis and Michael Shively, *An Overview of Anti-Demand Efforts in Atlanta: Summary Based Upon Research from the Study, "Developing a National Action Plan for Eliminating Sex Trafficking"* (August 16, 2010), 7.
[64] Ibid. 9.

a series of supportive editorials by the *New York Times* editorial board.[65] The periodic FBI Innocence Lost National Initiative raids on brothels across the country always generated a spate of news articles, reporting on how many adult facilitators were arrested and how many youth were "rescued."[66]

Like many activists, media stories juxtaposed international sex trafficking to domestic youth involvement in the sex trade. In addition to his columns on international child sex trafficking, Nicholas Kristof began to publish columns on sex trafficking of US youth within the United States. Kristof argued in a July 2010 column, "There's a misperception in America that 'sex trafficking' is mostly about foreigners smuggled into the US. That exists. But I've concluded that the biggest problem and worst abuses involve not foreign women but home-grown runaway kids."[67] Kristof described several cases of girls violently prostituted by adult men, and portrayed the "typical case" as a rebellious thirteen-year-old who runs away from home because her mother's boyfriend is hitting on her and meets a "pimp" at the bus station, who first seduces her and then violently coerces her into prostitution. To solve this problem, which he described as "21$^{st}$-century slavery," Kristof suggested that police should "go after pimps rather than girls" and prosecute the men buying sex from girls.

Claiming increased numbers of youth involved in commercial sex, media coverage often focused on the lost innocence of girls. A 2005 *US News and World Report* story, "Young Lives for Sale," quoted a Los Angeles police detective saying, "It's like America has lost its innocence. Little girls just aren't little girls anymore."[68] In 2006, *People* magazine published an article about the commercial sexual exploitation of adolescent girls at truck stops. "Nightmare at the Truck Stop" told the story of thirteen-year-old "Summer," a "bubbly, ponytailed girl from Oklahoma City, fond of volleyball and SpongeBob SquarePants," who suffered "hundreds of forced encounters with truckers two or three times her age." The article quoted former Oklahoma US attorney Robert McCampbell saying, "This isn't something that's happening on a distant shore, it's happening right in our communities. A family pulling into one of these truck stops wouldn't know that is going on. The truth is it's happening everywhere."[69] The article also reported on an FBI

---

[65] See, for example, Ian Urbina, "For Runaways on the Street, Sex Buys Survival," *New York Times* (October 27, 2009), A1; Bob Herbert, "Young, Cold and for Sale," *New York Times* (October 19, 2006), A27; Nicholas Confessore, "New Law Shields Children from Prostitution Charges," *New York Times* (September 27, 2008), A2; "Help for Victimized Children," *New York Times* (July 19, 2008), A16.

[66] See, for example, "Suspected Child Prostitutes Rescued in Federal Sweep," *Wall Street Journal* (February 24, 2009), A6.

[67] Nicholas Kristof, "Seduction, Slavery and Sex," *New York Times* (July 15, 2010), A31.

[68] See, for example, Bay Fang, "Young Lives for Sale," *US News and World Report* (October 24, 2005), 30–34.

[69] Alex Tresniowski, "Nightmare at the Truck Stop," *People* 65.17 (May 1, 2006).

Innocence Lost National Initiative sting, "code-named Stormy Nights," resulting in the conviction of fourteen traffickers in Oklahoma. Women's magazines like *Ms.* and *Essence* ran articles and television covered the issue as well, like Linda Smith's appearance on the talk show *Dr. Phil* in 2008 and Katie Couric's 2009 program on CBS, "The Lost Girls," about juvenile prostitution in Las Vegas and a special court set up to address the issue.[70]

In addition to media coverage, two widely distributed, feature-length documentary films brought the issue to many new audiences: *Very Young Girls* released in 2007 and *Playground* released in 2009.[71] *Very Young Girls*, produced by GEMS, circulated through community groups and at colleges, as well as playing on network television and on demand through Showtime. *Playground* circulated among community groups and played on Netflix. These films foregrounded the stories of survivors. While race was not discussed explicitly in either film, *Playground* focused primarily on the story of one white girl, whereas *Very Young Girls* focused mostly on the stories of African American girls. The facilitators portrayed in both films were African American. These films leveraged deeply held cultural beliefs of childhood innocence, as indicated in their titles – *Very Young Girls* and *Playground* – representing the victims of commercial sexual exploitation as young, naïve children. The promotional poster for the film *Very Young Girls*, which focused on older adolescent girls, used an image of a child's dangling feet with Mickey Mouse socks and sneakers (see Figure 5.5a), whereas *Playground* used a drawing of an empty swing set and a discarded toy with a pink background (see Figure 5.5b). These images were a dramatic contrast to YWEP's Street Youth Rise Up campaign image shown in figure 5.2.

These films varied in the degree to which they paid attention to systemic factors like poverty, failing schools, and lack of living wage jobs. Lloyd's film, featuring largely African American survivors, delved into the complex web of problems that lead to the commercial exploitation of girls, including poverty, childhood sexual abuse, and violence, and the failure of those in the criminal-justice system to understand and intervene in the commercial sexual exploitation of girls. The film critiqued how the criminal-justice system contributes to the sexual exploitation of girls by failing to respond to reports of abuse, by failing to investigate and arrest men who exploit girls, and by treating victims as perpetrators. In contrast to *Very Young Girls*, *Playground*, an excerpt from which was played at a hearing before Congress in 2010, explicitly downplayed the role of poverty and did not discuss other social factors. The media generally

[70] Jeannine Amber, "Black Girls for Sale," *Essence* (October 2010), 164; Letitia Campbell, "Selling Our Children," *Sojourners* (August 2010), 22–26; Carrie N. Baker, "Jailing Girls for Men's Crimes," *Ms.* (Summer 2010), 27–31; Shared Hope International on Dr. Phil (October 20, 2008); Katie Couric Reports, *The Lost Girls* (CBS) (July 23, 2009).

[71] *Very Young Girls*, dir. David Schisgall and Nina Alvarez, Swinging T Productions, 2007; *Playground*, dir. Libby Spears, Blueprint Films, Smokehouse Pictures and Sundial Pictures (2009).

FIGURE 5.5A Promotional image for the film *Very Young Girls* (2007).

hewed more closely to the simplistic narratives of *Playground* than the more complicated story of *Very Young Girls*. Increased media coverage about the issue of domestic youth trafficking combined with more extensive efforts of activists to educate the public on the issue to generate greater public awareness and community pressure on government officials to act.

FIGURE 5.5B Promotional image for the film *Playground* (2009).

## A NEW APPROACH: THE PUSH FOR SAFE HARBOR LAWS

Increased public awareness about youth involvement in the sex trade provided fertile ground for campaigns to help these youth. Activists approached the issue with differing strategies and with divergent results. Activists in New York waged a four-year campaign to convince the state legislature to pass the nation's first safe harbor law to divert youth away from prosecution for prostitution toward social services. On the other hand, despite a powerful local movement against child prostitution, activists in Georgia faced religious

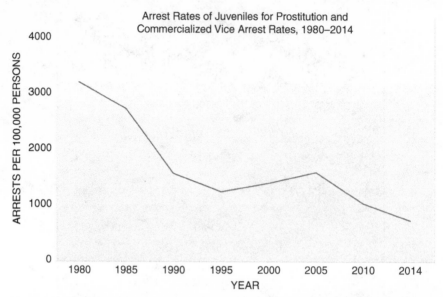

FIGURE 5.6 Arrests of Juveniles for Prostitution and Commercialized Vice, 1980–2014.[72]

opposition to a proposed safe harbor law, which the Georgia legislature declined to adopt. In Texas, activists pursued a different strategy – they filed a legal challenge to the criminal prosecution of a teenager for prostitution, which resulted in a stunning victory before the Texas Supreme Court.

While arrests of juveniles for prostitution decreased precipitously during the 1980s, no doubt due in part to activism against US youth sex trade at the time, the trend reversed in the early 1990s, when prostitution arrests of juveniles began to climb, peaking in 2004 (see Figure 5.6). When Rachel Lloyd arrived in New York in 1997 to work with adult women incarcerated for prostitution, she was shocked to find under-aged girls imprisoned for prostitution at Riker's Island. Then, over time, she noticed the girls were becoming younger and younger.[73] Out of this climate grew the country's first campaign to pass a "safe harbor law."

The campaign was inspired by the 2003 case of twelve-year-old Nicolette R., who was arrested for offering to perform oral sex on an undercover police

---

[72] Howard N. Snyder and Joseph Mulako-Wangota, Bureau of Justice Statistics, *Arrests of Juveniles for Prostitution and Commercialized Vice, 1980-2014* (generated using the Arrest Data Analysis Tool at www.bjs.gov, January 19, 2018). Many more, however, were arrested for other crimes, like drug possession or curfew violation. Michelle Stransky and David Finkelhor, *How Many Juveniles Are Involved in Prostitution in the U.S.?* (Durham, NH: Crimes Against Children Research Center, 2008), 5.

[73] Rachel Lloyd, *Girls Like Us* (New York: Harper Collins, 2011), 1–27.

officer for forty dollars.[74] Despite evidence of sexual and physical abuse as well as involvement of an adult male facilitator, a New York family court judge ruled that Nicolette was delinquent for engaging in prostitution. Katherine Mullen of the New York Legal Aid Society appealed the case, arguing that because of her age she was legally incapable of consenting to participate in a sexual act and that she was a victim, not a perpetrator, of child prostitution. An appellate court affirmed that Nicolette was delinquent, ruling that the plain language of the prostitution law did not limit its application based on age and that New York's statutory rape law setting the age of consent at seventeen was irrelevant to the prostitution law.[75] Angered by the court's decision, Mullen turned to the legislature. In the fall of 2004, a working group with representatives from the Juvenile Rights Practice of the Legal Aid Society of New York, the Juvenile Justice Project of the Correctional Association of New York, and GEMS drafted legislation to require commercially sexually exploited youth to be treated as victims and provided with services rather than being prosecuted.[76] The group arranged for young survivors from GEMS to meet with legislators in Albany to testify about the abuse and neglect that made them vulnerable to exploitation, the violence they experienced from facilitators and buyers, and the stigma and scorn they experienced in the criminal justice system. They convinced legislators to sponsor a bill. According to Mullen and Lloyd, J.R. Drexelius, Jr., Counsel to the Senate Codes Committee, made a "commitment to creating a 'safe harbor' in New York State for children who had been sexually exploited," which was the origin of the name they gave the proposed law.[77]

The first version of the safe harbor bill proposed to amend the penal code to exclude youth under eighteen from prostitution laws, but this met with strong opposition. Law enforcement officials and the Bloomberg administration opposed the bill because they feared that it would make it harder to prosecute prostitution. The mayor's criminal justice coordinator John Feinblatt and others argued for keeping the girls locked up because otherwise they would return to prostitution.[78] District attorneys argued that prosecutors would not be able to threaten youth with prosecution in exchange for their testimony against facilitators. According to Mullen and Lloyd, "some opponents of the

[74] Thomas Adcock, Nicolette's Story, *New York Law Journal* (October 3, 2008), 23–24.

[75] *In re Nicolette R.*, 9 A.D.3d 270 (N.Y. App. Div. 2004); Megan Annitto, "Consent, Coercion, and Compassion: Emerging Legal Responses to the Commercial Sexual Exploitation of Minors," *Yale Law and Policy Review* 30.1 (2011), 34–35.

[76] Katherine Mullen and Rachel Lloyd, "The Passage of the Safe Harbor Act and the Voices of the Sexually Exploited Youth," in Jill Laurie Goodman and Dorchen A. Leidholdt (eds.), *Lawyers' Manual on Human Trafficking: Pursuing Justice for Victims*, 129–140 (New York, NY: Supreme Court of the State of New York, Appellate Division, First Department and the New York State Judicial Committee on Women in the Courts, 2013).

[77] Ibid. 131.

[78] Sher, *Somebody's Daughter*, 254; Annito, "Consent, Coercion and Compassion, 47; Nicholas Confessore," "New Law Shields Children from Prostitution Charges," *New York Times* (September 27, 2008), B2.

bill viewed commercially sexually exploited youth as 'teen hookers' and 'Lolitas' who should be held criminally accountable for their actions."[79]

Instead of modifying the penal code, new versions of the bill attempted to change the definition of juvenile delinquent to exclude youth charged with prostitution and to provide them with services. Some legislators opposed funding for victim counseling and other services because they believed this would be too costly. The bill was redrafted several times and youth survivors continued to speak at legislative hearings, in meetings with individual legislators, and in the press. A wide range of advocacy groups joined the New York State Anti-Trafficking Coalition, including CATW, NOW NYC, ECPAT-USA, Equality Now, Catholic Charities, and the Women's National Republican Club, all lobbying for the bill. The Urban Justice Center's Sex Work Project also supported the passage of New York's safe harbor law. Beginning in 2006, GEMS organized an annual day to End Sexual Exploitation of Children in New York City. The *New York Times* came out in strong support of changing the law. Over time, public support increased. In June of 2007, activists pressured the New York City Council to pass a resolution calling upon state legislators to pass a safe harbor act. Nicolette's attorney Katherine Mullen testified in favor of the safe harbor bill at a hearing before the Council.[80]

The Assembly finally passed the New York State Safe Harbor for Exploited Children Act in 2008, the first of its kind in the nation.[81] The compromise bill that passed created a legal presumption that any person under the age of eighteen who is charged with prostitution is a "severely trafficked person," as defined by the TVPA. The Act required that youth under the age of sixteen be treated as status offenders, which means they were "persons in need of support" (PINS) and entitled to support through the Department of Social Services. However, the Act gave judges discretion to convert a case back into a delinquency proceeding if the minor is unwilling to cooperate with specialized services ordered or court mandates like testifying against facilitators or if the minor has a previous prostitution offense.[82] The law called for the creation of housing and services for exploited youth, but did not

---

[79] Mullen and Lloyd, "The Passage of the Safe Harbor Act and the Voices of the Sexually Exploited Youth," 132.

[80] New York State Anti-Trafficking Coalition, at www.tvpja.com/the-new-york-state-anti-trafficking-coalition.html; Interview with Sienna Baskin, April 22, 2016; Sher, *Somebody's Daughter*, 252; Opinion, "Children in Need of Safe Harbor," *New York Times* (September 15, 2007), A16; Opinion, "Safe Harbor for Exploited Children," *New York Times* (June 5, 2007), A22; *Oversight Hearing Before the Committee for Youth Services and the Committee for Juvenile Justice: New York's Sexual Exploited Youth* (N.Y. City Council, June 11, 2007), 42–43.

[81] Safe Harbor for Exploited Children Act, N.Y. Fam. Ct. Act § 311.4 (McKinney 2008).

[82] In one of the first published decisions to apply the safe harbor act, the New York Family Court refused to convert the charge of prostitution from a delinquency case to a PINS proceeding, using the child's desperate circumstances against her to justify prosecution. The girl in question was first prostituted at the age of twelve, she had no parental support because her parents' rights had

provide any direct funding for services.[83] The law took effect in 2010. Advocates subsequently pressed to expand the safe harbor law to cover sixteen- and seventeen-year-old youth as well.[84]

Soon after New York passed its safe harbor law, other states followed suit, adopting different variations of the law. The next year the state of Washington passed the Sex Crimes Involving Minors Act, which required that a first offense of prostitution for youth under the age of eighteen be diverted out of the juvenile court, although criminal prosecution for subsequent offenses was allowed.[85] Unlike New York, Washington created a fund to support youth involved in the sex trade, including mental health and substance abuse counseling, education and vocational programming, and housing.[86] In 2010, Connecticut totally eliminated criminal liability for minors under the age of sixteen accused of engaging in prostitution and created a rebuttable presumption that sixteen- and seventeen-year-olds charged with prostitution were coerced into committing the offense by another person.[87] Connecticut, like New York, did not fund specialized services for exploited youth. Also in 2010, Illinois enacted a more expansive law by forbidding criminal or juvenile penalties for all minors under the age of eighteen engaging in prostitution and mandating that the state provide such youth with services.[88]

The same year, however, a proposed safe harbor law in Georgia was defeated due to protests by conservative evangelicals who argued that a safe harbor law would legalize child prostitution. Religious groups became increasingly active against the US youth sex trade in the latter part of the decade, but they didn't always agree on how to approach the issue. Between 2005 and 2010, activism in Georgia expanded – with churches, corporations, and governments officials becoming more involved. In 2007, the Atlanta Women's Foundation and the Harold and Kayrita Anderson Family Foundation jointly donated one million dollars to launch, along with the Juvenile Justice Fund, a new organization called "A Future. Not a Past." (AFNAP), which focused on research, prevention, intervention, and education designed to fight demand for commercial sex from youth and to help child victims of sexual exploitation.[89]

---

been terminated, and she had an adult facilitator. *In re Bobby P.*, 907 N.Y.S.2d 540 (N.Y. Fam. Ct. 2010).

[83] N.Y. Fam. Ct. Act § 311.4.

[84] Scott Brinton, "Legislator Wants State to 'Raise the Age,'" *Long Island Herald* (February 1, 2016). At this time, New York was one of two states that prosecuted all sixteen- and seventeen-year-old youth in the justice system as adults, with no exception. These youth were also held in adult prisons, not juvenile detention facilities. The Correctional Association of New York's Juvenile Justice Project led a campaign, Raise the Age NY, to remove all minors from the adult criminal justice system. Raise the Age NY, at http://raisetheageny.com/.

[85] Wash. Rev. Code §13.40.070(7) (2010).    [86] Id. §43.63A.740.

[87] 2010 Conn. Acts 815 (Reg. Sess.); Conn. Gen. Stat. §53a-82(c)(2010).

[88] 2010 Ill. Laws 6931, Public Act 096-1464.

[89] YouthSpark, Our Programs, at http://youth-spark.org/programs/policy-advocacy/a-future-not-a-past/.

In 2008, they commissioned a study of hotel employees[90] and two years later a study of men who buy sex from adolescent girls.[91] AFNAP supported legislation in Georgia to require mandatory reporters to report facilitation of youth involvement in the sex trade by any adult as child abuse, which passed in 2009, and an AFNAP representative testified at Congressional hearings in September of 2010 on legislation to provide funding for victim care and enforcement training. The campaign also developed an accredited law enforcement and prosecutor training program and reached out to the business community by partnering with the National Association of Women Business Owners in Atlanta in 2009 to educate businesses across Atlanta about the problem.[92] Two months later the Westin Hotel of Atlanta became the first hotel to agree to train all their employees about commercial sexual exploitation of youth.

Around the same time, other members of the religious community concerned about the commercial sexual exploitation of youth in Atlanta organized Street Grace.[93] In March of 2007 and January of 2008, Dr. Scott Weimer of North Avenue Presbyterian Church and Rev. Dr. James Milner at Chapel of Christian Love Baptist Church hosted a series of summits for the Atlanta faith-based community on commercial sexual exploitation of children with the goal of assisting nonprofits working on the issue with resources and volunteers. Eight churches collaborated to create Street Grace, which received its 501(c) status in 2009.[94] They formed a speaker's bureau and organized an annual lobby day at the Georgia legislature. They produced a mobilization toolkit called *Out of the Shadows* to help churches and other community groups to organize against commercial sexual exploitation of youth. They sponsored a campaign to support the production of a 30-minute film called *The Candy Shop*. This Tim Burton-style allegory portrayed a young boy rescuing even younger girls from an effeminately portrayed, demonic man who lured innocent girls into his candy factory then turned them into lollipops, which he sold to old men.[95] This film framed heterosexual patriarchy as the solution to child sex trafficking by using a traditional tale of a heroic boy saving girls from a genderqueer trafficker (see Figure 5.7).[96] This film is one of the most extreme examples of a gendered rescue narrative. Street Grace also created an initiative aimed at

[90] Davis and Shively, *An Overview of Anti-Demand Efforts in Atlanta*, 8.

[91] The Shapiro Group, *Men Who Buy Sex with Adolescent Girls: A Scientific Research Study* (Atlanta, GA: The Shapiro Group, 2010).

[92] A Future. Not a Past. "Year-Three Recap" (2010), at http://wp.jjf.glulife.net/wp-content/uploads/2012/06/AFNAP-Year-3-Recap1.pdf.

[93] Street Grace, Mission, at www.streetgrace.org/mission/.

[94] Breauna Hagan, "Street GRACE: Building Partnerships that Save Exploited Kids," Georgia Center for Nonprofits (November 2012), at www.gcn.org/articles/Street-GRACE-Building-Partnerships-that-Save-Exploited-Kids.

[95] *The Candy Shop*, dir. Brandon McCormick, Whitestone Pictures, 2011.

[96] For further discussion, see Baker, "Moving Beyond 'Slaves, Sinners, and Saviors.'"

FIGURE 5.7 Image of trafficker in *The Candy Shop* (2010).

fathers – Fathers Against Child Exploitation (FACE) – with the mission of creating "a generational shift that empowers men of all ages to stand up and protect those most affected by domestic minor sex trafficking."[97] FACE asked men to pledge that they would not buy sex, that they would work to "reverse today's distorted perception of sex," and that they would mentor the next generation to do the same.

---

[97] Street Grace, Fathers Against Child Exploitation, at www.streetgrace.org/face/.

In response to this expansive and diverse movement, the state of Georgia created a new office in 2009 – the Georgia Care Connection Office, located in Decatur – to provide a central location for the coordination of activities of anyone working against the commercial sexual exploitation of youth, including community members, law enforcement, medical personnel, and service providers.[98] In 2010, the Juvenile Justice Fund rebranded itself as YouthSpark Voices and focused on prevention by working with girls deemed at high risk for commercial sexual exploitation. Partnering with the Fulton County Juvenile Court and Probation Department, YouthSpark offered a direct-service, early-intervention program for youth at risk of involvement in the sex trade.[99]

Despite this strong movement, activists were not able to convince the Georgia legislature to pass a safe harbor law in 2010 because of resistance from conservative Christians. A Republican state senator named Renee Unterman introduced a bill that would have offered rehabilitative services rather than jail time to youth under sixteen years old found selling sex. She justified the bill by arguing that arresting and jailing youth would likely make them resistant to cooperating with police investigations. Unterman told *Atlanta-Journal Constitution,* "You put handcuffs on a twelve-year-old kid, put them in the back of a police car, they shut up just like that. But if you get them into therapy, they never have those handcuffs put on them – they're more apt to talk."[100] But the representatives of the Christian Coalition and Concerned Women for America of Georgia argued that decriminalizing youth in prostitution would make the problem worse. The Georgia Christian Coalition, the Georgia Baptist Convention, the Georgia Eagle Forum, Ralph Reed's Faith and Freedom Coalition, and other conservative organizations staged protests and letter writing campaigns, claiming the law would legalize child prostitution and arguing that arresting girls was the best way to get them off the streets and out of the hands of "pimps."[101] In opposing the law, Sue Ella Deadwyler, a conservative Christian activist commented in her newsletter *Georgia Insight,* "some boys and girls know the law, defy the law, and decide to choose prostitution as a way to make money."[102] The bill died that year. The following year, Georgia passed a new law imposing a twenty-five-year

[98] The office is now known as Georgia Cares. Georgia Cares, About Georgia Cares, at www .gacares.org/about.html.

[99] YouthSpark Voices, Early Intervention, at http://youth-spark.org/programs/youth-services-center/voices-early-intervention/.

[100] Sher, *Somebody's Daughter,* 256.

[101] Jim Galloway, "Georgia's Christian Right Comes Out Against Bills Aimed at Child Prostitution," *Atlanta Journal Constitution* (February 1, 2010); Buzz Brockway, "A Bill To Help Child Prostitutes Incorrectly Called 'Legalization' By 'Christian' Opponents," *Peach Pundit* (February 1, 2010).

[102] "Unbelievable: Two Georgia Bills Decriminalize Juvenile Prostitution," *Georgia Insight* (January 2010); "New Version Worse: S.B. 304, Juvenile Prostitution Decriminalized," *Georgia Insight* (February 19, 2010).

minimum sentence for people convicted of trafficking minors under eighteen and mandatory minimum sentences for buyers of sex with minors – five years if the minor is sixteen or seventeen, and ten years if below the age of sixteen. Conservative Christians supported this law, as did politicians in Georgia who were more comfortable with enhancing punishments for facilitators than decriminalizing youth in the sex trade. It would take several more years before Georgia would pass a safe harbor law.

In another state with a strong conservative evangelical presence – Texas – a legislative campaign for a safe harbor law might have met a similar fate, but activists pursued an alternative strategy: they challenged a prostitution conviction of an adolescent girl in court in the case of *In Re B.W.*, described in the introduction.[103] While twelve-year-old Nicolette lost the appeal of her conviction for prostitution, hence sparking the safe harbor act campaign in New York, the Supreme Court of Texas issued a groundbreaking contrary ruling in 2010. The Texas Supreme Court majority ruling reflected changing attitudes toward young people involved in prostitution. Advocates, policymakers and now judges were recognizing the contradiction between statutory rape laws, which treated youth as legally incapable of consenting to sex, and prosecuting youth for prostitution. They also recognized the contradiction between new anti-trafficking laws, which defined youth under the age of eighteen who were involved in commercial sex as victims of a severe form of human trafficking without regard to consent, and the criminal prosecution of minors. Finally, they recognized the double standard of criminally prosecuting youth for prostitution while the adult men who were buying sex from them and their adult facilitators were not being prosecuted. The facts of the *In Re B.W.* case vividly exposed these contradictions – the criminal prosecution of a thirteen-year-old girl exploited by a thirty-two-year-old man, who was not even investigated, in a state with a statutory rape law that set the age of consent at fourteen. This ruling was an important sign of changing times. *In Re B.W.*, however, only applied to minors under the age of fourteen, leaving older teens vulnerable to criminal prosecution. Therefore, advocates for commercially sexually exploited youth in Texas turned to lobbying for a safe harbor law, which they would achieve several years later.

Campaigns for safe harbor laws in New York, Georgia, and Texas illustrate how activists used varying tactics with varying results. Arguments that youth involved in prostitution were victims of manipulative and abusive adults were persuasive in some contexts, but old beliefs that they were bad kids or that they needed to be locked up for their own protection were powerful. These beliefs wielded by the Christian Right in Georgia defeated the 2010 safe harbor proposal there, but in Texas activists only had to convince five justices on the Supreme Court to provide safe harbor for youth, which they were able to do.

---

[103] *In re B.W.*, 313 S.W.3d 818 (Tex. 2010).

These early campaigns for safe harbor laws inspired activists in other states to initiate legislative campaigns and litigation to decriminalize prostituted youth over the next decade. Safe harbor laws became a pivotal tactic in the movement to shift perceptions and treatment of youth involved in prostitution.

In addition to state-level efforts to address domestic sex trafficking, several law enforcement initiatives occurred at the local level. Between 2005 and 2010, police departments around the country created new units or programs to address juvenile prostitution. For example, Sergeant Bryon Fassett, head of the Child Exploitation Unit in Dallas, Texas, created the High Risk Victims and Trafficking Unit that would flag cases involving high-risk youth in order to prioritize prosecuting their abusers and getting the children help. Fassett also worked to change the contemptuous attitudes of police, prosecutors, and judges toward the youth involved in prostitution by conducting trainings with the entire police force.[104] Alameda County District Attorney Nancy O'Malley set up an anti-trafficking program called HEAT Watch (Human Exploitation and Trafficking Watch) in California, with a mission to "develop an effective comprehensive, collaborative, and regional response to human trafficking of all forms; to provide tools, education, and community engagement to change societal, legal, and institutional approaches; and to support victims and hold their offenders accountable."[105] The program sponsored a public awareness campaign with billboards and bus shelter posters and produced a record number of convictions against people for trafficking minors. In 2005, Las Vegas Judge William Voy developed a youth prostitution court, with specially trained attorneys to represent youth and procedures ensuring that social work agencies assisted youth.[106] Finally, the Los Angeles Police Department established a Human Trafficking Unit with the mission of "identification and rescue of juvenile victims lured into the sex trade."[107] These efforts created alternatives to criminal prosecution and enhanced services available to youth involved in prostitution.

## FEDERAL ACTION ON CHILD SEX TRAFFICKING

Between 2008 and 2010, activists came together to work on several federal initiatives. Their differing perspectives were often apparent in their testimony before Congress, as in the 2010 hearings described at the start of this chapter, but they were still able to work together as a collaborative adversarial

---

[104] Urbina, "For Runaways, Sex Buys Survival," A22; Sher, *Somebody's Daughter,* 44–47, 140, 302.

[105] H.E.A.T. Watch, at www.heatwatch.org/

[106] Associated Press, "Nevada Implementing Strict Child Prostitution Law," *The San Diego Union Tribune* (June 23, 2009), at www.sandiegouniontribune.com/sdut-nv-child-prostitution-nevada-062309-2009jun23-story.html.

[107] Los Angeles Police Department, Human Trafficking Section, at www.lapdonline.org/detective_bureau/content_basic_view/51926.

movement. Diverse activists joined together to support the reauthorization of the TVPA in 2008, including Vednita Carter, Rachel Lloyd, and Gary Bauer, president of the conservative American Values organization.[108] The reauthorization, passed as the William Wilberforce Trafficking Victims Protection Reauthorization Act of 2008, expanded social service assistance to United States citizens who were trafficked.[109] Supporters highlighted their belief that contemporary human trafficking was similar to the nineteenth-century slavery of Africans by naming the law after the famous British abolitionist, William Wilberforce. The Act also provided that prosecutors did not have to prove that the defendant knew that the person exploited had not attained the age of eighteen, as long as they had a reasonable opportunity to observe the minor. The Act provided that youth should be held in the least restrictive placement possible unless they were a danger to the community or were charged with a crime, and it removed the provision that required young people to provide reasonable assistance in investigating and prosecuting their trafficker in order to be able to receive assistance and services – achieving a goal youth advocates had sought for years.

Even after the 2008 reauthorization, however, TVPA funding was largely directed toward non-citizen victims of trafficking until 2009 when the Department of Justice Office for Victims of Crime began funding a grant specifically to provide services for US-citizen sex trafficking victims under the age of eighteen and to develop community responses to domestic minor sex trafficking.[110] During fiscal years 2009 and 2010, the federal government allocated approximately $42.5 million to address domestic trafficking, with $18.7 million dedicated to training and task forces. In 2010, the National Coordinator, Frances Hakes, testified at Congressional hearings on domestic minor sex trafficking that her office had allocated some of the funds authorized by the Act to three demonstration projects that provided services to domestic minor sex trafficking victims: $800,000 each over three years to Safe Horizon in New York City (which had a harm reduction approach), Salvation Army Metropolitan Division in Chicago, and SAGE in San Francisco (both of which were abolitionist).[111] The motivation for granting these funds, however, appeared to be to secure victims' cooperation with law enforcement. Hakes testified, for example, that secure housing allowed law enforcement to "build the necessary rapport and trust to allow the victims to assist in the investigation and prosecution of their abusers."[112]

[108] Sher, *Somebody's Daughter*, 255–256.
[109] William Wilberforce Trafficking Victims Protection Reauthorization Act of 2008, Pub. L. No. 110-457, § 213, 122 Stat. §§5063-5065 (2008).
[110] Memo to Honorable Carolyn Maloney, from Alison Siskin, Adrienne Fernandes, and Kristin Finklea, Re: Sex Trafficking of Minors in the United States, Congressional Research Service (dated April 27, 2010), 3 (on file with author).
[111] *Domestic Minor Sex Trafficking Hearing, 2010*, 125, 132.   [112] Ibid. 132.

To combat child pornography, Congress passed the PROTECT Our Children Act of 2008,[113] which called for the development of a national strategy for the prevention and interdiction of child sexual exploitation. The law focused on the use of the internet for sexual exploitation, and child pornography in particular, but the infrastructure set up by the act addressed child sex trafficking as well. The Act called for the Office of the Deputy Attorney General of the Department of Justice to create a National Coordinator for Child Exploitation, Prevention, and Interdiction, which served as the Justice Department's liaison to federal, state, and local agencies and organizations working on child sexual exploitation issues. The Department of Justice first published its National Strategy for Child Exploitation Prevention and Interdiction in 2010, which it reissued in 2016.[114]

In 2010, Congress held two major hearings on domestic sex trafficking. These hearings continued some of the themes from the early part of the decade, but introduced new themes and strategies as well. In February, the Subcommittee on Human Rights and the Law of the Senate Judiciary Committee and held a hearing titled *In Our Own Backyard: Child Prostitution and Sex Trafficking in the United States*. Similar to the 2005 hearing, the February 2010 hearing focused prominently on criminal justice approaches to domestic sex trafficking, including attacking demand. Also similar to the 2005 hearing, several witnesses emphasized that this was not just a problem abroad but exists "in our own backyard." However, whereas in the 2005 hearing, witnesses raised the alarm that domestic trafficking was a problem that was spreading from urban settings to the middle-class white girls of wealthy suburbs, witnesses at the 2010 hearing, especially Lloyd, suggested that race and class might in fact be contributing to the neglect of this problem because it disproportionately affected poor girls of color. Whereas the survivor witness in 2005 was a white middle-class girl, the survivor witness in February 2010 was an African-American girl from a working-class background. Lloyd emphasized systemic failures, including racism and poverty, that made youth vulnerable to trafficking, the criminal justice system's criminalization of youth in the sex trade, the lack of specialized services for youth survivors, and their needs for medical care and employment opportunities.

In her testimony, Lloyd pointed out multiple contradictions and double standards in society's treatment of children involved in prostitution – that the US condemned other countries for tolerating prostitution of children yet ignored the problem in the United States, that police arrested girls for

---

[113] Providing Resources, Officers, and Technology to Eradicate Cyber Threats to Our Children Act of 2008, Pub. L. 110-401, 42 USC §17601 et seq.

[114] Department of Justice, *National Strategy for Child Exploitation Prevention and Interdiction, A Report to Congress – April 2016*; Department of Justice, *National Strategy for Child Exploitation Prevention and Interdiction in 2010, A Report to Congress – August 2010*.

prostitution but allowed the adult men who bought and sold them to go free, and that young girls were arrested for prostitution even when they were under the legal age of consent. Referencing the title of the hearing, "In Our Own Backyard," Lloyd argued, "this is not something that is only happening in other countries to other people's children, but it is happening here."[115] Noting that it was only recently that there has been a concerted effort to view and treat American girls as trafficking victims, she argued,

As a nation, we've graded and rated other countries on how they address trafficking within their borders and yet have effectively ignored the sale of our own children within our own borders. We created a dichotomy of acceptable and unacceptable victims, wherein Katya from the Ukraine will be seen as a real victim and provided with services and support, but Keisha from the Bronx will be seen as a "willing participant," someone who's out there because she "likes it" and who is criminalized and thrown in detention or jail.[116]

Like others before her, Lloyd located some of the blame on a culture of tolerance for commercial sexual exploitation: she condemned that "we have allowed popular culture to glorify and glamorize the commercial sex industry and particularly pimp culture." But she also pointed out the economic causes that make children vulnerable to exploitation: "our policies and economic choices have left huge numbers of children at risk for so many things, including commercial sexual exploitation, simply because of the zip code they live in." Lloyd, however, testified that she believed significant progress in recognizing what was really happening to youth had been made. Drawing an analogy to the domestic violence movement, she emphasized the importance of accurately naming what was happening in order to change beliefs and behaviors:

Slowly we are beginning to use the appropriate language, recognizing that calling children who are victims of rape, sexual assault, and violence prostitutes is neither helpful nor accurate. Using the terminology of "child prostitution" or "child prostitute" conjures up stereotypes and misconceptions about who these children are and how we should treat them ... It is critical that we accurately label this crime against children as commercial sexual exploitation and domestic trafficking.[117]

Lloyd described the key role played by GEMS girls and young women in the passage of New York's safe harbor act, which she described as shifting the treatment of prostituted children from a juvenile justice approach to a child welfare issue. Despite this progress, emphasized Lloyd, there was a dearth of

---

[115] *In Our Own Backyard Hearing, 2010*, 14.    [116] Ibid. 15.

[117] Ibid. After this hearing, Katya vs. Keisha became a widely quoted meme. According to Sienna Baskin, this "marked a savvy complicating of the narrative of white citizen vs. foreigner of color by introducing the white foreigner vs. black citizen. This trope was successful at galvanizing US African American women around the rescue approach when they might have been natural allies of the harm reduction/empowerment approach. A white working class British woman, Lloyd also came across as a woman of color to American audiences because of her way of dressing and speaking." Correspondence with author, January 12, 2018.

shelter and services for these girls. Lloyd was the only witness to explicitly address race and class in the hearing. While acknowledging that commercial sexual exploitation could happen to any child, Lloyd testified that it disproportionately impacted low-income children and children of color. She argued that "issues of race, class and prior victimization have ensured that these children are frequently invisible in our national dialogue."[118] Lloyd concluded by emphasizing that survivors needed to be at the forefront of the movement.

Members of the committee and others testifying strongly agreed that youth involved in prostitution should be treated as victims, not criminals. Chairman Richard Durbin of Illinois opened the hearing by playing a clip from the documentary *Playground*, about the prostitution of two under-aged girls in the United States, then he pointed out the legal dichotomy between how the federal government treated prostituted children as victims, but that states often treated them as criminals. He called for states to treat child prostitution as human trafficking and to allow state social service agencies to play a role in helping youth. Senator Wyden described child prostitution as a "moral blot" and stated that "pimps have all the power" and that they "use violence to control and traumatize young girls." He called for more shelters and services for youth, so they "feel safe enough to come forward" so that prosecutors can "get the kind of testimony that builds the case, busts the pimps, and gets them behind bars where they belong."[119] He described pending legislation to provide block grants for the development of shelters. Luis CdeBaca, Ambassador-at-Large of the State Department's Office to Monitor and Combat Trafficking in Persons, testified that many young people in the sex trade may not be sympathetic, but they still warrant help:

It does not matter whether the victim once consented to do this. It does not matter if the victim returned to the trafficker after he or she had been freed. It does not matter whether the enslavement was through chains of mental dependency or psychological manipulation as opposed to being physically locked up ... children in prostitution may not all be saints, may not understand that they are victims, may consider our help to be unwanted interference, and may even be in love with those who abuse them. But that does not make them any less deserving of a compassionate response. Indeed, I think that these tendencies require more, not less, commitment and engagement on our parts.

He noted that many were "forced to steal, beg, or sell drugs on the streets" but we "need to look past these things and protect those children."[120] Anita Alvarez, State's Attorney of Cook County, Illinois, testified that she created an Organized Crime/Human Trafficking initiative in July of 2009 to conduct long-term, proactive investigations of organized crime engaged in trafficking children. She testified about how her office was working with the Chicago Police Department to train officers working vice to identify and investigate human

[118] Ibid. 17.    [119] Ibid. 4.    [120] Ibid. 7–8.

trafficking, especially involving children, and to "view prostituted children as victims, rather than criminal defendants."[121]

The hearing also addressed how systems were failing youth. Rachel Lloyd testified about inadequate responses to child sexual abuse and the failing child welfare system, especially foster homes and group homes from where youth were often recruited into the sex trade. Lloyd criticized social service providers for being "incredibly judgmental and stigmatiz[ing] young people" and called for training "first responders, child welfare workers, law enforcement, emergency room nurses, et cetera."[122] Shaquana, whose testimony began this chapter, illustrated this by describing her own experience of abuse at the hands of law enforcement, as well as the mistreatment of girls she worked with in juvenile detention facilities. Lloyd testified about youth survivors' need for better shelter and housing options, better counseling and mental health treatment, as well as medical treatment, education, employment training, and "viable employment opportunities to help them achieve economic independence."[123]

Later that year, in September of 2010, Congress held another hearing, entitled *Domestic Minor Sex Trafficking*, before the Subcommittee on Crime, Terrorism, and Homeland Security of the House Judiciary Committee.[124] Unlike the February hearing, this hearing did not focus on the exploitation of marginalized youth or the systemic failures leading to that exploitation. Instead, this hearing focused on law and order responses to domestic minor sex trafficking. A central topic of the hearing was the "adult services" section of Craigslist.com. As a result of a nationwide campaign against Craigslist led by activists and attorneys general alleging that children and youth were sold on Craigslist.com, in the spring of 2010 several members of Congress had called for a Congressional inquiry into the issue.[125] In addition to legislators and criminal justice representatives, participants at that hearing included SHI Executive Director Linda Smith; NCMEC President Ernie Allen; survivor Tina Frundt, Executive Director of Courtney's House in Washington, DC; and Deborah Richardson, Chief Program Officer of the Women's Funding Network of San Francisco, California. No youth survivors testified. Representatives from Craigslist also testified. Linda Smith submitted two SHI research reports into the record, *Domestic Minor Sex Trafficking: America's Prostituted Children* and *Demand*. Smith described the phrase "domestic minor sex trafficking" as "the name we have given to the sexual exploitation of US citizen children through prostitution, pornography, and sexual entertainment."[126] She emphasized that this exploitation was trafficking and therefore victims were

---

[121] Ibid. 13.  [122] Ibid. 26.  [123] Ibid. 16.
[124] *Domestic Minor Sex Trafficking Hearing, 2010.*
[125] Letter to Representatives Conyers, Smith, Scott and Gohmert, from Representative Jackie Spier et al. (dated May 28, 2010), *Domestic Minor Sex Trafficking Hearing, 2010*, 326.
[126] Ibid. 116.

entitled to the full range of protections, services, and rights provided in the TVPA.

Coded racial appeals were repeated throughout the hearing, both in the focus on victims as daughters of white middle- and upper-class families and in racialized calls for extreme punishment of traffickers that recalled white supremacist historical treatment of African Americans. Representative Chris Smith (R-NJ) emphasized in his testimony, "These are our daughters. These are our children."[127] Representative Mike Quigley (D-IL) repeated the common refrain that this child sex trafficking does not only happen in "third world countries" or to poor people, but that it affects "the nicest neighborhoods":

[C]hild sex slavery, child sex trafficking, prostitution of children ... you would like to think or unfortunately imagine this would be in some Third World country, or at least not in nice neighborhoods. But I will tell you, you can go out in Lakeview, one of the nicest communities in the city of Chicago and the nicest areas that you would ever want to live in, you will see the vans out there of social service agencies trying to find the kids, runaway kids who are exposed to – who are vulnerable to these offenses right there in some of the nicest neighborhoods ... [T]he people who are committing these offenses ... are not far away.[128]

Quigley's testimony made explicit the concern for the sexual exploitation of middle-class and upper-middle class youth. The reactionary tone of this hearing was also expressed in repeated calls for extreme punishment of traffickers. Representative Ted Poe (R-TX) suggested that lynching would be an appropriate response to trafficking when he said, "... traffickers are the filth of humanity, and they are criminals. And as one Texas Ranger friend of mine ... said, 'When you see one, Judge, get a rope.'"[129] Before serving in Congress, Poe had been a district judge in Harris County, Texas. Poe repeated the threat to "get a rope" later in the hearing in response to the testimony of African American survivor and service provider Tina Frundt.[130] Representative Chris Smith emphasized the "huge and escalating crisis of child sex trafficking in the United States" and called for "very long prison sentences, including up to life imprisonment itself" for traffickers.[131] Linda Smith condemned the "men who buy their innocence," demanding for the "full penalty called for in the law," reflecting SHI's position that the government should prosecute men who buy sex from youth as traffickers. Several witnesses and members of Congress focused on demand – including stings and criminal prosecution of the men who buy sex from youth and public shaming campaigns. For example, Judge Poe stated, "if these guys all of a sudden start seeing their photographs on the Internet they may stop this conduct."[132]

A form of this racialized discourse was also employed in the description of the crimes against youth, with speakers throughout the hearing repeatedly describing child sex trafficking as slavery, including NCMEC's CEO Ernie

[127] Ibid. 21.     [128] Ibid. 4.     [129] Ibid. 16.     [130] Ibid. 217.     [131] Ibid. 21.     [132] Ibid. 218.

Allen, who said, "this is truly 21st century slavery."[133] Nicholas Sensley, Chief of Police, Truckee Police Department, Truckee, California, made an explicit parallel to the transatlantic slave trade: "from the street level we can attest that what is going on in this domestic minor sex trafficking is, in fact, an act of slavery. Where the problem exists is that there is not the emphasis in responding to this problem of slavery that we saw some 200 years ago." He characterized domestic minor sex trafficking as "an atrocity that is being perpetrated against our children."[134] In light of the frequent racialized framing of youth involvement in the sex trade, with the focus on white girls lured into prostitution by African American men, the use of the term "slavery" to describe the phenomena was ironic at best, and sinister at worst.[135]

While most of those testifying agreed that youth were victims of prostitution and that the federal government should act to combat the problem, some participants expressed reservations. Representative Robert Scott (D-VA) conceded that "tossing kids in jail while ignoring the broader problem" was "certainly a Federal issue," but expressed concern about "a gradual move toward federalization of local prostitution or local prostitution-related crimes."[136] Contradicting his previous statement about domestic minor sex trafficking as a form of slavery, Truckee Police Chief Sensley testified that some youth were culpable for their involvement in the sex trade: "My experiences do not allow me to draw a blanket conclusion that all minors involved in this crime are without measures of culpability. Often, their circumstances do not neatly satisfy the evidences that would point to them as victims." However, he said, the justice system must presume minors were victims "until clear evidence shows otherwise, that a minor has not been forced or coerced into the crime."[137] This testimony highlighted a misunderstanding of federal law, even by policymakers and law enforcement officials. The TVPA established that all youth under the age of eighteen involved in commercial sex are victims, with no requirement of force or coercion.

But advocates continued to leverage the trafficking framework to put pressure on the United States to address on domestic minor sex trafficking.

---

[133] Ibid. 138, 2, 4, 6, 9.    [134] Ibid. 145.

[135] The use of the term "slavery" to refer to sex trafficking and prostitution has been extensively criticized in the literature as inaccurate and historically anachronistic. Julia O'Connell Davidson, *Children in the Global Sex Trade* (Malden, MA: Polity Press, 2005), 41 (arguing that "the language of slavery deflects attention from questions about the structural conditions that encourage many children independently to use prostitution as a strategy for survival"); Robin Maynard, "#Blacksexworkerslivesmatter: White-Washed 'Anti-Slavery' and the Appropriation of Black Suffering," *The Feminist Wire* (September 9, 2015) (arguing that the anti-trafficking movement has "hijacked" the word "slavery" and used "abolition" to promote human rights abuses, which she finds to be a "deeply disrespectful appropriation of Black suffering").

[136] *Domestic Minor Sex Trafficking Hearing*, 2010, 3.    [137] Ibid. 136.

At the September 2010 hearing, ECPAT-USA submitted a statement to Congress applauding the State Department for evaluating the United States' progress in combatting trafficking within its own borders for the first time in the 2010 Trafficking in Persons (TIP) Report, but questioning the United States' Tier 1 ranking because of "the government's dismal efforts to identify and protect sexually exploited children," noting that the report reveals that the United States arrested three times as many children for prostitution as were offered protection and assistance.[138] In fact, the TIP report acknowledged that "the prostitution of children has traditionally been handled as a vice crime or a juvenile justice issue and the anti-trafficking approach of the TVPA has been slow to fully permeate the state child protection and juvenile justice systems."[139] By highlighting the hypocrisy of the United States' condemnation of countries for arresting sex trafficking victims while at the same times states were arresting victims of "domestic minor sex trafficking," ECPAT hoped that Congress would put pressure on states to change their approach to minors involved in prostitution.

CONCLUSION

As the movement against the US youth sex trade matured in the latter part of the decade, it became a collaborative adversarial movement. Sex worker organizations worked side by side with abolitionist organizations, and evangelical groups worked with feminist groups, even if sometimes at arms-length. The expansion and diversification of the movement was due in part to increased resources made available as a result of new funding streams at the state and federal levels, as well as increased private funding from individuals and foundations. However, the historical moment might also have contributed to the increased interest in the issue. Activism against youth involvement in prostitution across time has consistently spiked during times of social and economic change. The 2007 economic crisis, the election of the first African American president, and the legalization of gay marriage, as well as the ongoing "war on terror," may have fueled anxiety about youth sexuality, especially among conservatives.

The strategies and framings of the movement diversified as well between 2005 and 2010, as illustrated by the juxtaposition of the Congressional testimonies of youth survivor Shaquana and Congresswoman Linda Smith at the start of this chapter. Conservative groups, particularly religiously affiliated ones, framed the problem in terms of the threat of lost innocence, rescue, and protection, and envisioned themselves as saviors or defenders. Feminist groups,

---

[138] ECPAT-USA Comment on the 2010 US State Department Trafficking in Persons Report, in *Domestic Minor Sex Trafficking Hearing, 2010*, 318–319.

[139] United States Department of State, *Trafficking in Persons Report*, 10th Edition (Washington, DC: US Department of State, June 2010), 342.

on the other hand, tended to use an empowerment framework, centering the voices of survivors and pushing for increased social services for youth. Many groups worked with law enforcement and courts, but some, like YWEP, considered police and social service providers to be part of the problem rather than part of the solution. Some activists, like Rachel Lloyd, spoke explicitly about the role of race in the criminalization of girls involved in prostitution, and condemned systemic inequities that made girls vulnerable to entering the sex trade. Despite these significant differences, most of these activists could agree on certain things: that juveniles should not be prosecuted for prostitution; that they should instead be provided with services to help them avoid commercial sexual exploitation; that adults who facilitate youth involvement in the sex trade should be aggressively prosecuted; and that the adults who purchase sex from youth should be punished and educated. As a result, ideologically diverse activists could collaborate on particular goals, like safe harbor laws in the states or the reauthorization of the TVPA with expanded funding for youth services. These groups came together as a collaborative adversarial movement, which powerfully mobilized diverse constituencies to support shared goals.

By 2010, when "domestic minor sex trafficking" entered the political lexicon at the September Congressional hearing of the same name, activists had fully leveraged the trafficking framework.[140] They achieved this goal by making four key arguments for why this issue was important and should be addressed. They reiterated arguments made earlier in the decade that it was hypocritical for Americans to condemn child prostitution abroad while ignoring the same behavior within their own borders. They also reiterated their condemnation of the widespread police practice of arresting girls for prostitution and not arresting the adult men who bought and sold them. But they introduced two new arguments. First, they contended that it was inconsistent for a state to prosecute a girl for prostitution when she was younger than the age of consent set by the state's statutory rape law. Second, they pointed out the contradiction between prosecuting youth for prostitution when, under federal anti-trafficking laws and sometimes new state laws as well, anyone under the age of eighteen engaged in commercial sex was defined as a victim of a severe form of trafficking, without regard to force, fraud, or consent. Activists made these arguments in legislative hearings, courts of law, and public education campaigns to support their core argument that youth involved in prostitution were victims of sexual abuse, not perpetrators of the crime of prostitution, and they deserved support and services rather than condemnation and incarceration. The US government was condemning countries around the world for treating prostituted children as criminals, yet many states did just that. These arguments were very effective in convincing policymakers at the

---

[140] See, for example, Shared Hope International, *National Report on Domestic Minor Sex Trafficking: America's Prostituted Children* (Vancouver, WA: Shared Hope International, 2009).

federal, state, and local levels to take the issue of domestic minor sex trafficking seriously, and to act on the issue.

The diversity of the movement contributed to its success by recruiting a wide range of supporters, but some advocates were more influential than others, especially those who were most strongly connected to policy-makers and those who framed the issue in ways that were consistent with existing cultural scripts about childhood. Some advocates' ways of framing the issue, geared toward broad mainstream audiences, had the effect of obscuring the experiences of marginalized youth and reinforcing problematic gender and racial stereotypes. The relentless focus on innocent young girls kidnapped and forced to sell sex, which generated widespread concern about the issue, suggested that other, less "perfect" victims, might not be worthy of support. Rescue narratives intertwined with religiously inflected savior narratives to tell a very traditional tale of damsels in distress, evil dark perpetrators, and shining white knights. Law and order conservatives seized on the issue in racialized ways by repeating stories of African American "pimps" targeting innocent white girls, echoing similar characterizations from the 1970s, the 1990s, and even the 1910s.

The racialized themes that trafficking was targeting "our children" and the fear of "lost innocence" continued to reverberate in Congressional hearings, media coverage, and activist discourses between 2005 and 2010. Politicians and activists called for harsher and heavier punishment of traffickers, including life in prison and even to "get a rope" as Representative Poe repeatedly suggested in the September 2010 hearing. Race was just below the surface, "hidden in plain sight," even if rarely directly addressed. Nevertheless, young survivors of color were speaking out more and more at state legislative hearings for safe harbor laws and in federal Congressional hearings, telling their stories of survival and empowerment and challenging the discourses that would stigmatize and dismiss them. Some activists, like Rachel Lloyd, repeatedly highlighted the systemic inequities that made girls vulnerable to commercial sexual exploitation, especially poor girls of color. Others, like members of YWEP, focused on the institutional violence of the criminal justice, social service, and medical systems, and advocated turning away from these systems to solve the problem faced by youth in the sex trade and relying instead on self-help and community building. These varied framings and discourses would proliferate on all sides in the second decade of the twenty-first century.

# 6

## "Locked in Like a Dog in a Kennel": Expanding Tactics, Challenging Systems

"Suffering, isolated, helpless and tired, at the age of 15, the concrete box that represented myself in Zenoff Hall, the largest juvenile facility in Las Vegas, Nevada, seemed no less invasive than the horror of the streets," testified the young African American survivor Withelma T. Ortiz Walker Pettigrew on March 26, 2014, at a Congressional hearing titled "Innocence for Sale: Domestic Minor Sex Trafficking" before the House Judiciary Committee's Subcommittee on Crime, Terrorism, and Homeland Security.[1] She continued, "As much of a real physical confinement that it was, it was not all too different than the mental confinement that I endured from my pimp. I was interrogated for hours on end, reminded that my opinions did not matter, and locked in like a dog in a kennel. Unless I was saying the answers to the questions that they wanted to hear, my voice was irrelevant." Seven years later, Pettigrew was honored by *Glamour* magazine as "The Bravest Truth-Teller" in the 2011 Woman of the Year issue[2] and, in 2013, *Time* magazine included her on its list of "30 people under 30 changing the world" as "The Survivor's Advocate."[3] Pettigrew, who at the time of her testimony worked for the Washington, DC-based Human Rights Project for Girls, was raised in the foster care system and was involved in the sex trade from age ten until she was seventeen years old. Pettigrew condemned both the foster care and criminal justice systems. The foster care system, she testified, was "where I learned to accept and normalized being used as an object of financial gain by people who were supposed to love and care for me, got used to various people controlling my

---

[1] *Innocence for Sale: Domestic Minor Sex Trafficking: Hearing Before the Subcommittee on Crime, Terrorism, & Homeland Security, Committee on the Judiciary*, House of Representatives, 113th Cong., 2nd Sess. (March 26, 2014), Serial No. 113–80 [hereinafter *Innocence for Sale Hearing, 2014*], 16.

[2] Sarah J. Robbins, "Withelma 'T' Ortiz-Macey: The Bravest Truth-Teller," *Glamour* (October 31, 2011).

[3] Denver Nicks, "These Are the 30 People Under 30 Changing the World," *Time Magazine* (December 5, 2013).

life." In detention, she was "retraumatized every day ... watched naked while I showered. No one ever assessed me or even asked me what got me there, and there were no rehabilitation services offered. I just sat locked in a box being interrogated and talked down to." The police "always wanted to detain me and my pimp, both people of color, instead of focusing on the buyers who were adults and primarily White. No one seemed to care about them." Pettigrew called for "alternative, gender specific and trauma informed services" for children rather than detention, and "more investigation and prosecution of buyers as child rapists."[4]

Pettigrew's testimony was representative of the consolidation of survivor leadership in the movement in the 2010s and activists' turn toward broader critiques of society for failing young people involved in the sex trade. During this period, the movement employed new strategies, like survivor memoirs and social media campaigns, to convince the public of the problem's urgency and to persuade federal and state governments to improve child welfare and criminal justice system responses to young people in the sex trade. Activists mobilized federal funding available under the TVPA, forming new organizations and expanding campaigns against domestic minor sex trafficking. They targeted men buying sex from youth through "end demand" campaigns and, to the ire of free speech advocates, organized against internet service providers for allowing sexual service advertisements on their websites. While the traditional gendered and racialized narrative of youth victimization continued to prevail, activists began to call attention to a wider range of youth, including girls of color, LGBT youth, and boys. This chapter will trace this maturation of the movement in the 2010s.

## SURVIVOR ACTIVISM/SURVIVOR POLITICS

Survivors played an increasingly central role in the movement against domestic minor sex trafficking in the 2010s, serving as leaders in the movement and sharing their stories, which became woven throughout the movement from widely circulated memoirs to Congressional testimony. Survivors wrote opinion editorials, made films, and spoke out at conferences, police trainings, and john schools. Many survivors founded and led organizations. Some focused primarily on public education, like Survivors for Solutions founded by Autumn Burris[5] or Nola Brantley Speaks, which provided training, public speaking, and consultation.[6] Others worked for service providers, like MISSSEY, My Life My Choice, Breaking Free, GEMS, or Courtney's House. Many shelters and outreach organizations preferred to hire survivors to counsel the young women they served. Like activists in the child sexual abuse movement,[7] the direct

---

[4] Ibid. 17–18.    [5] Survivors for Solutions, at www.survivors4solutions.com/.
[6] Nola Brantley Speaks, at www.nolabrantleyspeaks.org/.
[7] Nancy Whittier, *The Politics of Child Sexual Abuse: Emotion, Social Movements and the State* (New York, NY: Oxford University Press, 2009), 59.

experience of survivors lent credibility to their activism and made them uniquely qualified to speak about youth involvement in the sex trade. The individual stories of survivors generated new knowledge, theory and action against domestic minor sex trafficking.

Survivor politics is based on the idea that people in stigmatized groups internalize society's negative stereotypes about themselves, leading them to believe the myths and misinformation circulated about their group. By "coming out" through speaking about their experiences and making themselves visible, stigmatized groups challenge these negative ideas. Feminist speak outs of the 1960s and 1970s on rape, domestic violence, sexual harassment, and abortion, as well as the imperative to "come out" of the gay liberation movement, were built on the idea that embracing one's stigmatized identity could challenge society's devaluation of a group. As Nancy Whittier has said about the child sexual abuse movement, "Visibility issued a fundamental challenge to stigma and blame" and was a "key to social change."[8]

Survivors of domestic minor sex trafficking, by speaking out, challenged society's longstanding belief that young women were to blame for their involvement in prostitution, that they were "bad girls" and that they chose to engage in prostitution. Survivor narratives dramatically illustrated parental abuse and neglect, the manipulation and violence of the adults who entrapped them, and their own emotional vulnerability as young people. Survivor advocacy is based on the "politicization of emotion and identity" and "entails changing individuals' feelings and identities, changing the culture, and changing policy."[9] The movement transformed survivors into activists by using popular means of disseminating their points of view – in newspapers, magazines, memoirs, and film – to reshape the discourses used to define them.

Stories by and about survivors played a central role in raising awareness about sex trafficking of youth in the United States. Survivors traveled the country on speaking tours, produced TED talks and YouTube videos, and told their stories through art, music, theater, and film. Many published memoirs about their experiences. Theresa Flores' *The Slave Across the Street* in 2010, Rachel Lloyd's *Girls Like Us* in 2011, Carissa Phelps' *Runaway Girl* in 2012, Holly Austin Smith's *Walking Prey* in 2014, and Barbara Amaya's *Nobody's Girl* in 2015 were some of the most widely circulated among the many memoirs published by survivors of commercial sexual exploitation in the United States. In these memoirs, the authors described speaking out about their experiences as beneficial both personally, to generate healing, and politically, to challenge society's stigma and disregard toward youth involved in prostitution. For example, at the beginning of her memoir *Nobody's Girl*, survivor Barbara Amaya says, "Breaking my silence is a political statement for me, one of choosing to never again be a voiceless victim. It is a deliberate choice to take my life back and to help others do the same for

[8] Ibid. 63. [9] Ibid. 6, 12.

themselves."[10] The theme of individual transformation as a political act ran throughout survivor memoirs, although some focused on systemic change as well. The memoirs of Carissa Phelps, Theresa Flores, and Barbara Amaya centered their stories on individual triumph over adversity, whereas Smith and especially Lloyd analyzed the community and society-level factors that contributed to the commercial sexual exploitation of youth. All of these memoirs encouraged readers to act on the issue by offering resource lists of social service and political advocacy organizations working on domestic minor sex trafficking.

These memoirs contained remarkably similar stories of girls fleeing neglect and abuse in their families and ending up under the control of "pimps," most of whom were men of color. In her memoir *Runaway Girl*, Carissa Phelps recounted how at the age of twelve she ran away from a large impoverished family with an abusive stepfather and neglectful mother, ending up in the hands of a brutal African American man. Phelps, who is Latina, eventually escaped prostitution and graduated with a JD and MBA from UCLA. In 2008, Phelps made a documentary short about her life, titled *Carissa*,[11] which won several awards and was featured on *USA Today* and *Good Morning America*.[12] In contrast to Phelps' impoverished and chaotic childhood, Theresa Flores grew up in an upper-middle-class white family with a stay-at-home mother and a father with a successful corporate career. In *The Slave Across the Street*,[13] Flores recounted how at the age of fifteen while living in Detroit, she was sexually assaulted by a boy from her high school and then tricked into prostitution by a group of boys and men with the threat of photographs of the assault being shared with her parents and made public. Her abusers were "Chaldeans," a Catholic minority in Iraq who were forced to leave the country because of their religion. After two years of abuse, her dad was transferred to another city and the abuse stopped. In her memoir, Flores emphasized how she was an "all-American teenager" and how this could happen to "an average kid from the suburbs."[14]

Similar to Phelps and Flores, Barbara Amaya's 2015 memoir, *Nobody's Girl: A Memoir of Lost Innocence, Modern Day Slavery and Transformation,* was a story of personal triumph over adversity. Growing up in a white, middle-class neighborhood of Fairfax, Virginia, Amaya experienced incest from an uncle, her brother, and her father. When she was twelve years old, she ran away from home and ended up under the control of a violent African American man in

---

[10] Barbara Amaya, *Nobody's Girl: A Memoir of Lost Innocence, Modern Day Slavery and Transformation* (Pittsburgh, PA: Animal Media Group LLC, 2015), 5.

[11] *Carissa*, dir. by David Sauvage, Tenth Street Films, 2008.

[12] Carissa Phelps, The Documentary, at http://carissaphelps.com/documentary/.

[13] Theresa L. Flores with PeggySue Wells, *The Slave Across the Street: The True Story of How an American Teen Survived the World of Human Trafficking* (Boise, ID: Ampelon Publishing, 2010), 14.

[14] Ibid. 14.

New York City, who forced her into prostitution. She became addicted to heroin when she was fourteen. After years on the streets, and many arrests, Amaya finally escaped the sex trade, but the psychological trauma and a criminal record haunted her for years. Not until she began telling her story, and becoming an activist, was she healed. For Amaya, speaking out and helping young girls gave her a sense of purpose, and enabled her to recover from her traumatic childhood. The memoirs of Phelps, Flores, and Amaya focused on individual-level factors that shaped their lives.

The memoirs of Holly Austin Smith and Rachel Lloyd, on the other hand, dedicated considerable attention to the larger social context in which their abuse occurred. In her book, Lloyd, who is white, told her own story but also told the stories of girls she worked with at GEMS, many of whom were African American and whose facilitators were African American men. Smith, who is white and middle-class, told how when she was fourteen years old she was lured from a mall by an African American man.[15] Smith focused her critique on how America's culture of materialism, consumerism, and the sexual objectification of women made girls vulnerable to commercial sexual abuse. She also identified other social risk factors that made girls vulnerable including poverty, the presence of the illegal or legal sex industry, the presence of a transient male population, high transit areas, proximity to truck stops, proximity to international borders, gangs, and homeless youth culture. Like Smith, Lloyd emphasized the social, economic, and political factors that contributed to the commercial sexual exploitation of youth, like "race, poverty, homelessness, abuse, ineffective city systems, and a public policy that blames the victims," as well as drug epidemics and the war on drugs, the AIDS crisis resulting in many children in foster care, and larger social and governmental policy decisions like substandard education, lead paint, high rates of asthma, and no recreational or green spaces.[16] These five memoirs represented two poles of child sex trafficking narratives – individual triumph over adversity versus the failures of social systems and the need for reform of those systems. All of these survivors became activists, forming organizations, working on public policy, writing columns, appearing on television, and speaking around the country.[17]

While survivors played a critical role in getting the movement's message out in the 2010s by writing about their experiences, the memoirs that circulated most widely were ones that reinforced the dominant narrative of sex trafficking – vulnerable girls, often white,

[15] Holly Austin Smith, *Walking Prey: How America's Youth are Vulnerable to Sex Slavery* (New York, NY: Palgrave MacMillan, 2014).

[16] Rachel Lloyd, *Girls Like Us* (New York, NY: Harper Collins, 2011), 44.

[17] For example, Phelps founded Runaway Girls, Inc. (http://runawaygirl.org/highlights/), Flores founded S.O.A.P. (www.traffickfree.com/) and Amaya does policy work, writes for the *Washington Post*, has appeared on NPR and Fox, and speaks on college campuses (www .barbaraamaya.com/).

targeted by men of color. Three of the five memoirs – Flores, Smith, and Amaya – are stories of middle-class or upper-middle-class white girls from "intact" families who end up lured into the sex trade by men of color. All the authors were white except for Phelps, who is Latina, and all of the authors describe their abusers as men of color. Flores' abusers were immigrant men. Survivors' experiences in these memoirs also followed the dominant societal narrative of individual tribulation and triumph, victimization and individual empowerment. The memoir form itself supports this individualistic framing of problems, downplaying structural failures that heighten youth vulnerabilities.[18] In other respects, however, these memoirs challenge the standard rescue narrative. These survivors largely save themselves, although intervention from teachers and counselors played a role in helping them to leave prostitution. But more importantly, some of these memoirs contained radical critiques of society's failures and calls for societal responsibility for the commercial sexual exploitation of youth.

In addition to memoirs, survivors told their stories in film. Over thirty documentaries and dramatic films on US youth involvement in the sex trade were released between 2006 and 2017. These films and programs circulated broadly, contributing to increased public awareness about the issue. Many of these films prominently featured survivors and several were made by survivors themselves telling their own stories, like *Carissa* (2008) or *I Was A Teenage Prostitute* (2011) about a young survivor Juliana Piccillo who told a story of being trafficked from her suburban neighborhood as a seventeen-year-old high school junior. Some of the films were set in particular locales, like *Rape for Profit* (2012), made by several young male activists based in Seattle; *Your American Teen* (2013) about Portland, Oregon; *Too Close to Home* (2010) about Tampa Bay, Florida; *Turning a Corner* (2006) about Chicago; and *California's Forgotten Children* (2016). *International Boulevard* (2013), which also focuses on California, was made by a young activist, Rebecca Dharmapalan, and another film, *Sex+Money: A National Search for Human Worth* (2011), was made by a group of journalism students as they travelled across the United States learning about commercial sexual exploitation of youth. Suffolk University law professor Kate Nace Day produced *A Civil Remedy* (2014), advocating for state laws allowing survivors to bring civil cases against their traffickers for monetary damages. Activist organizations produced many films as well, like GEMS' *Very Young Girls*. Shared Hope International produced *Chosen* (2013), to be used to educate high school students about child sex trafficking. Breaking Free in Minneapolis produced a documentary in 2014 titled *Breaking Free from the Life of Sex Trafficking and Prostitution*, which was screened at the Twin Cities Film Fest Changemaker

---

[18] Cynthia G. Franklin, *Academic Lives: Memoir, Cultural Theory and the University Today* (Athens, GA: University of Georgia Press, 2009), 17.

Series in 2014.[19] Evangelical filmmakers made films with a faith-based approach to the issue, such as *In Plain Sight: Stories of Hope and Freedom* (2014). These documentary films sometimes included dramatic reenactments of child sex trafficking, like *Cargo: Innocence Lost* (2007). There were also multiple dramatic films about youth in the US sex trade[20] and the issue appeared as part of documentaries about global trafficking as well, such as in *Nefarious: Merchant of Souls* (2011), *Not My Life* (2011), and *The Abolitionists* (2014).

Survivor stories in memoirs and films increased public awareness about the issue, but often reproduced the gendered and racialized narrative of white men rescuing white girls from men of color. The victims were almost always cisgender female, often white, and they were usually victimized by African American men and saved by white men. For example, the 2013 documentary *Tricked*, which aired on Netflix, told the story of a white male police officer seeking to save white girls from African American "pimps."[21] Similar to the 2009 documentary *Playground*, which also aired on Netflix, *Tricked* leveraged western ideologies of childhood innocence and demonstrated the resilience of the racialized narrative of youth prostitution from decades past in the contemporary cultural imagination. Another example was the 2017 documentary *I Am Jane Doe*, about the campaign against online sex advertising. The film told the stories of two girls, one white and one African American. All but one the advocates portrayed were white and the sole "pimp" interviewed was African American. However, the film also focused on the three white men who own the largest online advertiser of sex – Backpage.com – portraying them as facilitators of child sex trafficking.[22] Furthermore, portrayals of the issue rarely delved very deeply into the societal causes behind the youth sex trade, but focused primarily on the victim's families – fatherlessness, neglect, and drug abuse. Films often framed the solution to the problem as stronger enforcement of criminal laws against facilitators and services for the victims, only rarely focusing on the deeper economic and political causes of youth vulnerability to entering the sex trade.[23]

Similar patterns persisted in the proliferating media coverage of the issue in the 2010s. Television and cable covered youth involvement in the sex trade with increased frequency in the 2010s. Halogen TV produced a series beginning in

[19] "Sex Trafficking of Teen Girls Subject of New Documentary," *CBS Minnesota* (October 24, 2014).

[20] See, for example, *A Dance for Bethany* (2007) (which has an evangelical approach), *Gardens of the Night* (2008), *Where There is No Light* (2008), *Delicate Innocence* (2009), and *Eden* (2012). Activists produced several dramatic films about child sex trafficking as well, including *The Candy Shop* (2010) and *The Package: A Tale of Human Trafficking* (2011).

[21] *Tricked*, dir. Jane Wells and John Keith Wasson, First Run Pictures, 2013.

[22] *I Am Jane Doe*, dir. Mary Mazzio, 50 Eggs Films, 2017.

[23] Carrie N. Baker, "An Intersectional Analysis of Sex Trafficking Films," *Meridians: feminism, race, transnationalism* 12.1 (Spring 2014): 208–226.

2011 called *Tainted Love*, which featured many anti-trafficking activists including Linda Smith of SHI, Ernie Allen of NCMEC, Tina Frundt of Courtney's House, and Bradley Myles of Polaris Project. CNN correspondent Amber Lyon conducted a year-long investigation of internet child sex trafficking across the United States, including in Maryland, Missouri, Tennessee, and Nevada, and produced the documentary *Selling the Girl Next Door*, which aired in 2012.[24] In 2014, MSNBC aired a three-part series *Sex Slaves: Fighting Human Trafficking* on sex trafficking of girls and women in the United States[25] and CNN aired *Children for Sale: The Fight to End Human Trafficking* in 2015 with Jada Pinkett Smith about trafficking in Atlanta.[26] A three-part PBS series with Diane Sawyer about child sex trafficking in the United States, *A Path Appears* (2015), was based on a book of the same name by Nicholas Kristof and Cheryl WuDunn.[27] In addition to documentary and news programs, child sex trafficking in the United States was the focus of several television series, like *True Detective, Law and Order: Special Victims Unit,* and *American Dad.*[28] These programs varied in their approach to the issue, but they reliably included the stories of survivors as well as interviews with activists, law enforcement officers, government officials, and politicians.

Mainstream and independent print media significantly expanded coverage of the US youth sex trade in the 2010s. Articles appeared in magazines and newspapers, as well as news blogs. Much of the media coverage centered on FBI stings, trials involving sex trafficking, legislative action on the issue, new initiatives against trafficking, or activist campaigns. In the first six months of 2016, the *Huffington Post* alone published fifteen stories on child sex trafficking. CNN had multiple stories on child trafficking with a focus on Atlanta.[29] Much of the media coverage focused on cisgender girls, although sometimes alternative media published stories on boys.[30] By touching on a wide

---

[24] *Selling the Girl Next Door*, dir. Amber Lyon (CNN, 2012). "CNN's Amber Lyon Investigates Teen Trafficking in America," *CNN Press Room* (January 18, 2011).

[25] "MSNBC Premieres Three New Hours on Fighting Human Trafficking," *MSNBC* (July 9, 2014).

[26] "CNN, Jada Pinkett Smith Join Forces for Special Report on Sex Trafficking," *CNN Press Room* (July 14, 2015).

[27] Melissa Locker, "A Path Appears: Can Celebrities Really Help Tackle Humanity's Biggest Problems?" *The Guardian* (February 2, 2015).

[28] *True Detective* (season 1, episode 2, "Seeing Things" in 2014); *Law and Order: Special Victims Unit* (season 12, episode 4, "Merchandise" in 2010); *American Dad* (season 3, episode 8, "The Most Adequate Christmas Ever" in 2006).

[29] See, for example, Patricia Leigh Brown, "A Court's All-Hands Approach Aids Girls Most at Risk," *New York Times* (January 29, 2014), A11; Priscilla Alvarez, "When Sex Trafficking Goes Unnoticed in America," *The Atlantic* (February 23, 2016); Huffington Post, Child Sex Trafficking, at www.huffingtonpost.com/news/child-sex-trafficking/; Leif Coorlim and Dana Forb, "Sex Trafficking: The New American Slavery," *CNN* (July 21, 2015); Jane O. Hansen, "Selling Atlanta's Children: What Has and Hasn't Changed," *CNN* (July 18, 2015).

[30] Jodie Gummow, "Demystifying Commercial Sexual Exploitation of Boys: Our Forgotten Victims," *Alternet* (October 18, 2013).

range of concerns in contemporary America, particularly those related to race, gender, sexuality, and immigration, these stories resonated with people across the ideological and political spectrum and mobilized broadened participation in the movement.

## PROLIFERATION OF ORGANIZATIONS AND STRATEGIES TO COMBAT YOUTH TRAFFICKING IN THE 2010S

By mid-decade, hundreds of organizations had formed across the United States working on youth sex trafficking. A database of non-governmental organizations working on human trafficking created by Polaris Project listed two hundred and seventeen organizations working on the US youth sex trade as of July 2017.[31] These organizations were working on policy advocacy, public education, legal support, and service provision. About a quarter of the organizations were explicitly religious, mostly Christian. States with the most organizations were California (29), Florida (15), New York (15), Ohio (13), and Texas (12).

In addition to memoir and film, anti-trafficking activists engaged in a variety of other strategies to raise awareness about the issue. Activists sought to educate youth about sex trafficking by creating curricula to be used in schools. Over twenty non-profit organizations developed school curricula to raise awareness about commercial sexual exploitation and trafficking of youth and teach students how to protect themselves.[32] For example, ECPAT developed the Empower Youth to Take the Lead toolkit, using a peer-to-peer learning model, and FAIR Girls, a Washington-based advocacy and education organization, produced a curriculum called Tell Your Friends that combined videos, art, and songs. Advocacy groups also ran prevention groups in schools, group homes, and in communities, such as My Life My Choice Prevention Groups in Boston.[33] In Atlanta, YouthSpark produced several public service announcements about child sex trafficking directed toward youth.[34] These efforts raised awareness about child sex trafficking.

Shifting discourse around youth involvement in the sex trade from blame to sympathy was a central focus of activists. The Washington, DC-based Human Rights Project For Girls (HRPG), an advocacy and education organization with a human rights approach to gendered violence in the United States, created the No Such Thing campaign seeking to shift the narrative around girls in the sex

---

[31] Global Modern Slavery Directory at www.globalmodernslavery.org/.

[32] National Educators to Stop Trafficking, Curriculum Summaries, at http://nesteducators.org/curriculum-summaries/.

[33] My Life My Choice, Prevention, at www.fightingexploitation.org/prevention-education-and-solutions/.

[34] YouthSpark, PSA – Do the Math, September 12, 2013, at www.youtube.com/watch?v=2dOGi2Nm_AE.

trade by eliminating the concept of "child prostitution" in both language and law.[35] HRPG and The Raben Group, a public affairs consulting firm, researched the use of the phrase "child prostitute" and related terms (underage, minor, or juvenile prostitute/prostitution) in national and local print, wire, and online news outlets over five years, finding that these terms were very commonly used. The report on this research argued that phrases like "child prostitute" did not accurately represent what was really happening – the statutory rape or sexual abuse of a minor. Referencing the TVPA definition of sex trafficking and noting that most of the girls involved were under the statutory age of consent, the report argued that the use of the phrase "child prostitute" suggested consent and "can paper over the violence, harm, trauma and coercion that a trafficked child is subject to."[36] The report recommended that media use language that reflects the coercive nature of the sexual exploitation of minors, like "sex-trafficked child."

In addition to the study, HRPG had a change.org petition, authored by Pettigrew, addressed to the Associated Press Style Guide Editor David Minthorn, asking AP to stop using the term "child prostitute." Pettigrew described her experiences of sexual exploitation from ages ten to seventeen throughout the western United States and her experiences of being charged with solicitation and prostitution and being jailed. She said: "I was not a child prostitute or child sex worker. I was a victim and survivor of child rape. And so are the other kids out there now who are being bought and sold for sex. They are victims and survivors of child rape." Referencing the HRPG research on how often the media used phrases like "child prostitute," she critiqued the media's reporting on child sex trafficking for misleading the public because it "suggests consent and criminality."[37] HRPG's No Such Thing campaign website directed visitors to the change.org petition with prominently displayed slogans like "There is no such thing as a child prostitute"; "It is time to eradicate the term 'child prostitute.' There are only victims and survivors of child rape"; and "How you are named is how you are treated."[38] HRPG's goal was to shift cultural narratives around youth in the sex trade so they would be seen as victims rather than criminals. The campaign succeeded when in April of 2016, AP adopted a new policy recommending against using "child prostitute."[39] An analysis of the use of the terms "child prostitution" and "child sex trafficking" in print news media between 2000 and 2016 showed an increased use of "child sex trafficking"

[35] HRPG was later known as Rights4Girls. Rights4Girls, No Such Thing Campaign, at http://rights4girls.org/campaign/.

[36] The Raben Group, *The Use of the Phrase "Child Prostitute" in the Media: A Critical Examination and Course for Action* (Washington, DC: The Raben Group, 2015).

[37] Human Rights Project for Girls, Petitioning Editor, Associated Press Style Guide David Minthorn, Stop Using the Term "Child Prostitute" (November 2015), at www.change.org/p/associated-press-stop-using-the-term-child-prostitute-2.

[38] Human Rights for Girls, There is No Such Things as a Child Prostitute, at http://rights4girls.org/campaign/

[39] Merrill Perlman, "A Matter of AP Style," *Columbia Journalism Review* (April 4, 2016).

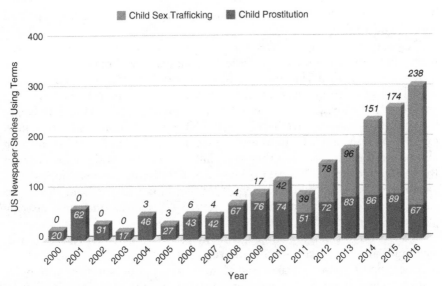

FIGURE 6.1 Use of "Child Prostitution" and "Child Sex Trafficking" in US Newspapers, 2000–2016.[40]

over "child prostitute" during this time period (see Figure 6.1). The use of "child sex trafficking" became more prevalent than "child prostitution" beginning in 2012 and overall coverage of the issue expanded dramatically during this time period, showing the impact of the movement.

This effort to shift the language in the media was part of a larger effort to change beliefs about the youth involved in the sex trade, which opened the way for changes in practice and policy. In February 2015, the US Senate passed a resolution stating that "there is no such thing as a 'child prostitute'" and encouraging states to treat youth in prostitution as victims, not perpetrators.[41] Later that year, Los Angeles Sheriff Jim McDonnell's announced that his force would stop arresting minors on prostitution charges and directed his employees to stop using the terms "child prostitute" and "underage prostitution."[42] The movement had made some progress toward achieving youth survivors' first demand in the 1998 Declaration and Agenda for Action – eliminating the use of the term "child prostitute," although the fight was ongoing.[43] Even as new

---

[40] Newspaper stories were retrieved from LexisNexis Academic in April of 2017.

[41] Senate Resolution 81, Cong. Rec., Vol. 161, No. 24, S1009 (February 12, 2015).

[42] Marisa Gerber and Garrett Therolf, "Sheriff to Staff: Stop Arresting Children on Prostitution Charges, Stop Saying 'Child Prostitute,'" *Los Angeles Times* (October 21, 2015).

[43] Youth Delegates of Out from the Shadows: International Summit of Sexually Exploited Youth, *Declaration and Agenda for Action of Sexually Exploited Children and Youth*, March 12, 1998, Victoria, B.C. Canada, 2.

solutions were put forth, existing systems and structures criminalized youth had yet to be dismantled.

Other advocates criticized the language used to refer to the men who buy sex from youth. Shared Hope International argued that use of the word "john" or "client" to refer men who buy sex from minors normalized the commercial sexual abuse of youth. Instead, they suggested using "perpetrator" or "sex abuser."[44] In a 2014 hearing before a subcommittee of the House Judiciary Committee, Representative Ted Poe (R-TX) noted, "I don't call those guys johns because, you know, John was a good buy in the Bible. I call them child abusers because that is what they are, child abusers."[45] At the same hearing, Representative Karen Bass (D-CA) said, "It kills me to hear 'johns' and 'customers' used for child molesters."[46] A *Ms.* blog asked, "What should we call men who buy young girls for sex?"[47] Responses included "paying pedophile" and "child sex trafficker," among others.

In addition to changing language, many activists, including Rachel Lloyd, Vednita Carter, and survivor/memoirist Holly Austin Smith critiqued the glorification of "pimp culture" and glamorization of prostitution in popular culture. They pointed to many examples from the news media, music, television, and movies: Comedy Central's The Daily Show featuring pimp Bishop Don "Magic" Juan; Simon and Schuster publishing "Pimpin' Ken" Ivy's book *Pimpology*; the video game *Grand Theft Auto* that allowed players to kill prostitutes; the 2006 Academy Award for Best Original Song going to Three Six Mafia's "It's Hard Out Here for a Pimp" from the movie *Hustle and Flow*; former pimp Ice-T's leading role in *Law and Order: Special Victims* and his receipt of the NAACP Image Award twice despite his role in a movie called *Pimpin' 101*; and Snoop Dogg and 50 Cent performing "P.I.M.P." at the 2003 MTV Video Music Awards while leading scantily clad women around the stage on leashes.[48] Missing from their critique, however, is an analysis of race: "pimp culture" is highly racialized in American culture, and is used to reinforce stereotypes of African American men as hypersexualized and violent.

Many advocates argued that popular culture lured girls into sexual abuse. Holly Austin Smith contended that "advertisers and popular culture promote misogynistic messages, causing many girls to accept, and even expect, exploitation."[49] Shared Hope International attributed the increase of commercial sexual exploitation of youth in part to a "culture of tolerance of commercial sex" characterized by a "sexualized popular culture that glamorizes

[44] Shared Hope International, ECPAT-USA, and the Protection Project of the John Hopkins School of Advanced International Studies, *Report from the U.S. Mid-Term Review on the Commercial Sexual Exploitation of Children in America* (2006), 27.

[45] *Innocence for Sale Hearing*, 2014, 42.    [46] Ibid. 46.

[47] "What Should We Call Men Who Buy Young Girls for Sex?" *Ms. Blog* (July 21, 2010), at http://msmagazine.com/blog/2010/07/21/what-should-we-call-men-who-buy-young-girls-for-sex/.

[48] Lloyd, *Girls Like Us*, 87–91; Smith, *Walking Prey*, 59–80.    [49] Smith, *Walking Prey*, 43.

pimping and prostitution and reduces the moral barriers to accessing commercial sex without regard to the origin or conditions of the trafficked women and children."[50] NCMEC's former director Ernie Allen condemned the sexualization of youth in American culture: "Increasingly, our society is sexualizing children at younger and younger ages, leading some kids to view sexual exploitation as normal. We must keep them from becoming compliant victims," referring to the 2007 report of the American Psychological Association's Task Force on the Sexualization of Girls.[51]

Another strategy used by some activists was to work with corporations on anti-trafficking campaigns. From 2009 to 2013, ECPAT-International partnered with the Body Shop in a "Stop Sex Trafficking of Children and Young People" campaign. The Body Shop created the Soft Hands Kind Heart Hand Cream and contributed the $3 million in profits from its sales to ECPAT's regional groups, including ECPAT-USA. ECPAT and the Body Shop launched the campaign at stores around the world, attracting extensive media attention. The campaign provided customers with information about child sex trafficking and asked them to sign a petition opposing trafficking of children for sexual exploitation and asking governments to take action. The petition, addressed to the UN Human Rights Council, obtained more than seven million signatures worldwide over three years.[52]

EPCAT-USA also pursued a corporate responsibility campaign consisting of encouraging hotels and other tourism-related companies to sign the Tourism Child-Protection Code of Conduct, an internationally recognized set of guidelines to address child sex trafficking, and to agree to train their employees to identify and report sex trafficking. With the American Hotel & Lodging Educational Institute, ECPAT-USA developed an online course in child sex trafficking.[53] They also offered customized training for employees. Speaking to corporate America's bottom line, if social responsibility were not enough, ECPAT's Carol Smolenski commented, "We are sending the message that in fact signing it is a way to protect yourself from a lawsuit that might be coming down the pike."[54] These diverse strategies all contributed toward

---

[50] Shared Hope International, *Demand. A Comparative Examination of Sex Tourism and Trafficking in Jamaica, Japan, the Netherlands, and the United States* (Vancouver, WA: Shared Hope International, 2007), 2–3.

[51] Sher, *Somebody's Daughter*, 139; American Psychological Association, Task Force on the Sexualization of Girls, *Report of the APA Task Force on the Sexualization of Girls* (Washington, DC: American Psychological Association, 2007).

[52] ECPAT International, *ECPAT 25 Years: Rallying the World to End Childhood Sexual Exploitation* (Bangkok, Thailand: ECPAT International, May 2015), 112–115.

[53] *The Role of Hospitality in Preventing and Reacting to Child Trafficking*, at www.youtube.com /watch?v=g-j1OsGPC90.

[54] Chris David, "Carol Smolenski, ECPAT-USA," *Means: The Art of Social Justice* (blog) (December 2, 2015).

raising awareness about domestic minor sex trafficking and shifting attitudes and behavior on the issue.

In addition to diversifying their strategies, activists in the movement were calling for more attention to marginalized girls and to social factors contributing to their vulnerability to entering the sex trade. Human Rights Project for Girls had a particular focus on the commercial sexual exploitation of African American girls. HRPG produced an important report in 2015 titled *The Sexual Abuse to Prison Pipeline: The Girls' Story*, with the Georgetown Law Center on Poverty and Inequality and Ms. Foundation for Women.[55] The report argued that girls in the juvenile justice system, especially girls of color, were disproportionately victims of sexual violence, that girls' behavioral reaction to sexual abuse and trauma was criminalized, and that the juvenile justice system typically failed to address, and often exacerbated, the trauma that caused girls to be there. The jailing of victims of sex trafficking was a prime example. The report argued that the juvenile justice system was ill-equipped to identify and treat violence and trauma that lie at the root of victimized girls' arrests, and recommended better mechanisms for identifying and treating trauma in the child welfare system.

Girls of color in particular were negatively affected by this system, and LGBT and gender nonconforming youth were overrepresented in the system. The increase of girls' rate of arrest and incarceration for all crimes over the last two decades, the report argued, was not due to girls increasing criminal activity or increasing violence, but was due to more aggressive enforcement of non-serious offenses that were rooted in the experience of abuse and trauma. Girls were arrested for minor offenses, and the decision to arrest was often "based in part on the perception of girls' having violated conventional norms and stereotypes of feminine behavior, even when that behavior is caused by trauma."[56] The system typically overlooked the context of abuse, which shielded the abusers from accountability and resulted in failure to address the trauma that was the underlying cause of the delinquent behavior. According to the report, "the choice to punish instead of support sets in motion a cycle of abuse and imprisonment that has harmful consequences for victims of trauma."[57] Detaining victimized girls in order to protect them and provide them with services, which were often inadequate anyway, ignored how the system's routine processes "including the use of restraints and strip searches, as well as the isolating punitive environment itself"[58] could re-traumatize girls. Furthermore, criminal records, especially for prostitution, could stigmatize girls for life.

---

[55] Malika Saada Saar, Rebecca Epstein, Linsay Rosenthal, and Yasmin Vafa, *The Sexual Abuse to Prison Pipeline: The Girls' Story* (Washington, DC: Georgetown Law Center on Poverty and Inequality, 2015).
[56] Ibid.    [57] Ibid. 12.    [58] Ibid. 14.

The HRPG made a series of recommendations to reform the juvenile justice and child welfare systems in order to better serve girls, including enacting universal safe harbor laws, providing law enforcement training on gender bias and gender stereotyping, prohibiting child welfare agencies and providers from rejecting or ejecting girls, improving identification of victims of abuse, and implementing a gender-responsive approach to victims of abuse.

Human Rights Project for Girls, like many organizations in the movement, framed youth involvement in the sex trade as a public health and mental health issue by using therapeutic ideas and language to create "alternative models of individuals' identities and interior lives."[59] Many activists used the idea of the "Stockholm syndrome" to explain girls' reluctance to leave their adult facilitators or their uncooperative behavior with law enforcement. HRPG's Director of Law and Policy Yasmin Vafa argued that many youth in the sex trade suffered from trauma that prevented them from seeing their victimization: "Because many victims have been arrested/detained for juvenile 'prostitution,' they internalize the view that they are 'bad girls' instead of victims of crime ... Despite their appearance in court, their seemingly rude or aggressive behavior and attitude, it is critical to remember these girls are simply exhibiting signs of complex trauma from years of abuse and sexual slavery."[60] This mental health framing of youth behavior portrayed youth as injured rather than delinquent, and as worthy of treatment as opposed to punishment. However, the language of trauma also continued to locate the problem in the girls themselves rather than in the social systems that harmed them and neglected their needs. This framing focused solutions on treating trauma rather than addressing the social causes of youth vulnerability.

Another important advocacy group that worked to help girls of color was the Minnesota Native Women's Research Center (MNWRC), which conducted research into the commercial sexual exploitation of Native American women and girls in Minnesota and published two reports. The first report, published in 2009 and titled *Shattered Hearts*, documented the prevalence and patterns of commercial sexual exploitation of Native American women and girls in Minnesota, as well as the factors that facilitate entry and the barriers to exiting the sex trade.[61] The report highlighted how the Native American history of colonization, including anti-Indian attitudes and stereotypes, the boarding schools, assimilation policies, involuntary sterilization, the Indian

---

[59] Whittier, *The Politics of Child Sexual Abuse*, 7.

[60] Yasmin Vafa, *Domestic Child Sex Trafficking: Prevalence and Dynamics* (Powerpoint presentation)(n.d.), at www.ncjfcj.org/sites/default/files/B3-ac2013.pdf

[61] Alexandra Pierce, *Shattered Hearts: The Commercial Sexual Exploitation of American Indian Women and Girls in Minnesota* (Minneapolis, MN: Minnesota Indian Women's Resource Center, 2009).

adoption policy, and generational trauma made Native American females particularly vulnerable to entering the sex trade.[62] The second report in 2012 was a cost-benefit analysis of investing in early intervention to avoid sex trafficking of female youth.[63] The executive director of MNWRC, Suzanne Koepplinger, testified before Congress in 2013 about sex trafficking of Native American women and girls.[64] A second important study on sex trafficking of Native Americans in Minnesota, published in 2011 and titled *Garden of Truth*, was produced by the Minnesota Indian Women's Sexual Assault Coalition in Minneapolis and Prostitution Research & Education in San Francisco.[65] The study was based on interviews and surveys of one hundred and five Native Women in prostitution, almost forty percent of whom had entered the sex trade before reaching the age of eighteen.

Another area of increased research was the vulnerability of LGBTQ youth to homelessness and survival sex. The Urban Institute and Streetwise and Safe in New York City published two research reports in 2015 on LGBTQ youth who engage in survival sex. The first was *Surviving the Streets of New York: Experiences of LGBTQ Youth, YMSM, and YWSW Engaged in Survival Sex*, published in February 2015, and the second was *Locked In: Interactions with the Criminal Justice and Child Welfare Systems for LGBTQ Youth, YMSM, and YWSW Who Engage in Survival Sex*, published in September of 2015.[66] These studies found that many LGBTQ youth trading sex experienced discrimination and harassment from social service workers and police, that few services were available to them, and that these youth were often arrested for "quality-of-life" and misdemeanor crimes other than prostitution offenses, so they were not eligible for services under New York's safe harbor law. These reports recommended increasing the availability of safe and supportive services for these youth, including housing, healthcare, food, and jobs; prohibiting

---

[62] Ibid. 5–13.

[63] Lauren Martin, Richard Lotspeich, and Lauren Stark, *Early Intervention to Avoid Sex Trading and Trafficking of Minnesota's Female Youth: A Benefit-Cost Analysis* (Minneapolis, MN: Minnesota Indian Women's Resource Center, 2012).

[64] *Combating Human Trafficking: Federal, State, and Local Perspectives: Hearing Before the Committee on Homeland Security and Governmental Affairs*, United States Senate, September 23, 2013 (testimony of Suzanne Koepplinger).

[65] Melissa Farley, Nicole Matthews, Sara Deer, Guadalupe Lopez, Christine Stark, and Eileen Hudon, *Garden of Truth: Prostitution and Trafficking of Native Women in Minnesota* (Minneapolis, MN: Minnesota Indian Women's Sexual Assault Coalition and Prostitution Research & Education, 2011).

[66] Meredith Dank, Jennifer Yahner, Kuniko Madden, Isela Bañuelos, Lilly Yu, Angela Ritchie, Mitchyll Mora, and Brendan Conner, *Surviving the Streets of New York: Experiences of LGBTQ Youth, YMSM, and YWSW Engaged in Survival Sex* (New York, NY: Urban Institute, 2015); Meredith Dank, Lilly Yu, Jennifer Yahner, Elizabeth Pelletier, Mitchyll Mora, and Brendan Conner, *Locked In: Interactions with the Criminal Justice and Child Welfare Systems for LGBTQ Youth, YMSM, and YWSW Who Engage in Survival Sex* (New York, NY: Urban Institute, 2015).

arrest of these youth; training law enforcement, child welfare, and court personnel on how to serve LGBTQ youth; holding these officials accountable for treating this population appropriately; offering less restrictive child welfare placements that respect the sexuality and gender identity of these youth; and involving LGBTQ youth themselves in developing policies and programs that will serve their needs. An increasing number of LGBT organizations began serving youth experiencing the sex trade in the 2010s, including BreakOut in New Orleans and Lyric and Huckleberry Youth Programs in San Francisco.

Most of the movement's focus has been on girls involved in the sex trade, but some organizations began to focus on boys as well in the 2010s. For example, in 2013, ECPAT-USA published a research report on the commercial sexual exploitation of boys (CSEB) titled *And Boys Too* based on interviews with forty service providers and youth agencies.[67] The report challenged the common notion that boys were willing participants in commercial sex or even exploiters, but not victims. The report concluded that CSEB was "vastly under reported," and that gay boys and transgender youth disproportionately experience exploitation.[68] While boys were less likely than girls to have a facilitator, commercial sexual exploitation posed very significant risks to boys' health and lives, and there was a shortage of services for these boys. The report recommended raising awareness about CSEB and expanding research into which boys experience exploitation and how to meet their needs. Local service providers also began to pay attention to boys. For example, My Life My Choice in Boston, Massachusetts, originally only served girls but as of 2014 served boys and transgender youth as well.[69] Surviving Our Struggle formed in the Boston area specifically to focus on boys in the sex trade.[70] The development of organizations that focus on girls of color, LGBT youth, and boys, and that began to bring attention to the structural and cultural causes for their vulnerability expanded the scope of the movement and pushed against narrow mainstream framings of the issue.

## END DEMAND CAMPAIGNS

In her 2014 testimony before Congress, Withelma Pettigrew's call for criminal prosecution of buyers of sex from youth as child rapists illustrates a shift in the movement toward focusing on the men who buy sex from youth, known as "end demand" strategies. This approach had deep roots in the movement, going back to the 1970s, but it was in the 2010s that it gained traction on a wide scale.

---

[67] ECPAT-USA, *And Boys Too* (Brooklyn, NY: ECPAT-USA, 2013).

[68] The study is unclear as to whether transgender youth includes transgender girls, transgender boys, or both.

[69] My Life My Choice, Survivor Empowerment, at www.fightingexploitation.org/survivor-empowerment/.

[70] Justice Resource Institute Trauma Center, Surviving Our Struggle, at www.traumacenter.org/initiatives/SOS.php.

Activists argued that there were two sides to a commercial sexual transaction –
the "supply" and the "demand." Historically, they noted, attempts to eradicate
prostitution have focused on arresting the women selling sex. They offered up
statistics of the disproportionate arrest and prosecution of women and girls
selling sex. Studies repeatedly showed that women were much more likely to be
arrested than the men buying sex from them. In 2005, a Congressional survey
found that women selling sex were six times more likely to be arrested than men
buying sex. Other surveys showed an even higher discrepancy.[71] But, they
argued, the root of the problem was not the vulnerable females selling sex,
but the men who were buying sex.

In the early 2000s, "end demand" campaigns popped up all over the country,
from Boston, to Chicago, from Atlanta to LA. These campaigns used a range of
strategies to decrease the demand for commercial sex, including encouraging
prosecution of sex buyers, public education to combat common perceptions of
prostitution, "john schools," and shaming campaigns. The 2005
reauthorization of the TVPA incorporated provisions about "ending demand
for commercial sexual services" as a solution to sex trafficking for the first time,
although Congress at the time declined to pass a provision that would have
treated buyers as sex traffickers.[72] Two prominent end demand organizations
that formed were Demand Abolition in Boston and End Demand Illinois.
In May 2010, Demand Abolition and the Embrey Family Foundation hosted
the National Planning Meeting to Eliminate Demand for Commercial Sex,
which resulted in a report spelling out a "national plan" to end demand.[73]
Two central tactics of the plan were to educate buyers of commercial sex and to
shift social norms that tolerate or support commercial sex. End Demand Illinois
also engaged in public education. Their Ugly Truth Public Awareness
Campaign, created by The Voices and Faces Project, was a multi-media
communications campaign seeking to raise awareness about the "realities of
the sex trade"[74] and the "harms endured by those in the sex trade."[75]
The campaign, which included print and radio ads, targeted public attitudes
about prostitution that denied or naturalized the sex trade. Their posters
featured "prostitution myths" in large type, like "It's the world's oldest
profession," "If a woman chooses to sell her body that's her business," or
"I don't know anyone who pays for sex," then at the bottom of the poster in
small type, "the ugly truth," with statistics and stories about violence and
exploitation in the sex trade and contact information for End Demand Illinois.

---

[71] *Exploiting Americans on American Soil Hearing*, 2005, 29.

[72] End Demand for Sex Trafficking Act of 2005, H.R. 2012, 109th Congress, 2005.

[73] Michael Shively et al., *Developing a National Plan for Eliminating Sex Trafficking* (Cambridge,
MA: Abt Associates, Inc., 2010).

[74] Voices and Faces, "It's Not Marketing, It's a Movement: Our Anti-trafficking Campaign
Reaches the European Union, and Beyond" (April 2015), at www.voicesandfaces.org/emails/
apr2015-UglyTruth/index.html.

[75] End Demand Illinois, The Ugly Truth, at http://Voicesandfaces.org/new/EDI.html.

By contrast, Hollywood celebrities Ashton Kucher and Demi Moore attempted to use humor to discourage demand. In April of 2011, the Ashton and Demi Foundation launched the "Real Men Don't Buy Girls" interactive video campaign with the goal of discouraging "child sex slavery."[76] Kucher and Moore were inspired to create the campaign after seeing an NBC Dateline feature on child sex trafficking in Cambodia.[77] With a soundtrack of elevator music, the one-minute videos feature men doing household tasks in quirky and incompetent ways with a voiceover at the end saying "real men don't buy girls." In the video featuring Ashton Kucher, titled "Real Men Do Their Laundry," Kucher throws his dirty socks in the waste basket and then opens a new package of socks. In another video, "Real Men Know How to Use an Iron," Sean Penn is portrayed ironing a grilled cheese sandwich. Many of the videos feature celebrities, like Justin Timberlake, Jamie Foxx, and Isaiah Mustafa. Viewers were invited to upload their own photographs or videos pledging that "real men don't buy girls, and I am a real man." According to Kucher, "Once someone goes on record saying they are or aren't going to do something, they tend to be a bit more accountable."[78] Women also appeared in some of the videos, including Demi Moore and Ariana Huffington, professing that they prefer real men who do not buy girls.

On a more serious note, Kucher and Moore created Thorn Digital Defenders of Children, a non-profit organization with the goal of developing innovative technology to combat online commercial sexual exploitation of youth. With the support of private technology companies like Microsoft, Facebook, Twitter, and Google, as well as the National Center for Missing and Exploited Children, they created a technology task force "to bring the brightest minds in technology together to brainstorm" on how to fight the commercial sexual exploitation of children on the internet.[79] The Thorn Innovation Lab in San Francisco developed digital technologies to scour the internet to identify victims, disrupt platforms, and deter predators, including a computer program called Spotlight, which they distributed across the country to prosecutors and police departments, who were the intended users.

The evangelical organization Shared Hope International led the research effort into demand. With a federal grant from the Department of State, SHI conducted research into demand in several countries, including the United States, and produced an extensive report and a video based on this report in 2007.[80] Beginning in 2013, SHI has released yearly "Demanding Justice" assessments

[76] Lucas Kavner, "Ashton Kutcher and Demi Moore Launch 'Real Men Don't Buy Girls' Campaign," *Huffington Post* (April 11, 2011).

[77] *Children for Sale*, NBC Dateline, 2009.    [78] Ibid.

[79] Julie Cordua, Executive Director, Thorn, at www.wearethorn.org/child-sexual-exploitation-and-technology/.

[80] Shared Hope International, *DEMAND. A Comparative Examination of Sex Tourism and Trafficking in Jamaica, Japan, the Netherlands, and the United States* (Vancouver, WA: Shared Hope International, 2007); *Demand Documentary* (Vancouver, WA: Shared Hope International, 2011).

that evaluated each state's penalties for buying sex acts with minors, whether states had eliminated the mistake of age defense for buyers of sex acts with minors, and whether states were prosecuting buyers.[81] Some of the deterrents that SHI recommended were threat of punishment, inclusion on a sex offender registry, public exposure on a billboard, a newspaper notice or webpage, a letter to the family or employer, suspension of a driver's license, impounding a car, or increased fines. In 2014, SHI published a report on prosecutions of buyers in child sex trafficking cases in four localities, finding "excessive leniency and low sentencing."[82] They subsequently produced two more reports, *Demand Justice Report* in 2014 on "anti-demand enforcement methods" and *Demanding Justice Arizona* in 2015 on "demand deterrence and enforcement" in the state of Arizona,[83] and the same year they produced a video on demand, "Buyers Beware: Mobilizing to End Demand."[84]

Government officials have also supported public education and shaming campaigns to discourage demand. In Miami, Children's Trust of Miami Dade and the Women's Fund of Miami Dade produced a "Dear John" campaign similar to Atlanta's in 2012 with print, radio, and television ads featuring US Congresswomen Ileana Ros-Lehtinen, Debbie Wasserman Schultz, and Frederica Wilson, as well as State Attorney Katherine Fernandez-Rundle, Miami-Dade County.[85] In 2014, the Los Angeles District Attorney's Office sponsored a billboard campaign with the message: "Buying a teen for sex is child abuse. Turning a blind eye is neglect," and "Teens sold for sex aren't prostitutes. They're rape victims."[86] In late 2015, the Los Angeles County Board of Supervisors voted to publish the names and booking photos of those convicted of soliciting prostitution from minors.[87]

Some end demand activists advocated for rigorous prosecution and sentencing of buyers of sex with minors, including attempts to prosecute buyers as traffickers. Shared Hope International, for example, supported charging buyers under the TVPA and the Mann Act. In the case of *United States of America v. Laura Evet Lambden and Ben Allen Riggs*, SHI filed an amicus curiae brief in support of tougher sentencing. They argued for viewing the buyer of sex acts in a sex trafficking case as distinct from a "john" in a prostitution case, and for prosecuting the two types of cases differently.

---

[81] Shared Hope International, Demanding Justice, at www.demandingjustice.org/home/.
[82] Shared Hope International, *Demanding Justice Report* (Vancouver, WA: Shared Hope International, 2014).
[83] Shared Hope International, Resources, at http://sharedhope.org/resources/.
[84] Shared Hope International, *Buyers Beware: Mobilizing the End Demand* (2015).
[85] The ads ran in Spanish and English. See www.womensfundmiami.org/media/video-gallery; justicewomen.com/images/not-in-district.jpg.
[86] Dana Littlefield, "Ads to Warn of 'Ugly Truth' of Human Trafficking," *The San Diego Union Tribune* (June 27, 2016).
[87] Hillary Jackson, "'Shame Campaign' Targets Child Sex Seekers: If You're Convicted, Your Name and Photo to be Published," *Mylanews.com* (November 3, 2015).

In their brief, they argued, "purchasing sex acts with a 13-year-old is wholly different from prostitution, amounting essentially to purchased child rape."[88] They described the buyer as the "primary cause of the crime of child sex trafficking."[89] SHI has also pushed for amending the TVPA to explicitly allow for prosecution of buyers for sex trafficking under the "obtaining" prong of the definition of trafficking,[90] although others in the movement, such as Polaris Project and Rachel Lloyd, disagreed with that approach because they preferred to focus resources on assisting survivors.[91]

Encouraged by anti-trafficking activists, local, state, and federal prosecutors increasingly targeted men for buying sex from minors. In 2006, US Attorney Cynthia Cordes in Missouri set up the Human Trafficking Rescue Project to go after facilitators, but in 2008 expanded her focus to include buyers of sex from minors by using sting operations.[92] In Operation Guardian Angel, Cordes' team placed ads on Craigslist advertising young girls for sex. After hundreds of inquiries, seven men went every step of the way, offering cash for sex with under-aged girls. The men arrested included an insurance executive, a car dealership's finance manager, and a US Navy recruiter.[93] In Peachtree City, outside Atlanta, Georgia, a similar sting netted over 20 men from all walks of life, whose photographs were published in the *Atlanta Journal-Constitution*.[94] In 2013, the Eighth Circuit Court of Appeals issued a decision upholding prosecution of buyers for trafficking under the TVPA in the case of *United States v. Jungers and Boonestroo*.[95] This case involved a police sting resulting in the arrest of two South Dakota men who responded to ads for sex with girls aged eleven and fourteen. The Eighth Circuit ruled that persons arranging for or having sex with a child under the age of eighteen could be prosecuted for human trafficking under the TVPA. Taking a different approach, North Carolina passed a law prohibiting convicted sex offenders from accessing commercial social-networking websites that permit children to use them, but the Supreme Court struck down the law as a violation of the First Amendment.[96]

---

[88] Brief of Amicus Curiae Shared Hope International in Support of Sentencing, *United States of America v. Laura Evet Lambden and Ben Allen Riggs*, In the United States District Court for the District of Oregon, Portland Division, Case No. 3:13-cr-00294-JO (October 7, 2014), 3.

[89] Ibid.

[90] Samantha Healy Vardaman and Christine Raino, "Prosecuting Demand as a Crime of Human Trafficking: The Eighth Circuit Decision in *United States v. Jungers*," *University of Memphis Law Review* 43 (Summer 2013), 917–962. Both Vardaman and Raino worked for SHI's Protected Innocence Project.

[91] Interview with Brittany Vanderhoof, October 25, 2015 (on file with author); GEMS, "Four Reasons Why We Don't Support the JVTA and Why You Should Call Your Senator Today" (March 18, 2015) (on file with author).

[92] Sher, *Somebody's Daughter*, 266.      [93] Ibid. 266–267.

[94] Saeed Amed and Kathy Jefcoats, "The Sex Predator Next Door: Web Snares Pedophiles," *Atlanta Journal Constitution* (May 21, 2006), A8–9.

[95] 702 F.3rd 1066 (8th Cir. 2013).      [96] *Packingham v. North Carolina*, 137 S. Ct. 1730 (2017).

Sex worker organizations have pushed back against end demand campaigns. In 2006, the Desiree Alliance produced a fact sheet arguing that end demand approaches resulted in more danger for sex workers and redirected public funds away from social service toward policing efforts.[97] In a 2007 position paper, the Sex Workers Project argued that focusing on the factors creating vulnerability to entering the sex trade, like poverty, unemployment, and gender inequality was a much more effective way to protect the rights of sex workers and trafficked persons than attempting to curb demand.[98] In 2012, journalist Noy Thrupkaew wrote an opinion editorial in the *New York Times*, arguing that end demand strategies harmed sex trafficking victims and sex workers because they drive the sex trade further underground and increased the criminalization of those selling sex. Instead, Thrupkaew argued that the best solution to sex trafficking was "shelter, job opportunities, and a responsive and sensitive law-enforcement system."[99] The Freedom Network, a coalition of sex workers rights organizations, has adopted a policy statement against end demand campaigns. But despite this opposition, many advocates fighting the US youth sex trade have supported these campaigns. The anti-trafficking movement has been starkly divided on end demand, although groups like Alliance to End Slavery and Trafficking (ATEST) and Polaris Project have been largely silent on the issue.

## CRAIGSLIST AND BACKPAGE CAMPAIGNS

Another major focus of the movement against child sex trafficking has been online advertising for commercial sex, which has been countered by free speech advocates and sex worker rights groups. As early as 2005, Norma Hotaling raised the issue of the use of Craigslist as a tool to sell sex with young girls in the United States.[100] Anti-trafficking activists have pressured internet websites to cease hosting ads for sexual services, alleging that minors were advertised and sold through these websites. The first target was Craigslist.com. Police and attorneys general notified Craigslist that they believed that the website was being used by sex traffickers. In 2007, Chicago police used Craigslist to apprehend people engaged in prostitution, using undercover officers to nab both sellers and buyers of sexual services. In July of 2007, Craigslist began posting a notice on its website warning users that they would report human trafficking and child exploitation to the police. In late 2007, Craigslist entered into negotiations with representatives from Connecticut Attorney General

---

[97] Desiree Alliance, *End Demand Factsheet* (2006).

[98] Emilia Casella, Irene Martinetti, and Stephan Sastrawidjaja, *Critique of Focus on Demand in the Context of Trafficking in Persons: A Position Paper of the Sex Workers Project at the Urban Justice Center* (New York, NY: Urban Justice Center, 2007).

[99] Noy Thrupkaew, "A Misguided Moral Crusade," *New York Times* (September 22, 2012), SR 14.

[100] *Exploiting Americans on American Soil Hearings*, 2005, 27.

Richard Blumenthal's office and other attorneys general. In November, Craigslist made a deal with attorneys general from forty states that it would start charging a small fee for the "erotic services" ads and require the use of a credit card so that users could be tracked. They also manually screened ads and filtered out ones that might involve trafficking, child exploitation, or child pornography.[101] On the entry pages to the erotic services section of the website, they placed warnings, NCMEC's cyber tip line number, and requests for users to report suspicions of illegal activity.[102]

Despite these actions, Cook County Sheriff Tom Dart announced at a press conference in March of 2009 that he was suing Craigslist in federal court to get them to remove their "erotic services" section, citing FBI evidence that the website was being used to promote child prostitution. On May 13, 2009, Craigslist announced that it was closing down the "erotic services" section of its website and replacing it with an "adult services" section that they pledged would be closely monitored by employees for illegal activity. A federal court dismissed Tom Dart's lawsuit,[103] ruling that host companies were not responsible for posts by users under the 1996 Communications Decency Act,[104] but the pressure continued. In May of 2009, Rachel Lloyd wrote an open letter to Craigslist CEO Jim Buckmaster imploring him to stop accepting ads trafficking youth, telling the story of several GEMS girls who had been sold on the website, including an eleven-year-old child. Buckmaster responded by insisting that his company was working closely with law enforcement to identify any illegal activity on the website. In July, a coalition of eighty-five anti-trafficking organizations staged a protest outside of the Craigslist headquarters in San Francisco. Activists also organized a change.org petition titled "Petition to End Craigslist Sex Slave Trafficking." The Georgia based Rebecca's Project for Human Rights published an open letter in the *San Francisco Chronicle* in May of 2010. The letter, addressed to "Dear Craig" and from "AK & MC, Survivors of Craigslist Sex Trafficking," told the stories of two girls who were forced into prostitution by older men using Craigslist.com. The letter implored the company to close down its adult services section.[105] In August of 2010, Connecticut attorney general Richard Blumenthal along with sixteen other state attorneys sent a letter to Craigslist demanding that the company take down the "adult services" page.

In September, Buckmaster closed down the adult services section, which at the time was bringing in $36 million a year. The company at first blackened out

---

[101] *Domestic Minor Sex Trafficking Hearing, 2010,* 174, 179 (testimony of Elizabeth L. McDougall, attorney for Craigslist.com).

[102] Ibid. 175.   [103] *Dart v. Craigslist, Inc.,* 665 F. Supp. 2d 961 (N.D. Ill. Oct. 20, 2009).

[104] Section 230 of the Act says that "No provider or user of an interactive computer service shall be treated as the publisher or speaker of any information provided by another information content provider." The Communications Decency Act, 47 U.S.C. § 230.

[105] Paid Advertisement by The Rebecca Project for Human Rights, *San Francisco Chronicle* (May 19, 2010), A9.

the link with the word "censored," and eventually removed the page. Immediately after this closure, a September 14, 2010, letter signed by ninety-eight anti-trafficking activists implored Jim Buckmaster and Craig Newmark of Craigslist to shut down the adult and erotic services sections of their websites in other countries.[106] The letter challenged Craigslist's claim that human trafficking ads on their site were rare and, in response to Buckmaster's claim that users will just migrate to other websites, they argued that "user volume and name recognition of those sites pales in comparison to yours. They are not a household name like Craigslist."[107] The activists came from a wide range of organizations, collaborating across the political and ideological spectrum. They included service providers like GEMS and My Life My Choice, public policy organizations like Polaris Project and ECPAT-USA, feminist groups like NOW NYC, Ms. Foundation for Women, and more than fifteen other women's funds and foundations,[108] sexual assault centers, and religious organizations like Catholic Charities, Salvation Army, and Evangelicals for Social Action. Signers included Rachel Lloyd, Vednita Carter, Carol Smolenski, Frank Barnaba, Tina Frundt, Linda Smith, and Laura Lederer. On September 15, Congress held a hearing on how the internet was used in the commercial sexual exploitation of youth in the United States. Craigslist customer service director William Powell testified that Craigslist.com had discontinued its adult services section as of September 3, 2010, and they had no plans to reinstate it.[109]

The closure of the adult services section of Craigslist.com led to heated arguments about free speech, moral policing of sexuality, and endangering adult sex workers by driving them underground and reducing their ability to work independently. Sex worker rights advocates argued that online advertising was a useful tool for adult sex workers to avoid pimps and traffickers by working independently, pointing to evidence that after an earlier website, Redbook, was shut down many sex workers were forced to the streets.[110] The Electronic Frontier Foundation submitted written testimony to Congress for the 2010 hearing objecting to the pressure placed by governmental officials on Craigslist based on free speech grounds. Senior researcher at Microsoft Research danah boyd argued against censoring Craigslist on the grounds that visibility made it easier to help victims and investigate perpetrators because law enforcement could work with ISPs to collect data and do systematic online stings. She argued, "Censorship online is nothing more than whack-a-mole, pushing the issue elsewhere or more underground." She also argued that

---

[106] *Domestic Minor Sex Trafficking Hearing, 2010*, 273–280.    [107] Ibid. 275.

[108] Sara Gould of Ms. Foundation reported that Chris Grumm of the Women's Funding Network, inspired by an Atlanta donor particularly committed to this issue, recruited women's funds from around the country to sign on to the letter. Interview with Sara Gould, August 25, 2016 (on file with author).

[109] *Domestic Minor Sex Trafficking Hearing, 2010*, 169.

[110] Correspondence with Sienna Baskin, January 12, 2018.

Craigslist increased the safety of sex workers by enabling them to work without facilitators.[111] The Center for Democracy and Technology submitted written testimony opposing the imposition of obligations on service providers to police online content. This controversy also led to claims that activists used falsely inflated numbers of sexually exploited youth, a position advanced in a series of articles in the *Village Voice*, owner of Backpage.com, which then became the most popular venue for adult service ads and the target of anti-trafficking activists.[112]

In May of 2009, when Craigslist implemented the credit card payment procedure, and on September 3, 2010, when Craigslist took down its adult services section, activity on Backpage.com spiked, according to Backpage's counsel Liz McDougall's testimony before Congress in 2010.[113] In August of 2011, attorneys general from forty-eight states and nineteen US senators wrote to Village Voice Media demanding that it stop advertising sex with minors on Backpage.com.[114] A coalition of religious leaders called Groundswell in New York City published a full-page ad in the *New York Times* urging Village Voice Media to shut down the adult section on Backpage.com and in March of 2012 delivered a petition to Backpage with over 225,000 signatures at a protest in front of the VVM headquarters in Cooper's Square.[115] Around the same time, the Coalition Against Trafficking in Women (CATW) organized a change.org petition[116] and staged street protests against Backpage, including one at the headquarters of Village Voice Media in New York City in June of 2012.[117] In September of that year, because of the loss of advertisers, VVM split off Backpage into a separate company from the thirteen alternative weeklies owned by the company.[118] The same year, the US Senate passed a resolution calling upon VVM to "act as a responsible global citizen and immediately eliminate the 'adult entertainment' section of the classified advertising website Backpage.com to terminate the website's rampant facilitation of online sex trafficking."[119]

In 2012, three under-aged girls filed a lawsuit against Village Voice Media in Washington State alleging that they were advertised and sold for sex by adults

---

[111] *Domestic Minor Sex Trafficking Hearing, 2010*, 209.
[112] Martin Cizmar, Ellis Conklin, and Kristen Hinman, "Real Men Get Their Facts Straight: Ashton and Demi and Sex Trafficking," *Village Voice* (June 29, 2011).
[113] *Domestic Minor Sex Trafficking Hearing, 2010*, 175, 176 (statement of Liz McDougall, Partner, Perkins Coie LLP, Seattle, WA).
[114] Letter from the National Association of Attorneys General to Samuel Fifer, dated August 31, 2011, available at www.law.alaska.gov/pdf/press/083111-NAAGletter.pdf
[115] Village Voice/Backpage Petition Delivery, Groundswell, at www.groundswell-mvmt.org/vvm-petition-delivery/#Photos
[116] Groundswell, Petition to Tell Village Voice Media to Stop Child Sex Trafficking on Backpage.com, at www.change.org/p/tell-village-voice-media-to-stop-child-sex-trafficking-on-backpage-com.
[117] Backpage.com Protest, Facebook, at www.facebook.com/events/430221443669476/.
[118] Sher, *Somebody's Daughter*, 327.     [119] S. Res. 439, 112th Cong. (2012).

on Backpage.com beginning when they were between the ages of thirteen and fifteen. In response, VVM argued that it was immune from suit under the Communications Decency Act of 1996. The lower court denied VVM's motion to dismiss, so VVM appealed to the Washington Supreme Court. The plaintiffs' attorneys argued that Backpage actively coached advertisers about how to avoid criminal liability for trafficking children. Several advocacy groups filed amicus curiae briefs supporting the plaintiffs in the case, including one by the Coalition Against Trafficking in Women[120] and another by the National Crime Victim Law Institute, Shared Hope International, Covenant House, and Human Rights Project for Girls.[121] A diverse group of activists signed onto the CATW brief, including Vednita Carter, the President of New York NOW Sonia Ossorio, and several religious groups. The brief emphasized young people's economic, emotional, and psychological vulnerability, as well as their need for "protection from decisions relating to sexual activity" and their lack of choice in whether to engage in commercial sex because of the coercive tactics of traffickers.[122] They concluded that granting immunity to VVM under the Communications Decency Act would cut off victims' ability to seek redress against the websites that facilitate the sexual exploitation of children.

In September of 2015, the Supreme Court of Washington State refused to dismiss the lawsuit against Village Voice Media, allowing the case to go to trial. However, a similar case against Backpage filed by three young women in Boston in 2014 was dismissed by a federal court, which ruled that the Communications Decency Act of 1996 shielded Backpage from liability for the content of its ads.[123] A similar array of activist groups filed briefs in the Boston case, including CATW, Legal Momentum, and FAIR Girls, as well as the NCMEC. Washington, Tennessee, and New Jersey passed laws imposing criminal penalties on internet service providers that host advertisements for sex with minors, but Backpage successfully challenged these laws in court.[124] Taking a different approach, the Sheriff of Cook County Tom Dart successfully pressured Visa, American Express, and MasterCard to cut their ties with Backpage in 2015.

[120] Amicus Curiae Brief of the Coalition Against Trafficking in Women (C.A.T.W.) in Support of Respondents, *J.S., S.L., and L.C. v. Village Voice Media Holdings*, Supreme Court of the State of Washington, No. 905-10-0 (September 3, 2014).
[121] Brief of Amici Curiae National Crime Victim Law Institute, Shared Hope International, Covenant House, and Human Rights Project for Girls, *J.S., S.L., and L.C. v. Village Voice Media Holdings*, Supreme Court of the State of Washington, No. 905-10-0 (September 4, 2014).
[122] Ibid. 7, 10-11. A similar case was dismissed in Missouri in 2011. *M.A. v. Village Voice Media*, 809 F.Supp.2nd 1049 (E.D. Mo. 2011).
[123] *Jane Doe No. 1 et al. v. Backpage.com*, 104 F. Supp. 3rd 149 (D. Mass. 2015), 817 F. 3rd 12 (1st Cir. 2016), *cert. denied* No. 16-276, Supreme Court of the United States (January 9, 2017).
[124] *Backpage.com v. McKenna*, 881 F. Supp. 2nd 1262 (W.D. Wash. 2012); *Backpage.com v. Cooper*, 939 F.Supp.2nd 805 (M.D. Tenn. 2013); *Backpage.com v. Hoffman*, Civil Action No. 2:13:03952 (CCC-JBC) (United States District Court for the District of New Jersey, May 14, 2014).

Backpage sued Dart, arguing that he used his legal authority to suppress its protected speech in violation of the First Amendment. Judge Richard Posner for the Seventh Circuit Court of Appeals ruled in favor of Backpage.[125]

The CEO of Backpage.com, Carl Ferrer, and Backpage's controlling shareholders, James Larkin and Michael Lacey, have also been targeted. In 2016, Texas police raided the Dallas headquarters of Backpage.com and arrested Ferrer. California prosecutors charged Ferrer, Lacey, and Larkin with pimping a minor, pimping, and conspiracy to commit pimping, but the charges were later dismissed as violating the Communications Decency Act, which established that internet service providers are not liable for the words of third party users of their services.[126] Prosecutors then refiled pimping and money laundering charges. At the federal level, the Senate Permanent Subcommittee on Investigations initiated an investigation into Backpage. com. On March 17, 2016, the Senate voted to hold Backpage.com in contempt for refusing to comply with a subpoena to Ferrer to testify and to hand over documents relating to how it handles ads that might involve minors on the adult services section of its website, which Ferrer unsuccessfully challenged in court.[127] In late 2016, the Senate Permanent Subcommittee on Investigations issued a report accusing Backpage.com of knowingly facilitating online sex trafficking. The Report alleged that Backpage.com used a computer program to delete words like "young" and "teenager," which amounted to "coaching" facilitators on how to make their ads appear legitimate.[128] The Subcommittee then subpoenaed Ferrer and several other Backpage.com executives to testify, but the executives invoked their Fifth Amendment rights against self-incrimination.[129] On January 9, 2017, the evening before the executives were to appear before Congress, Backpage.com shut down its adult services ads, posting a notice on the website saying "the government has unconstitutionally censored this content" under the word "CENSORED" in red.[130]

In March of 2018, Congress passed the Stop Enabling Sex Traffickers Act and the Allow States and Victims to Fight Online Sex Trafficking Act, referred to as SESTA-FOSTA, which allows states to criminally prosecute internet

---

[125] *Backpage.com v. Thomas J. Dart*, 807 F.3rd 229 (7th Cir., 2015), *cert. denied*, 137 S. Ct. 46 (2016).

[126] *California vs Ferrer, Lacey and Larkin*, Case No. 16FE019224, Dept. No. 61 (Cal. Super December 9, 2016).

[127] S. Res. 377, 114th Congress, March 17, 2016; *Ferrer v. Senate Permanent Subcommittee on Investigations*, 137 S.C. 28 (Mem.) (September 13, 2016).

[128] Senate Permanent Subcommittee on Investigations, Backpage.com's Knowing Facilitation of Online Sex Trafficking, Staff Report (January 9, 2017).

[129] "Backpage Execs Refuse to Testify at Sex Trafficking Hearing," *New York Times* (January 10, 2017).

[130] Derek Hawkins, "Backpage.com Shuts Down Adult Services Ads After Relentless Pressure from Authorities," *Washington Post* (January 8, 2017).

service providers who "promote or facilitate" prostitution of another person, and also allows individuals to sue internet service providers for civil damages for harm resulting from such actions.[131] Sex workers condemned the law for decreasing their ability to screen their clients and work independently, whereas civil libertarians warned of the chilling effects of the law on internet speech. Others, including some sex trafficking survivors and their advocates, argued that the law would impede investigations into sex trafficking because it would make it harder to identify victims.[132]

## IMPROVING THE CHILD WELFARE AND CRIMINAL JUSTICE SYSTEMS' RESPONSE TO YOUTH INVOLVED IN THE SEX TRADE

In addition to campaigns focused on ending demand and decreasing internet-facilitated child sex trafficking, activists also pushed for improvements to the child welfare system because youth in foster care were particularly vulnerable to commercial sexual exploitation. There have been state-level efforts to address this issue as well as Congressional action. In 2008, the state of Illinois engaged the International Organization for Adolescents (IOFA) and the Center for Human Rights of Children at Loyola University Chicago to assess the child welfare response to sex and labor trafficking of youth in Illinois and to make policy recommendations for how better to identify and serve those youth. These organizations created a project called ChildRight with the goal "to identify and address systemic gaps in knowledge, behavior, policies, and procedures in child welfare systems."[133] In 2011, they published a handbook, *Building Child Welfare Response to Child Trafficking*, "to build the capacity of state and public child welfare agencies to respond to human trafficking cases involving children."[134] The handbook covered identification and investigation, case management, legal protections and advocacy, and referral and resources. The ChildRight project conducted trainings with child welfare professionals around the state and generated new protocols and policies to guide child welfare investigations.[135] In 2013, New York State's Office of Children & Family Services subcontracted with IOFA to create ChildRight New York to conduct a similar assessment in New York

[131] Public Law No. 115-164 (2018).
[132] Melissa Gira Grant, "Proposed Federal Trafficking Legislation Has Surprising Opponents: Advocates Who Work with Trafficking Victims," *Injustice Today* (January 26, 2018), at https://injusticetoday.com/proposed-federal-trafficking-legislation-has-surprising-opponents-advocates-who-work-with-bf418c73d5b4.
[133] International Organization for Adolescents, *ChildRight Illinois* (2008–2012).
[134] Katherine Kaufka, Shelby French, Heather Moore, and Sehla Ashai, *Building Child Welfare Response to Child Trafficking* (Chicago: Loyola's Center for the Human Rights of Children and the International Organization for Adolescents, 2011), 19.
[135] *ChildRight Illinois* (2008–2012).

State and to develop a plan to implement its safe harbor law.[136] The project trained child welfare professionals and local service providers across the state, convened a statewide Blueprint steering committee and subcommittees, facilitated the drafting of a statewide Blueprint/Operational Framework and a handbook for New York, and provided technical assistance. In eight pilot regions, eighty-eight partners continued to meet monthly and developed customized action plans.

In 2013, Congress held two hearings on the relationship between the child welfare system and child sex trafficking, and considered multiple bills.[137] Representatives working with youth in child services and foster care participated in these hearings, reflecting the expanding scope of advocates working on sex trafficking of youth. The Senate Committee on Finance held a hearing, entitled "Sex Trafficking and Exploitation in America: Child Welfare's Role in Prevention and Intervention," on June 11, 2013.[138] The purpose of this hearing was to discuss the limitations of the child welfare system in preventing sex trafficking of foster youth. Asia Graves, an African American youth survivor and program coordinator at FAIR Girls in Washington, DC, testified about her experience of being trafficked in Boston as a youth in foster care and made recommendations about how to improve the child welfare system to better serve trafficked youth, including funding for specialized homes, educating social workers and teachers about youth sex trafficking, and prevention education for youth.[139] Several witnesses argued for expanding child welfare services beyond familial abuse and neglect to include any abuse. A second hearing, "Sex Trafficking of Foster Youth," was held on October 23, 2013, before the Subcommittee on Human Resources of the House Ways and Means Committee.[140] Several witnesses from nongovernmental organizations that advocate for youth in the child welfare and juvenile justice systems testified about the strong connection between experiences in foster care and vulnerability to commercial sexual exploitation.

---

[136] *Child Right New York* (2013–present); Interview with Sienna Baskin, April 22, 2016 (on file with author).

[137] Child Sex Trafficking Data and Response Act (H.R. 2744), Child Welfare Response to Human Trafficking Act (H.R. 1732), End Sex Trafficking Act (H.R. 2805), Improving Outcomes for Youth at Risk for Sex Trafficking Act (S.1518), and Strengthening Child Welfare Response to Trafficking Act (H.R. 1732).

[138] *Sex Trafficking and Exploitation in America: Child Welfare's Role in Prevention and Intervention: Hearing Before the Committee on Finance, Senate*, 113th Cong., 1st Sess. (June 11, 2013).

[139] Jennifer B. McKim, "From Victim to Survivor," *Boston Globe* (November 27, 2012).

[140] *Sex Trafficking of Foster Youth, Before the Subcommittee on Human Resources of the House Ways and Means Committee*, 113th Cong., 1st Sess. (October 23, 2013) [herinafter *Sex Trafficking of Foster Youth Hearing*, 2013]. The House Ways and Means Committee also held a field hearing in Seattle in February 2014. *Field Hearing on Ways to Prevent and Address Child Sex Trafficking in Washington State, Before the Subcommittee on Human Resources of the House Ways and Means Committee*, 113th Cong., 2nd Sess. (February 19, 2014).

Withelma T. Ortiz Walker Pettigrew of Human Rights Advocates for Girls (Rights4Girls) testified that the foster care system made youth vulnerable to control by "pimps" because it "inadvertently, objectifies the presence of youth for monetary purposes, and it also normalizes the idea to youth that other people are supposed to control their lives and circumstances," as well as preventing "the opportunity to gain meaningful relationships and attachments."[141] Congress was persuaded to address the foster care system in two federal laws in the following two years.

In the 2013 reauthorization of the Trafficking Victims Protection Act, Congress passed new provisions to address youth sex trafficking in the United States.[142] The Act required state foster care and adoption programs to develop prevention measures and victim assistance regarding commercial sexual exploitation of youth. The Act funded twelve-month block grants of $1,500,000 to $2,000,000 to be awarded to up to six qualified nongovernmental organizations in different regions to support the housing needs of youth who have experienced domestic minor sex trafficking. The next year, Congress passed the Preventing Sex Trafficking and Strengthening Families Act,[143] which required that States develop policies and procedures to identify and assist youth in the foster care system who were victims of sex trafficking, or were at risk of being trafficked. The Act required reporting and data collection on sex trafficked youth and created a National Advisory Committee on the Sex Trafficking of Children and Youth in the United States to advise the Secretary of Health and Human Services and the Attorney General on how to improve the nation's response to the sex trafficking of youth in the United States.

There were also efforts to provide training for judges about domestic minor sex trafficking, particularly for youth in state care. In 2015, the National Council of Juvenile and Family Court Judges (NCJFCJ) and the NCMEC published a technical assistance brief for the judiciary on missing children, state care, and child sex trafficking.[144] Sponsored by the Office of Juvenile Justice and Delinquency Prevention, the report sought to educate judges about child sex trafficking and how to use the services of the NCMEC for locating and recovering children missing from state care. Starting in 2015, the NCJFCJ began sponsoring an annual two-day intensive workshop, The National Judicial Institute on Domestic Child Sex Trafficking, to train judicial officers on "victim behavior, ethics and judicial decision-making"

---

[141] *Sex Trafficking of Foster Youth Hearing*, 2013.

[142] The Trafficking Victims Protection Reauthorization Act of 2013, Pub. L. 113-4 (March 7, 2013), 127 Stat. 56, 42 USC §13701 (2013).

[143] H.R. 4980, Pub. L. 113-183 (September 29, 2014), 128 Stat. 1919, 42 USC §1305 (2014).

[144] Melissa Snow and Mimari Hall, *Missing Children, State Care, and Child Sex Trafficking: Engaging the Judiciary in Building a Collaborative Response*, Technical Assistance Brief (Alexandria, VA and Reno, NV: National Center for Missing & Exploited Children and National Council of Juvenile and Family Court Judges, 2015).

related to domestic child sex trafficking.[145] The goal of these efforts was to increase awareness, understanding, and sensitivity among law enforcement, child welfare, and court personnel encountering youth involved in the sex trade.

There were also efforts to reform state criminal justice systems. Despite federal anti-trafficking policy that defined youth involved in prostitution as victims of a severe form of human trafficking, in many states, youth involved in the sex trade were still arrested, charged, and convicted for prostitution or related offenses.[146] Polaris Project and Shared Hope International were the leading national organizations pushing for state law reform, including safe harbor laws. Both organizations evaluated states on their progress toward adopting laws that they believed were crucial to a comprehensive anti-trafficking legal framework. Polaris Project rated each state on ten categories of laws, including safe harbor laws, protection for sex trafficked minors, and lowering the burden of proof for sex trafficking of minors.[147] They also drafted model policies and provided policy consultation to activists and legislators around the country. They used social media, including Facebook, Twitter, and online petitions to educate the public about juvenile sex trafficking and the need for safe harbor laws and pressured legislators to adopt them.[148] For example, the Director of Client Services at Polaris Project, Caroline De Los Rios, initiated a change.org petition in 2012 titled "Kids Not Criminals – Support Safe Harbor Laws," which petitioned state lawmakers to support safe harbor legislation.[149] At the federal level, Polaris Project worked on legislation to create incentives for states to pass safe harbor laws and they advocated for federal funding to support services for commercially sexually exploited youth. Polaris supported broad safe harbor laws that guaranteed immunity from arrest and prosecution for youth until age eighteen. Shared Hope International issued a report evaluating each state's laws, similar to the federal Trafficking in Persons annual report on nations' response to trafficking. SHI's criteria for evaluation were whether the states criminalized domestic minor sex trafficking, including the facilitators and buyers; whether states provided "protection for child victims"; and whether states expanded law

---

[145] National Council of Juvenile and Family Court Judges, National Judicial Institute on Domestic Child Sex Trafficking, 2016, at www.ncjfcj.org/DCST2016.

[146] Tamar R. Birckhead, "The 'Youngest Profession': Consent, Autonomy, and Prostituted Children," *Washington University Law Review 88* (2011), 1055–1115, at 1062.

[147] Polaris Project, *How Does Your State Rate on Human Trafficking Laws in 2012?* (Washington, DC: Polaris Project, 2012). The ten categories were: (1) Sex trafficking, (2) Labor trafficking, (3) (a) Asset forfeiture and/or (b) Investigative tools, (4) (a) Training on human trafficking and/or (b) Human trafficking task force, commission, or advisory committee, (5) Posting of a human trafficking hotline, (6) Safe harbor; protecting sex trafficked minors, (7) Lower burden of proof for sex trafficking of minors, (8) Victim assistance, (9) Access to civil damages, and (10) Vacating convictions for sex trafficking victims.

[148] Interview with Britanny Vanderhoof, October 25, 2015.

[149] Polaris Project, Petitioning State Lawmakers, Kids Not Criminals – Pass Safe Harbor Laws, at www.change.org/p/state-lawmakers-kids-not-criminals-pass-safe-harbor-laws.

enforcement and criminal justice tools to aid in investigations and prosecutions.[150]

In addition to Polaris Project and SHI, the American Bar Association (ABA) worked for reform of state laws. The ABA adopted a child trafficking policy that recommended that states prohibit arresting or charging young people "with the crimes of prostitution, solicitation, or loitering as well as other offenses, including status offenses that are incident to their trafficking situation."[151] In 2013, the American Bar Association's Uniform Law Commission released a model human trafficking law with several provisions relating to minors, including a model safe harbor law.[152] Even Congress put pressure on states to reform their laws by passing the Justice for Victims of Trafficking Act, which explicitly encouraged states to adopt safe harbor laws.[153]

At the state level, activists pushed for safe harbor laws to protect youth from prostitution charges, but faced some opposition. A range of arguments have been made against safe harbor laws. Some law enforcement professionals have argued that arrest was the only way to protect minors, and that without it, youth returned to abusive situations. They argued that prosecution protected youth from their own self-destructive behavior and that it was the only way to ensure youth would receive services. Law enforcement professionals have also argued that the threat of prosecution was the best way to persuade youth to give information or to testify against their traffickers. Opponents of safe harbor laws argued that these laws would encourage the prostitution of youth, leading to more sexual exploitation of youth, because precluding prosecution through decriminalization would create a loophole for those who exploit minors for prostitution. Some expressed concern about how expensive it was to provide services for youth exiting the commercial sex trade. Others argued that some children freely choose to enter prostitution in order to profit financially, so that they should be held criminally liable. In Florida, arguments against a proposed safe harbor law included that "some kids are bad kids," that kids would flood into Florida from around the country if juvenile prostitution was decriminalized, and that survivors would absorb a disproportionate share of Florida's "Road to Independence" scholarships available to foster children for education. Some people pushed for a mandatory lock-down period of ten

[150] Shared Hope International & American Center for Justice and Law, *Protected Innocence Legislative Framework: Methodology* (Vancouver, WA: Shared Hope International, 2010) and *Protected Innocence State Report Card* at http://sharedhope.org/what-we-do/bring-justice/reportcards/#reportcards.

[151] American Bar Association, *Policies on Human Trafficking* (2011).

[152] National Conference of Commissioners on Uniform State Laws, *Legislative Fact Sheet – Prevention of and Remedies for Human Trafficking*, Section 15: Immunity of a Minor, 10. See, for example, Minnesota Department of Public Safety Office of Justice Programs, *No Wrong Door: A Comprehensive Approach to Safe Harbor for Minnesota's Sexually Exploited Youth* (2013).

[153] Public Law 114-22 (May 29, 2015), 129 Stat. 228, 18 USC §3014.

months for survivors of prostitution based on the belief that they were "brainwashed" by their facilitators.[154]

In response to arguments against safe harbor laws, advocates countered that these laws would not decriminalize the prostitution of youth because other laws prohibited individuals from facilitating and purchasing sex from youth. They argued that decriminalizing commercial sex acts by youth would allow law enforcement to build relationships of trust with youth because they were not at risk of prosecution. They also argued that youth would be more likely to seek services of police or medical professionals if they were not at risk of prosecution. Finally, they argued that laws already existed or could be amended to permit child welfare agencies to provide medical and therapeutic services. The Florida legislature passed a safe harbor law in 2009, without the lockdown provision.

As of 2015, thirty-four states had passed some form of safe harbor law, but these laws varied widely with regard to level of services, the age to which immunity from criminal prosecution extended, and the type of immunity. For example, Tennessee provided complete immunity from criminal prosecution until the age of eighteen, but offered very few services to assist youth trying to leave the sex trade. Law enforcement who encountered youth trading sex were required to provide a national human trafficking hotline number to the youth, but could not arrest or otherwise detain them. Illinois, on the other hand, provided immunity and full services until the age of eighteen. Other states limited immunity to youth under the age of sixteen, first offenders, or youth who comply with treatment protocols. Some states that do not provide immunity direct or allow law enforcement to refer minors to child welfare or other system-based services instead of arrest or diversion. Kansas does not provide youth immunity from prostitution charges, but requires that law enforcement place minors in protective custody in a staff-secure facility.[155]

In addition to safe harbor laws, many states passed laws specifically prohibiting domestic minor sex trafficking.[156] These laws enhanced penalties, allowed for asset forfeiture, provided training and enhanced investigative tools to law enforcement, created state-level task forces on trafficking, created human trafficking hotlines, lowered the burden of proof for convicting defendants accused of trafficking youth, provided victim assistance, allowed victims to sue traffickers for civil damages, and vacated convictions for sex trafficking victims. In 2011, a Minnesota safe harbor law created the No Wrong Door program, a model for serving sexually exploited youth.[157] This statewide, trauma-informed, victim-centered program brought together multiple

---

[154] Interview with Sandy Skelaney, May 27, 2016 (on file with author).

[155] National Conference of State Legislatures, *Human Trafficking Overview* (May 19, 2014); Shared Hope International, *JuST Response State Systems Mapping Report* (Vancouver, WA: Shared Hope International, 2015), 42.

[156] Polaris Project maintains updated information on state anti-sex trafficking laws on their website at www.polarisproject.org/what-we-do/policy-advocacy/state-policy/current-laws.

[157] 2015 Minnesota Statutes 260B.007.

government and non-governmental stakeholders to address the problem of sexually exploited youth. The program created a statewide director and regional "navigators," who coordinate anti-trafficking activities in their region. After the passage of a safe harbor Act in 2009, the Florida State Attorney created an "in-house, one-stop human trafficking unit," dismantling local units working on the issue. In New York, Judge Fernando Camacho, an administrative judge for criminal matters in Queens County, created a specialized "human trafficking court" in 2011 for adults charged with prostitution, including 16- and 17-years-olds who are treated as adults in New York. Rather than just fines or incarceration, the court provided services as part of sentencing.[158] Similar courts have been created in Hawaii, California, Texas, and Ohio.[159] The Attorney General in Georgia, Sam Olens, who served on the board of Street GRACE, led his own campaign against domestic minor sex trafficking, creating the "Not Buying It" Initiative to encourage other states to prosecute buyers, train mandated reporters, and "incentivize" businesses and community organizations to fight against sex trafficking.[160] As part of the campaign, Olens produced a public service announcement featuring sports stars from the Atlanta Falcons, Hawks, and Braves speaking out against child sex trafficking.[161] These were just a few of the many state-level efforts to combat child sex trafficking.

At the federal level, anti-trafficking activists pushed Congress to strengthen criminal justice responses to trafficking. In March of 2014, the Subcommittee on Crime, Terrorism, and Homeland Security of the House Judiciary Committee held a hearing entitled "Innocence for Sale: Domestic Minor Sex Trafficking."[162] Witnesses included a federal prosecutor, a state police officer, a juvenile court judge, and the survivor activist Pettigrew. Some witnesses and members of Congress called for stronger criminal justice responses to domestic minor sex trafficking, repeatedly employing the "lost innocence" framing of the problem. In one of the rare occasions when race was explicitly addressed, African American Representative John Conyers, Jr. (D-WI) questioned a Maryland police officer about the race of buyers and youth involved, noting that he "wanted to get the color question in here because I think if we do not, we will not get a real clear picture," suggesting the police failure to arrest johns, who were usually white, might be due to race.

In 2015, Congress passed the Justice for Victims of Trafficking Act.[163] The law required people convicted of sexual exploitation of children to pay

---

[158] "Changing Perceptions: A Conversation on Prostitution Diversion with Judge Fernando Camacho," Center for Court Innovation, January 2012.

[159] Kristin Finklea, *Juvenile Victims of Domestic Sex Trafficking: Juvenile Justice Issues* (Washington, DC: US Congressional Research Service, 2014), 12–13.

[160] Street Grace, Not Buying It, at www.streetgrace.org/notbuyingit.

[161] AG Sam Olens, "Georgia's Not Buying It" PSA, at www.youtube.com/watch?v=EqBoThjeuyk.

[162] *Innocence for Sale Hearing,* 2014.

[163] Justice for Victims of Trafficking Act, Pub. L. 114-22, 129 Stat. 227 (May 29, 2015).

a $5,000 fine to go into a new Domestic Trafficking Victims' Fund, which provided block grants to states to be used for investigation and prosecution of child sex trafficking and services for youth survivors. The Act also encouraged states to adopt safe harbor laws, defined individuals who patronize or solicit persons for a commercial sex act as culpable for sex trafficking, and required that defendants in child sex trafficking cases prove by clear and convincing evidence that they reasonably believed that a minor was eighteen or over.[164] Many anti-trafficking organizations supported the law, including the Human Rights Project for Girls, but others opposed it, like GEMS. Rachel Lloyd did not support the Act because it prioritized the criminal justice system response to trafficking over services for youth or support for prevention efforts. GEMS objected to four aspects of the law in particular: funding was prioritized for law enforcement and prosecutors over victims' services; the law strongly encouraged cooperation with law enforcement; the law authorized courts to exercise extended jurisdiction over youth considered at risk for trafficking; and buyers would be charged as traffickers.[165] These objections stemmed from GEMS's preference for supporting a social service response to the problem rather than directing resources to the criminal justice system.

In addition to Congressional action, the FBI continued to work on the issue of child sex trafficking. By September of 2016, the FBI Innocence Lost National Initiative was coordinating seventy-four dedicated task forces on child sex trafficking and working groups of federal, state, and local law enforcement agencies throughout the US, working in tandem with the US Attorney Offices. To support these efforts, NCMEC created a Child Sex Trafficking Team to provide assistance to law enforcement agencies in identifying and recovering victims of child sex trafficking and prosecuting traffickers.[166] Between 2003 and 2016, the FBI had conducted ten cross-country stings that claimed to remove over 6000 youth from the sex trade, convicted more than 2500 adults for facilitating youth involvement in prostitution, and seized more than $3 million in assets.[167] One investigation, named "Stormy Nights," focused on the interstate prostitution of children at truck stops in Oklahoma, and resulted in the conviction of a man who trafficked two minor girls.[168] Another investigation, "Precious Cargo," targeted trafficking at truck stops in Harrisburg, Pennsylvania. The FBI reported that over one hundred and fifty

---

[164] Summary: S. 178 – 114th Congress (2015-2016).

[165] GEMS, Four Reasons Why We Don't Support the JVTA and Why You Should Call Your Senator Today, March 18, 2015.

[166] National Center for Missing and Exploited Children, Child Sex Trafficking Team, at www .missingkids.com/CSTT.

[167] FBI Innocence Lost National Initiative, at www.fbi.gov/investigate/violent-crime/cac.

[168] *United States v. Carlos Curtis*, No. 06-3047, United States Court of Appeals, District of Columbia Circuit, March 20, 2007.

victims were identified, forty-five of whom had been in the sex trade when they were underage and the youngest of whom was twelve. This investigation resulted in the indictment of eighteen individuals, and several were sentenced to long prison terms.[169] Sex worker advocates, however, have questioned these numbers, alleging that youth were arrested in the raids and many more adult sex workers were arrested than youth "rescued." They also question whether youth were provided with the services they needed to stay out of the sex trade.[170]

Throughout his presidency, Barack Obama took action against international human trafficking but, unlike his predecessor George W. Bush, Obama also addressed domestic sex trafficking of American youth. In August of 2008, Barack Obama, before winning the presidency, called on the nation to address domestic sex trafficking.[171] In September of 2012, President Obama delivered a speech on human trafficking in which he called attention to the plight of the "teenage girl, beaten, forced to walk the streets."[172] In 2012, President Obama created an interagency anti-trafficking task force with representatives from seventeen agencies, including Attorney General Eric Holder, Secretary of Health and Human Services Kathleen Sebelius, and Secretary of Homeland Security Jeh Johnson. The task force created a five-year action plan to strengthen "coordination, collaboration, and capacity" across governmental and nongovernmental entities that support victims of human trafficking, including survivors of domestic minor sex trafficking.[173] The plan advocated a victim-centered approach to treatment, public awareness, and outreach efforts, including expanded access to services and research to support evidence-based practices in victim services. In 2013, President Obama also supported the reauthorization of the TVPA.[174]

The Department of Justice's Office of Juvenile Justice and Delinquency Prevention (OJJDP) has also been very active in combatting the commercial sexual exploitation of youth with several programs focusing on child sex trafficking, including the Mentoring Child Victims of Commercial Sexual Exploitation and Domestic Minor Sex Trafficking Initiative, which supports organizations working with youth victims of domestic sex trafficking. To further professional education, they produced seventeen webinars on child sex trafficking between September of 2014 and October of 2015, and they

[169] *Domestic Minor Sex Trafficking Hearing, 2010*, 131.

[170] Correspondence with Sienna Baskin, January 12, 2018.

[171] Sher, *Somebody's Daughter*, 251.

[172] President Barack Obama, Clinton Global Initiatives Speech, September 25, 2012, at www .whitehouse.gov/issues/foreign-policy/end-human-trafficking.

[173] US Department of Justice, Department of Health and Human Services, and Department of Homeland Security, *Coordination, Capacity, Collaboration: Federal Strategic Action Plan on Services for Victims of Human Trafficking in the United States 2013-2017* (Washington, DC: US Department of Justice, 2014).

[174] Trafficking Victims Protection Reauthorization Act of 2013, Pub. Law 113-4, § 1201 et seq., 42 USC 13701.

disseminated information on child sex trafficking through their National Training and Technical Assistance Center. They have also supported multiple research projects on commercial sexual exploitation of youth and have produced several publications on child sex trafficking as well, including a technical assistance brief for judges on the intersection of the juvenile justice and child welfare systems in the lives of missing and trafficked youth.[175] In 2013, OJJDP issued policy guidance discouraging the placement of girls and young women who were status offenders or domestic minor sex trafficking victims in the juvenile justice system.[176]

By 2015, the movement had clearly succeeded in convincing the public and policymakers that domestic minor sex trafficking was a serious problem that warranted strong responses at the local, state, and federal levels. The movement has made some progress in reforming the criminal justice and child welfare systems by decreasing the criminal prosecution of youth involved in prostitution, expanding services to youth, and increasing criminal prosecution of adult facilitators.

## CONCLUSION

Withelma T. Ortiz Walker Pettigrew's call for reforms to the foster care and criminal justice systems before Congress in 2014 signified a shift in the movement against child sex trafficking in the United States. In the first decade of the century, policymakers focused primarily on criminal justice solutions to the problem of child sex trafficking, especially enhancing criminal penalties for trafficking and prosecuting traffickers, and to a lesser extent providing services to youth, especially to encourage them to testify against their traffickers. They framed the issue in terms of victimized children and the adults who preyed upon them. In the 2010s, advocates and policymakers, while continuing to use these traditional strategies and framings, also began turning toward improving system responses – the criminal justice system's treatment of youth in the sex trade and the child welfare system's neglect of them. Others targeted demand for sex from youth or the internet as a tool to traffic youth. While systems critiques had been made before by activists like Norma Hotaling and Rachel Lloyd, the movement had not gained much traction for system reform at the policy level until the 2010s.

Pettigrew's 2014 testimony also signified the consolidation of survivor leadership in the movement. Survivors spoke out in greater and greater

---

[175] Office of Juvenile Justice and Delinquency Prevention, Commercial Sexual Exploitation of Children, at www.ojjdp.gov/programs/csec_program.html; Snow and Hall, Missing Children, State Care, and Child Sex Trafficking.

[176] Office of Juvenile Justice and Delinquency Prevention, *Policy Guidance, Girls and the Juvenile Justice System* (Washington, DC: Office of Juvenile Justice and Delinquency Prevention, 2013), at www.ojjdp.gov/policyguidance/girls-juvenile-justice-system/.

numbers over the course of the decade, challenging the stigma and blame that society traditionally placed on youth involved in prostitution. Many published memoirs or made films about their experiences. They produced TED talks, testified before legislators, traveled the country on speaking tours, wrote opinion editorials, appeared on television, and founded organizations. The survivors who received the most attention were white and middle-class, but survivors of color, like Pettigrew, were speaking out more and more, testifying before Congress and state legislatures and working at anti-trafficking organizations. Research and advocacy focused on girls of color also increased during this period. Several organizations were founded that had a particular focus on girls of color, like Pettigrew's Human Rights Project for Girls and the Minnesota Native Women's Research Center. The number of organizations fighting the US youth sex trade swelled in the 2010s and there were increasing resources for this work. By 2017, over two hundred organizations in the United States offered services, public education, and policy advocacy on youth sex trafficking. Some of these organizations specifically served the needs of Latina, Asian and Pacific Islander, and LGBT youth.[177]

Despite this diversification of activism against child sex trafficking, media still often framed the issue in exaggerated, sensationalist, and extreme ways, focusing on dramatic and violent cases and "sympathetic" victims. Public discourses continued to rely on racialized and gendered narratives of innocence, perpetration, and rescue. Divisions continued to mark the movement, deepening as the decade progressed. Activism by religious groups grew significantly, sometimes generating tension with progressive groups, and critiques of the movement by the left and sex-worker organizations proliferated, especially related to online advertising of sexual services on Craigslist.com and Backpage.com. Despite differences in the movement, activists still functioned as a collaborative adversarial movement by working together to achieve common goals, like safe harbor laws.

As a collaborative adversarial movement, activists were able to mobilize a broad base of support to successfully pass laws at the federal and state levels. In the 2010s, Congress passed legislation encouraging states to pass safe harbor acts and by mid-decade over half of states had done so. As the decade progressed, more and more states set up central offices to address child sex trafficking and dedicated resources to creating programs to assist youth. Congress also considered and passed legislation to improve the child welfare

---

[177] See Polaris Project, Global Modern Slavery Directory (searched United States, minor), at www
.globalmodernslavery.org/#/0016000000zIi74AAC,41.65380859375,-83.53626251220703.
For example, UMOS Latina Resource Center Metro Milwaukee Rescue & Restore Trafficking
Initiative (www.umos.org/social_services/human_trafficking.html) serves US youth involved in
the sex trade, and My Sister's House (www.my-sisters-house.org/) in Sacramento, California,
serves API girls in the sex trade.

system response to youth in the sex trade and to enhance programs for runaway and homeless youth at risk of entering the sex trade. Prosecution of traffickers at the federal and state levels expanded, and states expanded their services to trafficked youth.

Despite these successes, or maybe because of them, the movement generated many critics, from multiple perspectives, including scholars, sex workers, and civil libertarians, and these critics proliferated as the decade progressed. This pushback called for the recognition of the heterogeneity of youth experiences and a renewed focus on empowerment over rescue, and systemic change over criminalization and punishment.

# 7

# "Quick Fixes and Good Versus Evil Responses": Criticisms of the Movement

The contemporary movement against the US youth sex trade achieved many of its goals, including increased numbers of prosecutions for facilitating and buying sex from youth, stronger penalties for these crimes, and shifting perceptions and treatment of youth in the sex trade. But vocal critics have emerged both from inside and outside the movement. In 2012, Rachel Lloyd published a *Huffington Post* blog critiquing the movement: "In an effort to get people to care about this issue, we've been less than careful with the statistics and in an effort to get the media to cover this story we've often reduced it to the most basic elements. I've been guilty of this too. We've focused on quick fixes and good vs. evil responses that rarely address the true causes or empower the young people that we're serving."[1] Three years later, her tone had become more urgent. In response to widespread support in the movement for the Justice for Victims of Trafficking Act, Lloyd posted an open letter on the GEMS website addressed to "the anti-trafficking movement" pleading:

Please let's not (continue to) lose our minds. Nuance is a good thing, critical thinking is a good thing, not coming from a purely emotionally driven place is a good thing, long-term, strategic planning is a good thing. These are not things to be afraid of or shut down. This is a complex issue that requires myriad complex solutions not just a black and white response. Let's be better than this and smarter than this. We can do it, there are enough of us critically thinking, nuance-having folks out there who work with youth and survivors daily and we know what's needed. We don't tend to be the loudest voices, the most funded or the people in power, but we can take power if we move and work collectively and collaboratively.[2]

Lloyd condemned "short-sighted and reactionary thinking and policies" and implored the movement to "work on all the root causes," including racism and

---

[1] Rachel Lloyd, "Urban Legends and Hoaxes: How Hyperbole Hurts Trafficking Victims," *Huffington Post* (February 3, 2012).

[2] Rachel Lloyd, "Dear Anti-Trafficking Movement" (March 19, 2015), at www.gems-girls.org /shifting-perspective/dear-anti-trafficking-movement.

classism, gender inequality and poverty, child abuse and domestic violence, affordable housing, and living wage jobs. She beseeched the movement to "push the conversation beyond the sensational and simplistic" and to "push all the excited, well-intentioned people to use this energy and momentum for real social justice and long-term change."[3] Lloyd was not alone in criticizing activism against the youth sex trade.

Criticisms of the movement fall into three main areas. First, critics have argued that movement advocates and the media have created a "moral panic" by exaggerating and sensationalizing the issue through narratives of victimization that obscure the heterogeneity of youth experiencing prostitution. As a result, they argue, this framing ignores the needs of many youth, undermines their agency, and results in a focus on criminal justice solutions that fail to address the root causes for youth involvement in the sex trade. Second, critics have argued that the movement has advanced a "carceral feminism" that has led to increased state power to surveille, regulate, and control the behavior and sexuality of youth through diversion programs and a growing anti-trafficking bureaucracy. They also argue that law and order solutions to trafficking have expanded law enforcement funding and powers, resulting in the targeting of communities of color and contributing to the build-up of the prison industrial complex. Third, critics have argued that the movement against domestic minor sex trafficking has put in place policies and practices that endanger adult sex workers and that act as a Trojan horse for an attack on the sex industry and sexuality more generally. These arguments seriously call into question the achievements and even the intentions of the anti-trafficking movement as a whole.

## MORAL PANICS: NARRATIVES OF VICTIMIZATION

As the issue of "child sex trafficking" entered the mainstream in the 2010s, appearing more and more in the news and on social media, and even as the subject of bus tours and a museum,[4] a simplistic and sensational framing stoked moral outrage and calls for rescue and retribution. Meanwhile, improved research yielded a much more complex picture of what was really going on with youth. The predominant narrative of innocent children, evil pimps, and heroic rescuers was challenged as a much more complicated and heterogeneous reality emerged from new research. Some activists within the movement, such as Lloyd, as well as activists outside the movement and several scholars criticized

---

[3] Ibid.

[4] Some groups around the country are offering bus tours of red light districts, and one has even opened a museum. For example, Georgia Public Service Commissioner Tim Echols runs a semi-annual bus tour of metro Atlanta's sex trade. Chris Joyner, "AJC Watchdog: Atlanta Sex-trafficking Tour Reveals 'The Hell of It,'" *Atlanta Journal Constitution* (January 19, 2017). A Houston, Texas-based group, Elijah Rising, runs the Museum of Modern Day Slavery and offers van tours of "high-probability trafficking areas." Elijah Rising, Museum, at www .elijahrising.org/museum/.

the mainstream movement's characterization of the issue and the resulting public policies, calling for a more measured, data-informed, and systemic approach to addressing the commercial sexual exploitation of youth.

One way the issue has been sensationalized is through exaggerated, speculative claims about the scope and nature of the problem. The media and activist organizations commonly claimed that as many as 100,000 to 300,000 (sometimes even 600,000) youth were at risk of entering the commercial sex trade in the United States (some say 100,000 to 300,000 were *in* the sex trade[5]), that most of these victims were cisgender girls, and that these girls on average entered prostitution (or first become prostituted) between the ages of twelve and fourteen. These claims have been hotly contested in the academic literature as speculative and based on flawed studies.[6] According to Michelle Stransky and David Finkelhor of the University of New Hampshire's Crimes Against Children Research Center, "[These numbers] are mostly educated guesses or extrapolations based on questionable assumptions ... The reality is that we do not currently know how many juveniles are involved in prostitution. Scientifically credible estimates do not exist."[7] The claim that cisgender girls are disproportionately the victims of domestic minor sex trafficking has also been challenged in a study of youth in New York City conducted by the Center for Court Innovation and John Jay College, which found that boys and transgender youth were 58% of the commercially exploited youth in New York City.[8] In addition to academic critiques of the movement's

---

[5] Martin Cizmar, Ellis Conklin, and Kristen Hinman, "Real Men Get Their Facts Straight: Ashton and Demi and Sex Trafficking," *Village Voice* (June 29, 2011) (attacking Ashton Kucher for saying that 300,000 youth *were* in the sex trade in the United States).

[6] See, for example, Ronald Weitzer, "The Social Construction of Sex Trafficking: Ideology and Institutionalization of a Moral Crusade," *Politics & Society* 35.3 (2007), 447–475. Georgetown University Professor Elżbieta M. Goździak suggests that commercially sexually exploited youth in the United States have been "subsumed under the trafficking label" because they are "important to the numbers game" in order to justify the anti-trafficking "moral crusade." Elżbieta M. Goździak, *Trafficked Children and Youth in the United States: Reimagining Survivors* (New Brunswick, NJ: Rutgers University Press, 2016), 30, 32. See Sally Engle Merry, *The Seductions for Quantification: Measuring Human Rights, Gender Violence, and Sex Trafficking* (Chicago, IL: University of Chicago Press, 2016), 112–139, for a discussion of the difficulty of estimating the number of people involved in sex trafficking and the widespread use of numbers lacking any scientific basis.

[7] Michelle Stransky and David Finkelhor, *How Many Juveniles Are Involved in Prostitution in the U.S.?* (Durham, NH: Crimes Against Children Research Center, 2008), 2; see also Alexandra Lutnick, *Domestic Minor Sex Trafficking: Beyond Victims and Villains* (New York, NY: Columbia University Press, 2016), 4–8; Jennifer Musto, *Control and Protect: Collaboration, Carceral Protection, and Domestic Sex Trafficking in the United States* (Oakland, CA: University of California Press, 2016), 12–15; Carrie N. Baker, "An Examination of the Central Debates on Sex Trafficking in Research and Public Policy in the United States," *Journal on Human Trafficking* 1:3 (August 2015): 191–208.

[8] Ric Curtis, Karen Terry, Meredith Dank, Kirk Dombrowski, and Bilal Khan, *The Commercial Sexual Exploitation of Children in New York City* (New York, NY: Center for Court Innovation and John Jay College, 2008), 34.

numbers, journalists and activists have criticized the movement's claims about the scope of the problem. For example, the *Village Voice,* which at the time owned Backpage.com, published an article debunking the trafficking movement's statistics.[9] Portland, Oregon-based sex worker activist emi koyama characterized the widely circulating numbers on youth involved in commercial sex as "common myths" of the anti-trafficking movement[10] and the Urban Institute in New York City has challenged movement research on men who buy sex from girls as lacking scientific merit.[11]

Critics have also questioned the movement's dominant trafficking narrative that portrays a young and vulnerable girl forced or coerced into prostitution and controlled by a manipulative and violent "pimp." This sensationalist narrative often included graphic detail of extreme violence and explicit sexual abuse.[12] Some advocates focused on very young girls or described girls as old as seventeen as children.[13] They emphasized histories of childhood sexual abuse, neglect, and trauma bonding (a strong emotional attachment between abuser and abused as a result of the cycle of violence). Advocates commonly referred to involvement of youth in the sex trade as a form of "slavery." Almost half of the 217 organizations working on child sex trafficking in the United States listed on the Global Modern Slavery Directory used the term "slavery" and frequently used imagery of chains and bondage on their websites.[14] In the face of evidence that many girls trading sex believed that they made a choice to do so, did not believe they were victims, and would repeatedly return to their adult facilitators, even after they had been "rescued," some advocates have portrayed girls as being too young or naïve to understand the implications of their decisions. A 2005 ECPAT report, for example, argued that girls "often cling to the false belief that they are doing what they want."[15] ECPAT attempted to finesse the contradiction between what girls say and the movement's claim that they are enslaved by distinguishing between actions

---

[9] Cizmar et al., "Real Men Get Their Facts Straight."

[10] emi koyama, *War on Terror & War on Trafficking: A Sex Worker Activist Confronts the Anti-Trafficking Movement* (Portland, OR: Confluere Publications, 2011), 4–12.

[11] The Women's Funding Network sponsored a study by the Shapiro Research Group titled *Men Who Buy Sex With Adolescent Girls: A Scientific Research Study,* which was criticized by the Urban Institute in a statement submitted to Congress at the September 2010 hearing on domestic minor sex trafficking. See *Domestic Minor Sex Trafficking, A Hearing Before the United States House Judiciary Subcommittee on Crime, Terrorism and Homeland Security,* 111th Cong., 2nd Sess. (September 25, 2010) [hereinafter *Domestic Minor Sex Trafficking Hearing, 2010*], 289–293, 300–312, 340–355.

[12] See, for example, Hofstede Committee Report, *Juvenile Prostitution in Minnesota* (St. Paul, MN: Minnesota Attorney General's Office, November 1999).

[13] Linda Smith of Shared Hope International, for example, has referred to older teens as "little girls." Author observation, Third Annual Northwest Conference Against Human Trafficking, January 15, 2011.

[14] Global Modern Slavery Directory at www.globalmodernslavery.org/ (data on file with author).

[15] See, for example, Sara Ann Friedman, *Who Is There to Help Us? How the System Fails Sexually Exploited Girls in the United States: Examples from Four American Cities* (New York, NY: ECPAT-USA, Inc., 2005), 4.

that are voluntary and those that are chosen: "there is usually little individual choice ... teens usually turn to prostitution as a result of desperation or due to manipulation by adults."[16] Advocates also emphasized the "unbalanced power dynamic" between youth and the adults who exploit them to argue that youth lack of agency in their relationships to adult facilitators.[17]

Despite these simplistic narratives put forth by many activists and portrayed in the media, evidence was building that youth in the sex trade were quite heterogeneous. Many young people trading sex do not have facilitators, and many are not directly forced to participate in the sex trade. A study by scholars at the Center for Court Innovation and John Jay College found that only sixteen percent of youth involved in prostitution in New York City had a facilitator.[18] Based on a survey of "underage sex workers" in New York City, an ethnographic study of street prostitution in Atlantic City, and a study of facilitators in New York City, Anthony Marcus et al. from John Jay College argue that the dominant narrative of "pimp trickery and coercion distorts reality in three ways: it (1) overestimates the role of adult facilitators in street sex markets, (2) overemphasizes the impact of the initial recruitment stage on subsequent practices, and (3) masks or simplifies the difficult and complex choices and contingencies faced by minors who sell sex."[19] Challenging the dominant narrative that adults entice adolescent girls into prostitution by "five powerful forces: love, debt, addiction, physical might and authority," this study found that the primary concern of "underaged sex workers" was not a controlling pimp but was their economic vulnerability.[20] In fact, these researchers found that many facilitators avoided minors because they were perceived as unreliable and lacking the "sexual performativity or education to charge high prices and attract affluent regulars."[21] The youth they interviewed mostly avoided anti-trafficking service organizations for fear they would "criminalize their adult support networks, imprison friends and loved ones, prevent them from earning a living, and return them to the dependencies of youth."[22]

Senior research scientist at Research Triangle Institute International Alexandra Lutnick argues that local and federal responses to sex trafficking

---

[16] Ibid. 27.

[17] H.E.A.T. Watch, HEAT Watch Myth Busters, at www.heatwatch.org/human_trafficking/myth_busters.

[18] Curtis et al., *Commercial Sexual Exploitation of Children in New York City.*

[19] Anthony Marcus, Amber Horning, Ric Curtis, Jo Sanson, and Efram Thompson, "Conflict and Agency Among Sex Workers and Pimps: A Closer Look at Domestic Minor Sex Trafficking," *Annals of the American Academy of Political and Social Science* 653 (May 2014), 225–246, at 227.

[20] Ibid. 232. Alexis Kennedy, Carolin Klein, Jessica Bristowe, Barry Cooper, and John Yuille, "Routes of Recruitment: Pimps' Techniques and Other Circumstances that Lead to Street Prostitution," *Journal of Aggression, Maltreatment, and Trauma* 15.2 (2007), 1–19.

[21] Marcus et al., "Conflict and Agency Among Sex Workers and Pimps," 232.    [22] Ibid. 242.

increase young people's vulnerability to trading sex. She contests the mainstream anti-trafficking movement's claim that most youth are coerced and controlled by facilitators.[23] Based on a review of existing research as well as her own community-based research with service providers at SAGE and GEMS, Lutnick argues that the needs of youth forced into prostitution by third parties are very different than the needs of youth engaging in survival sex, and that anti-trafficking laws often focus on the former group, even though the latter group is likely larger. Programs that require identification of a facilitator in order to receive assistance, she argues, fail to serve the latter group. Lutnick suggests a perverse motivation when she characterizes a police training video from California as "rescue porn" because it focused "exclusively on young cisgender women who have a third party forcing them to trade sex" and "where the young cisgender women are provocatively dressed and are being exploited by a person of color until police officers come in and save them."[24] This framing, she argues, can be harmful by reinforcing the stereotypes that make many victims invisible, like LBGTQ young people, young cisgender men, or young people who are not in an exploitative dynamic with a third party.

Youth are heterogeneous in other ways as well. Many are homeless, thrown out of their homes or fleeing physical and sexual violence in the home. Others are housed, but experiencing neglect in other ways. Some young people enter the sex trade in an attempt to meet unfulfilled emotional needs – love and attention they are not receiving at home. LGBTQ youth are particularly vulnerable to entering the sex trade because of individual and institutional homophobia and transphobia, which can result in homelessness and social isolation. Some enter the sex trade because it is seen as glamorous and exciting, or as a way to earn easy money to buy clothes or support a drug habit.[25] And youth often offer and receive assistance from peers.

Sex worker activist emi koyama has suggested that the movement distorts the reality of youth involvement in the sex trade for two reasons. First, she argues that conservative groups use the trafficking issue to push their anti-abortion and anti-sex agendas. She gives the examples of Shared Hope International "shamelessly using its mailing list to distribute anti-abortion propaganda" and producers of the anti-trafficking film "Sex+Money" "using its screenings to hand out 'purity bands' that encourage viewers to pledge abstinence until

[23] Lutnick, *Domestic Minor Sex Trafficking*, 29. Heather Montgomery's study of child prostitutes in Thailand similarly challenges the "stereotypes of martyrdom" and shows that children's stories "were much less neat than the ones used for campaigning purposes or written up in the newspapers." She argues that you can't "look only at prostitution while ignoring the wider social forces of family, community, economy and globalisation" and emphasizes the importance of talking to the children themselves. Healther Montgomery, *Modern Babylon? Prostituting Children in Thailand* (New York, NY: Berghahn Books, 2001), 21, 25.
[24] Lutnick, *Domestic Minor Sex Trafficking*, 91–92.   [25] Ibid. 14–26.

they are married."[26] Second, she argues that other groups focus on the least-common, worst-case scenario because they know that "the public would care less about the youth if they understood the reality that most of them are not 'forced,' at least not in slavery-like conditions, but are simply doing what it takes to survive."[27] Whether prompted by ulterior motives or expediency, these campaigns result in policies that don't address the needs of most youth, argues koyama.

Furthermore, critics have argued that the movement's framing of the issue denies youth agency and, ultimately, their human rights. Penelope Saunders, former Executive Director of HIPS in Washington, DC, has argued that the movement's shift from the language of "child prostitution" to "commercial sexual exploitation of children" or "CSEC" undermines youth agency. Whereas "child prostitute" was an identity that defined the child as inherently at fault, CSEC defines youth as always victimized and innocent, and sexuality as a dangerous perversion. She argues, "these narratives endure because the drama of purity besmirched at the hands of adults plays neatly into cultural notions of the sacred nature of childhood, where children must necessarily be preserved in a state of innocence outside of the reality of economics and sexuality."[28] This framing has resonated with liberal social rhetoric and has inspired moral outrage and social change but, notes Saunders, the majority of abuses occur to individuals "who are not innocent, not very young, and not unknowing of sexual activity and the world of work."[29] She warns, "by exclusively focusing world attention on extreme forms of CSEC, more pervasive forms of injustice may be obscured." Calling on the movement to develop "a new formulation of the child as a human-rights-bearing subject," she argues that "the notion of children developing self-determination must be part of any protective framework."[30]

In resisting this narrative of victimization, some critics refer to youth using the language developed by sex worker advocates. For example, a 2012 article appearing in the magazine *Working In These Times* used the phrase "youth sex worker."[31] *The New Republic* writer Noah Berlatsky referred to "child sex workers" in a January 2016 article.[32] These framings imply that youth and even

[26] emi koyama, "Youth in the Sex Industry: How Recognizing 'Push' and 'Pull' Factors Can Better Inform Public Policy" (October 19, 2011), at http://eminism.org/blog/entry/275.

[27] Ibid.

[28] Penelope Saunders, "How 'Child Prostitution' Became 'CSEC,'" in Elizabeth Bernstein and Laurie Schaffner (eds.), *Regulating Sex: The Politics of Intimacy and Identity* (New York, NY; Routledge, 2005), 183.

[29] Ibid. 184.

[30] Ibid. See also the work of Julia O'Connell Davidson, *Children in the Global Sex Trade* (New York, NY: Polity, 2005).

[31] Kari Lydersen, "Youth Sex Workers Organize for Their Rights," *Working In These Times* (June 19, 2012).

[32] Noah Berlatsky, "Child Sex Workers' Biggest Threat: The Police," *The New Republic* (January 20, 2016).

children *can* consent to sell sex. Some have gone even farther, arguing that youth should be allowed to sell sex because doing so can be an avenue for youth to escape abusive situations in parental or foster homes and give youth an opportunity to provide for themselves.[33] To call them victims "robs them of autonomy" and prevents them from meeting their needs.[34] The victim tropes can be a way of silencing young people, framing them as not knowing better or not being able to help themselves.[35]

Discourses around the issue of youth in the sex trade, however, are sometimes confused, reflecting both framings of choice and coercion. For example, in the spring of 2016, the magazine *Social Work Today* had an article, "Fighting Youth Sex Trafficking: The Social Worker's Role," that described youth sex trafficking both as "slavery" and as a "lifestyle."[36] The article noted that sometimes "a victim has no intention to leave the trafficking lifestyle," but that if they later consider "leaving the lifestyle," social workers should discuss the "pros and cons of trafficking and start to develop a plan to leave." The article encouraged social workers to be "nonjudgmental and to not impose their own beliefs about sex trafficking on the child."[37]

In order to push back against the discourse of rescue that is so prevalent in the movement, GEMS created a Survivor Leadership Institute and Resource Center, with the mission of "developing authentic leadership roles and sustainable economic opportunities for survivors across the country both within and outside the movement."[38] The Institute has a campaign called More Than a Survivor, More Than A Story that has a traveling photography exhibit with twenty-two portraits of survivor leaders who are accomplished in a variety of fields, including the arts, sciences, and politics. The goal of the campaign was to provide an "antidote to the stereotypes of commercially sexually exploited and trafficked victims perpetually broken and forever limited by their trauma."[39] Young Women's Empowerment Project also pushed back against framings that undermine the agency of girls and respect for girls' choices. Their 2009 research report *Girls Do What They Have To Do To Survive* centered on the voices of youth and emphasized their strength and resilience.[40] An example of a survivor

---

[33] See, for example, Young Women's Empowerment Project, *Girls Do What They Have To Do To Survive* (Chicago: Young Women's Empowerment Project, 2009).

[34] Lutnick, *Domestic Minor Sex Trafficking*, 111.

[35] Sarah Hunt, "Representing Colonial Violence: Trafficking, Sex Work, and the Violence of Law," *Atlantis* 37.2.1 (2015/2016): 25–39, at 34.

[36] Christina Reardon, "Fighting Youth Sex Trafficking: The Social Worker's Role," *Social Work Today* (March/April 2016), 10, 13–14.

[37] Ibid. 13–14.

[38] GEMS, Survivor Leadership Institute and Resource Center, at www.gems-girls.org/survivor-leadership.

[39] GEMS, More Than a Survivor Campaign, at www.gems-girls.org/survivor-leadership/resources/more-than-a-survivor-campaign.

[40] Young Women's Empowerment Project, *Girls Do What They Have To Do To Survive*, 2009.

resisting the dominant discourse of victimhood occurred at the February 2010 Congressional hearing on domestic minor sex trafficking before the Senate Judiciary Committee's Subcommittee on Human Rights and the Law when Senator Richard Durbin asked a youth survivor named Shaquana about why girls don't leave their facilitators. Durbin asked, "So are they afraid of the pimps, that if they leave the pimps will come after them?" Shaquana responded, "A lot of the times the girls, you know, are just scared or they love them and they do not want to do it."[41] Shaquana resisted Durbin's suggestion that youth behavior can be explained simply by fear of their facilitators.

As a result of the simplistic narratives of victimization promoted by the movement, anti-trafficking interventions often misconstrue the needs of youth, say critics. As Alexandra Lutnick has noted, experts' attention has often focused on mental health and poor self-esteem as a central problem for youth in the sex trade, which has diverted attention away from the social, economic, and cultural systems that maintain the conditions that make youth vulnerable to the sex trade. In surveys of youth, rather than identifying the problem as within themselves (or more specifically in their mental state), youth identified structural problems that contributed to their participation in the sex trade, like police abuse of youth, sexual abuse, homophobia and transphobia of families and schools, and limited social services.[42] Similarly, YWEP targeted its attention on the problems youth encountered with accessing needed services from institutions, particularly barriers related to biases against youth based on age, race, gender identity or expression, sexuality, clothing, or because they were homeless and/or home free.[43]

Whereas service providers report that the greatest need of young people in the sex trade is mental health services, the youth themselves report that employment and housing are their most pressing needs.[44] Many young people are reluctant to access services for fear they will be reported to their parents or child welfare and forced back into the abusive situations they fled. Their status as minors means that they cannot independently access many services, and are reliant on the approval of parents or child welfare workers, which may not be forthcoming. Within the child welfare system, high caseloads and staff turnover means that youth often do not find the attention or consistency that they need to develop trust in their caseworkers. Lutnick argues that the lack of employment opportunities for youth in fact push some into the sex trade, so living wage jobs

---

[41] *In Our Own Backyard: Child Prostitution and Sex Trafficking in the United States, A Hearing Before the United States Senate Judiciary Subcommittee on Human Rights and Law.* 111th Cong., 2nd Sess. (February 24, 2010) [hereinafter *In Our Own Backyard Hearing, 2010*], 19–20.

[42] Lutnick, *Domestic Minor Sex Trafficking*, 47–49.

[43] Young Women's Empowerment Project, *Denied Help! How Youth in the Sex Trade & Street Economy Are Turned Away from Systems Meant to Help Us & What We Are Doing to Fight Back* (Chicago, IL: Young Women's Empowerment Project, 2012), 53.

[44] Lutnick, *Domestic Minor Sex Trafficking*, 47.

accessible to youth would help some of them avoid the sex trade. Based on these facts, Lutnick recommends policy changes to empower youth, like allowing youth to request and receive services such as housing, healthcare, and food assistance without parental permission; allowing young people to enter into binding contracts for property if they can provide sufficient proof that they are financially able to honor the contract; allowing youth to work (some states prohibit youth under the age of 16 from working); and ensuring living wage jobs for youth. Lutnick argues that an empowerment model for youth in the sex trade would involve youth in identifying their needs and determining how to meet them. Young Women's Empowerment Project lived out this vision of empowerment through youth leadership, participatory action research, peer-led support groups, and youth-defined and led programming.

Critics have also argued that racial stereotypes often underlie the rhetoric and policies of the movement.[45] As shown in previous chapters, the portrayal of sex trafficking often relies on racialized framings of victims and perpetrators. Nevertheless, race is rarely explicitly acknowledged or addressed.[46] One activist reported that race rarely came up explicitly in her conversations with other activists or legislators. She suggested that people avoided conversations on race because no one knew how to talk about it.[47] Race is the movement's "elephant in the room." Nevertheless, the "ideal victim" is raced and classed, often portrayed as a white, middle-class suburban girl, whereas girls of color have often been absent or marginalized from anti-trafficking discourses. The portrayal of men is also very racialized. Facilitators are almost always portrayed as African American men, buyers as white, middle-class men, and rescuers as almost always white. These portrayals fuel racialized ideologies of innocence and guilt, blame and exculpation. The social structures that push African American men toward facilitating the sex trade, like exclusion from the formal economy due to mass incarceration, failing schools, race discrimination, and media glorification of "pimp culture," never receives attention.

Patricia Hill Collins has argued that Black femininity is defined in white supremacist society through stereotypes or "controlling images," including "the jezebel, whore, or 'hoochie.'" She argues that stereotypes of the deviant, sexually aggressive African American female lie at the heart of Black women's oppression, justifying sexual abuse, while also constructing

---

[45] See, for example, Jasmine Phillips, "Black Girls and the (Im)Possibilities of a Victim Trope: The Intersectional Failures of Legal and Advocacy Interventions in the Commercial Sexual Exploitation of Minors in the United States," *UCLA Law Review* 62 (August 2015), 1642; Cheryl Nelson Butler, "The Racial Roots of Human Trafficking," *UCLA Law Review* 62 (August 2015), 1464; Emily Chaloner, "Anybody's Daughter? How Racial Stereotypes Prevent Domestic Child Prostitutes of Color from Being Perceived as Victims," *Children's Legal Rights Journal* 30.3 (Fall 2010), 48–60.

[46] Phillips, "Black Girls and the (Im)Possibilities of a Victim Trope."

[47] Interview with Brittany Vanderhoof, October 23, 2015 (on file with author).

white womanhood as normal female sexuality.[48] These controlling images explain why African American girls are underrepresented in anti-trafficking discourses, despite the fact that they are disproportionately involved in the sex trade.[49] In arguing that youth are victims, not perpetrators of child prostitution, activists, either consciously or unconsciously, make a strategic decision to focus on white girls in order reinforce their message of blamelessness and to avoid triggering the stereotypes of deviant African American sexuality that would weaken their argument. The "our daughters" discourse and the disproportionate representation of white girls as victims in anti-trafficking discourses make activists' message of victimhood and blamelessness more persuasive in a white supremacist society. As Kimberlé Crenshaw has argued in the context of domestic violence, this rhetorical strategy "may simultaneously reify and erase 'othered' women as victims" of violence because of the "thin line between debunking the stereotypical beliefs that only poor or minority women are battered, and pushing them aside to focus on victims for whom mainstream politicians and media are more likely to express concern."[50] Advocates may not intend to play into these sensibilities, and favorable responses to this rhetorical strategy might not necessarily be based on these sensibilities, but the "our daughters" framing could nevertheless contribute to policy responses that are most responsive to the needs of white, middle-class girls and less responsive to the needs of marginalized girls and boys.

A few activists, however, like Rachel Lloyd, explicitly acknowledge race, suggesting at times that the reason the United States tolerates child prostitution is that it is not seen as affecting white girls, but only low-income African American girls. We see this in Lloyd's 2010 Congressional testimony when she contrasts the treatment of "Katya from the Ukraine" to "Keisha from the Bronx." She argued that we have created a "dichotomy of acceptable and unacceptable victims, wherein Katya from the Ukraine will be seen as a real victim and provided with services and support, but Keisha from the Bronx will be seen as a 'willing participant,' someone who's out there because she 'likes it' and who is criminalized and thrown in detention or jail."[51] Here Lloyd was arguing that African American girls were "acceptable victims" because, in line with Collins' argument about controlling images, they were seen as responsible

---

[48] Patricia Hill Collins, *Black Feminist Thought: Knowledge, Consciousness, and the Politics of Empowerment* (New York, NY: Routledge, 2000).

[49] Bureau of Justice Statistics, *Characteristics of Suspected Human Trafficking Incidents, 2008–2010* (April 2011).

[50] Kimberlé Williams Crenshaw, "Mapping the Margins: Intersectionality, Identity Politics, and Violence Against Women of Color," in Martha Albertson Fineman and Roxanne Mykitiuk (eds.), *The Public Nature of Private Violence: The Discovery of Domestic Abuse* (New York, NY: Routledge, 1998), 105.

[51] Ibid. 15.

for, or at least not harmed by, sexual behavior.[52] The white Katya, however, was considered to be a victim. She was not held responsible for her victimization, and she was seen as harmed by it. Lloyd's challenge, however, is rare. Most of the movement as well as mainstream media and policymakers rely on racialized narratives of victimization to garner attention to the issue and support for new policies.

## CARCERAL FEMINISM: STATE SURVEILLANCE AND CONTROL

The second criticism of activism against youth involvement in the sex trade is that the movement's law and order orientation has contributed to the build-up of the prison industrial complex to the detriment of communities of color. Politicians have focused on creating new crimes and increasing punishments, yet historically tough-on-crime measures have had a disproportionately negative impact on communities of color and African American men in particular.[53] Some have alleged that men of color are disproportionately prosecuted for prostituting minors. Defendants in a 2016 case in Portland, Oregon, for example, alleged racially biased enforcement of trafficking laws because most defendants were African American men in a city that is predominately white, but the court ruled against the claim.[54] While in the mainstream anti-trafficking discourse police are often praised and politicians prioritize funding for law enforcement training and investigation, some critics have argued that police are the biggest threat to youth in the sex trade.[55] Through in-depth research with service providers, Alexandra Lutnick found that police abuse of youth was common.[56] YWEP's Bad Encounter research revealed that youth involved in the sex trade in Chicago report highly negative experiences of their interactions with law enforcement.[57] A 2015 Urban Institute study found a similar result for LGBT youth in New York City.[58] Anti-

[52] Rachel Lloyd, "Acceptable Victims: Sexually Exploited Youth in the U.S.," *Encounter* 18.3 (2005), 6–18.

[53] Marie Gottchalk, *Caught: The Prison State and the Lockdown of American Politics* (Princeton, NJ: Princeton University Press, 2015); Michelle Alexander, *The New Jim Crow: Mass Incarceration in the Age of Colorblindness* (New York, NY: New Press, 2012).

[54] Defendant Thomas' Motion for Discovery on the Issue of Racial Profiling and Selective Prosecution, *U.S. v. DeJuan Antonio Thomas*, Case No. 3:14-CR-00214-MO (U.S.D.C. Oregon, Portland Division) (April 4, 2016). See also Defendant Ford's Motion for Discovery on the Issue of Racial Profiling and Selective Enforcement and/or Prosecution, *U.S. v. Taquarius Kaream Ford*, No. 3:14-cr-00045-1-HZ (March 31, 2016); Reply to Government's Response to Motion to Dismiss for Selective Prosecution and Motion for Relevant Discovery, *U.S. v. Derrick Malik Patterson*, CR 14-1395-TUC-RM (BMG) (U.S.D.C. Arizona) (July 9, 2015).

[55] Berlatsky, "Child Sex Workers' Biggest Threat: The Police."

[56] Lutnick, *Domestic Minor Sex Trafficking*, 39–40, 67–69.

[57] Young Women's Empowerment Project, *Denied Help!*

[58] Meredith Dank, Lilly Yu, Jennifer Yahner, Elizabeth Pelletier, Mitchyll Mora, and Brendan Conner, *Locked In: Interactions with the Criminal Justice and Child Welfare Systems*

trafficking policies have, in fact, significantly expanded law enforcement powers, including wiretaps, stiffer penalties, RICO prosecutions, state–federal collaboration, forfeiture, administrative subpoenas, and extraterritorial jurisdiction. Furthermore, these laws have channeled millions of dollars a year toward law enforcement, much of which goes toward street-level enforcement of prostitution laws.[59] Lois Lee, who favors decriminalization of the sex trade, argues that this money would be better spent on creating good homes for youth.[60] This build-up of the criminal justice system and the movement's alliance with law enforcement is directly contrary to anti-racist efforts to shrink the prison industrial complex.[61] Some have criticized service organizations that work with law enforcement, particularly if they require or pressure youth to testify against traffickers. Others have criticized the movement for an "appropriation of Black suffering" through the use of the language of slavery to bolster the criminalization of communities of color, including African American sex workers.[62]

Critics have also questioned the movement's push for increasing criminal penalties for buyers of sex from minors and for third party facilitators. Rachel Lloyd opposed the part of the 2015 federal legislation on domestic minor sex trafficking that allowed buyers to be prosecuted as traffickers under the "obtain" prong of law.[63] Others have opposed broadening laws to punish those who facilitate trafficking for fear that they would sweep within their reach youth who help other youth as well as harm-reduction-oriented programs. According to Lutnick, "young people help coordinate other young people's sex trade. Common harm reduction techniques on the street such as working in pairs, using condoms, and providing information about potential clients are criminalized and can result in young people being charged as traffickers," which "criminalizes young people's support systems and their fundamental right to health-promoting materials such as condoms."[64]

Concern about this kind of proposal in Illinois was a major factor in the closing of YWEP in 2013. According to one member, "anybody that assists somebody who is a trafficked person and doesn't report it counts as

for *LGBTQ Youth, YMSM, and YWSW Who Engage in Survival Sex* (New York, NY: Urban Institute, September 2015).

[59] Melissa Ditmore and Juhu Thukral, "Accountability and the Use of Raids to Fight Trafficking," *Anti-Trafficking Review* 1 (2012), 134, 136–137.

[60] Interview with Lois Lee, September 7, 2017 (arguing that criminal records lock women into prostitution; on file with author).

[61] Alexander, *The New Jim Crow*; Angela Davis, *Are Prisons Obsolete?* (New York, NY: Seven Stories Press, 2003).

[62] Robyn Maynard, "#Blacksexworkerslivesmatter: White-Washed 'Anti-Slavery' and the Appropriation of Black Suffering," *Feminist Wire* (September 9, 2015).

[63] Open letter to the Anti-Trafficking Movement, from Rachel Lloyd, March 18, 2015.

[64] Lutnick, *Domestic Minor Sex Trafficking*, 87, 114.

a trafficker."[65] YWEP did not insist that young people leave the sex trade and they served youth under the age of eighteen, who were automatically considered victims of sex trafficking if they engaged in the sex trade, even in the absence of force, fraud, or coercion. Therefore, YWEP was concerned that members eighteen and over assisting other members under the age of eighteen in any way might be criminally liable for facilitating the trafficking of minors. YWEP's concern increased when their office reportedly experienced police surveillance. This, combined with the difficulty of securing funders willing to support harm reduction and youth empowerment approaches to youth involved in the sex trade, contributed to YWEP's demise.

Even safe harbor laws have been controversial. Some activists and scholars argue that these laws often allow for the punitive detention of youth. Based on extensive ethnographic research with activists, service providers, and law enforcement personnel, scholar Jennifer Musto has argued that anti-trafficking programs are a form of "carceral feminism" that is coercive and paternalistic, entangling youth and adults in a "burgeoning, though largely unscrutinized, combination of law-enforcement punishment combined with psychosocial, social-service, and technologically mediated efforts to assist them."[66] Musto draws on the work of Elizabeth Bernstein, who criticizes the broader anti-trafficking movement's use of the criminal justice system to achieve social justice ends through "punitive systems of control,"[67] and Kristin Bumiller, who has argued that the neoliberal state has appropriated the feminist movement against sexual violence to fuel the growth of a coercive and punitive criminal justice system as well as social service bureaucracies that coercively regulate women's lives.[68] Neoliberalism's deregulation of the economy, according to Bumiller, led to "increased social stratification and a generalized sense of insecurity that then led to more regulation of the poor and minorities," particularly crime control as a "new form of social exclusion reinforcing other forms of discrimination against minorities and directed against potentially unruly classes of persons."[69] Racialized discourses of sexual violence toward women – "driven by fear of dangerous strangers, who were implicitly or explicitly

---

[65] Blake Nemec, *YWEP Still Works* (audio documentary) (2016), 18:06, at https://soundcloud.com /intermodal-1/ywep-wasnt-she-as-501c3.

[66] Musto, *Control and Protect*, 3.

[67] Elizabeth Bernstein, "Militarized Humanitarianism Meets Carceral Feminism: The Politics of Sex, Rights, and Freedom in Contemporary Antitrafficking Campaigns," *Signs* 36.1 (2010), 45–71, at 65; see also Elizabeth Bernstein, "Introduction: Sexual Economies and New Regimes of Governance," *Social Politics* 21.3 (2014), 345–354; Elizabeth Bernstein, "Carceral Politics as Gender Justice? The 'Traffic in Women' and Neoliberal Circuits of Crime, Sex, and Rights," *Theory and Society* 41.3 (2012), 233–259; Elizabeth Bernstein, "The Sexual Politics of 'New Abolitionism,'" *Differences* 18. 3 (2007), 128–151.

[68] Kristin Bumiller, *In An Abusive State: How Neoliberalism Appropriated the Feminist Movement Against Sexual Violence* (Durham, NC: Duke University Press, 2008), 6.

[69] Ibid.

marked as dark-skinned men"[70] – became a tool by which the state justified this increasing "culture of control." At the same time, the state expanded the regulation of women's personal lives through shelters and welfare programs that were "increasingly value-laden" and "tied to the promotion of the traditional nuclear family, fear of dependency, and distrust of women as mothers."[71] The movement against child sex trafficking, one could argue, falls into this dynamic by contributing to the growth of the prison industrial complex and supporting the expansion of a state-controlled social service infrastructure.

Through safe harbor laws, some argue, the movement has bolstered coercive social service bureaucracies that have increasing control over the lives of young people, particularly youth of color. Activists Brendan Conner of Streetwise and Safe in New York City has warned that safe harbor laws could potentially increase the number of arrests of youth, extend the length of court supervision and institutionalization, and perpetuate "endemic law enforcement harassment and brutality" against young people. Conner argues that the law's "unintended consequences" are that the "penalty for a violation or Class B misdemeanor – which, in the rare case where a maximum sentence is imposed, is ninety days of jail time – is raised to indefinite state custody, including in custodial placement in a geographically isolated and restrictive 'staff secure' facility until the age of majority if deemed necessary," a situation reminiscent of the days before the deinstitutionalization of status offenders in the 1970s.[72] On the other hand, Lois Lee argues that safe harbor laws have resulted in police turning youth found in the sex trade over to social workers who put them in group homes that lack services to treat them, which often leads them right back into the sex trade.[73]

Lee and others have also been critical of pressure placed upon youth to testify against the adults who have facilitated their participation in the sex trade.[74] According to Lee, widespread federal and state prosecution of "pimps" has resulted in gangs taking over child prostitution. As a result, argues Lee, many young people in the sex trade today are members of gangs and are engaging in crimes like carjacking and robbery. Lee contends that police hold the youth as material witnesses and threaten to prosecute them for crimes unless they testify in sex trafficking cases against their fellow gang members, placing them and their families in danger without adequate witness protection programs.[75]

---

[70] Ibid. 10.    [71] Ibid. 5.

[72] Brendan M. Conner, "In Loco Aequitatis: The Dangers of 'Safe Harbor' Laws for Youth in the Sex Trades," *Stanford Journal of Civil Rights & Civil Liberties* 12 (February 2016), 43, 49; see also Shelby Schwartz, "Harboring Concerns: The Problematic Conceptual Reorientation of Juvenile Prostitution Adjudication in New York," *Columbia Journal of Gender and Law* 18 (2008), 235.

[73] Interview with Lois Lee, September 7, 2017; Vednita Carter also expresses concern about how safe harbor laws enable youth to return immediately to their adult facilitators. Interview with Vednita Carter, July 27, 2017 (on file with author).

[74] Lutnick, *Domestic Minor Sex Trafficking*, 72.

[75] Interview with Lois Lee, September 7, 2017.

Finally, both safe harbor laws and anti-trafficking programs have led to the increasing professionalization and bureaucratization of responses to child sex trafficking. Since 2003, the government has funded many anti-trafficking task forces across the country, but some have questioned whether these task forces have produced results.[76] Lois Lee has argued that these funds, as well as funds for end demand campaigns, would be better spent on services for youth.[77] As the movement succeeded in convincing government officials of the importance of taking this issue seriously, states began to take over the handling of commercially sexually exploited youth, using a centralized, bureaucratized approach to youth that sometimes displaced small service providers who had maintained personal relationships with their clients. Activist Sandy Skelaney, for example, has criticized Florida's response to trafficking, which has increased institutionalization of services for youth trafficking survivors, on the grounds that it has resulted in the loss of personalized care. She has argued that the increasing involvement of state agencies like the Department of Children and Family and the Attorney General after the passage of the safe harbor law in Florida meant that youth often had to tell their stories multiple times to a range of state government employees, which could be traumatizing and risked violating confidentiality. She also noted the proliferation of people involved in the process who bring their own agendas and sometimes lack a holistic perspective.[78] The build-up of these bureaucracies, argue some critics, have increased interference and control over the lives of youth, limiting their freedom and controlling their behavior.[79]

## NEGATIVE IMPACTS ON ADULT SEX WORKERS

In addition to potentially harmful effects on youth, sex worker advocates have argued that anti-child-trafficking reforms have had a negative impact on adults in the sex trade. They argue that law enforcement action against traffickers, like the FBI Innocence Lost National Initiative stings, have led to the arrest of adults consensually engaging in the sex trade. They criticize end demand campaigns for driving sex work further underground, making it more dangerous.[80] Furthermore, sex workers argue that campaigns to shut down online advertising of sexual services have decreased their ability to work independently and safely. Civil libertarians have protested campaigns against online advertisers of sexual services as a violation of free speech. Lois Lee opposed the campaign to shut down Backpage.com because it was a useful

---

[76] Lutnick, *Domestic Minor Sex Trafficking*, 94.

[77] Interview with Lois Lee, September 7, 2017.

[78] Interview with Sandy Skelaney, May 27, 2016 (on file with author).

[79] Musto, *Control and Protect*.

[80] See, for example, Center for Democracy and Technology, Written Submission for the House Committee on the Judiciary, Subcommittee on Crime, Terrorism and Homeland Security, September 15, 2010, at *Domestic Minor Sex Trafficking Hearing, 2010*, 284–288.

way to find youth involved in the sex trade and help them.[81] Appeals to protect youth have sometimes functioned as a Trojan horse for a broader attack on the sex industry. Like with the Craigslist and Backpage campaigns, advocates argued for policies based on the impact on youth but the policies impacted adults as well. For example, Georgia voters overwhelming passed a statewide referendum in November of 2016 to impose an annual $5,000 fee on strip clubs to go toward housing, counseling, and other services for victims of child prostitution.[82] Advocates are more able to gain support if they frame their argument around youth because there is more public consensus about the harm caused by the prostitution of youth than there is about prostitution involving adults. Focusing on youth, and claiming that minors are a large percentage of people in the sex trade, enabled the movement to avoid difficult questions about female sexual agency because most people agree that youth, especially adolescent girls, could not, or should not, consent to commercial sex. Whereas activists encountered resistance when adult women were at issue, because whether women were subject to force, fraud, or coercion was a question to be determined, with youth that question was seemingly irrelevant – youth were assumed to be coerced by older men who bought sex from them and sold them for sex. The focus on young girls, and their innocence, gullibility, and vulnerability, reinforced this assumption. Activists argued that juvenile prostitution was "nested" in adult prostitution so that to eliminate the former you had to also eliminate the latter. By contrast, others argued that legalizing sex work was important in order to free up resources to focus on youth in the sex trade.

An example of how appeals to youth involvement in the sex trade can hamper sex worker rights efforts is a 2014 controversy about use of the word "prostitution" by the Associated Press. Sex Worker's Outreach Project NYC (SWOP-NYC) and Sex Workers Action New York (SWANK) organized a social media campaign calling on the Associated Press to stop using the word "prostitute" and instead to use the phrase "sex worker." They argued that sex workers "typically self-identify as something else entirely and that this difference may actually be quite crucial to their jobs and livelihood."[83] They requested that journalists not use the word "prostitute" to describe sex workers unless they expressly consent to the use of the term in reference to themselves. SWOP-NYC offered guidance on their website for journalists about appropriate language and how to respect the privacy concerns of sex workers. Abolitionists responded with an open letter to AP signed by over 300

---

[81] Interview with Lois Lee, September 7, 2017.

[82] Rhonda Cook, "Voters Overwhelmingly Adopt Three Constitutional Amendments," *Atlanta Journal Constitution* (November 9, 2016).

[83] Victoria Taylor, "Campaign Urges AP Stylebook to Replace Use of 'Prostitute' with 'Sex Worker,'" *New York Daily News* (October 15, 2014); Twitter, Sex Worker AP, at https://twitter .com/search?f=realtime&q=sex%20worker%20ap&src=typd.

organizations around the world opposing this change. In the letter, they argued that the term "sex worker" was "invented by the sex industry and its supporters in order to legitimize prostitution as a legal and acceptable form of work," but that it conceals the harm done to people in the sex trade. They then argued that "approximately two million children are exploited in the global sex trade and 325,000 American youth are at-risk of sexual exploitation." They also objected to the terms "prostitution" and especially "teen prostitute," and recommended instead that AP use the terms "person in prostitution," "prostituted person," or "commercially sexually exploited person."[84] This slippage between youth and adults is not uncommon. Another example is the February 2010 Congressional hearing on domestic minor sex trafficking when Senator Al Franken at one point made the comment that because most prostitutes start in the sex trade as children, adult males patronizing adult prostitutes continued this exploitation of children. He said, "the victims are the children and the women who are adult children who are the result of this exploitation."[85] Characterizing women in the sex trade as "adult children" then opens the door to condemning the entire sex trade. It also infantilizes adult women and suggests that they should be treated as children.

More generally, sex worker activist Ava Rose argues that the feminist anti-trafficking movement's focus on the victimized sex worker contributes to increased stigmatization and poorer working conditions for sex workers. Reflecting on her experiences in the sex trade as a youth, Rose argues, "criminalizing those purchasing my services would have certainly limited my income and added to the precarious situation in which I found myself," noting that this approach would not have addressed the economic insecurity and lack of opportunity she experienced at the time.[86]

Finally, some have noted that conservatives have used the anti-trafficking movement to attack sexual liberalism and women's rights. Some religious advocates have argued that teen prostitution resulted from the sexual revolution. Georgia pastor Jack Whedbee argued, "Basically, the sexual revolution was a failure – it didn't liberate anyone ... The culture of promiscuity that kicked in in the '60s and '70s is almost the same as the culture of prostitution. Promiscuity, prostitution. It's almost the same thing."[87] In Atlanta, activists successfully persuaded the Atlanta City Council to raise the minimum age of exotic dancers in the city from 18 to 21, which the

---

[84] Letter to David Minthorn, Stylebook Editor, The Associated Press, dated October 31, 2014, at http://media.virbcdn.com/files/14/39cd5a9c5d79b349-LettertotheAssociatedPress103114.pdf

[85] *In Our Own Backyard Hearing, 2010*, 23.

[86] Ava Rose, "Punished for Strength: Sex Worker Activism and the Anti-Trafficking Movement," *Atlantis*, 37.2.1 (2015–2016), 57–64, at 60, 62.

[87] Alan Judd, "Capital Rally Targets Teen Prostitution," *Atlanta Journal Constitution* (August 12, 2001), 2E.

Georgia Supreme Court overturned as a violation of free speech.[88] There is also overlap between the anti-trafficking movement and the movement against abortion and contraception. For many years, the Department of Health and Human Services allowed the US Conference of Catholic Bishops to put conditions on federal anti-trafficking grants by prohibiting subcontracting organizations from providing contraception to trafficking victims, but in 2012 a federal court ruled that this practice was a violation of the First Amendment separation of church and state.[89] On the other hand, the United States has required that organizations receiving federal anti-trafficking funds make an anti-prostitution pledge, which prevented some organizations from applying, like the Urban Justice Center's Sex Workers Project, which works with trafficking victims as well as sex workers.[90]

## CONCLUSION

The attitudes that led to the prosecution of youth for prostitution, especially a racialized sexual double standard, have lived on in the ways these new policies, especially safe harbor laws, have been applied. The public policies that leave youth vulnerable to involvement in the sex trade in the first place, including economic inequality, an inadequate social safety net, and failing schools, are still firmly in place, as are the racism, sexism, classism, and homophobia that justify these policies (or lack of policies). The movement as a whole has yet to address the root causes that drive youth involvement in the sex trade, but there have been strong advocates in the movement, from Norma Hotaling to Rachel Lloyd, who have repeatedly raised these concerns before state and federal legislatures, at conferences and community meetings, and in blogs and books.

Critics have suggested that moral panics, law and order responses, and attacks on the sex industry and sexuality more generally have not effectively helped youth and that they in fact bolster conservative political, economic, and moral agendas that make youth more vulnerable to abuse in the sex trade. Whether the movement, politicians, and the public will find these critiques persuasive seems unlikely, especially with the election of Donald Trump and the sharp turn toward neoliberal, law and order approaches to social problems and the new clout of evangelical Christians. Meanwhile, the hyperbolic narratives of victimization that have fueled the movement's success in motivating legislators to act have been politically expedient, but have played

---

[88] Stephanie Davis and Michael Shively, *An Overview of Anti-Demand Efforts in Atlanta: Summary Based Upon Research from the Study, "Developing a National Action Plan for Eliminating Sex Trafficking"* (August 16, 2010), 2.

[89] American Civil Liberties Union, "Court Prohibits Religious Restrictions on Government Funded Trafficking Victims' Program" (March 24, 2012), at www.aclu.org/news/court-prohibits-religious-restrictions-government-funded-trafficking-victims-program.

[90] Interview with Sienna Baskin, April 22, 2016 (on file with author).

into long-standing, racialized narratives of African American male predation toward white females that contributed to the build-up of the prison industrial complex to the detriment of communities of color, making youth in these communities ever more vulnerable to abuse. Furthermore, the unintended consequences of these narratives may be counterproductive. When the youth who end up in the diversion programs inspired by safe harbor laws are not the cowering cisgender girls of the dominant narrative, the movement's rhetoric is on a collision course with reality. The programs developed based on these narratives, often connected to or embedded in the criminal justice system, serve some youth better than others, and the differences often fall along the predictable lines of race, class, sex, and sexuality.

# Conclusion: Ending the US Youth Sex Trade?

> It is my hope that in 10 years, it will seem ludicrous that we once incarcerated some of our nations' most victimized and vulnerable children.
>
> Rachel Lloyd, Testifying Before the Senate Judiciary Subcommittee on Human Rights and the Law, February 2010[1]

The interplay of social, political, demographic, economic, and technological factors have contributed to the emergence of concern about the youth sex trade in different historical periods. These campaigns arose during times of expanding rights for women, and changing sexual norms that heightened anxieties about youth sexuality. Campaigns against the US sex trade surged when girls and young women were moving beyond traditional roles, entering the workplace or traveling away from home to pursue economic opportunities or flee abuse. In the late nineteenth century, industrialization and urbanization brought young women into the workplace in increasing numbers; parents' control over the courtship and marriage decisions of their children was waning; and political campaigns to extend property rights and suffrage to women were challenging traditional ideas about gender. In the mid to late twentieth century, women won the legal right to contraception and abortion, entered the labor force in record numbers with increased access to the professions and occupations that had been traditionally closed to them, and were more likely to be single mothers as a result of the advent of no-fault divorce laws and increased out-of-wedlock childbirth. The movements for civil rights, women's rights, and gay rights challenged white heterosexual male dominance in society, generating a political backlash. "Family values" conservatives organized against these social changes, particularly to abortion, sex education, and gay marriage.

---

[1] *In Our Own Backyard: Child Prostitution and Sex Trafficking in the United States, A Hearing Before the United States Senate Judiciary Subcommittee on Human Rights and Law.* 111th Cong., 2nd Sess. (February 24, 2010), 72.

Beginning in the 1990s, they turned to sex trafficking as a central issue after making little headway on issues like school prayer and abortion.

Occurring during times of high immigration and changing race relations, as well as economic changes, these campaigns tapped into racism and xenophobia as well as related economic anxieties. The 1880s to 1920s saw increased immigration from Central, Eastern, and Southern Europe, waning when restrictions were put in place after World War I; after passage of the 1965 Immigration Naturalization Act immigration increased from Latin America and Asia; and post 9/11 Islamophobia spiked and opposition to "illegal immigration" surged. These were also times of racial conflict – the nadir of American race relations post-Reconstruction, at the height of the civil rights movement, and during the "War on Terror." Racial anxieties laced public discourses on youth in prostitution during each period – from the late nineteenth century and early twentieth century "white slave trade" campaigns, to the 1970s campaigns against juvenile prostitution via the "Minnesota pipeline," to contemporary campaigns to protect "our daughters." These campaigns also arose during times of economic stress – the recessions following the Panic of 1893, the 1970s oil crisis, the recession in the 2000s, and the financial crisis of 2007–2008. The expansion of neoliberal economic policies since the 1980s, which destabilized the middle class, placed tremendous stress on working class and poor families, and eviscerated the social safety net, made youth more vulnerable to entering the sex trade. Anxieties about these changes were reflected in the recurrent tales of naïve white girls from the countryside moving or running away to the city and being tricked and ensnared in prostitution by foreign men or men of color.

Finally, increased visibility of the sex trade, resulting at least in part from technological changes, occurred during each period of activism against the US youth sex trade. In the nineteenth century, the invention of photography and later motion pictures quickly led to the distribution of pornography. The 1970s campaigns against juvenile prostitution occurred as the Supreme Court's liberalization of obscenity laws led to the proliferation of adult book stores and movie theaters. Video pornography began to make its way into homes with the launch of Betamax in 1975 and VHS in 1976. In the 1990s, activism against the commercial sexual exploitation of youth increased as the internet made the world of pornography and transactional sex visible on one's home computer at the touch of a key. Concern expanded significantly as internet technology developed in the 2000s with streaming and social media, and as the proliferation of iPhones and iPads provided youth unsupervised access to the internet. Each technological development significantly expanded the commercial sex trade and made it more visible and more likely to reach youth, which stoked adults' anxieties and fueled campaigns against youth prostitution.

From the mid-nineteenth century to the early twenty-first century, reformers used gendered and racialized narratives of sexual danger to argue for state intervention to protect cisgender girls and young women, and sometimes cisgender boys, from adult male predators, often imagined as men of color. Nineteenth-century campaigns to criminalize seduction and raise the age of consent sought to protect young, innocent white girls from older, predatory men, while the white slavery scare sought to protect white girls from foreign men who might coerce them into brothels. Campaigns against juvenile prostitution and trafficking from the mid-twentieth to the early twenty-first centuries were often framed in terms of African American men luring suburban or rural white girls into prostitution in the city. Activists warned against the dangers of a highly sexualized popular culture that taught girls to sexually objectify themselves and romanticized men who prostituted women and girls, as well as promoted materialistic values that might encourage girls to trade sex in order to obtain consumer goods. The movement both drew upon and amplified cultural discourses on childhood innocence and need for protection, as well as widespread "crisis discourses of 'girls at risk.'"[2]

The contemporary movement against the US youth sex trade built upon the successes of the 1970s' anti-rape movement and 1980s' child sex abuse movement, which raised awareness about the extent and impact of sexual assault and abuse, generally and in particular against children, and reformed laws to more effectively hold men accountable. The anti-rape movement challenged the sexual double standard that blamed women for sexual assault and excused perpetrators. Similarly, the sex workers' rights movement challenged the enforcement of prostitution laws whereby police arrested women selling sex but not male buyers. While the latter argument was never very successful with regard to adults, contemporary advocates' arguments against "jailing girls for men's crimes" were very effective. Challenging mid-twentieth century social scientists and psychologists who had portrayed incest as infrequent and innocuous and children as active participants, the child sexual abuse movement conducted their own research revealing the prevalence and harmful impact of incest, which they used to fight for stronger laws against child sexual abuse. Building on this legacy, activists opposing juvenile prostitution conducted research claiming to show the widespread existence and harmful impact of youth involvement in the sex trade. These activists asked why, if money changed hands, a child molester becomes just a "john." They also drew upon views of child sexual abuse offenders as pathological and incurable to support enhanced criminal prosecution of adults involving youth in the sex trade. Relying on statutory rape laws that went back to the early twentieth-century age of consent campaigns, activists pointed out the contradiction

---

[2] Emma Renold and Jessica Ringrose, "Feminisms Re-Figuring 'Sexualisation,' Sexuality and the 'The Girl,'" *Feminist Theory* 14.3 (2013), 247 (arguing that "the figure of the contemporary girl is overdetermined, weighted down with meaning and commonly represented through binary formations of celebratory postfeminist 'girl power' vs. crisis discourses of 'girls at risk'").

between prosecuting youth for prostitution when they were younger than the age of consent laws set by state law.

The movement took advantage of political opportunities to advance their cause. They leveraged the passage of the Trafficking Victims Protection Act in 2000, which focused on international trafficking, by arguing that child prostitution was a form of human trafficking and by pointing out the hypocrisy of concern about international victims of child sex trafficking while ignoring domestic victims. They pointed out the contradiction between federal anti-trafficking law and state and local police practices of arresting youth for prostitution. Evangelical activists in the broader anti-trafficking movement were able to convince President George W. Bush to make sex trafficking a priority issue and to facilitate the channeling of funds to nongovernmental organizations working on the issue, including religious organizations, so when Congress appropriated funds for domestic minor sex trafficking, evangelical groups like Shared Hope International became one of the primary recipients. The movement had several strong allies in Congress, like Chris Smith (R-NJ) and John Conyers (D-MI), and in the executive branch, like the anti-trafficking movement founder Laura Lederer. At the state level, rightward shifts in state legislatures in the early 2000s proved fertile ground for the law and order messaging of the mainstream movement, leading to tougher criminal laws and more funds for law enforcement to investigate and prosecute child sex trafficking. The movement also took advantage of cultural opportunities that became available by tapping into participants' anxieties and emotions about social change and providing an opportunity for participants to articulate their opposition to these developments through activism against youth involvement in the sex trade.

By 2010, the movement against the US youth sex trade was a collaborative adversarial movement, consisting of organizations from a range of political and social locations. The movement included evangelicals and feminists, law and order Republicans and liberal Democrats, proponents of human rights, and sex worker advocates. Unlikely alliances were built around campaigns for safe harbor laws to create immunity for youth from prostitution charges and laws to expunge or vacate criminal convictions for prostitution if a defendant could prove that they were a victim of human trafficking at the time they were arrested. Feminists and evangelical Christians testified side-by-side at Congressional hearings, filed amicus curiae briefs on the same side in legal cases, and co-signed letters to politicians and business leaders demanding action against child sex trafficking. Despite this political diversity, however, the movement was not racially diverse. With some notable exceptions, like Vednita Carter, Shirley Franklin, Tina Frundt, and Withelma Pettigrew, most of the movement's leaders have been white women. Similar to how African American women declined to join white reformers' age of consent campaigns in the early twentieth century, contemporary women of color may be skeptical about whether new anti-trafficking laws would help young women of color, and how they might be used against men of color.

Activists framed the issue of youth in the sex trade in diverse ways in order to inspire the public, policymakers, law enforcement, and social service workers to change their perceptions and treatment of these youth, as well as their perceptions of the adults involved. Feminist advocates, like the Coalition Against Trafficking in Women, framed the issue in terms of male violence against women and girls, condemning the commodification of female bodies and the sexualization of popular culture. Conservatives framed the issue as a crime control problem, whereas some evangelicals framed it as a problem of declining moral values, lost innocence, and materialism. Some criticized the criminal justice and child welfare systems for not recognizing and addressing the sexual exploitation of youth. Others framed the issue as a mental health problem – girls brainwashed or suffering from "Stockholm syndrome" – using therapeutic ideas and language to recharacterize youth as injured rather than delinquent and therefore worthy of treatment as opposed to punishment. The movement also sometimes used therapeutic language to reframe the men who buy sex from youth, from "johns" to pedophiles. The human rights framing of the problem focused on how American society had failed children by not addressing child poverty and abuse, racism, sexism, and homophobia. Vednita Carter of Breaking Free framed the prostitution of African American girls and women as a form of racism with roots going back to the nineteenth-century slavery of African Americans. Resisting victimization narratives, other activists pushed empowerment and survivor leadership – sometimes framed as an individual endeavor, other times as a collective effort for institutional change. These varied frames enabled the movement to recruit a wide range of supporters, both conservative and liberal, evangelical and feminist. Funders and the media, however, predominately elevated conservative, individualized frames that called for law and order responses rather than systemic change.

The direction of the movement has been shaped by public and private funding decisions. Government funding influenced research and activism, favoring some movement organizations and goals over others. Organizations that received government anti-trafficking funds typically employed conservative approaches that did not interrupt mainstream understandings or priorities. For example, Shared Hope International, led by former Congresswoman Linda Smith who was an evangelical Christian, received extensive government funding under the Bush administration, who favored evangelical organizations. With federal funding, Shared Hope conducted research that played a significant role in shaping knowledge about the issue and became the new basis for public policies. They also used federal funds for public education campaigns and to conduct training of law enforcement and prosecutors, thereby giving the organization significant influence on government approaches to the US youth sex trade. Shared Hope's individualized framing of the problem led to calls for law and order responses, rather than structural changes. SHI is an example of how the underlying politics of knowledge production shaped perceptions of the problem and policy responses. In addition to research, education and advocacy, the federal government has also funded private organizations to perform state functions, like running youth diversion programs or shelters. While these public/private collaborations have supported critical services for youth, they allowed for public funding of religious organizations and have had less accountability than public institutions.

In addition to government funding, private funding also played an important role in the development of the movement. In the late 1970s, private foundations and churches funded some of the earliest organizations working on the issue like Children of the Night and the Paul and Lisa Program. Beginning in 1999, the leftist Fund for Nonviolence based in Santa Cruz, California, funded much early activism against the youth sex trade, including the work of organizations providing services to youth like SAGE, GEMS, and the Paul and Lisa Program as well as advocacy organizations like ECPAT-USA and government advisory councils like the Atlanta Women's Agenda. They also funded the influential 2001 Estes and Weiner study, the US Campaign Against the Commercial Sexual Exploitation of Children, and the 2003 Breaking the Silence youth survivor summit.[3] In selecting grantees, the Fund for Nonviolence prioritized organizations that "pursue structural changes to root causes of race, class, and gender injustice," that "value the active involvement of members of the communities most impacted by the violence and social injustice being addressed," and that "promote the leadership of women within the organization."[4] Through their funding decisions, the Fund for Nonviolence supported the development of a survivor-led movement against exploitation of youth in the sex trade.

Media coverage also shaped the direction of the movement. Echoing muckraking journalism of the early twentieth century when media coverage of the "white slave trade" led to panic about foreign men forcing white girls into brothels, contemporary news coverage made exaggerated claims about the number of youth involved in the sex trade and repeatedly portrayed the most extreme cases involving the violent exploitation of young girls. The 1970s coverage focused on adult men buying sex from boys and African American men luring white, middle-class girls to cities. In the 2010s, the media coverage focused mainly on girls. Activists sought mainstream coverage to raise awareness about the issue, to expand support for legislative and policy reforms, and to decrease silence and stigma surrounding youth involved in the

---

[3] Between 1999 and 2005, the Fund for Nonviolence contributed close to half-a-million dollars to organizations combatting the commercial sexual exploitation of children. Fund for Nonviolence, CSEC Grants List, at www.fundfornonviolence.org/grants-list/earlier-grants/. Betsy Fairbanks was the president and CEO of the Fund for Nonviolence at the time.

[4] Fund for Nonviolence, Grantmaking Priorities, at www.fundfornonviolence.org/.

sex trade. How the media covered the issue, however, was influenced by selection processes driven by factors such as the activists' credibility and access to the media, publishers' demands for stories that would sell, conventions about how stories should be framed, and the degree to which movement formulations of issues were seen as relevant or comprehensible within prevailing understandings of the world, like hegemonic assumptions of childhood innocence, or whether they meshed with the state's pre-existing priorities, like harsh punishment of child molesters.

As a result, the perspectives of some movement actors were more likely to receive media attention than those of others. Media selection processes resulted in the elevation of stories with the deepest cultural resonance – racialized stories of "slaves, sinners and saviors" – rather than the more complex and demanding stories of failed social institutions and systemic bias.[5] Media coverage focused on adults brutally exploiting youth and ignored networks among homeless youth that facilitated engagement in the sex trade as a survival strategy. Activists who offered criminal justice solutions to youth involvement in the sex trade were more successful in gaining media attention than those calling for more transformative change. Credibility assessments also played a role in media coverage. The perspectives of advocates who were federally funded or affiliated with established institutions like universities or with the state were more likely to be perceived as credible and be cited and quoted in media coverage.

Mainstream discourses on the youth sex trade were highly racialized and sometimes functioned as a racial dog whistle. Scholar Ian Haney López has defined dog whistle politics as "coded racial appeals that carefully manipulate hostility toward nonwhites," such as "blasts about criminals and welfare cheats, illegal aliens and sharia law in the heartland."[6] These appeals communicated messages to a targeted audience about threatening nonwhites, although the cloaked language hid the racial character of the overture to some listeners.[7] Both in the 1970s and in the 2000s, condemnations of the youth sex trade were framed as an "urban" problem invading white middle-class communities and affecting "our daughters," suggesting a racial subtext, and portrayals of the issue often focused on white girls victimized by African American men. Echoing the nineteenth century "white slave trade" narratives of foreign men luring white girls into prostitution, and tapping into white supremacist narratives of African American male sexual predation that fueled lynching in the late nineteenth and early twentieth centuries, these frames appealed to whites anxious about social change and also justified the build-up

[5] Julia O'Connell Davidson, *Global Child Sex Trade* (Cambridge, England: Polity Press, 2005), 4; Carrie N. Baker, "Moving Beyond 'Slaves, Sinners, and Saviors': An Intersectional Feminist Analysis of U.S. Sex Trafficking Discourse, Law and Policy," *Journal of Feminist Scholarship* 4 (Spring 2013).

[6] Ian Haney López, *Dog Whistle Politics: How Coded Racial Appeals Have Reinvented Racism and Wrecked the Middle Class* (New York, NY: Oxford University Press, 2014), ix.

[7] Ibid. 5.

of the criminal justice system and the neglect of poor communities of color. The bitter irony was that these frames often occurred side by side with the characterization of the youth sex trade as a form of "modern day slavery."

In order to make the case that minors in the sex trade were victims rather than delinquents, activists relied heavily on deeply-rooted Western ideologies of childhood that children are innocent, asexual, and dependent–ideologies inflected by race and class. In image and word, as in the promotional images for the FBI Innocence Lost National Initiative (see figure 4.1) or the film *Very Young Girls* (see figure 5.5), campaigns against child prostitution have attempted to garner sympathy for youth in the sex trade by portraying them as young, naïve, vulnerable to manipulation by adults, and in need of rescue and protection. The media enthusiastically proliferated these sensationalistic stories that grabbed readers. These portrayals, however, contradicted the realities of the majority of youth in the sex trade, who were generally older and experienced, but still in need of support. Anti-trafficking discourses reinforced the ideology of youth incapacity underlying child labor laws that restricted youth employment and compulsory education laws that required youth to attend school until at least age sixteen and even eighteen in some states. Statutory rape laws assumed that youth cannot consent to sex with older people. For girls in particular, persistent cultural messages about the value of virginity, while obsolete in many respects, continued to live on in anti-trafficking discourses. These conceptions of childhood contributed toward an emerging distinction between adult prostitution and youth involved in prostitution, who came to be seen as victims of child sexual abuse. But these conceptions also justified denying self-determination to youth, making them more vulnerable to abuse in the absence of a strong, well-functioning social safety net to support children who lack family resources. In a neoliberal economic system that privatized child rearing, failed to provide effective alternatives when families cannot meet the needs of youth, and created barriers to youth supporting themselves through legal means, the street economy, including the sex trade, was one of the few remaining viable options for survival.

Furthermore, these portrayals of victimized youth were shaped by gendered and racialized middle-class notions of respectability that reinforced a "hierarchy of victimization."[8] For example, cisgender females were more likely to be perceived as victims in need of protection and rescue because of gendered stereotypes of "girls as soft, passive, fragile, and in need of intervention and support, but boys as hard and tough, able to take care of themselves."[9] Because of cultural stereotypes about women of color as promiscuous, girls of color were

---

[8] Chris Greer, "News Media, Victims, and Crime," in Pamela Davies, Peter Francis, and Chris Greer (eds.), *Victims, Crime, and Society* (London, England: Sage, 2007), 20–39.

[9] Jeffrey P. Dennis, "Women are Victims, Men Make Choices: The Invisibility of Men and Boys in the Global Sex Trade," *Gender Issues* 25.1 (2008), 11–25, at 21.

less likely to be seen as innocent and in need of protection. When youth were perceived to be complicit in their victimization or when they were angry or uncooperative with law enforcement, they were less likely to be seen as victims and more likely to be held responsible for their exploitation. Narratives of ideal victims obscured the heterogeneity of real victims, and the resourcefulness and resilience that they exhibited in order to survive. Youth, who rarely see themselves as victims, are often alienated by these narratives of victimization, which might dissuade them from accessing services. Activists' use of traditional ideologies of youth as innocent, asexual, and dependent, however, reinforced the justification for denying their agency and rights. Furthermore, framing youth involvement in prostitution as sexual abuse narrowed the focus to an individual experience of abuse and obscured the broader gendered, racialized, and classed context in which some youth might end up in the sex trade, thereby ignoring the larger structural problems that contributed to youth prostitution.

While the mainstream movement repeated narratives of youth victimization, some activists focused instead on empowerment. As opposed to evangelical groups like Shared Hope International, which used a "rescue approach" to youth and supported aggressive intervention, other groups like YWEP and GEMS were oriented around empowerment and youth leadership. YWEP, for example, argued that youth may need to participate in the sex trade in order to survive, and that therefore adults should not try to tell them what to do, especially in the absence of effective social programs to assist them in meeting their survival needs. YWEP was careful not to judge or second-guess the decisions of youth in its programs, instead using a harm reduction approach, offering them services to stay safe no matter what they decided to do. GEMS, on the other hand, took a strong stand that youth should leave the sex trade and tried to provide the financial and psychological support to enable them to do so. Both YWEP and GEMS developed strong youth leadership programs, which were seen as a path to empowerment. YWEP, however, went one step further, focusing not only on individual empowerment, but also on collective empowerment by engaging in participatory action research and fighting for institutional reforms in social service and health care systems in Chicago. But anti-trafficking policies contributed to the closure of YWEP because of police harassment and members' fear of prosecution under anti-trafficking laws, which were being redefined broadly to criminalize anyone who helps youth engaged in the sex trade, including older teens helping younger teens. GEMS, on the other hand, has thrived because they work closely with courts and law enforcement.

The campaigns against youth involvement in prostitution have significantly changed the law and its enforcement, and resulted in more youth services. A 2010 study funded by the Office of Juvenile Justice and Delinquency Prevention examining the TVPA's impact on the prosecution of CSEC cases showed a significant increase in federal investigations, case filings, and prosecutions for CSEC between 1998 and 2005, especially after the passage of the TVPA in 2000 and the PROTECT Act in 2003.[10] Filings increased the most in California, Utah, Ohio, Georgia, and New York.[11] Many of these cases involved child pornography, but they also included prostitution and other forms of sexual exploitation. FBI's Innocence Lost National Initiative claimed to remove 6000 youth from the sex industry (although it's unclear how many were arrested and how many were provided with what they need to stay out of the sex trade) and convicted over 2500 adults for facilitating youth involvement in the sex trade by 2016. At the end of 2015, there were at least seventy-four state and local task forces and working groups fighting domestic minor sex trafficking around the country.[12] Another indication that the movement against domestic minor sex trafficking was having an impact came from a 2014 study by the Urban Institute of the underground commercial sex economy in eight states. The study found that facilitators were increasingly avoiding minors because law enforcement had placed a heightened emphasis on arresting and prosecuting facilitators of underage youth in prostitution.[13]

In addition to increased prosecution of adults facilitators, there has been a decrease in arrest and prosecution of youth for prostitution. Since the passage of the TVPA in 2000, arrests of youth peaked in 2004, with over 1150 minors arrested for prostitution, approximately 850 girls and 300 boys.[14] After 2004, however, rates have dropped significantly. According to FBI crime reports, the number of minors arrested for prostitution or commercialized vice in the United States decreased significantly between 2008 and 2012, dropping 49.5% for boys (from 277 to 140) and 46.5% for girls (864 to 462).[15] In 2012, there were no arrests of children under ten years of age for prostitution,[16] down from thirty-one such arrests in 1995.[17] Some evidence indicated that the movement against the youth sex trade may have had some impact on law enforcement

---

[10] Williams Adams, Colleen Owens, and Kevonne Small, "Effects of Federal Legislation on the Commercial Sexual Exploitation of Youth," *OJJDP Juvenile Justice Bulletin* (July 2010), 4 (figure 1).

[11] Ibid. 5 (figure 2).

[12] FBI, Innocence Lost National Initiative, Statistics (September 30, 2016), at www.fbi.gov/investigate/violent-crime/cac.

[13] Meredith Dank, Bilal Khan, P. Mitchell Downey, Cybele Kotonias, Deborah Mayer, Colleen Owens, Laura Pacificci, and Lilly Yu, *Estimating the Size and Structure of the Underground Commercial Sex Economy in Eight Major US Cities* (Washington, DC: Urban Institute, March 2014), 151.

[14] Alexandra Lutnick, *Domestic Minor Sex Trafficking: Beyond Victims and Villains* (New York, NY: Columbia University Press, 2016), 77.

[15] FBI Uniform Crime Reports, Table 35, Five-Year Arrest Trends by Sex, 2008–2012, at www.fbi.gov/about-us/cjis/ucr/crime-in-the-u.s/2012/crime-in-the-u.s.-2012/tables/40tabledatadecoverviewpdf.

[16] FBI Uniform Crime Reports, Table 40, Arrests, Female, By Age, 2012, at www.fbi.gov/about-us/cjis/ucr/crime-in-the-u.s/2012/crime-in-the-u.s.-2012/tables/40tabledatadecoverviewpdf/table_40_arrests_females_by_age_2012.xls#overview.

[17] FBI, Crime in the United States, 1995, p. 218, at www.fbi.gov/about-us/cjis/ucr/crime-in-the-u.s/1995/95sec4.pdf.

attitudes toward and treatment of youth. A study of police responses to juvenile prostitution indicated evolving views about the nature of juvenile prostitution away from seeing it as juvenile delinquency and toward viewing it as a form of abuse.[18] Some states had developed coordinated state-wide responses to domestic minor sex trafficking that linked law enforcement, child welfare services, non-governmental organizations, and other stakeholders, like Minnesota's No Wrong Door initiative and the Georgia Cares program. However, even when there are safe harbor laws, police have continued to arrest youth for prostitution.[19] Furthermore, the state takeover of services has led to professionalization and bureaucratization of service delivery that may make these services more impersonal and alienating to youth.[20]

Specialized services for youth have also increased, although they were still deemed inadequate by advocates. By 2016, over two hundred organizations in the United States were working on trafficking of minors, some providing services to youth and other engaging in public education, research, and policy advocacy.[21] A 2013 nationwide study conducted by the Illinois Criminal Justice Information Authority and funded by the Department of Justice found that at the time of the survey in August 2012, there were thirty-seven programs offering services for sex trafficking survivors in the country, eighteen of which opened between 2007 and 2012. Fourteen programs were exclusive to domestic sex trafficking victims, twenty-two were open to domestic and international victims, and one was open to international victims only. Of the 682 beds in the thirty-seven existing shelters, 438 were reserved for minors and another sixty-six beds were available to minors or adults. However, fewer than twenty-eight beds were available for male survivors and only one program indicated that it would accept transgender girls.[22] A majority of the beds were in the western part of the country: California had ten residential programs, which provided fifty-four percent of all beds for sex trafficking victims.[23] At the time of the study, twenty-seven more shelters were preparing to open, fifteen for domestic victims and twelve for both domestic and international victims, which amounted to 354 more beds, mostly for minors. This is a ninety-three

---

[18] Kimberly J. Mitchell, David Finkelhor, and Janis Wolak, "Conceptualizing Juvenile Prostitution as Child Maltreatment: Findings from the National Juvenile Prostitution Study," *Child Maltreatment* 15.1 (February 2010), 18–36.

[19] Kristin Finklea, *Juvenile Victims of Domestic Sex Trafficking: Juvenile Justice Issues* (Washington, DC: US Congressional Research Service, 2014), 10 (recommending better police training).

[20] Interview with Sandy Skelaney, May 27, 2016 (reporting youth in Florida's system have to tell their stories repeatedly to multiple people: on file with author).

[21] See Polaris Project, Global Modern Slavery Directors (searched United States, minor), at www .globalmodernslavery.org/#/0016000000zIi74AAC,41.65380859375,-83.53626251220703.

[22] Jessica Reichert and Amy Sylwestrzak, *National Survey of Residential Programs for Victims of Sex Trafficking* (Chicago, IL: Illinois Criminal Justice Information Authority, October 2013), 15.

[23] Ibid. i.

percent increase over what was previously available.[24] This growth of services to youth leaving the sex trade was evidence that the movement against domestic minor sex trafficking has had some success in achieving its goals. However, twenty-eight states had no residential programs for youth and had no plans to create any.[25] While there was some federal and state funding, many of these programs were privately funded, including by churches.[26] In addition to these services specifically geared toward sex trafficking victims, there were homeless youth shelters around the country that accepted them and may have had some programming specifically for them. Service providers had begun to develop therapeutic treatment protocols for trafficked youth, but the American Psychological Association Task Force on the Trafficking of Girls issued a report in 2014 calling for better research and treatment programs for survivors.[27]

Finally, the movement has inspired some institutional reforms. In 2014, Congress passed the Preventing Sex Trafficking and Strengthening Families Act,[28] which required that states develop policies and procedures to identify and assist youth in foster care system who were victims of sex trafficking, or at risk of being trafficked. Homeless youth advocates also attempted to leverage the trafficking frame to access more resources. In 2014, members of Congress sponsored the Runaway and Homeless Youth and Trafficking Prevention Act,[29] which proposed funding grants to public agencies for street-based services to homeless youth who had experienced trafficking or were at risk of trafficking or sexual exploitation.[30] In 2015, Congress passed the Justice for Victims of Trafficking Act, which included such grants and also supported reform of the criminal justice response to youth involved in the sex trade by urging states to adopt safe harbor laws.[31]

While in some cases these changes have protected young people, safeguarding their bodily integrity, diverting them out of the criminal justice system, and providing them with support and services as they recover from exploitation, these shifts have also policed young people's sexual activities, at times increasing restrictions on their freedom, decreasing their sexual autonomy, and interfering with their ability to make decisions about their lives. As historian Shoshanna Ehrlich has argued, "social anxiety about youthful female sexuality has been channeled into statutory regimes that regulate young women's bodies in ways that are both potentially liberating and

---

[24] Ibid. 16.   [25] Ibid. i.   [26] Ibid. 18–19.

[27] Task Force on Trafficking of Women and Girls, *Report of the Task Force on Trafficking of Women and Girls* (Washington, DC: American Psychological Association, 2014).

[28] H.R. 4980, Pub. L. 113-183 (2014).   [29] S.262 and H.R. 1779 (2016).

[30] Congressional Research Service, Summaries for the Runaway and Homeless Youth and Trafficking Prevention Act, at https://www.govtrack.us/congress/bills/114/s262/summary. This bill did not pass, but a 2015 version of this Act was incorporated into the Justice for Victims of Trafficking Act.

[31] Justice for Victims of Trafficking Act, Pub. L. 114-22, 129 Stat. 227 (May 29, 2015).

stifling."[32] The movement's support of laws restricting legal recognition of minors' ability to consent to sexual behavior can protect some youth, but can also bolster efforts to restrict youth rights in other areas. Both statutory rape and safe harbor laws assume that youth cannot consent to sexual behavior – or that their consent should not be legally recognized. This assumption could weaken the legal recognition of youth's ability to consent in other areas, like birth control, abortion, or even sexual behavior with other teenagers.[33] Furthermore, while there has been an increasing shift toward viewing youth in the sex trade as victims rather than delinquents, services for youth are still significantly underfunded, and youth are still often stigmatized and detained against their will. A disproportionate share of funding to address domestic minor sex trafficking goes toward law enforcement and criminal prosecution rather than social services.

Calls to address the systemic causes of youth trafficking are often left unheeded, while criminal justice approaches to the problem predominate and disproportionately target men of color, buttressed by racialized and gendered narratives of sexual predation and victimization that reinforce the very systems that make many girls vulnerable to sex trafficking in the first place. The movement's dominant narrative of coercive assault by strangers has obscured the more complicated and common manifestation of youth involvement in the sex trade: survivor sex facilitated by peers and necessary because of the lack of social services for homeless youth. Ironically, whereas feminists in the anti-rape movement had pressed for the decentering of "stranger rape" – the stranger with a weapon attacking a woman in the dark of night – and the recognition of acquaintance rape and date rape, many in the anti-trafficking movement moved in the opposite direction – disproportionately characterizing the involvement of youth in the sex trade as caused by strangers preying on youth, resulting in expansion of the criminal justice response rather than an expansion of social services and policies addressing structural inequalities that make youth vulnerable to entering the sex trade.[34]

These criminal justice approaches to the youth sex trade have contributed to the build-up of the prison industrial complex. Congress and state legislatures have allocated significant funds to law enforcement and to US and state attorneys to investigate, arrest, and prosecute child sex traffickers. Anti-trafficking laws have authorized and sometimes encouraged pressuring victims to testify against traffickers by connecting assistance to cooperation. Law enforcement is increasingly engaged in technologically mediated

---

[32] J. Shoshanna Ehrlich, *Regulating Desire: From the Virtuous Maiden to the Purity Princess* (Albany, NY: SUNY Press, 2014), 31.

[33] Megan Annitto, "Consent, Coercion, and Compassion: Emerging Legal Responses to the Commercial Sexual Exploitation of Minors," *Yale Law and Policy Review* 30.1 (2011), 21.

[34] See Sandy Skelaney, *A Novel Solution to Sex Trafficking*, TEDxMiama, 2013, at www.youtube .com/watch?v=OLuJALGTpQ8, urging reforms that address youth vulnerability rather than addressing focusing on criminal prosecution of facilitators and buyers.

surveillance of people exchanging sex for money.[35] For youth, programs that divert youth out of the criminal justice system are still inadequate, are not responding to their real needs, and are often coercive and punitive.[36] This build-up is likely to fall disproportionately on communities of color, which weakens the communities from which survivor/victims often come, leaving youth without the community support they need. In fact, trafficking defendants have filed selective prosecution cases around the country.[37] At a time when social justice movements are pushing back against the build-up of police and prisons, the anti-trafficking movement has contributed to that build-up.

Activists against the youth sex trade have often framed the state as the protector of youth, thereby absolving the state of responsibility for creating, maintaining, or allowing the very conditions that make youth vulnerable to exploitation in the first place. In her analysis of international sex trafficking, scholar Jennifer Suchland argues that states enact "economies of violence" through neoliberal, capitalist policies that support global systems of precarious labor, thereby making people vulnerable to trafficking. She criticizes the international anti-trafficking movement for framing human trafficking as a violation of bodily integrity and a problem of criminal behavior, thereby absolving capitalist states from their role in creating conditions that give rise to human trafficking. "Neither bodily harm nor criminal behavior," she argues, "exposes how trafficking is intertwined in the constitutive operations of economic systems."[38] Hence Suchland calls for more attention to the economic and social causes of sex trafficking.

Similarly, youth involvement in the US sex trade is rooted in neoliberal economic policies, which are deeply intertwined with the racial history of the United States. Public benefits and protections developed in the progressive area and after the Depression largely excluded African Americans, who were often not covered by workplace protections and were barred from accessing welfare. Beginning in the 1940s and picking up speed in the 1950s and 1960s, the Civil Rights Movement demanded the inclusion of African Americans in these protections and social programs, which they eventually achieved. These developments were then used by the New Right to argue for shrinking the welfare state and deregulating business, which began in earnest under the Reagan administration in the 1980s.[39] Conservatives blamed poverty on individual irresponsibility rather than economic conditions. A racialized and

---

[35] Jennifer Musto, *Control and Protect: Collaboration, Carceral Protection, and Domestic Sex Trafficking in the United States* (Oakland, CA: University of California Press, 2016), 51.

[36] Barry C. Feld, "Violent Girls or Relabeled Status Offenders? An Alternative Interpretation of the Data," *Crime & Delinquency* 55.2 (April 2009), 261; Musto, *Control and Protect.*

[37] See chapter 7, note 54, for a discussion of racially biased enforcement of trafficking laws.

[38] Jennifer Suchland, *Economies of Violence: Transnational Feminism, Postsocialism, and the Politics of Sex Trafficking* (Durham, NC: Duke University Press, 2015), 1.

[39] Nancy MacLean, *Democracy in Chains: The Deep History of the Radical Rights Stealth Plan for America* (New York, NY: Penguin Random House, 2017).

gendered discourse developed that characterized poor people as lazy and irresponsible. The welfare queen stereotype birthed by Reagan condemned dependency on government benefits and portrayed women on welfare as promiscuous and dishonest. In 1996, Congress jettisoned entitlement to welfare granted by AFDC for the time-limited and highly conditioned TANF.[40] Furthermore, the increasingly neoliberal state allowed employers to back away from their traditional obligations to provide compensation and benefits that allowed employees to care for themselves and their families, while at the same time shrinking social welfare programs that traditionally filled gaps between the needs of families and the market.[41] Employers offered fewer benefits and suppressed wages, despite steadily increasing profits. Rather than raising the minimum wage, policymakers pushed poor mothers into low-wage jobs without adequate childcare. Meanwhile, to contain unrest from growing neoliberal economic conditions, particularly among people of color, lawmakers expanded the war on drugs and passed ever more stringent criminal laws and penalties, which vastly expanded the criminal justice system and the prison industrial complex, removing many parents from families and communities. These conditions perpetuated high rates of poverty and lack of opportunity. Parents were forced to work multiple low-wage jobs to make ends meet, schools were underfunded, crowded, and inadequately staffed, and the sex trade and sexualization of women and girls grew exponentially, all increasing youth vulnerability to commercial sexual exploitation. Finally, states increased criminal prosecution of juveniles, including youth involved in the sex trade.

The deregulation of business, the disinvestment in community welfare, and the criminalization of marginalized communities, justified by individualistic discourses condemning dependency and extolling "personal responsibility," has had a particularly devastating effect on children, adolescents, and teens. High child poverty rates combined with failing schools, lack of opportunities for youth, and underfunded social service programs as well as homophobia, racism, and sexism have contributed to youth vulnerability to involvement in the sex trade. The conservative move to blame individuals for social problems like poverty, falls particularly harshly when children are its victims. The combination of neoliberal societal abandonment of vulnerable youth and society's punitive response to the youth produced by this system created the crisis of child sex trafficking in the US. Youth involvement in the sex trade is part of the dark underbelly of neoliberal economic changes that eliminated many workplace protections and rights, particularly for low-income Americans, and eviscerated the social safety net. Concern about child sex trafficking, on the other hand,

---

[40] Laura Briggs, *How All Politics Became Reproductive Politics* (Oakland, CA: University of California Press, 2017).

[41] Jane L. Collins and Victoria Mayer, *Both Hands Tied: Welfare Reform and the Race to the Bottom of the Low-Wage Labor Market* (Chicago, IL: University of Chicago, 2010).

became a cultural reservoir for adult anxieties about the impacts of neoliberalism as well as the impacts of social changes related to gender, sex, sexuality, race, and immigration. Neoliberal economic policies combined with ongoing racism, sexism, and homophobia fueled youth vulnerability to the sex trade, but the social movement against the US youth sex trade has disproportionately relied on criminal justice solutions to the issue rather than tackling the underlying economic and social issues that make youth vulnerable.

In the campaign against the youth sex trade, protective policies that control youth have prevailed over human rights-based policies that empower youth and the communities from which they come. According to historian Barbara Bennett Woodhouse, the children's rights movement emerged in the 1970s seeking to "shift the focus away from adults' protection of children to children's own claims to autonomy,"[42] but adults have been uncomfortable with children's agency and voice, and fear that children's rights will compromise parental rights. The United States has been particularly resistant to recognizing and protecting children's rights, especially on issues relating to sexuality. Youth in foster care, for example, often lack the right to legal representation, the right to speak in their own court case, the right not to be deprived of property without due process, and the right to contact with their family.[43] The United States is one of the few nations in the world that has not ratified the UN Convention on the Rights of the Child and has one of the highest child poverty rates in the Global North.[44] According to Woodhouse, "the American macrosystem is characterized by a number of mutually reinforcing values and ideologies that [are] toxic to children, including a blind belief in individual responsibility; the myth of individual autonomy; a belief in free market efficiency as the measure of good and consumption as the engine of the free market; deep-seated prejudices dividing people along lines of race, class, gender, and religion, and a success ethic that rejects as unworthy those who falter in climbing the ladder of success."[45] She describes this system as "profoundly unjust to children" and leading to "our nation's underinvestment in children as a group."[46] Instead, Woodhouse argues, "the law must reflect children's dependency but also honor their emerging capacity for participation and, ultimately, control." This must include needs-based rights – the "positive rights to nurture, education, food, medical care, shelter, and other goods without which children cannot survive, let alone develop" – and capacity-based rights that "recognize children's agency and voice even

[42] Barbara Bennett Woodhouse, *Hidden in Plain Sight: The Tragedy of Children's Rights from Ben Franklin to Lionel Tate* (Princeton, NJ: Princeton University Press, 2008), 31.

[43] Ibid. 5–6.

[44] In 2014, 22% of American children live in poverty and 38% of African American youth. Anna E. Casey Foundation, Children in Poverty by Race and Ethnicity, at http://datacenter.kidscount.org/data/tables/44-childrenin-poverty-by-race-and-ethnicity#detailed/1/any/false/869,36,868,867,133/10,11,9,12,1,185,13/324,323.

[45] Woodhouse, *Hidden in Plain Sight,* 310.     [46] Ibid. 311.

before children reach the state of maturity that allows them to make decisions without adult assistance and guidance."[47] But children's rights arguments have been largely absent from public discourses on youth involvement in the sex trade.

The lack of a human rights perspective in the movement against the US youth sex trade has had a particularly negative effect on the human rights of cisgender girls. The movement has embraced and amplified a "sexualization of girls" discourse. In this discourse, "the primary objects of looking and fear are *girls*," argue sociologists Emma Renold and Jessica Ringrose. They critique several aspects of this discourse, including an overemphasis on protectionism, victimization, and objectification; the neglect of girls' sexual agency, rights, and pleasure; a "renewal of enduring binaries of active, predator male sexuality versus passive, non-agentic female sexuality"; and the legitimization of a "heteronormative and linear developmental trajectory of 'healthy' female *hetero*sexuality." Renold and Ringrose argue that this discourse operates as a "white middle class panic over the desire for and loss of a raced and classed sexual innocence, and thus reproduces the othering of working class/racialized cultures as evidence of hyper-sexuality."[48] Sensationalized media stories about girls in the sex trade portray "fantasies of the eroticized-innocent girl child," where "girls' sexual innocence is so fetishised that it has become an irretrievable lost object."[49] Australian philosopher Joanne Faulkner explains that "modern western society has reacted to problems plaguing the adult world by fetishizing children as innocents, who must be protected from social realities."[50] But the ideas that girls are asexual before they reach adolescence and then are no longer sexually innocent once they develop breasts[51] creates an inaccurate and harmful bifurcation that denies the sexuality of children and presumes sexual readiness in sexually developed adolescents.[52] Further complicating ideas of youth sexuality are the tensions between a highly sexualized popular culture in the US and religious purity movements that draw a bright line of appropriate sexuality at heterosexual marriage.[53] These movements press for abstinence-

---

[47] Ibid. 35–36.

[48] Emma Renold and Jessica Ringrose, "Feminisms Re-Figuring 'Sexualisation,'" Sexuality and the 'The Girl,'" *Feminist Theory* 14.3 (2013), 248–249.

[49] Ibid. 249.

[50] Joanne Faulkner, *The Importance of Being Innocent: Why We Worry About Children* (Melbourne: Cambridge University Press, 2010), vii.

[51] Interview with Carol Smolenski, July 21, 2017 (arguing that people have a hard time believing that sexually developed girls are not responsible for their involvement in the sex trade: on file with author).

[52] See Sharon Lamb and Zoë D. Peterson, "Adolescent Girls' Sexual Empowerment: Two Feminists Explore the Concept," *Sex Roles* 66 (2012), 703–712, rejecting both the "emotional readiness" discourses promoted by abstinence only sex education advocates and "biological readiness" discourses.

[53] Sara Moslener, *Virgin Nation: Sexuality Purity and American Adolescence* (New York, NY: Oxford University Press, 2015).

based sex education that keeps youth ignorant about their sexuality. Caught in this catch-22, youth become vulnerable to abuse and likely to blame themselves if they end up in the sex trade.

A focus on an exaggerated threat to childhood sexual innocence leads not only to bad policy, but also reinforces a neoliberal view of the state. Feminist legal theorist Martha Fineman has questioned the need to create victim status in order to justify assistance from the state, arguing that vulnerability is a universal human condition not unique to children, the elderly, and the disabled.[54] Fineman argues that society needs to recognize both the agency and the vulnerability of all citizens and provide a responsive state that enables all people to develop resilience. As an alternative to the autonomous and independent liberal subject, Fineman argues that a society structured around the vulnerable subject demands "a more responsive state and closer monitoring of societal institutions." By focusing on the failures of institutions rather than the deficiencies of individuals, states can be responsive in helping citizens develop resiliency – "the means and ability to recover from harm or setbacks."[55] Framing vulnerability as a characteristic of individuals and subgroups, argues Fineman, not only obscures universal vulnerability, decreasing empathy and solidarity that might result from its recognition, but also obscures the role of the state in creating and maintaining structural inequalities. Child sex trafficking discourses reinforce neoliberalism's autonomous subject by exaggerating and enforcing the vulnerability and dependence of the trafficked child in contrast to the ideal, autonomous, and invulnerable adult. Vulnerable adults then become deviant, lacking personal responsibility and therefore not entitled to state support, and youth are denied self-determination. Fineman urges recognition that "webs of economic, social, cultural and institutional relationships ... profoundly affect our individual destinies and fortunes ... structur[ing] our options, creating or impeding our opportunities." Therefore, trafficking is not just an individual experience, but a reflection on the very structures and institutions of society – its schools, families, and communities. These structures and institutions, argues Fineman, must be the focus of reform, not individuals.[56]

While the movement against the US sex trade has addressed institutions to some degree – particularly the treatment of youth in the criminal justice and the failures of the child welfare systems – these reforms have been partial. Child welfare systems are perennially understaffed and underfunded. The prison industrial complex disproportionately targets communities of color. Movement reforms have in fact contributed toward the expansion of state

[54] Martha Albertson Fineman and Anna Grear, eds., *Vulnerability: Reflections on a New Ethical Foundation for Law and Politics* (New York, NY: Routledge, 2013).

[55] Martha Albertson Fineman, "Vulnerability, Resilience, and LGBT Youth," *Temple Political and Civil Rights Law Review* 23 (2014), 311, 320.

[56] Ibid. 316, 318.

surveillance and criminalization of communities of color through both systems[57] as well as the criminalization of adult sex workers. These approaches have framed the problem in individualistic ways that have eclipsed social responsibility for the victimization of youth and neglected community-level reforms that would decrease the vulnerabilities of youth to sexual exploitation. The movement often relied on narratives of extreme victimization and sexual danger, which have been politically expedient, but have bolstered oppressive gender and racial systems that have disempowered marginalized communities. Parts of the movement have centered empowerment of youth rather than victimization, and some have advocated for policies that "recognize [young people's] dignity and autonomy; help them fight addictions, continue their education, obtain stable housing, build marketable skills; and address abusive parental relationships, rather than focus obsessively on their sex lives."[58] But even these approaches still frame the problem in individualistic ways that obscure how social systems make youth vulnerable.

Empowerment that focuses only on individuals is not enough. Social change requires the development of critical consciousness and attention to systemic bias and inequality, including a "more thorough analysis of how contextual factors, including non-sexual ones, shape young women's sexual choices and lives."[59] Individualized empowerment becomes a "self-improvement discourse" that locates the problem in individuals rather than systems – becoming more about coping with rather than solving social problems. According to sociologist Laina Bay-Cheng, "while coping models strive to strengthen individuals' abilities to accommodate the existing social environment, empowerment theory and practice in their fully realized states ... aim to transform the social environment to meet the needs, uphold the rights, and enable the well-being of those living within it."[60]

But in fact, the US has done little to address the social conditions that make youth vulnerable to entering the sex trade, conditions like high rates of child poverty, failing schools, urban blight, mass incarceration, unemployment and underemployment, racism, homophobia, and transphobia. And the Trump administration's neoliberal agenda is likely to worsen these conditions for youth and is already retreating from assistance to LGBT youth.[61]

---

[57] Dorothy Roberts, "Prisons, Foster Care, and the Systemic Punishment of Black Women," *UCLA Law Review* 59 (August 2012), 1474.

[58] Anthony Marcus, Amber Horning, Ric Curtis, Jo Sanson, and Efram Thompson, "Conflict and Agency Among Sex Workers and Pimps: A Closer Look at Domestic Minor Sex Trafficking," *Annals of the American Academy of Political and Social Science* 653 (May 2014), 243.

[59] Laina Y. Bay-Cheng, "Recovering Empowerment: De-personalizing and Re-politicizing Adolescent Female Sexuality," *Sex Roles* 66 (2012), 713.

[60] Ibid. 714.

[61] For example, OJJDP's 2016 solicitation for proposals from organizations to provide mentoring to child victims of commercial sexual exploitation and domestic minor sex trafficking specifically mentioned LGBT youth, but the 2017 solicitation no longer did.

Organizations that pursue collective empowerment and environmental transformation, like YWEP, are marginalized in the movement, while organizations that pursue an individualized, criminal justice oriented agenda, like Shared Hope International, thrive with large government grants and extensive media attention. But, as Julia O'Connell Davidson has said about children in the global sex trade, "children's rights to protection from commercial sexual exploitation cannot be separated from their rights to decent economic and social standards of living."[62] Davidson suggests that idealized views of childhood innocence are fueled by anxieties about the harsh conditions under advanced capitalist states. Joanne Faulkner suggests that adults' obsession with childhood innocence and protecting (some) children is rooted in adult anxieties about their own vulnerabilities and the failings of modern consumer capitalism. Into the child, she argues, we project "all our hopes and fears about the direction of society."[63] But instead of addressing society's failings, policymakers ignore the flaws of social and economic systems that underlie youth involvement in the sex trade and focus on individual level perpetrators. The privileged people who control these systems would rather blame individuals than change the structural inequalities that undergird their privileges. The commercial sexual exploitation of youth is a symptom of a society out of balance, and until those imbalances are addressed, the problem will not go away.

Has the movement against the US youth sex trade helped youth like B.W., whose story began this book? Perhaps safe harbor laws keep some of them out of jail. Increased youth services provide needed help to some. Enforcement of criminal laws against sex trafficking may have decreased the likelihood that adults will seek to facilitate youth involvement in the sex trade. But the movement has not done enough to address the underlying conditions that make youth vulnerable to entry into the sex trade in the first place. At the end of the film *Trading Women* about sex trafficking in Southeast Asia, anthropologist David Feingold argues that saving girls "has more emotional resonance than changing the conditions of [their] lives."[64] While saving girls might make us feel like heroes, the US youth sex trade will not end until we addresses the conditions that make youth vulnerable to commercial sex. Moving beyond rescue narratives requires adopting transformative approaches that center the lives and voices of youth and that enhance their life opportunities.

---

[62] Davidson, *Children in the Global Sex Trade*, 62.
[63] Faulkner, *The Importance of Being Innocent*, 14.
[64] *Trading Women*, dir. David A. Feingold, Documentary Educational Resources, 2003 (narrated by Angelina Jolie).

# Select Bibliography

Able-Peterson, Trudee, *Children of the Evening* (New York, NY: G.P. Putnam's Sons, 1981).

Able-Peterson, Trudee, and June Bucy, *The Streetwork Outreach Training Manual* (Washington, DC: US Department of Health and Human Services, 1993).

Able-Peterson, Trudee, and Richard A. Hooks Wayman, *Streetworks: Best Practices and Standards in Outreach Methodology to Homeless Youth* (Minneapolis, MN: StreetWorks Collaborative, 2006).

Adams, William, Colleen Owens, and Kevonne Small, "Effects of Federal Legislation on the Commercial Sexual Exploitation of Youth," *OJJDP Juvenile Justice Bulletin* (July 2010), 1–10.

Ahart, Gregory, *Sexual Exploitation of Children – A Problem of Unknown Magnitude. Report to the Chairman, Subcommittee on Select Education, House Committee on Education and Labor* (Washington, DC: General Accounting Office, 1982).

American Psychological Association Task Force on Trafficking of Women and Girls, *Report of the Task Force on Trafficking of Women and Girls* (Washington, DC: American Psychological Association, 2014).

Annitto, Megan, "Consent, Coercion, and Compassion: Emerging Legal Responses to the Commercial Sexual Exploitation of Minors," *Yale Law and Policy Review* 30.1 (2011), 1–70.

Arthur Young and Company, *Juvenile Prostitution: A Federal Strategy for Combatting Its Causes and Consequences, Report Submitted to the Youth Development Bureau, Office of Human Development Services, Department of Health, Education and Welfare* (June 1978).

Attorney General's Commission on Pornography, *Final Report* (Washington, DC: US Department of Justice, July 1986).

Baker, Carrie N., "An Examination of the Central Debates on Sex Trafficking in Research and Public Policy in the United States," *Journal on Human Trafficking* 1.3 (August 2015), 191–208.

"An Intersectional Analysis of Sex Trafficking Films," *Meridians: Feminism, Race, Transnationalism* 12.1 (Spring 2014), 208–226.

"Moving Beyond 'Slaves, Sinners, and Saviors': An Intersectional Feminist Analysis of U.S. Sex Trafficking Discourse, Law and Policy," *Journal of Feminist Scholarship* 4 (Spring 2013).

Barnitz, Laura A., *Commercial Sexual Exploitation of Children: Youth Involved in Prostitution, Pornography, and Sex Trafficking* (Washington, DC: Youth Advocate Program International, 1998).

Barry, Kathleen, *The Prostitution of Sexuality* (New York, NY: New York University Press, 1995).

Barry, Kathleen, Charlotte Bunch, and Shirley Castley, *International Feminism: Networking Against Female Sexual Slavery* (New York, NY: International Women's Tribune Centre, Inc., 1984).

Bell, Ernest A., *Fighting the Traffic in Young Girls or War on the White Slave Trade* (Chicago, IL: G. S. Ball, 1910).

Bernstein, Elizabeth, "Carceral Politics as Gender Justice? The 'Traffic in Women' and Neoliberal Circuits of Crime, Sex, and Rights," *Theory and Society* 41.3 (2012), 233–259.

"Introduction: Sexual Economies and New Regimes of Governance," *Social Politics* 21.3 (2014), 345–354.

"Militarized Humanitarianism Meets Carceral Feminism: The Politics of Sex, Rights, and Freedom in Contemporary Anti-Trafficking Campaigns," *Signs* 36.1 (Autumn 2010), 45–71.

"The Sexual Politics of the 'New Abolitionism,'" *Differences: A Journal of Feminist Cultural Studies* 18.3 (2007), 128–151.

Bernstein, Robin, *Racial Innocence: Performing American Childhood from Slavery to Civil Rights* (New York, NY: New York University Press, 2011).

Beyond Borders, ECPAT-USA, and Shared Hope International, *Report of the Canada–United States Consultation in Preparation for World Congress III Against Sexual Exploitation of Children and Adolescents, October 2–3, 2008* (Arlington, VA: Beyond Borders, ECPAT-USA, and Shared Hope International, 2008).

Birckhead, Tamar R., "The 'Youngest Profession': Consent, Autonomy, and Prostituted Children," *Washington University Law Review* 88 (2011), 1055–1115.

Boxill, Nancy A., and Deborah J. Richardson, "A Community's Response to the Sex Trafficking of Children," *Child Welfare League of America, The Link* 3.4 (2005), 1, 3–4, 9.

"Ending Sex Trafficking in Atlanta," *Affilia: Journal of Women and Social Work* 22.2 (Summer 2007), 138–149.

Bracey, Dorothy Heid, *"Baby-Pros": Preliminary Profiles of Juvenile Prostitutes* (New York, NY: John Jay Press, 1979).

Brennan, Denise, "Competing Claims of Victimhood? Foreign and Domestic Victims of Trafficking in the United States," *Sexuality Research & Social Policy* 5.4 (December 2008), 45–61.

Bromfield, Nicole Footen, *The Hijacking of Human Trafficking Legislation During its Creation: A U.S. Public Policy Study* (Saarbrücken, Germany: VDM Verlag Dr. Müller, 2010).

Bronstein, Carolyn, *Battling Pornography: The American Feminist Anti-Pornography Movement, 1976–1986* (New York, NY: Cambridge University Press, 2011).

Butler, Cheryl Nelson, "The Racial Roots of Human Trafficking," *UCLA Law Review* 62 (August 2015), 1464–1514.

California Office of Criminal Justice Planning, *Confronting Sexual Exploitation of Homeless Youth: California's Juvenile Prostitution Intervention Projects* (Sacramento, CA: California Office of Criminal Justice Planning, 1991).

Campagna, Daniel S., and Donald L. Poffenberger, *The Sexual Trafficking in Children: An Investigation of the Child Sex Trade* (Dover, MA: Auburn House, 1988).

Carter, Vednita, "Prostitution: Where Racism and Sexism Intersect," *Michigan Journal of Gender and Law* 1 (1993), 81–89.

"Providing Services to African American Prostituted Women," *Journal of Trauma Practice* 2.3/4 (2003), 213–222.

Carter, Vednita, and Evelina Giobbe, "Duet: Prostitution, Racism and Feminist Discourse," *Hastings Women's Law Journal* 10 (1999), 37–57.

Casella, Emilia, Irene Martinetti, and Stephan Sastrawidjaja, *Critique of Focus on Demand in the Context of Trafficking in Persons: A Position Paper of the Sex Workers Project at the Urban Justice Center* (New York, NY: Urban Justice Center, 2007).

Chaloner, Emily, "Anybody's Daughter? How Racial Stereotypes Prevent Domestic Child Prostitutes of Color from Being Perceived as Victims," *Children's Legal Rights Journal* 30.3 (Fall 2010), 48–60.

Child Interfaith Movement, *Child Sexual Exploitation and Trafficking in Georgia: A 10-Year Review of the Issue of Child Prostitution in Georgia with Special Emphasis on Child Prostitution in Atlanta* (August 2009).

Cohen, Marcia I., Mark C. Edberg, and Stephen V. Gies, *Final Report on the Evaluation of the SAGE Project's LIFESKILLS and GRACE Programs* (May 2011).

Collins, Patricia Hill, *Black Feminist Thought: Knowledge, Consciousness, and the Politics of Empowerment* (New York, NY: Routledge, 2000).

Conner, Brendan M., "In Loco Aequitatis: The Dangers of 'Safe Harbor' Laws for Youth in the Sex Trades," *Stanford Journal of Civil Rights and Civil Liberties* 12 (February 2016), 43–97.

Curtis, Ric, Karen Terry, Meredith Dank, Kirk Dombrowski, and Bilal Khan, *The Commercial Sexual Exploitation of Children in New York City* (New York, NY: Center for Court Innovation and John Jay College, 2008).

Dank, Meredith, Bilal Khan, P. Mitchell Downey, Cybele Kotonias, Deborah Mayer, Colleen Owens, Laura Pacificci, and Lilly Yu, *Estimating the Size and Structure of the Underground Commercial Sex Economy in Eight Major US Cities* (Washington, DC: Urban Institute, March 2014).

Dank, Meredith, Jennifer Yahner, Kuniko Madden, Isela Bañuelos, Lilly Yu, Angela Ritchie, Mitchyll Mora, and Brendan Conner, *Surviving the Streets of New York: Experiences of LGBTQ Youth, YMSM, and YWSW Engaged in Survival Sex* (New York, NY: Urban Institute, 2015).

Dank, Meredith, Lilly Yu, Jennifer Yahner, Elizabeth Pelletier, Mitchyll Mora, and Brendan Conner, *Locked In: Interactions with the Criminal Justice and Child Welfare Systems for LGBTQ Youth, YMSM, and YWSW Who Engage in Survival Sex* (New York, NY: Urban Institute, 2015).

Davis, Stephanie, and Michael Shively, *An Overview of Anti-Demand Efforts in Atlanta: Summary Based Upon Research from the Study, "Developing a National Action Plan for Eliminating Sex Trafficking"* (August 16, 2010).

Davidson, Julia O'Connell, *Children in the Global Sex Trade* (New York, NY: Polity Press, 2005).

Densen-Gerber, Judianne, "Child Prostitution and Child Pornography: Medical, Legal, and Societal Aspects of the Commercial Sexual Exploitation of Children," in Barbara McComb Jones, Linda L. Jenstrom, and Kee McFarlane (eds.), *Sexual Abuse of Children: Selected Readings* (Washington, DC: US Department of Health and Human Services, 1980), 77–81.

Densen-Gerber, Judianne, and Stephen Hutchinson, "Sexual and Commercial Exploitation of Children: Legislative Responses and Treatment Challenges," *Child Abuse & Neglect* 3 (1979), 61–66.

ECPAT International, *Commercial Sexual Exploitation of Children: Report of the First Year Following the Congress Against the Commercial Sexual Exploitation of Children Held in Stockholm, Sweden, August 1996* (Bangkok, Thailand: ECPAT International, August 1997).

*ECPAT 25 Years: Rallying the World to End Childhood Sexual Exploitation* (Bangkok, Thailand: ECPAT International, May 2015).

ECPAT-USA, *Who Is There to Help Us? How the System Fails Sexually Exploited Girls in the United States: Examples from Four American Cities* (New York, NY: ECPAT-USA, 2005).

Enablers, Inc., *Juvenile Prostitution in Minneapolis: The Report of a Research Project* (St. Paul, MN: Enablers, Inc., 1978).

Estes, Richard J., and Neil Alan Weiner, *Commercial Sexual Exploitation of Children in the United States, Canada and Mexico, Full Report* (Philadelphia, PA: University of Pennsylvania, 2002).

Farley, Melissa, Nicole Matthews, Sara Deer, Guadalupe Lopez, Christine Stark, and Eileen Hudon, *Garden of Truth: Prostitution and Trafficking of Native Women in Minnesota* (Minneapolis, MN: Minnesota Indian Women's Sexual Assault Coalition and Prostitution Research & Education, 2011).

Feinstein, Claire, and Clare O'Kane, "Children's and Adolescents' Participation and Protection from Sexual Abuse and Exploitation," *Innocenti Working Paper 2009–10* (Florence, Italy: UNICEF Innocenti Research Centre, February 2009).

Finklea, Kristin, *Juvenile Victims of Domestic Sex Trafficking: Juvenile Justice Issues* (Washington, DC: US Congressional Research Service, 2014).

Fisher, Bruce, Ernest Fazio, D. Kelly Weisberg, Edwin Johnson, Toby Marotta, and Sally Jones, *Juvenile Prostitution: A Resource Manual* (San Francisco, CA: Urban and Rural Systems Associates, July 1982).

Friedman, Sara Ann, *And Boys Too?* (New York, NY: ECPAT-USA, 2013).

Goulet, Lisa E., *Out From the Shadows: Good Practices in Working with Sexually Exploited Youth in the Americas* (Victoria, BC: University of Victoria, 2001).

Goździak, Elżbieta M., *Trafficked Children and Youth in the United States: Reimagining Survivors* (New Brunswick, NJ: Rutgers University Press, 2016).

Greene, Elizabeth, "Charity Run by Former Prostitutes Steers Girls Away From the Streets," *Chronicle of Philanthropy* 14:2 (November 1, 2001), 10.

Hofstede Committee Report, *Juvenile Prostitution in Minnesota* (St. Paul, MN: Minnesota Attorney General's Office, November 1999).

Hotaling, Norma, "Sex for Sale: The Commercial Sexual Exploitation of Women and Girls: A Service Provider's Perspective," *Yale Journal of Law and Feminism* 18 (2006), 181–190.

Hotaling, Norma, Autumn Burris, B. Julie Johnson, Yoshi M. Bird, and Kirsten A. Melbye, "Been There Done That: SAGE, A Peer Leadership Model Among Prostitution Survivors," in Melissa Farley (ed.), *Prostitution, Trafficking, and Traumatic Stress* (Binghamton, NY: Hawthorne Press, 2003), 255–265.

Illinois Legislative Investigating Committee, *Sexual Exploitation of Children: A Report to the Illinois General Assembly* (August, 1980).

International Organization for Adolescents, *ChildRight Illinois* (2008–2012). *Child Right New York* (2013–present).

Ives, Nicole, *Background Paper for the North American Regional Consultation on the Commercial Sexual Exploitation of Children* (Philadelphia, PA: University of Pennsylvania School of Social Work, December 2–3, 2001).

James, Jennifer, "Motivations for Entrance into Prostitution," in Laura Crites (ed.), *The Female Offender* (Lexington, MA: Lexington Books, 1976), 177–205.

Kaufka, Katherine, Shelby French, Heather Moore, and Sehla Ashai, *Building Child Welfare Response to Child Trafficking* (Chicago, IL: Loyola's Center for the Human Rights of Children and the International Organization for Adolescents, 2011).

Kennedy, Alexis, Carolin Klein, Jessica Bristowe, Barry Cooper, and John Yuille, "Routes of Recruitment: Pimps' Techniques and Other Circumstances that Lead to Street Prostitution," *Journal of Aggression, Maltreatment, and Trauma* 15.2 (2007), 1–19.

Koyama, Emi, *War on Terror & War on Trafficking: A Sex Worker Activist Confronts the Anti-Trafficking Movement* (Portland, OR: Confluere Publications, 2011).

Lederer, Laura, *Human Rights Report on Trafficking of Women and Children: A Country-by-Country Report on a Contemporary Form of Slavery* (Washington, DC: Paul H. Nitze School of Advanced International Studies, Johns Hopkins University, 2001).

Leidholdt, Dorchen, "Keynote Address: Demand and the Debate," in Morrison Torrey (ed.), *Demand Dynamics: The Forces of Demand in Global Sex Trafficking* (Chicago, IL: DePaul University College of Law, 2004).

Leigh, Carol, "Inventing Sex Work" in Jill Nagle (ed.), *Whores and Other Feminists* (New York, NY: Routledge, 1997), 83–93.

Linedecker, Clifford L., *Children in Chains* (New York, NY: Everest House Publishers, 1981).

Lloyd, Rachel, "Acceptable Victims: Sexually Exploited Youth in the U.S.," *Encounter* 18.3 (2005), 6–18.
*Girls Like Us: Fighting for a World Where Girls Are Not for Sale: A Memoir* (New York, NY: Harper Collins, 2011).

Lloyd, Robin, *For Money or Love: Boy Prostitution in America* (New York, NY: Vanguard Press, 1976).

Lutnick, Alexandra, *Domestic Minor Sex Trafficking: Beyond Victims and Villains* (New York, NY: Columbia University Press, 2016).

Marcus, Anthony, Amber Horning, Ric Curtis, Jo Sanson, and Efram Thompson, "Conflict and Agency Among Sex Workers and Pimps: A Closer Look at Domestic Minor Sex Trafficking," *Annals of the American Academy of Political and Social Science* 653 (May 2014), 225–246.

Martin, Lauren, Richard Lotspeich, and Lauren Stark, *Early Intervention to Avoid Sex Trading and Trafficking of Minnesota's Female Youth: A Benefit-Cost Analysis* (Minneapolis, MN: Minnesota Indian Women's Resource Center, 2012).

Maynard, Robyn, "#Blacksexworkerslivesmatter: White-Washed 'Anti-Slavery' and the Appropriation of Black Suffering," *The Feminist Wire* (September 9, 2015).

Minnesota Department of Public Safety Office of Justice Programs, *No Wrong Door: A Comprehensive Approach to Safe Harbor for Minnesota's Sexually Exploited Youth* (2013).

Mitchell, Kimberly J., David Finkelhor, and Janis Wolak, "Conceptualizing Juvenile Prostitution as Child Maltreatment: Findings from the National Juvenile Prostitution Study," *Child Maltreatment* 15.1 (February 2010), 18–36.

Moslener, Sarah, *Virgin Nation: Sexual Purity and American Adolescence* (New York, NY: Oxford University Press, 2015).

Mukasey, Michael B., Cybele K. Daley, and David G. Hagy, *Commercial Sexual Exploitation of Children: What Do We Know and What Do We Do about It?* (Washington, DC: US Department of Justice, Office of Justice Programs, 2007).

Mullen, Katherine, and Rachel Lloyd, "The Passage of the Safe Harbor Act and the Voices of the Sexually Exploited Youth," in Jill Laurie Goodman and Dorchen A. Leidholdt (eds.), *Lawyers' Manual on Human Trafficking: Pursuing Justice for Victims* (New York, NY: Supreme Court of the State of New York, Appellate Division, First Department and the New York State Judicial Committee on Women in the Courts, 2013).

Muntarbhorn, Vitit, *Report of the Second World Congress Against Commercial Sexual Exploitation of Children* (Yokohama, Japan, December 2001).

*Rights of the Child: Sale of Children* (New York, NY: United Nations Economic and Social Council, 1992).

Musto, Jennifer, *Control and Protect: Collaboration, Carceral Protection, and Domestic Sex Trafficking in the United States* (Oakland, CA: University of California Press, 2016).

National Center for Missing and Exploited Children, *Female Juvenile Prostitution: Problem and Response* (Washington, DC: National Center for Missing and Exploited Children, December 1992).

Palmquist, Al, with John Stone, *The Minnesota Connection* (New York, NY: Warmer Books, 1978).

Phillips, Jasmine, "Black Girls and the (Im)Possibilities of a Victim Trope: The Intersectional Failures of Legal and Advocacy Interventions in the Commercial Sexual Exploitation of Minors in the United States," *UCLA Law Review* 62 (August 2015), 1642.

Pierce, Alexandra, *Shattered Hearts: The Commercial Sexual Exploitation of American Indian Women and Girls in Minnesota* (Minneapolis, MN: Minnesota Indian Women's Resource Center, 2009).

Priebe, Alexandra, and Cristen Suhr, *Hidden in Plain View: The Commercial Sexual Exploitation of Girls in Atlanta* (Atlanta, GA: Atlanta Women's Agenda, September 2005).

Raymond, Janice G., and Donna M. Hughes, *Sex Trafficking of Women in the United States: International and Domestic Trends* (New York, NY: Coalition Against Trafficking in Women, 2001).

Reichert, Jessica, and Amy Sylwestrzak, *National Survey of Residential Programs for Victims of Sex Trafficking* (Chicago, IL: Illinois Criminal Justice Information Authority, October 2013).

Rush, Florence, *The Best Kept Secret: Sexual Abuse of Children* (New York, NY: McGraw-Hill, 1981).

Russell, Diana E.H., and Nichol Van de Ven, *The Proceedings of the International Tribunal on Crimes Against Women* (Millbrae, CA: LES FEMMES, 1976).

Saunders, Penelope, "How 'Child Prostitution' Became 'CSEC,'" in Elizabeth Bernstein and Laurie Schaffner (eds.), *Regulating Sex: The Politics of Intimacy and Identity* (New York, NY; Routledge, 2005), 167–188.

Schwartz, Shelby, "Harboring Concerns: The Problematic Conceptual Reorientation of Juvenile Prostitution Adjudication in New York," *Columbia Journal of Gender and the Law* 18.1 (2009), 235–280.

Sereny, Gitta, *The Invisible Children: Child Prostitution in America, West Germany and Great Britain* (New York, NY: Knopf, 1985).

Shared Hope International, *Demand. A Comparative Examination of Sex Tourism and Trafficking in Jamaica, Japan, the Netherlands, and the United States* (Vancouver, WA: Shared Hope International, 2007).

Shared Hope International, *Demanding Justice Report* (Vancouver, WA: Shared Hope International, 2014).

*JuST Response State Systems Mapping Report* (Vancouver, WA: Shared Hope International, 2015).

*National Report on Domestic Minor Sex Trafficking: America's Prostituted Children* (Vancouver, WA: Shared Hope International, 2009).

Shared Hope International and American Center for Justice and Law, *Protected Innocence Legislative Framework: Methodology* (Vancouver, WA: Shared Hope International, 2010).

Shared Hope International, EPCAT-USA, and The Protection Project of John Hopkins University School of Advanced International Studies, *Report from the U.S. Mid-Term Review on the Commercial Sexual Exploitation of Children in America* (May 2006).

Sher, Julian, *Somebody's Daughter: The Hidden Story of America's Prostituted Children and the Battle to Save Them* (Chicago, IL: Chicago Review Press, 2011).

Shively, Michael, Sarah Kuck Jalbert, Ryan Kling, William Rhodes, Peter Finn, Chris Flygare, Laura Tierney, Dana Hunt, David Squires, Christina Dyous, and Kristin Wheeler, *Final Report on the Evaluation of the First Offender Prostitution Program: Report Summary* (Cambridge, MA: Abt Associates, Inc., 2008).

Shively, Michael, Karen McLaughlin, Rachel Durchslag, Hugh McDonough, Dana Hunt, Kristina Kliorys, Caroline Nobo, Lauren Olsho, Stephanie Davis, Sara Collins, Cathy Houlihan, SAGE, Rebecca Pfeffer, Jessica Corsi, and Danna Mauch, *Developing a National Plan for Eliminating Sex Trafficking* (Cambridge, MA: Abt Associates, 2010).

Smith, Linda A., with Cindy Coloma, *Renting Lacy: A Story of America's Prostituted Children* (Vancouver, WA: Shared Hope International, 2009).

Smith, Linda A., Samantha Healey Vardaman, and Melissa A. Snow, *Domestic Minor Sex Trafficking: America's Prostituted Children* (Vancouver, WA: Shared Hope International, 2009).

Snow, Melissa, and Mimari Hall, *Missing Children, State Care, and Child Sex Trafficking: Engaging the Judiciary in Building a Collaborative Response, Technical Assistance Brief* (Alexandria, VA and Reno, NV: National Center for

Missing and Exploited Children and National Council of Juvenile and Family Court Judges, 2015).

Spangenberg, Mia, *Prostituted Youth in New York City: An Overview* (New York, NY: ECPAT-USA, 2001).

Spurlock, John C., *Youth and Sexuality in the Twentieth-Century United States* (New York, NY: Routledge, 2016).

Stransky, Michelle, and David Finkelhor, *How Many Juveniles Are Involved in Prostitution in the U.S.?* (Durham, NH: Crimes Against Children Research Center, 2008).

The Advocates for Human Rights, *Sex Trafficking Needs Assessment for the State of Minnesota* (Minneapolis, MN: The Advocates for Human Rights, 2008).

The Stockholm Declaration and Agenda for Action, First World Congress Against the Commercial Sexual Exploitation of Children, Stockholm, Sweden (August 27–31, 1996).

Thukral, Juhu, and Melissa Ditmore, *Revolving Door: An Analysis of Street-Based Prostitution in New York City* (New York, NY: Urban Justice Center, 2003).

US Department of Justice, Department of Health and Human Services, and Department of Homeland Security, *Coordination, Capacity, Collaboration: Federal Strategic Action Plan on Services for Victims of Human Trafficking in the United States 2013–2017* (Washington, DC: US Department of Justice, 2014).

US Department of Labor, *Forced Labor: The Prostitution of Children* (Washington, DC: US Department of Labor, 1996).

Vardaman, Samantha Healy, and Christine Raino, "Prosecuting Demand as a Crime of Human Trafficking: The Eighth Circuit Decision in *United States v. Jungers,*" *University of Memphis Law Review* 43 (Summer 2013), 917–962.

Weisberg, D. Kelly, *Children of the Night: A Study of Adolescent Prostitution* (Lexington, MA: Lexington Books, 1985).

"Children of the Night: The Adequacy of Statutory Treatment of Juvenile Prostitution," *American Journal of Criminal Law* 12.1 (1984), 39–45.

Whittier, Nancy, "Rethinking Coalitions: Anti-Pornography Feminists, Conservatives, and Relationships Between Collaborative Adversarial Movements," *Social Problems* 61.2 (2014), 1–19.

*The Politics of Child Sexual Abuse: Emotions, Social Movements and the State* (New York, NY: Oxford University Press, 2011).

Woodhouse, Barbara Bennett, *Hidden in Plain Sight: The Tragedy of Children's Rights from Ben Franklin to Lionel Tate* (Princeton, NJ: Princeton University Press, 2008).

Wosh, Peter J., *Covenant House: Journey of a Faith-Based Charity* (Philadelphia, PA: University of Pennsylvania Press, 2005).

Wynter, Sarah, "WHISPER: Women Hurt in Systems of Prostitution Engaged in Revolt," in Frédérique Delacoste and Priscilla Alexander (eds.), *Sex Work: Writings by Women in the Sex Industry* (San Francisco, CA: Cleis Press, 1987), 266–270.

Young Women's Empowerment Project, *Denied Help! How Youth in the Sex Trade & Street Economy Are Turned Away from Systems Meant to Help Us & What We Are Doing to Fight Back* (Chicago, IL: Young Women's Empowerment Project, 2012).

*Girls Do What They Have to Do to Survive: Illuminating Methods Used by Girls in the Sex Trade and Street Economy to Fight Back and Heal* (Chicago, IL: Young Women's Empowerment Project, 2009).

# Index

Able-Peterson, Trudee, 58–59, 67, 122–123
Abolition, defined, 9
*The Abolitionists* (film), 167
Abortion, 24, 205
Activism against sex trafficking
  overview, 3
  African-Americans in, 17–18
  child sex abuse and, 34–35, 222–223
  collaborative adversarial movement (*See*
    Collaborative adversarial movement)
  conservatives in, 8–9, 33–36
  corporations and, 173–174
  criticism of (*See* Criticism of activism)
  different approaches in, 4
  diversification of, 121–137
  "end demand" campaigns, 177–182
  evangelicals in, 3–4
  evolution of, 11, 14–23, 36–37
  expansion of activism, 121–137
  feminists in, 3–4, 8–9, 33–36, 223–224
  framing of issues and, 224
  funding of, 224–225
  gendered narratives and, 5, 131–134
  historical context, 4–5, 11–12
  ideological differences in, 8–9, 80–81,
    135–137, 223–224
  leveraging of political and cultural
    opportunities (*See* Leveraging of political
    and cultural opportunities)
  LGBT persons and, 177
  marital rape and, 33–34
  men in, 131–134
  morality narratives and, 20–22
  "pimp culture" and, 172
  popular culture and, 172–173
  racialized narratives and, 5, 76–77, 174–175
  safe harbor laws, 141–150 (*See also* Safe
    harbor laws)
  in school curricula, 169
  sexual liberation and, 23–26
  societal changes and, 24–25
  socioeconomics and, 19–20
  survivor movements, 162–169 (*See also*
    Survivor movements)
  TVPA and, 11–12, 78, 82–83, 85–86,
    162, 223
  victimization narrative in, 16
  "white slavery" and, 18–19, 20
  women's movement and, 35–36
  youth participation in, 169–177
Adams, Alesia, 112, 114
Adoption Reform Act of 1977, 48
Adult sex workers, criticism of activism by,
  215–218
Adults Saving Kids (Richfield, MN), 134
A Future. Not a Past (Atlanta), 145–146
Age of consent laws, 18–19
Aid to Families with Dependent Children
  (AFDC), 234
Alexander, Priscilla, 35–36
Allen, Ernie, 82–83, 105–106, 108, 155–157,
  167–168, 172–173
Alliance to End Slavery and Trafficking
  (Washington D.C.), 182
Allow States and Victims to Fight Online Sex
  Trafficking Act of 2018 (FOSTA),
  187–188
Alternatives for Girls (Detroit), 59, 109
Alvarez, Anita, 154–155
Amaya, Barbara, 163–166

American Bar Association, 192
American Civil Liberties Union (ACLU), 46–47
*American Dad* (television program), 167–168
American Express, 186–187
American Female Moral Reform Society, 16–17
American Hotel & Lodging Educational
    Institute, 173–174
American Psychological Association, 25, 44,
    172–173, 231
American Values (Merrifield, VA), 151
Amnesty International, 79, 80
Anderson, Kayrita, 114–115
Angela's House (Atlanta), 114–115
Anti-rape movement, 33–34, 222–223
Associated Press, 170–171, 216–217
*Atlanta Business Chronicle*, 115
*Atlanta Journal-Constitution*, 111–113,
    114–115, 117, 148, 181
Atlanta Women's Foundation, 112–113, 115,
    145–146
Autonomy of youth, 206–207, 231–232

Backpage.com, 185–188, 198, 216
Bad Encounter Line (Chicago), 126, 211
Barnaba, Frank, 33, 64, 67, 74, 75, 105–106,
    107–109, 122, 184
Barnaba Institute, 122
Barnitz, Laura, 81–84, 86–87, 97–99
Barry, Kathleen, 77–79
Baskin, Sienna, 136, 153
Bass, Karen, 172
Bauer, Gary, 151
Baxter, Karen, 39–40
Bay-Cheng, Laina, 238
Bayh, Birch, 30, 40
Beidel, Nicola, 19–20
Bell, Ernest A., 14, 20
Bell, Miriam, 80
Bennett, William, 80
Berlatsky, Noah, 206
Bernstein, Elizabeth, 213–214
Berry, Halle, 124
*The Best Kept Secret: Sexual Abuse of Children*
    (Rush), 34
Bill Wilson Center (Santa Clara), 60
Black feminist theory, 6–7
Blige, Mary J., 124
Bliss, George, 40, 46
Bloomberg, Michael, 143–144
Blum, Jeffrey, 30
Blumenthal, Richard, 182, 183
*Body and Sold* (play), 99

Body Shop, 173
Bono, 81
Booth, Bramwell, 19
Booth, Catherine, 19
*Boston Globe*, 93–94
Boston Social Services Department, 99
Boston Women's Fund, 99
Boxill, Nancy, 110–111
boyd, danah, 184–185
Boys in sex trafficking, 5, 40, 177, 202
Bracey, Dorothy Heid, 54–55
Brantley, Nola, 128
Breaking Free (Minneapolis), 65–66, 82, 88,
    98–99, 102, 109, 122–123, 127, 128, 135,
    162, 166–167
*Breaking Free from the Life of Sex Trafficking
    and Prostitution* (documentary), 166–167
Breaking the Silence (2003), 98–99, 225
BreakOut (New Orleans), 177
Breault, Susan, 97
Bridge for Runaway Youth (Minneapolis),
    52–53
Bridge Over Troubled Waters (Boston), 32
British Columbia Office of Ombudsman,
    70
Bronstein, Carolyn, 24
Brownback, Sam, 80–81, 86–87, 105–106
Brownmiller, Susan, 35
Brunson, Veronica, 38–40, 61–62
Bryant, Anita, 26
Buckmaster, Jim, 183–184
Bucy, June, 67
Bumiller, Kristin, 213–214
Burris, Autumn, 162
Busby, John, 80
Bush, George H.W., 84
Bush, George W., 93–94, 121, 196, 223,
    224–225
Bush, Michelle W., 1
Butler, Josephine, 19

California
    human trafficking courts in, 194
    juvenile prostitution in, 48, 54
    Office of Criminal Justice Planning, 60
    prosecution of sex trafficking in, 229
    specialized services for youth in, 230
*California's Forgotten Children* (film), 166
Call Off Your Old Tired Ethics (COYOTE)
    (San Francisco), 35–36
Campagna, Daniel, 61
Campbell, Bill, 113–114

Canadian International Development
   Agency, 70
*The Candy Shop* (film), 146–147
Capacity Building Initiative, 124
Carceral feminism, 211–215
Cardin, Benjamin, 106–107
*Cargo: Innocence Lost* (film), 167
*Carissa* (film), 166
Carson, Johnny, 64
Carter, Vednita, 65–66, 82–83, 123, 151, 172,
   184, 186, 223–224
Catholic Charities, 88, 123, 144, 184
Celebrity activism, 179
Center for Court Innovation (New York),
   202, 204
Center for Democracy and Technology, 185
Center for Human Rights of Children, 188
Centers for Disease Control, 115
Center to End Adolescent Sexual Exploitation
   (CEASE) (Atlanta), 114
Central City Hospitality House (San
   Francisco), 60
Chesney-Lind, Meda, 22
Chicago Street Youth in Motion, 126
*Chicago Sun-Times*, 46
*Chicago Tribune*, 39, 40, 46
Child, Kristy, 123
Child Abuse Prevention and Treatment Act of
   1977, 48
Child Exploitation and Obscenity Section
   (DOJ), 104–105
Child Online Protection Act of 1998, 88
Child pornography, 45–47, 152
Child prostitutes. *See also* Juvenile prostitution
   criticism of use of term, 169–172
   defined, 10
Child Protection Act of 1983, 57–58
Children
   defined, 10
   innocence of children paradigm, 14–16, 227,
      236–237
Children at Risk (Texas), 1
*Children for Sale: The Fight to End Human
   Trafficking* (television program),
   167–168
*Children of the Evening* (Able-Peterson), 58–59
Children of the Night (Los Angeles), 32–33, 64,
   82–83, 117–118, 122, 225
Children's rights movement, 235–236
Children's Trust of Miami Dade, 180
ChildRight Illinois, 188
ChildRight New York, 188

Child sex abuse
   activism against, 34–35, 222–223
   inadequate response to, 155
   LGBT persons and, 44
   prostitution and, 227
   societal attitudes toward, 108–109
   survivor movements and, 63–64, 127, 163
Child Sex Trafficking Team (NCMEC),
   195–196
Child sex workers, defined, 10
Child welfare system, challenging, 12
Christian Coalition, 148
*Christianity Today*, 81
*Christian Science Monitor*, 74–76, 89, 90–91
*A Civil Remedy* (documentary), 166
Civil Rights Act of 1964, 25
Civil Rights Movement, 220, 233
Cizik, Richard, 79–80
Class
   activism and, 19–20, 221
   causes of sex trafficking, 233–235, 238–239
Clayton, Mark, 76
Clinton, Bill, 80–81, 84
Clinton, Hillary, 80–81, 86
CNN, 167–169
Coalition Against Trafficking in Women
   (CATW), 77–78, 82–83, 84, 136, 144,
   185, 186, 224
Coalition to Abolish Slavery and Trafficking
   (Los Angeles), 109
Collaborative adversarial movement
   overview, 3, 8, 12, 120–121, 223–224
   diversification of activism, 121–137
   expansion of activism, 121–137
   feminists in, 135–137
   gendered narratives and, 131–134,
      146–147, 160
   government responses, 150–158
   media coverage of, 137–140
   racialized narratives and, 156–157, 160,
      223–224
   safe harbor laws and, 198–199
Collins, Patricia Hill, 209–211
Comedy Central, 172
Commercial sexual exploitation of children
   overview, 11, 63–64, 90–91
   defined, 10
   evangelicals on, 79–80
   global movement against, 68–72
   government responses, 87–90
   juvenile prostitution and, 87–90
   media coverage of, 72–77

in Minnesota, 88–89
racialized narratives and, 76–77, 91
survivor movement against, 64–68
US movement against international sex
trafficking, 77–81
Commission on Security and Cooperation in
Europe, 92, 105–106
Communications Decency Act of 1996, 88,
183, 185–188
Concerned Women for America of
Georgia, 148
Congressional hearings, 46–47, 120–121,
145–146, 151, 152–156, 160,
189–190, 194
Connecticut, safe harbor law in,
145
Conner, Brendan, 214
Consent
age of consent laws, 18
child prostitution and, 1–2
Conservatives
in activism, 8–9, 33–36
framing of issues by, 224
on sex trafficking, 233–235
Contraception, 24
Convention on the Rights of the Child, 68, 82,
85, 235
Conyers, John, Jr., 46, 136, 194, 223
Cook County Organized Crime/Human
Trafficking Initiative, 154–155
Cordes, Cynthia, 181
Corporations, activism and, 173–174
Correctional Association of New York,
142–143, 145
"Council of Daughters" (GEMS), 124
Couric, Katie, 139
Courtney's House (Washington D.C.), 128,
162
Covenant House (New York), 32,
129–130, 186
Craigslist.com, 117, 155, 182–185, 198, 216
Crenshaw, Kimberlé, 6, 210
Cricket Island Foundation, 124
Criminal justice system, challenging, 12,
232–233
Criminal Law Campaign Act (UK), 19
Criminal seduction, 16–17, 20–22
Criticism of activism
overview, 5–6, 12–13, 200–201, 218–219
by adult sex workers, 215–218
carceral feminism and, 211–215
moral panic and, 201–211

racialized narratives and, 209–211,
213–214
safe harbor laws and, 213–214
state surveillance and control and, 211–215
victimization narratives and, 201–211
Cultural opportunities. *See* Leveraging of
political and cultural opportunities
CyberTipline, 88

*The Daily Show* (television program), 172
Dallas
Child Exploitation Unit, 89–90, 150
High Risk Victims and Trafficking Unit, 150
Dart, Tom, 183, 186–187
*David Letterman Show*, 124
Davidson, Julia O'Connell, 239
Davis, Stephanie, 110–111, 115, 137
Day, Kate Nace, 166
Deadwyler, Sue Ella, 148
deBaca, Luis C., 154
Defenders USA, 131
Definitions of terms, 9–11
Deinstitutionalization of runaways, 29–32
Delinquency, paradigm shift to domestic minor
sex trafficking, 2–3
De Los Rios, Caroline, 191
Demand Abolition (Boston), 178
"Demanding Justice" assessments, 179–180
Densen-Gerber, Judianne, 43, 45–47
Desiree Alliance, 182
Detention of runaways, 28–29
Dharmapalan, Rebecca, 166
*Diagnostic and Statistical Manual of Mental
Disorders*, 25, 44
DIGNITY (Phoenix), 123
Distortion of youth involvement in sex
trafficking, 205–206
Diversification of activism, 121–137
Domestic minor sex trafficking
defined, 10
paradigm shift from delinquency, 2–3
reframing youth sex as, 2–3, 12
Domestic Minor Sex Trafficking Deterrence
and Victims Support Act of 2010, 136
Donovan, Brian, 20
Downtown Eastside Youth Activities Society
(Vancouver), 74
*Dr. Phil* (television program), 139
Drexelius, J.R., Jr., 143
Dudar, Helen, 47
Durbin, Richard, 154, 207–208
Dworkin, Andrea, 59

Echols, Tim, 201
ECPAT-International, 69–70, 134
ECPAT-USA, 72, 95–96, 122, 129–130,
    136–137, 144, 157–158, 169, 173–174,
    177, 184, 225
Edgewood Academy (San Francisco), 122
Educational Amendments of 1972, 25
Education and Prevention Services to Reduce
    Sexual Abuse of Runaway, Homeless, and
    Street Youth Program, 87
Education Department, 134
Ehrlich, Shoshanna, 24, 231–232
Electronic Frontier Foundation, 184
Elijah Rising (Houston), 201
Embrey Family Foundation, 178
Empire State Coalition, 67
Empowerment of youth, 228
Empower Youth to Take the Lead (toolkit), 169
"End demand" campaigns, 177–182
End Demand for Sex Trafficking Act of 2005,
    105–106, 108
End Demand Illinois, 178
Ending Child Prostitution in Asian Tourism
    (ECPAT), 68, 69, 72, 82, 90, 203–204
Equality Now (New York City), 79, 97, 144
*Essence* (magazine), 139
Estes, Richard, 97, 106, 225
Evangelicals
    in activism, 3–5, 8–9, 12, 121, 223
    on commercial sexual exploitation of
        children, 79–80
    "end demand" campaigns and, 179–180
    LGBT persons and, 121
    on safe harbor laws, 145–150
    on sexual liberation, 25–26
    survivor movements and, 167
Evangelicals for Social Action, 184
Exaggerated statistics, 202–203
Expungement laws, 8–9, 223–224

Facebook, 179, 191
Facilitators, 204–205
FAIR Girls (Washington D.C.), 169, 186
Faith and Freedom Coalition (Duluth, GA), 148
Fassett, Bryon A., 2, 89–90, 150
Fathers Against Child Exploitation (Atlanta),
    146–147
Faulkner, Joanne, 236–237, 239
Federal Bureau of Investigation (FBI), 88,
    104–107, 113–114, 195–196, 215,
    227, 229
Federalism, 157

Feinblatt, John, 143–144
Feingold, David, 239
Feldt, Gloria, 80
Feminist Majority Foundation, 80, 136–137
Feminists
    in activism, 3–4, 8–9, 33–36, 223–224
    carceral feminism, 211–215
    in collaborative adversarial movement,
        135–137
    framing of issues by, 224
    US Campaign Against Commercial Sexual
        Exploitation of Children and, 77–81
Fernandez-Rundle, Katherine, 180
Ferrer, Carl, 187
Fifth Amendment, 187
50 Cent, 103–104, 172
*Fighting the Traffic in Young Girls* (Bell), 20
Fineman, Martha, 237
Finkelhor, David, 202
First Amendment, 88, 181, 186–187, 218
First International Tribunal on Crimes Against
    Women, 35–36
First World Congress Against the Commercial
    Sexual Exploitation of Children (1996),
    10, 68, 69–70, 71, 81–82, 90
Flores, Robert, 87–88, 104, 165–166
Flores, Theresa, 163–164
Florida
    Children and Family Department, 215
    safe harbor laws in, 192–193
Flynt, Larry, 47
Focus on the Family, 129–130
*For Money or Love* (Lloyd), 40
Fortson, Deborah Lake, 99
Foster, Jodie, 46
Fourth World Conference on Women, 69,
    80–81
Foxx, Jamie, 179
Framing of issues
    activism against sex trafficking and, 224
    differences in, 4, 160
    empowerment, 158–159, 165–166
    gendered narratives, 43–44
    "lost innocence" narratives, 117–119, 194
    mental health and, 175
    "our girls" narratives, 94, 104
    pathologization of youth and, 127–128
    racialized narratives, 5, 76–77, 157
    state and, 233
    in TVPA, 86, 91
    victimization narratives, 201–211
Franklin, Shirley, 115–117

Freedom Network, 182
From Prostitution to Independence, Dignity and
    Equality (PRIDE) (Minneapolis), 53, 75,
    88, 89
Frundt, Tina, 128, 155–156, 167–168, 184,
    223–224
Fulton County Court Appointed Special
    Advocates, Inc., 114
Fund for Nonviolence (Santa Cruz), 96–97, 225
Funding of activism, 224–225

Gallagher, Tim, 89–90
Gangs, 214
Gay marriage, 158, 220–221
Gay rights movement, 40, 61, 220
Gendered narratives
    activism and, 5, 131–134
    collaborative adversarial movement and,
        131–134, 146–147, 160
    framing of issues, 43–44
    historical background, 221–222
    innocence of children paradigm and, 15–16
    juvenile prostitution and, 43–44, 50
    leveraging of political and cultural
        opportunities and, 91
    sex trafficking and, 227–228, 232
    survivor movements and, 167
Geneva Conventions, 93
Georgetown Law Center on Poverty and
    Inequality, 174
Georgia
    campaign against commercial sexual
        exploitation of girls in, 110–117
    Care Connection Office, 148
    Child Sexual Commerce Prevention Act, 113
    Georgia Cares, 148
    prosecution of sex trafficking in, 229
    safe harbor laws in, 141–142, 145–150
Georgia Baptist Convention, 148
Georgia Christian Coalition, 148
Georgia Eagle Forum, 148
Giles W. and Elise G. Mead Foundation, 32–33
Giobbe, Evelina, 59
Girls Educational and Mentoring Services
    (GEMS) (New York), 65, 66, 82, 95–96,
    98–99, 102, 109, 117–118, 120, 124, 127,
    128, 129–130, 131, 135, 136, 139,
    142–143, 144, 153–154, 162, 166–167,
    184, 194–195, 200, 204–205, 207,
    225, 228
Girls in Charge (Chicago), 100
*Girls Like Us* (Lloyd), 163

Glamorization of prostitution, 91, 108, 153,
    172–173
*Glamour* (magazine), 161
Glide Memorial Church (San Francisco), 27–28
Global Fund for Women, 74
Global Health Promise, 134
Goldman, Ron, 84–85
*Gonzales v. Mailliard* (1971), 29
Google, 179
Gould, Sara, 184
Government Accountability Office, 53, 54
Goździak, Elżbieta M., 202
Grace, Lisa Goldblatt, 101
*Grand Theft Auto* (video game), 172
Graves, Asia, 189, 223–224
Groundswell (New York), 185
Grumm, Chris, 184

Hakes, Frances, 151
Hamman, Emily, 128
Hansen, Jane, 111–113
Harm reduction, 59, 67–68, 71, 83, 99–102,
    117–118, 124, 212–213
Harold and Kayrita Anderson Family
    Foundation, 145–146
Harpold, Karen Clark, 1
Harvard, Beverly, 113–114
Harvard University, 78
Hatchett, Glenda, 110, 112, 117
Haugen, Gary, 79, 80
Hawaii
    human trafficking courts in, 194
    Task Force Against Human Trafficking,
        94–95
Haymarket Peoples' Fund, 99
Haymes, Richard, 73–74
Healing in Action (Chicago), 126–127
Health, Education and Welfare Department,
    27, 31
Health and Human Services Department,
    105–106, 134, 218
Hefner, Hugh, 32–33, 64
Helms, Jesse, 83
Helping Individual Prostitutes Survive (HIPS)
    (Washington D.C.), 82–83
Herbert, Bob, 137–138
Heterogeneity of youth in sex trafficking,
    204–205
Hickson, Nina, 110–113, 114, 117
Hill, Anita, 84–85
Hill, Kelly, 66, 82–83, 94–95, 96–97
Hofstede, Albert, 88–89

Holder, Eric, 196
Homeland Security Department, 134
Homophobia, juvenile prostitution and, 44
Horowitz, Michael, 79–80, 81
Hotaling, Norma, 63–64, 65, 68, 69, 74, 82–83,
    90, 94, 96–98, 105–106, 107–109, 122,
    123, 129–130, 182, 197, 218
House of Hope (St. Paul), 122–123
Howard, Paul, 110
Huckleberry House (San Francisco), 27, 177
Hudson Institute, 79–80, 81
Huffington, Ariana, 179
*Huffington Post*, 168–169, 200
Hughes, Donna, 97
Human Exploitation and Trafficking (HEAT)
    Watch (Alameda County), 150
Human rights framing of issues, 224
Human Rights Project for Girls (HRPG)
    (Washington D.C.), 161, 169–171, 174,
    175, 186, 194–195, 198
Human Rights Watch, 80
Human trafficking courts, 194
Human Trafficking Resource Project
    (Missouri), 181
*Hustle and Flow* (film), 172

*I Am Jane Doe* (documentary), 167
Ice-T, 172
Ideological differences in activism, 8–9, 80–81,
    135–137, 223–224
Illinois
    Criminal Justice Information Authority, 230
    juvenile prostitution in, 53–54
    Legislative Investigating Commission, 40–42,
        43, 53–54
    safe harbor laws in, 145, 193
    specialized services for youth in, 230
Image Award (NAACP), 172
Immigration and Nationality Act of 1965,
    25, 221
"Incorrigible girl" statutes, 22, 28
Indianapolis, juvenile prostitution in, 55
*In loco parentis*, 28
Innocence Lost National Initiative (FBI),
    104–105, 108, 137–139, 195–196, 215,
    227, 229
Innocence of children paradigm, 14–16, 227,
    236–237
Innocent Images National Initiative, 88
*In Plain Sight: Storied of Hope and Freedom*
    (film), 167
*In re B.W.* (Texas 2010), 1–2, 149

Institute for Child Rights and Development
    (University of Victoria), 70
*International Boulevard* (film), 166
International Human Rights Law Group, 78
International Human Rights Network, 78
International Justice Mission (Washington D.C.),
    79, 84
International Organization for Adolescents,
    95–96, 188
International Religious Freedom Act of 1998,
    79–80
*In These Times*, 206
Ireland, Patricia, 80
Irvine Foundation, 32–33
"It's Hard Out Here for a Pimp" (song), 172
Ivy, "Pimpin' Ken," 172
*I Was A Teenage Prostitute* (film), 166

James, Jennifer, 35–36
John Jay College, 202, 204
"Johns"
    criticism of use of term, 172
    defined, 10
Johns Hopkins University, 78, 129–130
Johnson, Jeh, 196
Jolie, Angelina, 81
Justice Department, 46–47, 97, 104–105, 134,
    151, 152, 196–197
Justice for Victims of Trafficking Act of 2015,
    192, 194–195, 200, 231
Juvenile Justice and Delinquency Prevention
    Act of 1974, 30, 56–57
Juvenile Justice Fund (Atlanta), 114, 148
Juvenile Justice Project (New York), 145
Juvenile prostitution
    overview, 11, 38–39, 61–62
    boys in, 40
    in California, 48, 54
    commercial sexual exploitation of children
        and, 87–90
    decline in prosecution for, 229–230
    gendered narratives and, 43–44, 50
    government responses, 104–109
    homophobia and, 44
    in Illinois, 53–54
    in Indianapolis, 55
    LGBT persons and, 44
    in Los Angeles, 55
    in Louisville, 55
    in Minnesota, 49–53
    morality narratives and, 56–58
    in New York, 48, 54–55

public discourse on, 39–45
racialized narratives and, 42–43
resistance to, 54–55
in Seattle, 55
specialized units, 55
unsubstantiated claims of, 40–42
in Washington D.C., 55
"white slavery" and, 43

Kansas, safe harbor laws in, 193
"Katya vs. Keisha," 153, 210–211
Kelly, William, 44
Kennedy School of Government, 78
King, Martin Luther, Jr., 56
Kingsley, Cherry, 70–71, 97
Knowles, Beyoncé, 124
Koepplinger, Suzanne, 175–176
koyama, emi, 203, 205–206
Kristi House Child Advocacy Center
    (Miami), 128
Kristof, Nicholas, 102, 115, 138, 167–168
Kutcher, Ashton, 179

Labor trafficking, 118
Lacey, Michael, 187
Land, Richard, 80
Landesman, Peter, 102–103
Language, 9–11, 43, 71, 103, 153, 157 n. 135,
    169–172, 206–207, 216–217, 226
Larkin, James, 187
Las Vegas Operation STOP (Stop Turning Out
    Child Prostitutes), 89
*Law and Order: Special Victims Unit* (television
    program), 167–168, 172
Law and order paradigm, 56, 223, 224
Lederer, Laura, 69, 77–79, 80, 86–87,
    184, 223
Lee, Lois, 32–33, 64, 67, 74–75, 212, 214,
    215–216
Legal Momentum (New York City), 186
Leidholdt, Dorchen, 77–78
Leveraging of political and cultural
    opportunities
    overview, 12, 92–94, 117–119, 223
    gendered narratives and, 91
    Georgia campaign against commercial sexual
       exploitation of girls, 110–117
    government responses, 104–109
    growth and connection of service providers,
       94–99
    media coverage of, 102–104
    new service providers, 99–102

racialized narratives and, 91, 103–104
LGBT persons
    activism against sex trafficking and, 177
    child sex abuse and, 44
    evangelicals and, 121
    juvenile prostitution and, 44
    prostitution and, 44, 61
    runaways, 27–29, 32
    sex tourism and, 72–73
    in sex trafficking, 174–175, 176–177, 205
    survivor movements and, 163
Lloyd, Rachel, 66, 70–71, 82–83, 95–98,
    118–119, 124, 129–130, 139, 142,
    143–144, 151, 152–154, 155, 159, 160,
    163, 165, 172, 181, 183, 184, 194–195,
    197, 200–202, 210–211, 212, 218, 220
Lloyd, Robin, 40–42
"Lolita syndrome," 91
López, Ian Haney, 226
Los Angeles
    Children's Hospital, 60
    Human Trafficking Unit, 150
    juvenile prostitution in, 55
    Sexually Exploited Child Unit, 55
"Lost innocence" narratives
    overview, 158
    conservatives on, 224
    framing of issues, 117–119, 194
    media coverage and, 137, 138–139
    racial narratives and, 160
Louisville
    Exploited and Missing Child Unit, 55
    juvenile prostitution in, 55
Love146 (Connecticut), 122
*Loving v. Virginia* (1967), 25
Loyola University Chicago, 188
Lutheran Immigration and Refugee
    Services, 134
Lutnick, Alexandra, 204–205, 208–209,
    211, 212
Lynching narratives, 5, 16, 17, 156, 226–227
Lyon, Amber, 167–168
Lyric (San Francisco), 177

MacDonald, John M., 22
MacKinnon, Catherine, 59
Mann, James, 19
Mann Act of 1910, 19, 36, 48, 180–181
Marcus, Anthony, 204
Marital rape, 33–34
MasterCard, 186–187
May, Susan, 110–111

McCampbell, Robert, 138–139
McConnell, Mitchell, 55
McDonnell, Jim, 171
McDougall, Liz, 185
McGinniss, Warren, 38, 43, 44, 61
McLaughlin, Karen, 134
Media coverage of sex trafficking, 72–77,
    102–104, 137–140, 225–226
Meese, Edwin, 58
Men Against the Trafficking of Others,
    131–134
Men in activism, 131–134
Mentoring Child Victims of Commercial Sexual
    Exploitation and Domestic Minor Sex
    Trafficking Initiative (OJJDP), 196–197
Methodological considerations, 6–11
    black feminist theory and, 6–7
    collaborative adversarial movements and, 8
    ideological differences and, 8–9
    language and, 9–11
    social movement theory and, 7
    terminology and, 9–11
Microsoft, 179
Mikulski, Barbara, 80–81
*Milk Money* (film), 76
Millett, Kate, 35
Milner, James, 146–147
*Minneapolis Star Tribune*, 76–77
*Minneapolis Tribune*, 42–43
Minnesota
    Alliance for Speaking Truths on Prostitution
        (A-STOP), 88
    commercial sexual exploitation of children
        in, 88–89
    Health and Human Services Department,
        52–53
    juvenile prostitution in, 49–53
    No Wrong Door Program, 193–194, 230
    Pimp/Juvenile Prostitution Task Force, 89
    Task Force on Juvenile Prostitution, 50–52
    Youth Development Bureau, 52–53
*The Minnesota Connection* (Palmquist), 43,
    49–50
Minnesota Indian Women's Sexual Assault
    Coalition, 175–176
Minnesota Native Women's Research Center,
    175–176, 198
Minthorn, David, 170–171
Mitchell, Kathleen, 123
Montgomery, Heather, 205
Moore, Demi, 124, 179
Morality narratives

in activism, 20–22
juvenile prostitution and, 56–58
sex trafficking and, 234–235
Moral panic, criticism of activism and, 201–211
"More Than a Survivor, More Than a Story"
    Campaign (GEMS), 207
Moseley, Ray, 40
Moses, Ericka, 75
Motivating, Inspiring, Supporting & Serving
    Sexually Exploited Youth (MISSSEY)
    (Oakland), 128, 162
*Ms.* (magazine), 47, 80, 139, 172
Ms. Foundation for Women, 174,
    184
MSNBC, 167–168
MTV, 66
Mullen, Katherine, 134, 142–144
Muntarbhorn, Vitit, 68–69
Mustafa, Isaiah, 179
Musto, Jennifer, 213–214
Myles, Bradley, 167–168
My Life My Choice (Boston), 99, 101, 162, 169,
    177, 184

*The Nation*, 39
National Academy of Television Arts and
    Sciences, 117
National Advisory Committee on the Sex
    Trafficking of Children and Youth in the
    United States, 190
National Association for the Advancement of
    Colored People (NAACP), 172
National Association of Evangelicals, 79–80
National Association of Sheriffs, 30
National Association of Women Business
    Owners, 145–146
National Center for Missing and Exploited
    Children (NCMEC), 57–58, 88, 104–105,
    134, 179, 183, 186, 190–191, 195–196
National Coordinator for Child Exploitation,
    Prevention, and Interdiction, 152
National Council of Juvenile and Family Court
    Judges, 56–57, 190–191
National Crime Prevention Council, 134
National Crime Victim Law Institute, 186
National District Attorneys Association,
    136–137
National Network for Youth, 30
National Network of Runaway and Youth
    Services, 30, 67
National Organization for Women (NOW), 47,
    80, 144, 184

National Planning Meeting to Eliminate Demand for Commercial Sex, 178

National Strategy for Child Exploitation Prevention and Interdiction, 152

National Training and Technical Assistance Center (OJJDP), 196–197

Nealon, Lina, 134

*Nefarious: Merchant of Souls* (film), 167

Neoliberalism, 213–214, 233–235

Neuwirth, Jessica, 79, 80

Neverdusky, Veronica, 123

New Connections (Charleston), 59

Newmark, Craig, 184

New Right, 4–5, 26, 57–58, 233

*Newsweek*, 103–104, 118–119

New York City
  Community Health Project, 73–74
  juvenile prostitution in, 54–55
  Public Safety Committee, 95–96
  Task Force on the Sexual Exploitation of Young People, 95–96
  Victim Services Agency, 58
  Women's Issues Committee, 95–96

New York Legal Aid Society, 142–143

New York State
  human trafficking courts in, 194
  juvenile prostitution in, 48
  Office of Children & Family Services, 188–189
  prosecution of sex trafficking in, 229
  Safe Harbor for Exploited Children Act, 142–145
  safe harbor laws in, 141, 142–145, 149–150
  Social Services Department, 144

New York State Anti-Trafficking Coalition, 144

*New York Times*, 39, 40, 42, 43, 49, 73–74, 76–77, 102–103, 115, 117, 124, 137–138, 144, 182

*New York Times Magazine*, 72–73

NGO Group for the Convention on the Rights of the Child, 134

Nicolette R., 142–144

*Nobody's Girl* (Amaya), 163–165

Nola Brantley Speaks (San Pedro, CA), 162

Nolan, Clare, 97–98

North American Free Trade Agreement, 84

North Star (Minneapolis), 53

"Not Buying It" Initiative (Georgia), 194

*Nothing Left to Loose* (Blum and Smith), 30

*Not My Life* (film), 167

Nye, Nancy, 82

Obama, Barack, 121, 196

O'Connor, Sinead, 124

Odem, Mary, 22

Odyssey Institute (New York), 43, 45–47

Office for Victims of Crime, 122, 151

Office of Juvenile Justice and Delinquency Prevention, 31, 57, 88, 98–99, 196–197, 228–229, 238

Office to Monitor and Combat Trafficking in Persons, 86–87, 129, 154

*Off the Minnesota Strip* (television program), 50

Ohio
  human trafficking courts in, 194
  prosecution of sex trafficking in, 229

O'Leary, Claudine, 99–100

Olens, Sam, 194

O'Malley, Nancy, 150

Online advertising. *See* Backpage.com; Craigslist.com

Operation Guardian Angel, 181

Osanka, Frank, 45–47

Ossorio, Sonia, 186

"Our girls" narratives, 22–23, 94, 96, 107

Out from the Shadows: International Summit of Sexually Exploited Youth (1998), 70–71

Out of the Shadows (toolkit), 146–147

Page Act of 1875, 16

Palermo Protocol, 85

*The Pall Mall Gazette*, 19

Palmquist, Al, 49–52, 53, 61

Paradigm shift, 2–3, 12

*Parens patriae*, 28

*A Path Appears* (television program), 167–168

Pathologization of youth, 127–128

Paul and Lisa Program (Westbrook, Connecticut), 33, 58, 59, 64–65, 76, 82–83, 93, 95, 97, 98–99, 102, 117–118, 122, 129–130, 225

PBS, 167–168

Pearson, Landon, 70

Peer Educator Training Program, 65

Penn, Sean, 179

*People* (magazine), 138–139

Personal Responsibility Act of 1996, 84, 233–234

Pettigrew, Withelma T. Ortiz Walker, 161–162, 170–171, 177, 190, 194, 197–198, 223–224

Phelps, Carissa, 163–164, 165–166
*Phil Donahue Show* (television program), 50
Piccillo, Juliana, 166
"P.I.M.P." (song), 172
*Pimpin' 101* (film), 172
*Pimpology* (Ivy), 172
Pimps
  defined, 10–11
  evidence regarding, 204–205
  "pimp culture," 172
Planned Parenthood, 59–60, 80
Playboy Foundation, 32–33, 64
*Playground* (documentary), 139–140, 154,
  167
Poe, Ted, 156, 160, 172
Poffenberger, Donald, 61
Polaris Project, 98–99, 136–137, 169, 181, 182,
  184, 191–192
*Police Story* (television program), 39–40, 49
Political opportunities. *See* Leveraging of
  political and cultural opportunities
Popular culture, 172–173
Pornography, 25
Posner, Richard, 187
Postal Service, 88
Powell, William, 184
Presidential Task Force Commission on Law
  Enforcement and the Administration of
  Justice, 29
*Pretty Woman* (film), 76
"*Pretty Woman* syndrome," 91
Preventing Sex Trafficking and Strengthening
  Families Act of 2014, 190, 231
Prison Fellowship, 80
Project GOLD (Miami), 128
Project Offstreets (Minneapolis), 88
Project PACE (Los Angeles), 60
Project Street Beat (New York), 59–60
Project Turnaround (San Francisco), 60
Prostituted women, defined, 9
Prostituted youth, defined, 10
Prostitutes' Empowerment, Education and
  Resource Society (British Columbia,
  Canada), 70
Prostitution
  child sex abuse and, 227
  defined, 9
  LGBT persons and, 44, 61
  paradigm shift to domestic minor sex
    trafficking, 2–3
  Texas, child prostitution laws in, 1–2
  use of term, 216–217

Prostitution Intervention Program
  (Honolulu), 66
Prostitution Research & Education (San
  Francisco), 175–176
PROTECT Act of 2003, 228–229
Protection of Children Against Sexual
  Exploitation Act of 1977, 48
Protection Project, 78–79, 84, 129–130, 134
PROTECT Our Children Act of 2008, 152
Protect Our Children from Sexual Exploitation
  (Hawaii), 94–95
Protocol to Prevent, Suppress and Punish
  Trafficking in Persons, especially Women
  and Children, 85
*The P.T.L. Club* (television program), 50
Public Health Services Act of 1967, 24

Quigley, Mike, 156

Raben Group, 170
Rabun, John, 55
Racialized narratives
  activism and, 5, 76–77, 174–175
  collaborative adversarial movement and,
    156–157, 160, 223–224
  commercial sexual exploitation of children
    and, 76–77, 91
  criticism of activism and, 209–211, 213–214
  framing of issues, 5, 76–77, 157
  historical background, 221–222
  innocence of children paradigm and, 15
  juvenile prostitution and, 42–43
  leveraging of political and cutural
    opportunities and, 91, 103–104
  sex trafficking and, 76–77, 227–228, 232
  survivor movements and, 165–166, 167
Racketeer Influenced and Corrupt
  Organizations Act of 1970 (RICO),
  113–114
Ramdas, Kavita, 74
Ramos, Norma, 77–78
*Rape for Profit* (film), 166
Raymond, Janice, 97
Reagan, Ronald, 55–58, 62, 84, 233
"Real Men Don't Buy Girls" Campaign, 179
Rebecca Project for Human Rights (Marietta,
  GA), 183
*Redbook*, 184
Reed, Ralph, 148
Reform attempts, 237–238
Rehabilitation of runaways, 30–31
Renold, Emma, 236–237

*Renting Lacey* (Smith), 130
*Requiem for Tina Sanchez* (television program), 43–44
Rescue narratives, sex trafficking and, 5, 16, 131–134, 146–147, 153, 160, 203–204
Richardson, Deborah, 110–111, 114, 155–156
Richette, Lisa Aversa, 30
Rights4Girls Campaign, 170–171
Ringrose, Jessica, 236–237
Ritter, Bruce, 32, 38, 47, 57
Rivera, Sylvia, 27–28
Rodarte, Adela Hernandez, 128
Rose, Ava, 217
Ros-Lehtinen, Ileana, 180
Runaway and Homeless Youth and Trafficking Prevention Act of 2014, 231
*Runaway Girl* (Phelps), 163–164
Runaway House (Washington D.C.), 27
Runaways
    deinstitutionalization of, 29–32
    detention of, 28–29
    gender differences, 28–29
    LGBT persons, 27–29, 32
    problems of, 26–27
    rehabilitation of, 30–31
    services for, 27–28
*Runaways* (musical), 50
Runaway Youth Act of 1974, 30–32
Rush, Florence, 34
Russell, Diana, 78–79

Safe harbor laws, 141–150
    overview, 192–193
    collaborative adversarial movement and, 198–199
    in Connecticut, 145
    criticism of, 213–214
    evangelicals on, 145–150
    in Florida, 192–193
    in Georgia, 141–142, 145–150
    in Illinois, 145, 193
    in Kansas, 193
    in New York, 141, 142–145, 149–150
    in Tennessee, 193
    in Texas, 142, 149–150
    in Washington, 145
Safe Horizon (New York), 97, 151
SAGE House (San Francisco), 122
St. James, Margo, 35–36
Salvation Army, 80, 151, 184
Saunders, Penelope, 206
"Save Our Children" Crusade, 26

Save the Children Canada, 97
Sawyer, Diane, 167–168
Scaggs Foundation, 77
School curricula, 169
Scott, Robert, 157
Seattle, juvenile prostitution in, 55
Sebelius, Kathleen, 196
Second World Conference Against the Commercial Sexual Exploitation of Children (2001), 96–98, 129–130
*Selling the Girl Next Door* (television program), 167–168
Sensationalization of problem, 202–203
Sensley, Nicholas, 157
Sentencing Reform Act, 56
Sereny, Gitta, 60–61
SESTA-FOSTA (Stop Enabling Sex Traffickers Act of 2018 and Allow States and Victims to Fight Online Sex Trafficking Act of 2018), 187–188
*Sex+Money: A National Search for Human Worth* (film), 166
Sex panic, criticism of activism and, 201–211
*Sex Slaves: Fighting Human Trafficking* (television program), 167–168
Sex trade, defined, 9
Sex trafficking, defined, 9
Sex trafficking victims, defined, 9
Sexual double standard, 4, 15–16, 17, 22, 37, 108, 222–223
Sexualization of girls, 236–237
Sexual liberation, activism and, 23–26, 217–218
Sexually transmitted diseases, 26
Sex work, defined, 9
Sex Workers Action New York (SWANK), 216–217
Sex Worker's Outreach Project NYC (SWOP-NYC), 216–217
Sex Workers Project (New York), 99, 101–102, 117–118, 136, 144, 182, 218
Sex workers' rights movement, 222–223
Shared Hope International (SHI) (Vancouver, WA), 86, 121, 128–134, 135, 136–137, 155–156, 172–173, 179–181, 186, 191–192, 205–206, 223, 224–225, 239
Shields, Brooke, 76
Simons, Marlise, 72–73
Simpson, Nicole Brown, 84–85
Simpson, O.J., 84–85

Sisters Offering Support (SOS) (Honolulu), 65, 66, 94–95, 96–97
*60 Minutes* (television program), 39–40
Skelaney, Sandy, 98–99, 128, 134, 215
*Slate* (magazine), 103–104
*The Slave Across the Street* (Flores), 163–164
Slavery
    defined, 9
    slavery narratives, sex trafficking and, 156–157, 203–204
Smalley, Suzanne, 103–104
Smeal, Eleanor, 80
Smith, Chris, 80–81, 92, 105–108, 156, 223
Smith, Holly Austin, 163, 165–166, 172–173
Smith, Jada Pinkett, 167–168
Smith, Judith, 30
Smith, Lamar, 136
Smith, Linda A., 86, 120–121, 128–129, 130–131, 134, 139, 155–156, 158, 184, 224–225
Smith-Mazariegos, Sarai T., 128
Smolenski, Carol, 72, 82–83, 95, 96–97, 134, 173–174, 184
Sneed, Michael, 40, 46
Snoop Dogg, 172
Social movement against exploitation. *See* Activism against sex trafficking
Social movement theory, 7
*Social Work Today* (magazine), 206
Societal changes, activism and, 24–25
Socioeconomics
    activism and, 19–20, 221
    causes of sex trafficking, 233–235, 238–239
Solinger, Rickie, 25–26
Southern Baptist Convention, 80
Speaks, Nola Brantley, 162
Specialized services for youth, 230–231
Standing Against Global Exploitation (SAGE) (San Francisco), 63, 65, 94, 98–99, 102, 109, 117–118, 122, 127, 128, 129–130, 135, 151, 204–205, 225
Stark, Christine, 98–99
State Department, 86–87, 129, 130–131, 134, 154, 179–180
Statutory rape laws, 1–2
Stead, William, 19
Steinem, Gloria, 47, 80
Sterry, David Henry, 98–99
"Stockholm Syndrome," 175, 224

Stop Enabling Sex Traffickers Act of 2018 (SESTA), 178–179
The Storefront (San Diego), 60
"Stranger rape," 232
Stransky, Michelle, 202
Street Grace (Atlanta), 146–147
Street Transvestite Action Revolutionaries (STAR) (New York), 27–28
Streetwise and Safe (New York), 176
Streetwork Project (New York), 58, 67
Streetworks Outreach Collaborative for Homeless Youth (Minneapolis), 122–123
Street Youth Rise Up Campaign (Chicago), 126, 139
Suchland, Jennifer, 233
Surveillance, criticism of activism and, 211–215
Surviving Our Struggle (Boston), 177
Survivor Leadership Institute and Resource Center (GEMS), 207
Survivor movements, 162–169
    child sex abuse and, 63–64, 127, 163
    "coming out" in, 163
    against commercial sexual exploitation of children, 64–68
    documentaries and, 166–167
    evangelicals and, 167
    film and, 166–167
    gendered narratives and, 167
    LGBT persons and, 163
    memoirs and, 163–166
    print media and, 168–169
    racialized narratives and, 165–166, 167
    survivor, defined, 9–10
    television and, 167–168
Survivor Services Education and Empowerment Network, 123
Survivors for Solutions (Denver, CO), 162
Swecker, Chris, 105

Tailhook Scandal, 84–85
*Tainted Love* (television program), 167–168
*Take Back the Night: Women on Pornography* (Lederer ed.), 78
Task Force on the Trafficking of Girls (APA), 231
*Taxi Driver* (film), 46
Tea Party Movement, 121
Technology, sex trafficking and, 221
Temporary Assistance for Needy Families (TANF), 84, 233–234
Tennessee, safe harbor laws in, 193

Terminology, 9–11
Texas
  child prostitution laws in, 1–2
  human trafficking courts in, 194
  safe harbor laws in, 142, 149–150
The Ugly Truth Public Awareness
  Campaign, 178
Third World Conference Against Sexual
  Exploitation of Children and Adolescents
  (2008), 134–135
"This Is to Mother You" (song), 124
Thomas, Clarence, 84–85
Thorn Digital Defenders of Children, 179
Thorn Innovation Lab, 179
Three Six Mafia, 172
*The Throwaway Children* (Richette), 30
Thrupkaew, Noy, 182
Timberlake, Justin, 179
*Time* (magazine), 39, 42, 43, 161
*Too Close to Home* (film), 166
Torre, C. Angel, 126
Tourism Child-Protection Code of Conduct,
  173–174
*Trade* (film), 103
*Trading Women* (film), 239
Trafficking in Persons (TIP) Reports, 86, 93,
  130–131, 158
Trafficking Victims Protection Act of 2000
  (TVPA)
  overview, 12, 155–156, 228–229
  activism and, 11–12, 78, 82–83, 85–86,
    162, 223
  enactment of, 91
  "end demand" campaigns and, 180–181
  framing of issues in, 86, 91
  ideological differences in proponents of, 8,
    79–81
  problems with, 93–94, 96
  prosecutions under, 181, 229
  safe harbor laws and, 144, 159
  survivor movements and, 90
  youth as victims under, 157, 158, 170
Trafficking Victims Protection Reauthorization
  Act of 2013, 190, 196
Transgender youth, 5, 27–28, 101, 177, 202
*Tricked* (documentary), 167
Truckers Against Trafficking, 131–134, 135
*True Detective* (television program), 167–168
Trump, Donald, 218, 238
Turner, George Kibbe, 19
*Turning a Corner* (film), 166

Turvey, Josh, 74
Twenty-Sixth Amendment, 25
Twitter, 179, 191

Uniform Law Commission, 192
United Nations
  Committee on the Rights of the Child, 68
  Convention on the Rights of the Child, 68,
    82, 85, 235
  Economic and Social Council, 77–78
  High Commission on Human Rights, 68
  Human Rights Council, 173
  Special Rapporteur on the Sale of Children,
    Child Prostitution and Child
    Pornography, 68
  UNESCO, 69, 77–78
  UNICEF, 68, 70, 134
University of Pennsylvania, 97
University of Victoria, 70
Unterman, Renee, 148
Urban Institute (New York), 176, 203, 211, 229
Urban Justice Center (New York), 101,
  117–118, 144, 218
US Campaign Against Commercial Sexual
  Exploitation of Children, 81–87, 90,
  96–97, 98–99, 225
US Conference of Catholic Bishops, 218
*US News and World Report*, 138–139
Utah, prosecution of sex trafficking in, 229

Vafa, Yasmin, 175
Vanguard (San Francisco), 27–28
Veronica's Voice (Kansas City), 123
*Very Young Girls* (documentary), 124,
  139–140, 166–167
Victimization narratives
  criticism of activism and, 201–211
  sex trafficking and, 16, 227–228, 232
Victims of Prostitution (Atlanta), 112–113
*Village Voice*, 185, 202–203
Village Voice Media, 185–188
VineyardUSA (Stafford, TX), 136–137
Violence Against Women Act of 1994,
  84–85, 87
Violent Crime Control and Law Enforcement
  Act of 1994, 84
Violent Crimes and Major Offenders Section
  (FBI), 104–105
Visa, 186–187
Voices and Faces Project (End Demand
  Illinois), 178

Voy, William, 150
Vulnerability of youth, 76–77, 169–177

*Walking Prey* (Smith), 163
War Against Trafficking Alliance, 129
"War on Terror," 93
Washington D.C.
  juvenile prostitution in, 55
  Juvenile Prostitution Unit, 55
Washington State
  safe harbor laws in, 145
  Sex Crimes Involving Minors Act, 145
Wasserman Schultz, Debbie, 180
Weaver, Sigourney, 81
Weimer, Scott, 146–147
Weiner, Neil Alan, 97, 106, 225
Weisberg, D. Kelly, 60
Welfare reform, 84, 233–234
Wells, Ida B., 16, 17
Wellstone, Paul, 80–81
Whedbee, Jack, 217
"White slavery," 18–19, 20, 43
White Slave Traffic Act of 1910, 19
Whittier, Nancy, 8, 135, 163
Whores, Housewives and Others (WHO) (San
  Francisco), 35–36
Wiesel, Elie, 81
Wilberforce, William, 151
William, Terrie, 67
William T. Grant Foundation, 97
William Wilberforce Trafficking Victims
  Protection Reauthorization Act of 2005,
  106–107, 109, 118, 151, 178
Wilson, Frederica, 180
Winfrey, Oprah, 94
Women Against Pornography (New York City),
  77, 91

Women Against Violence in Pornography and
  Media (San Francisco), 78
Women Hurt in Systems of Prostitution
  Engaged in Revolt (WHISPER)
  (Minneapolis), 59, 77, 89
Women's Christian Temperance Union,
  17–18
Women's Fund of Miami Dade, 180
Women's movement, activism and, 35–36
Women's National Republican Club,
  144
Woodhouse, Barbara Bennett, 235–236
World Wrestling Federation, 66
Wosh, Peter, 32
WuDunn, Cheryl, 167–168
Wyden, Ron, 154
Wynter, Sarah, 59

Xenophobia, 221

Young Women's Empowerment Project
  (YWEP) (Chicago), 94, 99–101, 102,
  117–118, 124–128, 129–130, 131, 135,
  139, 158–159, 160, 207, 208–209, 211,
  212–213, 228, 239
*Your American Teen* (film), 166
Youth, defined, 10
Youth Advocate Program International, Inc.,
  81–83, 96–97
Youth and Community Service (San Diego), 60
Youth Diversion Program (Minneapolis), 53
Youth leadership, 228
Youth participation in activism, 169–177
YouthSpark Voices (Atlanta), 148, 169
Yunus, Muhammad, 81

Zelizer, Viviana, 15